Accountability of International Territorial Administrations

Accountability of International Territorial Administrations

A Public Law Approach

Aleksandar Momirov

eleven
international publishing

Published, sold and distributed by Eleven International Publishing
P.O. Box 85576
2508 CG The Hague
The Netherlands
Tel.: +31 70 33 070 33
Fax: +31 70 33 070 30
Website: www.elevenpub.com

Sold and distributed in USA and Canada
International Specialized Book Services
920 NE 58th Avenue, Suite 300
Portland, OR 97213-3786, USA
Tel: 1-800-944-6190 (toll-free)
Fax: +1 503 280-8832
orders@isbs.com
www.isbs.com

Eleven International Publishing is an imprint of Boom uitgevers Den Haag.

ISBN 978-94-90947- 21-7

Printed in The Netherlands.

Ивани и Дејану, највољенијим родитељима

For my parents

ACKNOWLEDGMENTS

It takes the proverbial village to complete a PhD. I am grateful for the tremendous and diverse group of people around me who supported me and prevented the PhD-writing journey from becoming a solitary one.

First of all, I am deeply grateful to Ellen Hey, my PhD supervisor, for her ever-present trust and her enriching mentoring. I thank her for providing me with the necessary freedom to learn from conducting research independently and for always confronting me with the ramifications of my thoughts and choices.

My gratitude also goes out to Roel de Lange and Laurens Winkel for sharing their expertise with me regarding particular parts of my research, as well as to Sanne Taekema, Wouter Werner and Erika de Wet, the members of my Doctoral Committee, for reviewing my manuscript. I also thank the people from Eleven International Publishing as well as Donna Devine for their professionalism and smooth cooperation.

I am thankful to my 'former colleagues turn friends' Michael Karnavas, Mara Pilipović, Suzana Tomanović, Milan Vujin and Alan Yatvin for encouraging me to make the switch from my work at the International Criminal Tribunal for the Former Yugoslavia to the Erasmus School of Law to write a PhD and for supporting me throughout the process.

My current and former colleagues, and friends, at the Erasmus School of Law – the departments of Public International Law and European Law in particular – shaped an inspiring, pleasant and cosmopolitan working environment; for that I thank all of them. Andria Naudé Fourie and Zoltán Turbék, I could not have wished for better and more inspiring PhD-buddies. I am grateful to Elly Rood-Pijpers whose heartfelt engagement as PhD-coordinator often went above and beyond the call of duty. Finally, I want to thank Elaine Mak, Paulo da Rosa and Nathalie Weber, as well as student-assistants Ali Agayev, Raveen Moenesar, Jamaal Mohuddy and Michelle Rodenburg for assisting me during various phases of the PhD process.

My stay in Priština added real value to my research thanks to a lot of people. For contributing to my research, but most importantly for making me feel at home, I am grateful to Fatmir Celina, Shpend Emini, Remzije Istrefi, Flutura Kusari, Gjylbehare Murati, Edi Nimani, Liridon Shurdhani and all my colleagues at the Ombudsperson Institution in Kosovo.

Finally, my wonderful friends and family. Their continuing interest and patience – as well as the necessary distraction they provided – made the completion of this book possible and the whole process worthwhile; I am blessed to have them in my life – *другари и фамилијо, бескрајно вам хвала на стрпљењу и подршци*. I owe a special "thank you" to Sefton Nickless, Vladica Rakić and, my two *paranimfen*, Türkan Ertuna Lagrand and Malik Hinan: you are invaluable.

Most importantly, Ivana, my mom who passed away in 2006, and Dejan, my dad. Feeling their unparalleled devotion and unconditional love every day continues to make all the difference.

When the going gets tough, the tough get going... Sometimes, we are reminded that completing a PhD is a technicality in comparison to other challenges we face in life. I am deeply indebted to everyone for being near, one way or another, when having family and friends around mattered the most.

Rotterdam, April 2011

TABLE OF CONTENTS

LIST OF ACRONYMS AND ABBREVIATIONS

AI	Amnesty International
BiH	Bosnia and Herzegovina
CAT	Convention Against Torture and Other Cruel, Inhuman or Degrading Treatment and Punishment
CEDAW	Convention on the Elimination of All Forms of Discrimination Against Women
CERD	Committee on the Elimination of Racial Discrimination
CESCR	Committee on Economic, Social and Cultural Rights
CoE	Council of Europe
CommHR	Commission on Human Rights
CPT	European Convention for the Prevention of Torture and Inhumane or Degrading Treatment or Punishment
CRC	Convention on the Rights of the Child
CtAT	Committee Against Torture
CtEDAW	Committee on the Elimination of Discrimination Against Women
CtRC	Committee on the Rights of the Child
DRC	Detention Review Commission for Extra-Judicial Detentions based on Executive Orders (Kosovo)
ECHR	European Convention on Human Rights
ECommHR	European Commission on Human Rights
ECtHR	European Court of Human Rights
ERRC	European Roma Rights Centre
ESI	European Stability Initiative
EU	European Union
EUAM	European Union Administration of the City of Mostar
EULEX	European Union Rule of Law Mission in Kosovo
EUFOR	European Union Force Althea (Bosnia and Herzegovina)
EUPT	European Union Planning Team for Kosovo

GA	United Nations General Assembly
HRAP	Human Rights Advisory Panel (Kosovo)
HRC	Human Rights Council
HRCee	Human Rights Committee
HRW	Human Rights Watch
IAC	Interim Administrative Council (Kosovo)
IAD	Interim Administrative Department (Kosovo)
ICCPR	International Covenant on Civil and Political Rights
ICERD	International Convention on the Elimination of All Forms of Racial Discrimination
ICESCR	International Covenant on Economic, Social and Cultural Rights
ICG	International Crisis Group
ICO	International Civilian Office (Kosovo)
ICRC	International Committee of the Red Cross
IDP	Internally Displaced Persons
IPTF	International Police Task Force (Bosnia and Herzegovina)
ITA	International Territorial Administration
IWPR	Institute for War & Peace Reporting
JIAS	Joint Interim Administrative Structure (Kosovo)
KFOR	Kosovo Force
KTA	Kosovo Trust Agency
KTC	Kosovo Transitional Council
NCC	National Consultative Council (East Timor)
NGO	Non-governmental Organization
OHR	Office of the High Representative (Bosnia and Herzegovina)
OIK	Ombudsperson Institution of Kosovo
OSCE	Organization for Security and Co-operation in Europe
PAK	Privatisation Agency of Kosovo
PIC	Peace Implementation Council (Bosnia and Herzegovina)
PISG	Provisional Institutions of Self-Government (Kosovo)
SC	United Nations Security Council

SG	Secretary-General of the United Nations
SRSG	Special Representative of the Secretary-General
TA	Transitional Administrator (East Timor)
UN	United Nations
UNHCR	Office of the UN High Commissioner for Refugees
UNMIK	United Nations Interim Administration Mission in Kosovo
UNTAES	United Nations Transitional Authority in Eastern Slavonia, Baranja and Western Sirmium
UNTAET	United Nations Transitional Administration in East Timor
WHO	World Health Organization

"If men were angels, no government would be necessary. If angels were to govern men, neither external nor internal controls on government would be necessary. In framing a government which is to be administered by men over men, the greatest difficulty lies in this: you must first enable the government to control the governed; and in the next place oblige it to control itself. A dependence on the people is, no doubt, the primary control on the government, but experience has taught mankind the necessity of auxiliary precautions"

- *The Federalist No. 51*[*]

---

[*] Federalist Paper No. 51, 8 February 1788, authored by James Madison.

1 INTRODUCTION, METHODOLOGY AND DEFINITIONAL CONSIDERATIONS

"The innocence of the intention abates nothing of the mischief of the example"

- *Rev. Robert Hall*[1]

1.1 ILLUSTRATING THE ACCOUNTABILITY DEFICIT: THE ROMA LEAD-POISONING CASE

In the aftermath of the foreign intervention in 1999, as overall administration over the territory of Kosovo was assumed by an international presence pursuant to UN Security Council Res. 1244 (1999), Kosovo experienced a massive reflux of previously expelled persons, followed by a widespread expulsion of members of Kosovo's various local minorities. Between October 1999 and January 2000, the Office of the UN High Commissioner for Refugees (UNHCR) – together with its executive partners and under the overall authority of the United Nations Mission in Kosovo (UNMIK) – set up three temporary camps in order to house a large group of internally displaced persons (IDP) belonging to the Roma, Ashkali and Kosovo Egyptian local minorities.[2] Located in the northern part of

[1] Rev. Robert Hall, English Baptist Minister, during his sermon 'The sentiments proper to the present crisis', preached at Bridge Street, Bristol on 19 October 1803, as included in Tryon Edwards, *A Dictionary of Thoughts*, p. 154.

[2] According to a Kosovo Statistical Office estimate in 2002, the Roma, Ashkali and Kosovo Egyptian minorities make up 2% of the total population of Kosovo, roughly totalling some 38000 individuals, *see* <http://www.ks-gov.net/ESK/eng/>. Prior to the events of 1999, the area around the southern part of the city of Mitrovica housed around 8000 members of the mentioned minorities, most of which fled to camps in Montenegro, Serbia proper or joined their families throughout countries in western Europe, *see* Society for Threatened Peoples, The Kosovo Medical Emergency Group, *Dossier of Evidence Supporting the Call to Take Decisive Action to Implement Immediately an Emergency Evacuation and the Highest Level of Medical Treatment for all Roma, Ashkali and Kosovan-Egyptian Families in the Displaced Persons Camps of North Kosovo*, p. 8, at <http://www.gfbv.de/uploads/download/download/Dossier%20of%20Evidence.pdf> (all internet sites, unless stated otherwise, were last accessed 10 January 2011) (Dossier of Evidence). The Dossier of Evidence is compiled by the Society for Threatened Peoples, a German non-governmental organization actively

Mitrovica and Zvečan, the camps – Česmin Lug, Žitkovac and Kablare – were to house the families for 45 days until a permanent solution was found and the burned homes of the families in the southern part of Mitrovica were reconstructed.[3] At the time, the Special Representative of the Secretary-General (SRSG), Bernhard Kouchner, confirmed that the camps would be closed within 45 days.[4]

The camps were set up in an area surrounded by the Trepča mines, a complex of over 40 mining facilities. Burdened by mismanagement, a lack of interest in basic environmental standards and political tensions during the preceding decade, Trepča's lead emission rates had reached staggering levels.[5] In August 2000, citing health and environmental hazards, UNMIK took control of the mines and partially closed them: "[w]e are now the administration of all the complex of Trepča", Bernhard Kouchner reportedly proclaimed.[6]

Despite this closure, neighbouring toxic slag heaps continued to fill the air with lead dust while lead-contaminated soil affected local crops. This resulted in the IDPs' ongoing direct exposure to various heavy metals, predominantly lead.[7]The camps continued to remain operational, and in the summer of 2000 the first reports began to reach UNMIK and the World Health Organization concerning the alarming levels of lead found in blood samples taken during random tests conducted amongst the IDPs. However, the immediate relocation recommended by the reports did not take place.[8]

---

engaged in the matter. The dossier contains original data, analyses, reports and communications and is used throughout this introduction as a main point of reference. In general, *see also* HRW, *Kosovo: Poisoned by Lead, A Health and Human Rights Crisis in Mitrovica's Roma Camps*, Report, 23 June 2009 (HRW Report 2009). *See* Stone Sweet (1999), at 17: "Judicialization is a political process sustained by the interdependence of dyads and triads, and of rules and strategic behavior. It is observable, and therefore measurable, as modifications in the conduct of dispute resolution and social exchange".

[3] Dossier of Evidence, p. 9.

[4] *Id.*, p. 10.

[5] For a detailed analysis of the hazardous effects thereof, *see e.g.* Michael Palairet, *Trepča 1965-2000*, A report to the European Stability Initiative (ESI) & the Lessons Learned and Analysis Unit of the EU Pillar of UNMIK in Kosovo, 11 June 2003, at <http://www.esiweb.org/index.php?lang=en&id=156&document_ID=62>.

[6] ABC News, *U.N. Takes over Mining Complex in Kosovo*, 17 August 2000, at <http://abcnews.go.com/International/story?id=82865&page=1>.

[7] Once absorbed, lead affects all organs, causing, amongst other things, irreversible damage to the brain (encephalopathy), the kidneys, the nerve and immune system and impairment to bone growth. High exposure levels can cause death. Most vulnerable are children under the age of six, pregnant women and infants conceived at the site, *see* Dossier of Evidence, pp. 36-37.

[8] UNMIK did conduct additional tests amongst local UNMIK policemen who had been jogging in the area between Česmin Lug and Kablare. The test results prompted UNMIK to immediately repatriate the policemen for treatment, *see* Dossier of Evidence, p. 13.

In 2004, during which time the camps were still housing IDPs, the World Health Organization resumed random blood testing amongst inhabitants. Results showed that *all* children under the age of six had life-threatening levels of lead in their blood. With 45µg/dl being the lead level after which therapy is recommended,[9] most levels recorded were above 65µg/dl, the highest level readable by the instruments used to carry out the tests.[10]

International attention involving the situation in the IDP camps intensified from 2004. UNMIK organized discussions with relevant non-governmental organizations (NGO) and, in turn, NGOs provided aid to the affected population and organized trips to Belgrade where treatment was, at times reluctantly, provided. Other organizations, such as the International Committee of the Red Cross (ICRC)[11] and Amnesty International,[12] demanded that the IDPs be evacuated from the camps. Furthermore, the UN special envoy to Kosovo at the time, Kai Eide, called for the immediate removal of the camps, characterizing the situation as an "emergency".[13] Local institutions also voiced their dismay. The Ombudsperson Institution in Kosovo (OIK) called for UNMIK to take action. Moreover, Kosovo's international Ombudsperson, Marek Antoni Nowicki, on one occasion added that it was his "deep suspicion that these people are being treated this way for no other reason than that they are Roma".[14] Despite all of the attention, the camps remained as they were while medical tests continued to result in "some of the highest lead levels in medical history".[15]

In 2005, UNMIK announced the reconstruction of a deserted former French military compound, camp Osterode, aimed at providing new temporary housing for the IDPs. As it was located in the direct vicinity of the three original camps, SRSG Joachim Rücker and the World Health Organization declared camp Osterode "lead *safer*" and in 2006, some 400 inhabitants of camps Žitkovac and Kablare were moved to Osterode.[16] Since then, NGOs have continued to demand final evacuation of the camps, while various UN human rights bodies have paid considerable attention to the situation.[17] UNMIK responses have

---

[9] Dossier of Evidence, p. 43, citing the United States Centre for Disease Control.

[10] *Id.*, pp. 38-43.

[11] *Id.*, p. 11.

[12] Amnesty International (AI), *Kosovo: Protect the right to health and life*, News Service No. 189, 13 July 2005.

[13] Report to the UN SG by Ambassador Kai Eide, *A Comprehensive Review of The Situation in Kosovo*, UN Doc. S/2005/635, 7 October 2005, p. 11.

[14] International Herald Tribune, *In Kosova's Camps, a Story Waits for an Ending*, 12 January 2005.

[15] *See* Dossier of Evidence, p. 38 for an overview of results obtained through tests conducted in the period between 2005 and 2008,

[16] *Id.*, p. 20; HRW Report 2009, p. 29.

[17] *E.g.* Human Rights Council (HRC), 4th Session, *Report of the Special Rapporteur on the right to adequate housing as a component of the right to an adequate standard of living, Mr.*

ranged from joint efforts to rebuild the houses of the IDPs to controversial claims that the IDPs themselves were to blame for the lead contamination, citing the illegal smelting of car batteries in the camps as the cause of the pollution.[18]

Following the 2008 political turn of events in Kosovo, the responsibility for the camps was transferred by UNMIK to the local authorities. In February 2010, a full decade after establishment, the remaining camps – Česmin Lug and Osterode – still housed approximately 600 Roma, Ashkali and Kosovo Egyptian inhabitants.[19] Human Rights Watch (HRW) reported in December 2010 that the remaining camps were being shut down by the European Commission and the US Agency for International Development.[20] However, at the time of writing February 2011, the ICRC in Kosovo was not able to confirm the complete closure of the camps.[21]

The impact of the described situation cannot be established with absolute certainty, as medical records, including the registration of miscarriages, remain poor because autopsies have not been carried out. Estimates indicate that between the end of armed hostilities in 1999 and February 2009, approximately 80 persons have died in the camps.[22] The Council of Europe Commissioner for Human Rights, Thomas Hammarberg, concluded after a visit to the camps in February 2010 that "[t]he fact that the camps have been inhabited for a full decade is no less than a scandal. The international community has a large part of the responsibility for this situation".[23] Taken together, the claim made by

---

Miloon Kothari, Addendum, Summary of communications sent and replies received from Governments and other actors, UN Doc. A/HRC/4/18/Add.1, 18 May 2007, §§ 64-66; AI, *Briefing to the Human Rights Committee during the 87th Session in July 2006*, AI Index: Eur 70/007/2006, p. 25; CommHR, *Adverse effects of the illicit movement and dumping of toxic and dangerous products and wastes on the enjoyment of human rights, Report of the Special Rapporteur, Okechukwu Ibeanu, Addendum, Summary of communications sent to and replies received from Governments and other actors during 2005*, 62nd Session, UN Doc. E/CN.4/2006/42/Add.1, 27 March 2006, §§ 11-15; Human Rights Committee (HRCee), *Report Submitted by the United Nations Interim Administration Mission in Kosovo to the Human Rights Committee on the Human Rights Situation in Kosovo Since June 1999, Kosovo (Serbia and Montenegro)*, UN Doc. CCPR/C/UNK/1, 13 March 2006.

[18] HRCee, *Document submitted by the United Nations Interim Administration Mission in Kosovo under articles 16 and 17 of the Covenant, Kosovo (Serbia)*, UN Doc. E/C.12/UNK/1, 15 January 2008, § 557 and HRW Report 2009, p. 30.

[19] HRW Report 2009, pp. 41-42.

[20] HRW, *Lead-Contaminated Roma Camps in Kosovo Shut Down*, News Release, 9 December 2010.

[21] Information provided by the ICRC in Northern Mitrovica, 22 February 2011.

[22] Dossier of Evidence, p. 47. The casualty figures include children and persons who had to be returned to the camps after they underwent treatment in Belgrade.

[23] Council of Europe (CoE), *Kosovo: Commissioner Hammarberg calls for stop of forced returns and immediate evacuation of Roma from lead-contaminated camps*, at <http://www.coe.int/t/commissioner/News/2010/100215Kosovo_en.asp>. *See also* CoE,

Commissioner Hammarberg and the events underlying the lead-poisoning drama prompt the question as to through which mechanisms can Kosovo's international administration be held to account. In this book, the broader context of this question is addressed, namely the accountability of international territorial administrations and the emergence and possible added value of public law principles in the realm of international law.

1.2 THE SUBJECT MATTER

International territorial administration (ITA) has been the subject of extensive academic debate.[24] In this book, the focus is on the accountability of

---

Report of the Council of Europe Commissioner for Human Rights' Special Mission to Kosovo(1), Doc. CommDH(2009)23, 2 July 2009, pp. 24-26.

[24] Some authors discuss the issue of sovereignty and legal status of internationally administered territories, *e.g.* Knoll B. (2008), *The Legal Status of Territories Subject to Administration by International Organizations*, New York: Cambridge University Press; Zaum D. (2007), *The Sovereignty Paradox. The Norms and Politics of International Statebuilding*, Oxford: Oxford University Press; Smyrek D.S. (2006), *Internationally Administered Territories – International Protectorates?: An Analysis of Sovereignty over Internationally Administered Territories with Special Reference to the Legal status of Post-War Kosovo*, Berlin: Duncker & Humblot; Knoll B. (2002), 'UN Imperium: Horizontal and Vertical Transfer of Effective Control and the Concept of Residual Sovereignty in 'Internationalized' Territories', 7(3) *Austrian Review of International and European Law*, pp. 3-52. Others have focused on historical precedents, *e.g.* Wilde R. (2008), *International Territorial Administration. How Trusteeship and the Civilizing Mission Never Went Away*, Oxford: Oxford University Press. The linkage between peacekeeping, foreign occupation and international administration of territory has also been assessed, *e.g.* Brabandere E. (2009), *Post-conflict Administrations in International Law; international territorial administration, transitional authority and foreign occupation in theory and practice*, Leiden: Martinus Nijhoff Publishers; Caplan R. (2006), *International Governance of War-Torn Territories*, New York: Oxford University Press; Ratner S. (2005), 'Foreign Occupation and International Territorial Administration: The Challenges of Convergence', 16(4) *European Journal of International Law*, pp. 695-719; Wilde R. (2003), 'Taxonomies of International Peacekeeping: An Alternative Narrative', 9 *ILSA Journal of International and Comparative Law*, pp. 391-398. ITA has also been referenced extensively in the broader context of an emerging constitutionalization of international law, *e.g.* Klabbers J., Peters A. & Ulfstein G. (2009), *The Constitutionalization of International Law*, Oxford: Oxford University Press; De Wet E. (2004), 'The Direct Administration of Territories by the United Nations and its Member States in the Post Cold War Era: Legal Bases and Implications for National Law', 8 *Max Planck Yearbook of United Nations Law*, pp. 291-340. Finally, the issues of legitimacy and accountability of ITA missions has been discussed in some depth or as part of overall assessments of the ITA concept, *e.g.* Stahn C. (2008), *The Law and Practice of International Territorial Administration*, Cambridge: Cambridge University Press; Pacquée D. & Dewulf S. (2007), 'International Territorial Administrations and the Rule of Law: The Case of Kosovo', 4(1) *Essex Human Rights Review*, pp. 1-14; Knoll B. (2007)(1), 'Legitimacy and UN-Administration of Territory', 8(1) *German Law Journal*, pp. 39-56; Stahn C. (2005)(3), 'Governance Beyond the State: Issues of Legitimacy in International Territorial Administration', 2(1) *International organizations Law Review*, pp. 9-56; White N.D. &

international missions established under an ITA mandate. Before the topic is discussed any further, however, the ITA concept requires certain preliminary clarifications.

1.2.1 INTERNATIONAL TERRITORIAL ADMINISTRATIONS: LEGAL CONTOURS

ITA has been perceived as a peculiarity within the international legal order. The phenomenon is intriguing, as it goes against certain legal patterns to which we have become accustomed. Receiving a stamp with UN markings instead of the usual national insignia upon entering an internationally administered territory or seeing a UN mission listed amongst states in membership listings of certain international associations or amongst treaty signatories is simply at odds with the way in which we perceive the international legal order.[25]

Although ITA as a phenomenon reflects a development rather than a static concept, a working definition is indispensable at this point. Two main characteristics define ITA. In the first instance, an international administering entity, whether an international organization or a *sui generis* international body, enjoys virtually all-encompassing authority to exercise public power within a particular territory. In other words, international entities are charged with the administration of all facets of a particular society, ranging from healthcare to economy, from foreign policy to the administration of justice. In order to exercise this mandate, the international entity enjoys legislative and executive powers and is responsible for the judiciary. Over time, the international administrator will usually engage in a gradual transfer of powers to local authorities while retaining the final say. However, territories remain under international administration as long as the ultimate decision-making authority remains with the international entity. Thus, the second defining characteristic

---

Klaasen D. (eds.) (2005), *The UN, human rights and post-conflict situations*, Manchester: Manchester University Press; Chesterman S. (2005), *You, the people: the United Nations, transitional administration and state-building*, Oxford: Oxford University Press.

25 *See e.g.* the Central European Free Trade Agreement to which UNMIK became a party on behalf of Kosovo on 19 December 2006. The preamble, Art. 1 and the signatures on the last page of the agreement place UNMIK on an equal footing with other signatories, at <http://www.cefta2006.com/sites/default/files/CEFTAMAINTEXT2006.pdf>. In 2011 UNMIK took over the Chairmanship of CEFTA. Also on behalf of Kosovo, UNMIK signed the European Common Aviation Area agreement in June 2006. *See* in particular p. 5 and Protocol IX, at <http://ec.europa.eu/transport/air_portal/international/doc/reference/background/com_2006_0113_en.pdf>. As a final illustration, UNMIK used to be listed as a separate entity listed right after Ukraine on a site dealing with the Universal Human Rights Index of United Nations Documents, at <http://www.universalhumanrightsindex.org/en/geographical/7.html>. The entry was replaced by Kosovo following the political turn of events in 2008.

rests in the fact that the power enjoyed by the international actors is ultimate in nature and remains with the international administering entity throughout the process of gradual transfer of power. This means that an entity possessing a fully-fledged network of governmental bodies – for example Bosnia and Herzegovina (BiH) – is still considered to be an internationally administered territory, as long as the ultimate decision-making power is held by an international organ placed above local governing structures. This definition results in two main determinants of this book's theme.

Firstly, *international territorial administration typifies a unique interplay between the international and local legal domain.* ITA illustrates the fusion of two traditionally separate legal realms. The international administration engages in the legislative, executive and judicial administration of a territorial entity and its inhabitants. In so doing, the international administration exercises power traditionally belonging to states. Secondly, *this interplay results in international decision-making processes having direct impact at the local level.* As a consequence of the aforementioned interplay, local societies and legal orders are shaped directly through international decision-making processes. In other words, individuals at the local level are directly subjected to decisions taken by international entities that operate at the local level. These decisions impact individuals without being filtered by or embedded in national – or otherwise applicable – rules and legislation since at that moment these decisions in fact *are* the applicable rules and legislation.[26]

Together, these two determinants shape a 'common zone of impact' at the local level: namely, one in which individuals, and other subjects, are directly affected by the exercise of public power wielded by both local and international actors, and where the distinction between the two is blurred.[27] Perceived as such, ITA is most pointedly exemplified by the institutional design and practice of the UN's administration of East Timor[28] between 1999 and 2002 and the territory of

[26] *E.g.* Knoll (2006), 'Beyond the *Mission Civilisatrice:* The Properties of a Normative Order within an Internationalized Territory', 19(2) *Leiden Journal of International Law*, pp. 275-304.

[27] Stahn makes the same argument by stating "International territorial administration illustrates more vigorously than any other form of international governance that international organizations and other non-state actors can affect individual and group rights in the same manner as states. In this setting, governmental responsibility cannot strictly be tied to the concept of the state, but should be founded upon an impact-based assessment of responsibility, namely 'the degree to which actors can impact an individual's or group's human rights'", *see* Stahn (2005)(3), p. 55, quoting Mégret F. & Hoffmann F. (2003), 'The UN as a Human Rights Violator? Some Reflections on the United Nations Changing Human Rights Responsibilities', 25(2) *Human Rights Quarterly*, p. 321.

[28] Pursuant to an agreement between Indonesia and Portugal on the transfer of authority to the UN, on 25 October 1999, SC Res. 1272 (1999) was adopted establishing a United Nations Transitional Administration in East Timor (UNTAET). UNTAET was in charge of the overall

Kosovo from 1999 onwards,[29] as well as the international governance of BiH by the Office of the High Representative (OHR) since 1995.[30] With respect to Kosovo and BiH, emphasis is placed on UNMIK and the OHR, respectively. The European Union (EU) has steadily been increasing its engagement in the administration of these territories. This increased engagement has thus far been complex on paper and ambiguous in practice, resulting in an unclear relationship between the EU missions on the ground and the UN-led administrations. The legal complexities surrounding these EU-led missions merit separate research, however, and for that reason the EU's engagement in ITA missions will not be analyzed in this book.[31]

1.2.2 THE RESEARCH QUESTION: HOLDING INTERNATIONAL TERRITORIAL ADMINISTRATIONS TO ACCOUNT

The main theme of this book involves a reoccurring aspect of ITA missions: namely, their systemic accountability deficit. In this respect, the nature of missions such as UNMIK can be misleading. ITA missions avail themselves of a presupposed legitimacy based on their linkage with peacekeeping and they operate in conflict-affected areas where, one is inclined to argue, things can hardly get any worse. Such reasoning tends to push the question of ITA mission accountability to the sidelines of the debate, under the pretext that the international administrator can do no wrong. As a matter of principle, however, assumed benevolence is not considered sufficient to the extent that it warrants a marginalization of the need for accountability.

---

civil administration of the territory and contained a military component composed of a multinational force previously deployed pursuant to SC Res. 1264 (1999). UNTAET's mandate was formally terminated on 20 May 2002, upon the independence of East Timor, now officially named Timor-Leste.

[29] On 10 June 1999, SC Res. 1244 (1999) was adopted, deciding on an "international civil and security presence" and paving the way for the establishment of UNMIK.

[30] The General Framework Agreement for Peace in Bosnia and Herzegovina negotiated in Dayton, Ohio, USA, and signed in Paris on 14 December 1995 (Dayton Peace Agreement), established the OHR as an international administration holding the final authority with regard to the implementation of the peace agreement.

[31] For UNMIK, this means that the emphasis is placed on the period during which the UN mission was fully functional: *i.e.* the period between June 1999 and 9 December 2008, the deployment date of the European Union Rule of Law Mission in Kosovo (EULEX). Nominally, UNMIK continued to operate after that date based on its original mandate. Likewise, EULEX technically operates within the ambit of SC Res. 1244 (1999), despite the telling statement of Yves de Kermabon, first head of EULEX, in which he said that as of 9 December 2008, "EULEX will switch on and UNMIK will switch off", at <http://www.emportal.rs/en/news/serbia/72082.html>. For a brief overview of the EU's engagement in BiH and Kosovo, *see* Section 2.2.2 below.

The Roma lead-poisoning drama pointedly illustrates the need for accountability. Furthermore, the example highlights the actual accountability deficit. During the relevant period, accountability was pursued through various legal means. At the local level, the European Roma Rights Center in 2005 filed a criminal complaint with the Office of the Public Prosecutor in Priština on behalf of a resident of the IDP camps.[32] The complaint alleged a violation of the Provisional Criminal Code of Kosovo, a local law adopted by way of a UNMIK regulation.[33] Human Rights Watch reported that action was taken by the prosecutor's office pursuant to this complaint.[34] Complaints were also filed with the Ombudsperson Institution in Kosovo and the Human Rights Advisory Panel (HRAP), institutions established by UNMIK for precisely this purpose. Ultimately, these institutions were prevented from achieving their goal, as will be shown in Sections 5.2.2 and 5.2.3 below. At the international level, the European Roma Rights Center attempted to involve the European Court of Human Rights (ECtHR) by filing an application in 2006. The application alleged violations of the Convention for the Protection of Human Rights and Fundamental Freedoms (ECHR), and in particular the right to life, the right to a fair trial and the adjacent right to an effective legal remedy. One day after the application was filed, the ECtHR informed the applicants that it was not competent to accept the case, as UNMIK was not party to the ECHR.[35] Finally, internal UN mechanisms were set in motion. In 2006, a third-party compensation claim was filed under UN General Assembly Res. 52/247.[36] Internal UN oversight bodies were also informed about the state of affairs in the IDP camps.[37] The complaints were in vain.

The work of the International Law Association (ILA) and the International Law Commission (ILC) indeed recognizes that accountability issues arise in situations of territorial administration.[38] The emblematic situation as presented in the previous part of this introduction shapes the conditions in which accountability of relevant international actors can legitimately be demanded. In addressing this demand, it is taken as a point of departure that certain public law principles and accountability are interrelated. Accountability implies that there

[32] The complaint was filed on 31 August 2005.
[33] UNMIK Reg. 2003/25, 6 July 2003, as amended.
[34] HRW Report 2009, pp. 32-33.
[35] European Roma Rights Center, *European Court of Human Rights Has No Jurisdiction in Kosovo Lead Poisoning Case*, 3 April 2006, at <http://www.errc.org/cikk.php?cikk=2568>.
[36] GA Res. 52/247, 17 July 1998.
[37] Internal mechanisms are discussed in Sections 5.1.2, 5.1.4 and 5.2.1 below.
[38] ILA, Committee on Accountability of International Organizations, Final Report 2004, *Report of the Seventy-First Conference*, Berlin 2004 (ILA 2004). The ILC included the topic of "Responsibility of International Organizations" into its long-term program of work in 2000, at <http://www.ila-hq.org> and <http://www.un.org/law/ilc/>.

are limits as to how public power is to be exercised.[39] Such limits can be established by institutionalizing certain public law principles: namely, the rule of law, reviewability and an independent judiciary through the diffusion of powers. In other words, these public law principles are considered to enhance accountability. A second presupposition is that accountability has a legitimizing effect on the exercise of public power.[40] Taking this into consideration, the described accountability deficit is approached in this book from a public law perspective, guided by the following question:

What is the potential of public law principles in conceptualizing the systemic accountability deficit inherent to missions engaged in international territorial administration?

1.2.3 WHY A PUBLIC LAW APPROACH?

ITA missions are generally considered the most far-reaching embodiment of a steady evolution of UN peacekeeping and peacebuilding practice. However, this assumption is problematic. In short, peacekeeping and peacebuilding are conceptually unable to address the aforementioned accountability-related challenges.

While the ITA concept did gain momentum in the context of evolving peacekeeping and peacebuilding practice, it cannot be perceived as merely a part thereof. Admittedly, there is no precise distinction between ITA missions and adjacent international undertakings such as peacekeeping. However, emphasis is placed on the fact that ITA missions face decidedly distinct challenges compared to more traditional military undertakings: namely, challenges for which international law provides neither a clear legal framework nor institutional solutions.[41]

This book adopts as a point of departure that the functional parallel between states and internationally administered territories creates the basis upon which accountability issues should be addressed. This parallel rests on two foundations: similarity of power and similarity of problem. The extent of public power vested in ITA missions only nominally falls short of being identical to the

---

39 Bovens considers this to be the constitutional perspective of accountability, *see* Bovens M. (2007), 'Analysing and Assessing Accountability: A Conceptual Framework', 13(4) *European Law Journal*, p. 463.

40 *Id.*, p. 464.

41 Accountability related to these more traditional military undertakings, as well as the military components of ITA missions, is not discussed in this book. For a critique of mainstream approaches in terms of conceptualizing ITA missions, *see* Wilde R. (2004), 'Representing International Territorial Administration: A Critique of Some Approaches', 15(1) *European Journal of International Law*, pp. 71-96.

scope of public power exercised by states. Hence, the challenges faced by international institutions in their administering capacity are inclined to be similar in nature to problems faced by states. In the state context, public law principles shape an accountability regime with respect to the holders of public power, ultimately increasing their legitimacy. It is assumed that a public law approach to the ITA accountability deficit would have a similar effect.[42]

In summary, the aim is to add to the conceptualization of a particular field of public international law, by addressing how accountability is affected and arguably compromised by the present way in which ITA missions are set up. Through an analysis of the causes underlying the existing accountability deficit, the potential role of established public law principles in addressing this deficit is identified. Section 1.3 clarifies the applied methodology, while Section 1.4 provides definitional considerations regarding public law, accountability and legitimacy and places them in context.

1.3 THE METHODOLOGY

Principles of public law, which primarily regulate the relationship between states and (groups of) individuals, developed traditionally at the national level. In this book, public law is used as a lens to analyze the accountability deficit that characterizes the relationship between international administrations and individuals.[43] In this manner, it is postulated that the two settings – the traditional state and internationally administered territories – are comparable.[44] However, comparable does not mean identical: hence, the manner in which public law principles are employed requires sensitivity to context.[45]

The applied methodology builds upon certain postulates of comparative law and it implies the transplantation of legal concepts from a national to an *internationalized* context.[46] Such vertical transplantation has conventionally

---

[42] For an overview of the ongoing continental European debate on the role of public law in international law, *see* the special issue of the *German Law Journal* (2008, vol. 9, no. 11) on 'The Exercise of Public Authority by International Organizations: A Research Project of the Max Planck Institute for International Law'.

[43] To a large extent, ideas advanced in the following paragraphs were published in Momirov A. & Naudé Fourie A. (2009), 'Vertical Comparative Law Methods: Tools for Conceptualizing the International Rule of Law', 2(3) *Erasmus Law Review*, pp. 291-309.

[44] This premise is further substantiated in Sections 2.2 and 4.3.

[45] *See also* Bogdandy A. (von) (2008), 'General Principles of International Public Authority: Sketching a Research Field', 9(11) *German Law Journal,* pp. 1909-1938. Bogdandy analyzes the (public law) principles which "guide and tame the public authority of international institutions" and defends the added value of "comparative thinking" in this respect.

[46] *See* Chodosh H.E. (1999), 'Comparing Comparisons: In Search of Methodology', 84 *Iowa Law Review*, p. 1038: "[E]ach view of the increasingly penetrating role of an international law, institution, or a process in a traditionally national ambit of authority relies on a

been surrounded by scepticism due to an assumed inherent incompatibility between the national and international legal contexts.[47] This pervasive scepticism does not signify that such transplantations have not been employed already to a significant degree and for a significant time.[48] Before the methodological steps are set out, two considerations should be taken into account: the objective of the exercise and the importance of functionalism.

Firstly, the choice of a method is related to a clearly defined research objective. As David Gerber put it, "where are we going?" and "how can we get there?" are interrelated questions.[49] Here, the primary objective of the transplantation is to address a systemic problem in international law. In other words, the public law principles are used as a tool to shed light on a particular problem. With this goal the methodology is geared towards seeking a fit between certain public law principles and the ITA context.

---

comparison". With regard to comparative law in general, essentially legal comparison can be employed in four modes: (1) horizontally, among legal systems at the national level; (2) horizontally, among legal regimes at the international level. Legal comparison might also be (3) vertical, 'top-down' (*e.g.* typically reflected in the context of *internalization* of international norms and regulations by national legal orders, whereby national law is required to fit international concepts into the national legal system, terminology and ideology); or (4) vertical, 'bottom up'. *See also* Rosenblum D. (2007), 'Internalizing Gender: Why International Law Theory Should Adopt Comparative Method', 45 *Columbia Journal of Transnational Law*, pp. 759-828; Koopmans T. (2003), *Courts and Political Institutions: A Comparative View*, Cambridge: Cambridge University Press; Kiss A.C., 'Comparative Law and Public International Law' *in* Butler W.E. (ed.) (1980), *International Law in Comparative Perspective*, Alphen aan den Rijn: Sijthoff & Noordhoff.

[47] Gotteridge, for example, reflects this conventional position by arguing that "so far as it exists at all, any relationship or kinship between comparative law and the law of nations must, therefore, be of a shadowy nature, and the only possible link between the two disciplines is to be found in the extent to which the comparative study of private law can be regarded as an instrument to be employed in promoting the growth and development of the law of nations", as quoted in Butler (ed.) (1980), p. 27. *See also* Wiener J.B. (2001), 'Something Borrowed for Something Blue: Legal Transplants and the Evolution of Global Environmental Law', 27 *Ecology Law Quarterly*, p. 1301: "Whatever couplings or comminglings between national and international law have in fact occurred might have been so discreet, or perhaps so scandalous, that no one seems to talk about them in polite company (at least not for very long). Even if borrowing from national into international law occurs in practice, it seems to have been neglected or hushed, both in officialdom and in theory". *See finally* Dannemann G., 'Comparative Law: Study of Similarities or Differences?' *in* Reimann M. & Zimmerman R. (eds.) (2006), *The Oxford Handbook of Comparative Law*, Oxford: Oxford University Press, p. 390 for an overview of "difference theorists" who work with a presumption of dissimilarity.

[48] Principles entrenched in the international legal order such as good faith, *pacta sunt servanda* and *res judicata* all find their origin at the national level, *see* Bothe M. & Ress G., 'The Comparative Method and Public International Law' *in* Butler (ed.) (1980), pp. 51 and 58-62. *See also* Kiss, *in* Butler (ed.) (1980), p. 44.

[49] Gerber D. (1998), 'System Dynamics: Toward a Language of Comparative Law', 46(4) *American Journal of Comparative Law*, p. 719.

Secondly, the employed methodology embraces functionalism as its basic – though not sole – foundation. Functionalism emphasizes "a concrete social problem" instead of the formal aspects of laws or institutions.[50] It relies on the presumption that "the legal system of *every* society faces essentially *the same problems*, and solves these problems by quite different means though very often with similar results".[51] Functionalism has been the subject of critique which includes allegations of functionalism's unjustified emphasis on similarities[52] and of functionalism being inherently biased and implicitly hegemonic.[53] Still, functionalism should not be summarily rejected. As Myres S. McDougal remarked:

> The demand for inquiring into function is, however, but the beginning of insight. Further questions are "functional" for whom, against whom, with respect to what values, determined by what decision-makers under what conditions, how, with what effects.[54]

What, then, is the rationale behind the methodological choices *in casu*? The dynamic ITA concept has thus far been applied in several instances on an ad hoc basis. However, placing territories under direct rule of international organizations lacks an adequate legal framework and institutional backing. The ITA concept outgrows the confines, institutional capacity and terminology of public international law. This gives rise to new legal problems that in turn call for solutions that cannot be easily found within international law – at least not in its present stage of evolution. Hence, inspiration is sought within other bodies of law, especially national public law.[55] Such an approach is further justified by the emergence of the 'common zone of impact'. As individuals increasingly become the addressees of international law, expectations from international law – that

[50] Peters A. & Schwenke H. (2000), 'Comparative Law beyond Post-Modernism', 49 *International and Comparative Law Quarterly*, p. 808, quoting Ernst Rabel, founder of the functional approach.
[51] Zweigert K. & Kötz H. (1998), *An Introduction to Comparative Law*, Oxford: Oxford University Press, p. 34.
[52] *See also* Dannemann, in Reimann & Zimmerman (eds.) (2006), p. 390.
[53] Peters & Schwenke (2000), p. 827.
[54] McDougal, as quoted in Peters & Schwenke (2000), p.828.
[55] *See e.g.* Kingsbury B., Krisch N. & Stewart R. (2004), 'The Emergence of Global Administrative Law', 2004/1 *IILJ Working Paper*, pp. 1-48 and Hey E. (2004), 'International Public Law', 6 *International Law FORUM du droit International*, pp. 149-162. *See also* Wiener (2001), p. 1356, where he remarks that international lawyers "cannot examine 'the same branch of the law in other legal systems' under different conditions, because we only have one international law on this planet – only one Earth. We have no database for a cross-sectional empiricism of international law. To follow Watson's teaching [on comparison and similarities], we would somehow need to look at other planets also facing [similar problems] and evaluate how their legal systems responded in comparison to our own".

cannot be met by an 'autistic' approach to international law – continue to increase. It is this particular context that provides a compelling justification and an interesting opportunity for considering public law principles when looking for ways to address the accountability of ITA missions.

Four stages of the methodology are distinguished in the following sections. Understood together, these methodological stages underlie the findings presented throughout this book.

1.3.1 STAGE ONE

Stage one is triggered by the observance of a reoccurring ITA accountability deficit. In order to address this deficit, a hypothesis is formulated. The hypothesis rests on a *praesumptio similitudinis*: namely, on similarities observed between corresponding features (the scope of public powers held by ITA missions and states) and corresponding problems (accountability problems faced by ITA missions and states).[56] The question remains as to how far one has to account for contextual differences, since failure to properly consider context presents a prominent risk.[57] It is suggested that contextual differences remain important, but that being overly concerned about the risk may lead to "exaggerations and absurdities".[58] Stages two and three address this issue further.

At this point, the hypothesis posits that there is a link between the ITA accountability deficit and the absence of public law principles in the way ITA missions exercise their public powers. In order to address the deficit, ITA missions should be perceived as state-like entities rather than international institutions engaged in extensive peace-building operations.[59] Throughout this

---

[56] Whether one emphasizes differences or similarities remains a balancing act and depends on the research objectives, *see* Dannemann, *in* Reimann & Zimmerman (eds.) (2006), pp. 383-385.

[57] *Id.*, p. 388.

[58] *E.g.* Palmer V.V. (2005), 'From Lerotholi to Lando: Some Examples of Comparative Law Methodology', 53 *American Journal of Comparative Law*, p. 261; Peters & Schwenke (2000), p.803.

[59] For example, the UN Handbook on Multidimensional Peacekeeping Operations observes that UN peacekeeping operations have become 'multidimensional', as they increasingly began to include non-military components. This handbook also makes explicit reference to ITA by stating that "multidimensional peacekeeping operations [...] may be required to [...] [a]dminister a territory for a transitional period, thereby carrying out *all the functions that are normally the responsibility of a government*" which creates a situation in which the international presence is "responsible for *directly* managing *all aspects of civilian life* while simultaneously working to devolve its responsibilities to local authorities", *see* Handbook on United Nations Multidimensional Peacekeeping Operations, United Nations, Department of Peacekeeping Operations, Peacekeeping Best Practices Unit, December 2003, pp. 1-2 and 35, emphasis added. *See also* Nilsson, J. (2004), 'UNMIK and the Ombudsperson Institution in

book, the hypothesis will be referred to as the public law argument. Such a paradigm shift facilitates a better conceptualization of the problem. Taking the argument one step further, it is normatively asserted that the institutional design of ITA missions should embody principles and mechanisms that regulate the exercise of public power in the context of the state.

1.3.2 STAGE TWO

Stage two relates to public law as the *tertium comparationis*: that is, the benchmark against which the checks and balances that govern the exercise of public power are assessed.[60] The outcome of stage two depends strongly on the subject matter and on the aim of the research. In some cases, stage two can lead to a conceptual model that can then be applied meticulously to the subject of analysis.[61] The aim of the second methodological step *in casu* is decidedly more modest. It relates to the choice of public law as the perspective through which the subject matter is assessed, in keeping with the definitional considerations provided at the end of this introduction.[62] In order to serve as a *tertium comparationis,* our understanding of three key public law principles – the rule of law, judicial review and an independent judiciary achieved through the diffusion of power – has to capture the appropriate level of abstraction rather than to focus on the way in which these principles have been employed throughout various national legal systems.[63] Consider, for example, the diffusion of power. The aim of this principle is to facilitate checks and balances by preventing the concentration of power. Whether this aim is achieved through the division of power into two, three or more branches is of subsidiary importance. Likewise, the essence of judicial review is reviewability. Which acts should be reviewable, which institution should have the jurisdiction to do so and against which higher norms are context-dependent variables.

Kosovo: Human Rights Protection in a United Nations "Surrogate State"', 22(3) *Netherlands Quarterly of Human Rights*, pp. 389-411.

[60] Zweigert & Kötz explained the functionalist focus of the "common core" as follows: "[…] the solutions we find in the different jurisdictions must be cut loose from their conceptual context and stripped of their national doctrinal overtones so that they may be seen purely in the light of their function, as an attempt to satisfy a particular legal need", *see* Zweigert & Kötz (1998), p. 44.

[61] *E.g.* Naudé Fourie A. (2009), *The World Bank Inspection Panel and Quasi-Judicial Oversight: In Search of the 'Judicial Spirit' in Public International Law*, Utrecht: Eleven International Publishing.

[62] *See* Section 1.4.1 below.

[63] Peters & Schwenke (2000), p. 808. Zweigert and Kötz also emphasize the necessity to create an "abstract heuristic conceptual framework; free from the context of a particular system […] flexible enough to grasp a wide variety of 'heterogeneous institutions which are functionally comparable", *see* Chodosh (1999), p. 1051.

Only if the right level of abstraction is captured, can public law – detached from the traditional state concept and understood in terms more closely related to the exercise of public power rather than the context in which this power is exercised – serve "as a yardstick" for the exercise of public law.[64]

1.3.3 STAGE THREE

The third stage of the methodology relates to the core of the legal analysis: namely, the transplantation of the ideas behind legal concepts (if not, strictly speaking, the legal concepts themselves) from one setting to another. In general, the third stage explores the *prima facie* similarities observed in stage one. These similarities should not be accepted without questioning their significance, as they might be merely coincidental. Differences will also inevitably be encountered. As with similarities, differences should not be taken at face value. For instance, they might turn out to be artificial once the context is taken into account or when differences in terminology are better understood. *In casu,* this stage consists of two steps.

Firstly, the exercise of public power by ITA missions is assessed and essential features of ITA missions are conceptualized in terms of public law. For instance, the legal analysis at this stage shows that constituent documents of ITA missions entrust these entities with mandates to exercise public power that virtually mirror the scope and effect of public power exercised by states. The encountered differences – for example, the fact that states enjoy full sovereignty while ITA missions formally do not – prove to be immaterial in this respect. Overall, the boundaries of the analogy between states and ITA missions are determined.[65] Secondly, the applicable accountability regime is assessed and the main deficiencies in the ITA accountability regime are addressed in terms of public law. In particular, the extent to which certain features of ITA missions determine the structure of the ITA accountability regime is analyzed. At this stage, in the words of Vernon Palmer,

> [legal] transplants almost always undergo some modification and reform not only at an unconscious epistemological level (wherein borrowed rules receive a distinct local interpretation or "translation" by the local culture); there is often a conscious revision of the transplant to conform to an analogous or cognate legal idea already present in the system. The process is neither new nor abnormal in many mixed systems. It is actually a kind of

---

[64] Koopmans (2003), p. 9.
[65] *See* Chapter 4 below.

creative convergence – the construction of autonomous law out of borrowed elements.[66]

1.3.4 STAGE FOUR

In the fourth stage, findings from the preceding stages are integrated and the hypothesis formulated in the first stage is proved or disproved. Conclusions are drawn and final observations are presented

1.4 DEFINITIONAL CONSIDERATIONS PLACED IN CONTEXT

The following sections provide definitional considerations with respect to three concepts that reoccur throughout this book: public law, accountability and legitimacy. The meaning of these words can be understood in numerous ways. Firstly, Section 1.4.1 sets forth the essence of three public law principles used in relation to the ITA context: that is, outside their traditional state context. Hence, this section does not expound the various ways in which these principles have been embedded in various legal systems. Rather, the section explains succinctly how the essence of these principles is understood in the context of this book, in keeping with the section on methodology where it is stated that the 'idea' behind these concepts is used as a lens to look at a particular development in international law.[67] Sections 1.4.2 and 1.4.3 turn to accountability and legitimacy, respectively. Due to an abundance of interpretations, these concepts have often been used as 'weasel words', promising more than what is actually intended. The two sections define what is meant by the terms in the present context and explain the linkage between the two concepts.

1.4.1 THREE PUBLIC LAW PRINCIPLES IN CONTEXT

At the national level, public law regulates the exercise of public power – *i.e.* the full scope of activities carried out by public bodies in the exercise of their authority – and shapes the relationship between those exercising it and those who might be affected by it. In so doing, public law follows the tenet that the exercise of governmental authority must be limited and that these limits must be institutionalized. This conception of public law is influenced by liberal and constitutionalist ideas since these ideas – throughout their development in western legal thought in particular – have challenged absolutism as a way of

[66] Palmer (2005), p. 276.
[67] *See* Section 1.3.2 above.

exercising public power. Consider, for example, Carl Joachim Friedrich's claim that:

> [w]hat has persisted throughout the history of Western constitutionalism is the notion that the individual human being is of paramount worth and should be protected against the interference of his ruler, be he a prince, party, or a popular majority.[68]

The UN relies strongly on these ideas and values *i.e.* on this shared raison d'être of a limited government.[69] Moreover, the quote refers to different types of rulers, making it clear that the described notion applies to a variety of situations in which public power is exercised.[70] In time, this normative postulate developed and was gradually institutionalized through law.[71] Three public law principles are generally deemed indispensable in pursuing a limited and accountable exercise of public power: the rule of law, judicial review and an independent judiciary as the product of a diffusion of power. There is an intrinsic link that connects the three principles. Firstly, the rule of law refers to the exercise of public power limited by law. As the second principle, judicial review is accepted as the primary device through which limits can be upheld. Finally, the guarantee of independence of (quasi-) judicial bodies is considered as the institutional embedding of judicial review. Through these principles, public law provides a framework within which the exercise of public power can be conceptualized as limited and governments can be held to account if these limits are overstepped.

---

[68] Friedrich C.J. (1964), *Transcendent Justice, the religious dimensions of Constitutionalism*, Durham: Duke University Press, p. 17. The worth of individuals was not always considered the primary aim of constitutionalism. Plato's ideas about a constitutional government for example do not mirror the modern-day human rights-based underpinning of a limited government. The idea of a constrained government was, at the time, presented as a means to preserve the state. The rationale thereof should be understood in the light of the difference between what the state was considered to be at the time and nowadays. The *πόλις* (city-state) was not an administrative unit: it was a way of life. In other words, the Greek state was the sum of its citizens; "the citizen is not simply the counterpart of the state, nor the state of him. The citizen *is* the state in little", *see* McIlwain C.H. (1968), *The growth of political thought in the West: from the Greeks to the end of the Middle Ages*, New York: Cooper Square Publishers, pp. 10-11. *See also* Morrow J. (2005), *History of Western Political Thought. A Thematic Introduction*, New York: Palgrave Macmillan, (2005), p. 5.

[69] *See e.g.* <http://www.un.org/en/ruleoflaw/index.shtml>.

[70] Friedrich argued that constitutionalism is based on, amongst other things, the basic assumption that man is inclined to abuse power, *see* Friedrich (1947), p. 123.

[71] *See e.g.* McIlwain C.H. (rev.ed. 1947), '*Constitutionalism: Ancient and Modern*', Ithaca, New York: Cornell University Press, Chapters II-V, at <http://www.constitution.org/cmt/mcilw/mcilw.htm>. *See also* Gordon S. (1999), *Controlling the State – Constitutionalism from Ancient Athens to Today*, Cambridge: Harvard University Press on the evolution of constitutionalism.

By default, these three principles are associated with states. However, the demand for limits to the exercise of public power does not arise exclusively in the traditional state context. Rather, such a demand for constraint is generally applicable to constructs within which public powers are exercised. Hence, it is argued that the three public law principles can and should play a role in addressing the accountability of ITA missions. Worded differently, the argument is that the absence of these three principles underlies the ITA accountability deficit.

1.4.1.1 The Exercise of Public Power Confined by Law

The first principle relates to the rule of law, according to which everyone should be bound by law, including those exercising public power. Throughout history, rule of law has been employed to address the dichotomy between will and law and the underlying conundrum: should (as the normative aspect) and can (as the practical aspect) the entity entitled to make law be bound by it?[72] Thomas Hobbes, for example, argued it could neither be nor should it be.[73] For Hobbes, the notions of unlimited sovereignty and government needed to be embodied in one and the same entity. Absolute sovereignty was the only way to avoid the chaos of an unregulated and disordered society. Logic is also on Hobbes' side, for how can the creator of law be limited by it when he enjoys the power to alter it.[74] Hobbes was countered by the rise of liberalism, and the rule of law acquired its dominant contemporary underpinning with the positioning of individual

[72] For example, in his *Πολιτεία* (usually, though somewhat confusingly, translated as The Republic) and *Πολιτικός* (Statesman) Plato advocates the idea of a constitutional government, albeit only as a second best. He holds that "the best government theoretically or ideally is based upon the discretion of the ruler and *not* upon law", *see* McIlwain (1947), p. 16, emphasis added. A ruler should be uninhibited and his rule unhampered by law. However, Plato stresses that this ruler would need to be a philosopher king: "[u]ntil philosophers are kings, or the kings and princes of this world have the spirit and power of philosophy, and political greatness and wisdom meet in one [...] cities will never have rest from their evils, – nor the human race, as I believe, – and then only will this our State have a possibility of life and behold the light of day", from Plato's *The Republic*, translation by Benjamin Jowett (1892), p. 158. Aware of the impossibility of his ideal, Plato replaces the philosopher king by a constitutional government, being a better alternative than rule based on the discretion of unwise men. *See also* Tamanaha B. Z. (2004), *On the Rule of Law*, Cambridge: Cambridge University Press, p. 10.

[73] Hobbes T. (1996), *Leviathan*, edited by J.C.A. Gaskin, Oxford: Oxford University Press, pp. 176-177. However, Hobbes does accept that the absolute sovereign is bound by the laws of nature; *see* Leviathan, Chapter 17. In fact, according to Hobbes, the subjects of the sovereign do have the right not to follow orders of their sovereign when these orders pose a serious threat to them.

[74] Tamanaha (2004), p. 48.

freedom as the primary rationale behind limited government.[75] The concept developed over time and increasingly gained importance in legal thought and practice.[76]

Two different categories of theories regarding the rule of law emerged: "formal theories focus on the proper sources and form of legality, while substantive theories also include requirements about the content of the law".[77] In the words of former UN Secretary-General Kofi Annan, the rule of law combines procedure and substance:

> a principle of governance in which all persons, institutions and entities, public and private, including the State itself, are accountable to laws that are publicly promulgated, equally enforced and independently adjudicated, and which are consistent with international human rights norms and standards.[78]

Analyzing the substantive aspect of the rule of law would go beyond the scope of this book. Moreover, in this book no claim is made as to which substantive norms *in particular* should be considered to bind ITA missions, especially since substantive norms – written or unwritten – which bind governing entities "vary from time to time and from place to place".[79] Instead, claims made in this book

---

[75] *E.g.* ButleRitchie D.T. (2004), 'The confines of modern constitutionalism', 3(1) *Pierce Law Review*, p. 17. Liberals throughout different time periods – such as John Locke John Stuart – all within their own understanding of liberalism shared the ideal of individual liberty above tyranny and absolutism, *see e.g.* Tamanaha (2004), p. 50; Zuckert M. P., 'Hobbes, Locke, and the Problem of the Rule of Law' *in* Shapiro I. (ed.) (1994), *The Rule of Law*, New York: New York University Press, pp. 63-79.

[76] *See also* Tamanaha (2004), p. 26; McIlwain (1947), p. 32.

[77] *See* Tamanaha (2004), p. 92 and Chapters 7-8 for a detailed discussion about the two sets of theories. *See also* Allan T. (2001), *Constitutional justice: a liberal theory of the rule of law*, New York: Oxford University Press.

[78] Report by the SG, *Uniting our strengths: Enhancing United Nations support for the rule of law*, UN Doc. A/61/636-S/2006/980, 14 December 2006; UN GA Report of the Sixth Committee, *The rule of law at the national and international levels*, UN Doc. A/61/456, 17 November 2006.

[79] Friedrich (1974), p. 67. For example, in the context of the United States, the Bill of Rights codifies fundamental rights. The initial text of the U.S. constitution did not include individual rights and was predominantly focused on constitutional arrangements, reflecting the possible friction between human rights and constitutionalism. It was Thomas Jefferson who argued with respect to the Bill of Rights that it enshrines "what the people are entitled to against every government on earth", *see* Koopmans (2003), pp. 45, and 216-217. In the United Kingdom, due to different historical factors, codifying rights for a long time used to be considered as something that would curtail the potency of the – traditionally sovereign – parliament. Moreover, codifying rights was deemed unnecessary, for why would the parliament that represents the people adopt decisions contrary to their well-being in the first place? As Dicey argued, freedoms in England were sufficiently guaranteed by the fact that

build on the fact that ITA missions themselves acknowledge that their exercise of public power ought to be in line with human rights standards. Hence, human rights are touched upon indirectly, by assessing questions such as: 'to what extent can international human rights law be considered to apply vis-à-vis ITA missions' or 'to what extent can treaty-based legal frameworks – within which certain accountability mechanisms were developed – play a role in framing the exercise of public power by ITA missions'.[80] Emphasis is placed on the need for a legal framework and accompanying mechanisms through which substantive standards can be met and upheld: "the technique of establishing and maintaining effective restraints on [...] governmental action".[81]

In summary, the rule of law postulates that everyone, citizens as well as government, is bound by law and that exercise of public authority must be based on and limited by law. Based on this understanding, Brian Tamanaha argues that the rule of law "stands in the peculiar state of being the preeminent legitimating political ideal in the world today".[82] In order to become more than a normative statement, further institutionalization of the principle through auxiliary mechanisms is crucial:

> [F]or the rule of law to endure, you need more than the good intentions of the rulers, for they may change (both the intentions and the rulers). You need institutions within society whose strength is independent of the state.[83]

It is these institutions that this book focuses on, in the context of ITA missions and the procedures through which these missions can be held to account.

1.4.1.2 Reviewability of the Exercise of Public Power

Judicial review is the second cornerstone principle.[84] No other concept has been considered more indispensable to upholding the limits to government as

any parliament is chosen with the aim to protect the citizens and any such parliament which would adopt an act limiting the freedom of its citizens would lose popular support.

[80] *See* Sections 4.1.1 and 5.3.3 below.

[81] Friedrich C.J. (1937), *Constitutional Government and Politics*, New York: Harper and Row, p. 101.

[82] Tamanaha (2004), p. 4.

[83] Zakaria F. (2004), *The Future of Freedom*, New York: W.W. Norton and Company Inc., p. 33. With respect to pre-modern times, Tamanaha states that actual restraint came about either through acceptance by the ruler, an assumption that the ruler indeed acted within the law or, finally, was merely a result of routine conduct, *see* Tamanaha (2004), pp. 115-116. *See also* Koopmans (2003), pp. 240-241.

[84] The term 'review' or 'judicial review' will be used to connote judicial, constitutional, administrative and other types of review. For an article dealing with the development of

discussed in the foregoing paragraph than judicial review. As Chief Justice Marshall said:

> To what purpose are powers limited, and to what purpose is that limitation committed to writing, if these limits may at any time be passed by those intended to be restrained? The distinction between a government with limited and unlimited powers is abolished if those limits do not confine the persons on whom they are imposed, and if acts prohibited and acts allowed are of equal obligation.[85]

Judicial review denotes the review by judicial bodies of the exercise of public power against applicable procedural and normative standards. This definition does not imply that the judiciary is given primacy over other branches of government, since the main purpose of judicial review is in fact to avoid the uncontrolled supremacy of any branch.[86] Judicial review, just as the rule of law,

---

review mechanisms in the German legal system, emphasizing the differences between judicial, administrative and constitutional review, *see* De Wet E. (2008), 'Holding International Institutions Accountable: The Complementary Role of Non-Judicial Oversight Mechanisms and Judicial Review', 9(11) *German Law Journal,* pp. 1987-2011; Stolleis M. (2003), 'Judicial Review, Administrative Review and Constitutional Review in the Weimar Republic', 16(2) *Ratio Juris*, p. 266-280. *See also* Harutyunyan G. & Mavčič A. (1999), *Constitutional Review and its Development in the Modern World: A Comparative Constitutional Analysis*, at <http://www.iatp.am/resource/law/harutunyan/monogr3/book.htm> and Arne Mavčič at <http://www.concourts.net/introen.php>. In the context of ITA missions, *see e.g.* Perritt H.H. (2004), 'Providing Judicial Review for Decisions by Political Trustees', 15(1) *Duke Journal of Comparative and International Law*, pp. 1-74.

[85] The United States, Supreme Court, *Marbury v. Madison*, 5 U.S. (1 Cr.) 137, 24 February 1803. This case relates to the question of conformity with the constitution of congressional acts. Other forms of 'judicial review' were already established in the U.S. legal system. For example, state law was held to be invalid if it conflicted with a treaty in *Ware v. Hylton* while in the later case of *Fletcher v. Peck*, state law was declared void on the basis of its non-conformity with the constitution, *see* the United States Supreme Court, *Ware v. Hylton,* 3 U.S. (3 Dall.) 190, 7 March 1796 and *Fletcher v. Peck*, 10 U.S. (6 Cr.) 87, 16 March 1810.Although the concept of judicial review now represents the backbone of the U.S. legal system, the fact that it is not embedded in the constitution remains explicitly a subject of debate. Leaders such as Thomas Jefferson, Andrew Jackson and Abraham Lincoln all expressed their serious doubts regarding the validity of the court's newly acquired powers. *See e.g.* Hand L. (1965), *The Bill of Rights*, New York: Atheneum on the legitimacy of judicial review; Bickel A.M. (1962), *The Least Dangerous Branch: the Supreme Court at the bar of politics*, Indianapolis: Bobbs–Merrill, pp. 1-33.

[86] Alexander Hamilton argued in this respect "The interpretation of the laws is the proper and peculiar province of the courts. A constitution is, in fact, and must be regarded by the judges, as a fundamental law. It therefore belongs to them to ascertain its meaning, as well as the meaning of any particular act proceeding from the legislative body. If there should happen to be an irreconcilable variance between the two, that which has the superior obligation and validity ought, of course, to be preferred; or, in other words, the Constitution ought to be preferred to the statute, the intention of the people to the intention of their agents. Nor does this conclusion by any means suppose a superiority of the judicial to the legislative power. It

does imply a certain hierarchy of norms: that is, the supremacy of certain rules, whether codified or not, over 'other acts' of the governing authorities.[87] In the ITA context, this relates to any such set of national or international legal standards that would be considered to apply to the administering entity.

Institutionalizing review prompts various context-dependent questions.[88] While no model is suggested with respect to the ITA context, several points of attention that accompany every discussion on judicial review are briefly restated at this point. A primary concern deals with the question of whether a court or judicial body should be entrusted with the power to review. In this respect, essentially two systems have developed: the diffuse system and the concentrated European model.[89] Another point of discussion considers which acts ought to be

only supposes that the power of the people is superior to both", *see* Federalist Paper No. 78, authored by Alexander Hamilton, at <www.foundingfathers.info>. In order to overcome the uneasy relationship between the unelected judiciary and the legislative authority, it is crucial to accept that the activity of the judicial branch is profoundly different in nature than the way in which the other branches exercise their entrusted powers. The essential difference lies in the fact that the judicial branch, as opposed to the other branches, acts upon judgment instead of will; it responds and interprets. Furthermore, "[o]ne needs a theory about the way in which judges should exercise their powers or review that tells them how they can distinguish laws that are legitimate expressions of the coercive powers of the state from those that are not without being influenced by their own biases and personal points of view", *see* Beatty (2004), p. 5. For limits to judicial review in general, *see e.g.* Koopmans (2003), pp. 98-128.

[87] Hans Kelsen, in drafting the Austrian constitution of 1920, also based his defence of constitutional review on the *Stufenbaulehre*, the doctrine of hierarchical structure which according to him was essential in order for "the immanent meaning of the concept of constitution [to be] accessible", *see* Paulson S. L. (2003), 'Constitutional Review in the United States and Austria: Notes on the Beginnings', 16(2) *Ratio Juris*, p. 234.

[88] Recent studies suggest that the institutional design of the judiciary and the delineation of its competences has a positive effect on a nation's economic growth and political freedom, and can even be of crucial influence on the coherence of a society, *see* Ramos Romeu F. (2006), 'The Establishment of Constitutional Courts: A Study of 128 Democratic Constitutions', 2(1) *Review of Law and Economics*, p. 104, with reference to research by Feld and Voigt (2004), La Porta *et al.* (2002) and Sweet and Brunell (1998). *See also* Ginsburg T. (2001), 'Economic Analysis of the Design of Constitutional Courts', 3(1) *Theoretical Inquiries in Law,* pp. 1-38.

[89] According to the American model, the power to review is given to the judiciary in general. In this system, the decisions have effect only in the specific case, taking into consideration the principle of *stare decisis*. Consequently, it is the Supreme Court that guarantees legal certainty and uniformity. Conversely, the concentrated or European system, modeled predominantly on the basis of Kelsen's design, attributes the power to review to a special (constitutional) court. In addition, a variety of systems exists in which elements of both models have been implemented. Whether the choice falls on one system or the other can depend on many factors, including distrust of the sitting judiciary, political uncertainty, legal certainty, federalism and imitation, *see* Ramos Romeu (2006). Taking Germany as an example, the debate on whether to establish a constitutional court or to opt for a diffuse system of judicial review reflects that such factors were taken into account, some of which proved decisive. At the time, Germany's recent past, its federal structure, Kelsen's neighboring Austrian constitutional court and a continental legal tradition were a driving force

subjected to review?[90] This question relates to the various channels through which public power is exercised. Legislative, executive and other acts might be subjected to different levels of scrutiny and different review procedures. In the ITA context, the distinction between the various categories of acts is blurred. While acts differ in terms of effect, the source and procedure behind these acts is essentially the same: the international administrator governs by decree. A final matter concerns the review procedure, and in particular the question of whether it can be initiated by (groups of) individuals.[91] For example, the issue was heavily debated during the adoption process of the new German Constitution in 1949. While some considered the inclusion of a constitutional complaint to be of "enormous importance", others argued it would overwhelm the Court. Powered by the tradition of constitutional complaints in Bavaria, voices in favour of the constitutional complaint were predominant: "basic rights [needed to be] justiciable".[92] Thus, as well as guaranteeing the constitutional order, judicial review can fulfill the role of guardian of citizens against the governing authorities.[93] In the context of the adoption of Germany's 1949 Constitution and as a response to the preceding period of Germany's history – "[t]he institutions of the Weimar Republic reflected what proved to be an undue optimism about things democratic"[94] – it was concluded that

> all basic rights are once again given substantive import. Given that a constitutional complaint may be filed, the basic rights acquire greater legal force, *and the guarantee that the state cannot enter this sphere willy nilly is established.*[95]

---

behind the adoption of a concentrated system, *see* Borowski (2003), 'The Beginnings of Germany's Federal Constitutional Court', 16(2) *Ratio Juris*, p. 164.

90 As well as legislation, one could also think of the review of lower–court decisions, executive regulations, acts of state officials (often through impeachment proceedings), international agreements and so forth.

91 Individuals in many systems have the right to address the constitutional court though a constitutional or popular complaint. Legal entities are also sometimes allowed to file a constitutional complaint, as is the case, for example, in Austria, Switzerland and Serbia. At the same time, the Croatian system of constitutional review explicitly denies legal entities this right.

92 Constitution of Bavaria, 14 August 1919, Section 1, § 70. Both sides in the debate proved to be right. While the constitutional complaint is considered to be 'the flagship power' of the German Federal Constitutional Court, it is also the Court's most burdensome mechanism, *see* Borowski (2003), pp. 168-174.

93 Borowski (2003), p. 160, n. 22.

94 *Id.*, pp. 159-161. *See also* Koopmans (2003), pp. 241-242 on the decline of trust in democratic decisions.

95 Hans Nawiasky, as quoted in Borowski M. (2003), p. 160, n. 23 from the Protocol of the 4th Session of the Subcommittee I of the Herrenchiemsee Conference of 18 August 1948, emphasis added. *See also* Zakaria (2004), p. 19: "To have 'democracy' mean, subjectively, 'a

In conclusion, what is essential is that the exercise of public power should be subjected to review and that such review should be institutionalized. Judicial review implies and upholds a certain hierarchy amongst legal norms and balances the different centers of authority within a system. Finally, reviewability of the exercise of public power – for example through constitutional complaints – offers a mechanism through which guaranteed rights can be effectuated. Ernst Friesenhahn observed with respect to constitutional courts that they themselves, as a mechanism through which judicial review is exercised, cannot "prevent revolution; they can, however, contribute to the *feeling of the citizens* that they are being treated according to the law", and consequently increase the perception of legitimacy of a legal system.[96]

good government' makes it analytically useless". Throughout Europe, vaguely institutionalized concepts of judicial review were often replaced after World War I by the establishment of constitutional courts. The Austrian Federal Constitution of 1920, drafted by Kelsen, established the Constitutional Court, entrusting it broad powers regarding constitutional review and thereby creating arguably the most prominent amongst such systems at the time. Kelsen himself admitted that the drafting of the provisions related to constitutional review "meant the most to him", *see* Hans Kelsen as quoted in Paulson S.L. (2003), pp. 232-237. Soon, several European states such as Greece, Liechtenstein and Spain followed and after World War II, constitutional review was embedded in national legal systems throughout the world, *see e.g.* Ramos Romeu (2006), p. 104, n. 9; Harutyunyan & Mavčič (1999). *See also* Tremblay L.B. (2003), 'General Legitimacy of Judicial Review and the Fundamental Basis of Constitutional Law', 23(4) *Oxford Journal of Legal Studies*, pp. 525-562.

[96] Ernst Friesenhahn, as cited in Borowski M. (2003), p. 159, emphasis added.

In the famed U.S. case *Marbury v. Madison*, Justice Marshall argued "To what purpose are powers limited, and to what purpose is that limitation committed to writing, if these limits may at any time be passed by those intended to be restrained? The distinction between a government with limited and unlimited powers is abolished if those limits do not confine the persons on whom they are imposed, and if acts prohibited and acts allowed are of equal obligation. It is a proposition too plain to be contested that the Constitution controls any legislative act repugnant to it, or that the Legislature may alter the Constitution by an ordinary act. [...] It would be giving to the legislature a practical and real omnipotence, with the same breath which professes to restrict their powers within narrow limits. It is prescribing limits, and declaring that those limits may be passed at pleasure."

Conversely, Justice John B. Gibson's dissent in the otherwise inconsequential case of *Eakin v. Raub* is widely regarded to be the most elaborate 'attack' on Justice Marshall's defense of judicial review. Justice Gibson does not deny the constitution's supremacy, but argues that it is not the courts but the people who have the ultimate power to uphold it: "It rests with the people, in whom full and sovereign power resides to correct abuses in legislation, by instructing their representatives to repeal the obnoxious act". While both branches are "not infallible", he argued, mistakes by the legislator are easier to repair. Allowing the courts to declare a law void would be tantamount to placing the courts above the legislator: "[...] in what part of the constitution are we to look for this proud pre–eminence? Viewing the matter in the opposite direction, what would be thought of an act of assembly in which it should be declared that the Supreme Court had, in a particular case, put a wrong construction on the constitution of the United States, and that the judgment should therefore be reversed? It would doubtless be thought a usurpation of judicial power".

The United States, Supreme Court, *Marbury v. Madison*, 5 U.S. (1 Cr.) 137, 24 February 1803 & *Eakin v. Raub*, 12 S & R Penn. Rep. 330 Pa, 16 April 1825.

1.4.1.3 Independent Judiciary through the Diffusion of Public Power

Finally, for judicial review to work in practice, it is generally accepted that a third principle needs to be institutionalized: an independent judiciary as one of the separated branches of government. The aim of dispersing public power is to prevent its exercise from becoming unlimited and institutionally uncontrolled. Power accumulated in the same hands is bound to render the rule of law principle redundant and judicial review ineffective.

In 1985, the UN General Assembly endorsed a list of "Basic Principles on the Independence of the Judiciary" in order to promote the independence of the judiciary amongst member states.[97] The set of principles highlights various aspects of the judicial branch – such as appointments, conditions of service, tenure and removal from office – that should be regulated in order for the

[97] GA Res. 40/146, 13 December 1985.

judiciary to be able to act freely upon its judgment when required by law to do so. The set of principles reflects a broad consensus on the importance of the diffusion of public power as a precondition of judicial independence.

The diffused exercise of public power is most often discussed in relation to the separation-of-powers doctrine. Being a means rather than an aim, this doctrine is consequently not mentioned as such amongst the principles endorsed by the UN.[98] It is widely accepted that it was Montesquieu who laid the foundations of the doctrine through his analysis of – what he perceived to be – the essence of the British constitutional system at the time. Montesquieu argued in his *De l'esprit des lois* that the diffusion of power is to be achieved best by dividing government into three independent branches. This doctrine is one means by which diffusion is achieved. Indeed, other options exist,[99] while some legal scholars have explicitly rejected the claim that this doctrine is essential in upholding judicial independence. Charles McIlwain, for example, argues that the independence of the judiciary and the separation of powers can and should be seen as unrelated.

> Among all the modern fallacies that have obscured the true teachings of constitutional history, few are worse than the extreme doctrine of the separation of powers and the indiscriminate use of the phrase 'checks and balances'.[100]

Already limited by law, a government should not be undermined by unnecessary separations that, according to him, have no historical foundation apart from the "imaginations of closet philosophers like Montesquieu".[101] Somewhat comparable are the views of Hobbes, according to whom a strict separation of governmental authority would "generate conflict within the divided sovereign" and disable the sovereign from preserving social order.[102]

For the purpose of this study, references to the separation or diffusion of power connote any such legal construct that aims at preventing a concentration of power that would jeopardize the independence of the judiciary.[103] In the words of James Madison:

---

[98] The document carefully omits the term 'separation of powers'.

[99] The traditional conception of the doctrine involves a tripartite division of powers. Other divisions are thinkable which include additional branches, usually tasked with the control of finance–related decision–making processes, such as for example a possible auditory branch.

[100] McIlwain (1947), p. 67.

[101] *Id.*, p. 67.

[102] Tamanaha (2004), p. 48.

[103] Koopmans, for example, argues that the traditional concept of separation of powers is gradually replaced by a 'bipolar distinction', one between the judiciary on the one side and the other branches on the other, *see* Koopmans (2003) p. 247. In the Federalist Papers,

> The accumulation of all powers, legislative, executive and judiciary, in the same hands, whether of one, a few, or many, and whether hereditary, self appointed, or elective, may justly be pronounced the very definition of tyranny.[104]

A diffusion of power implies that the branches entrusted with their specific tasks are independent vis-à-vis each other, although independence of the judiciary does not imply unlimited power.[105] In addition to institutionalized limitations, limitations can be developed by the judiciary itself. Illustrative is the 'political question' doctrine as developed by the U.S. Supreme Court, dealing with issues deemed non-justiciable by the judiciary,[106] or the concept of '*acte de gouvernement*', as applied by the French Conseil d'Etat, mostly covering issues related to the French foreign policy.[107]

Alexander Hamilton also emphasizes the independence of the judiciary vis-à-vis the other branches of power: [...] though individual oppression may now and then proceed from the courts of justice, the general liberty of the people can never be endangered from that quarter; I mean so long as the judiciary remains truly distinct from both the legislature and the executive. For I agree, that "there is no liberty, if the power of judging be not separated from the legislative and executive powers", *see* Federalist Paper No. 78, authored by Alexander Hamilton; at <www.foundingfathers.info>.

[104] Federalist Paper No. 47, authored by James Madison; at <www.foundingfathers.info>.

[105] As to the extent of independence, the following quote is illustrative: "[...] where the whole power of one department is exercised by the same hands which possess the whole power of another department, the fundamental principles of a free constitution are subverted. This would have been the case in the constitution examined by him, if the king, who is the sole executive magistrate, had possessed also the complete legislative power, or the supreme administration of justice; or if the entire legislative body had possessed the supreme judiciary, or the supreme executive authority. This, however, is not among the vices of that constitution. The magistrate in whom the whole executive power resides cannot of himself make a law, though he can put a negative on every law; nor administer justice in person, though he has the appointment of those who do administer it". In fact, the essence is the following: "It is agreed on all sides, that the powers properly belonging to one of the departments ought not to be directly and completely administered by either of the other departments. It is equally evident, that none of them ought to possess, directly or indirectly, an overruling influence over the others, in the administration of their respective powers". Federalist Paper No. 47 and 48, authored by James Madison; at <www.foundingfathers.info>, emphasis omitted.

[106] *E.g.* Allan (2001), pp. 161-199.

[107] *E.g.* Koopmans (2003), pp. 98-104. *See also* Federalist Paper No. 78, authored by Alexander Hamilton, at <www.foundingfathers.info>, footnote omitted and emphasis omitted: "Whoever attentively considers the different departments of power must perceive, that, in a government in which they are separated from each other, the judiciary, from the nature of its functions, will always be the least dangerous to the political rights of the Constitution; because it will be least in a capacity to annoy or injure them. The Executive not only dispenses the honors, but holds the sword of the community. The legislature not only commands the purse, but prescribes the rules by which the duties and rights of every citizen are to be regulated. The judiciary, on the contrary, has no influence over either the sword or the purse; no direction either of the strength or of the wealth of the society; and can take no active resolution whatever. It may truly be said to have neither force nor will, but merely

In summary, power should be diffused in order to facilitate institutional checks and balances and to allow for an independent judicial branch that, based on the rule of law, has the liberty to review the exercise of public power by other branches of government without having to fear unreasonable repercussions.

1.4.2 ACCOUNTABILITY IN CONTEXT: WHO, TO WHOM AND FOR WHAT?

The concept of accountability is elusive: "it resembles a dustbin filled with good intentions, loosely defined concepts and vague images of good governance", often used to "patch up rambling argument, to evoke an image of trustworthiness, fidelity and justice, or to hold critics at bay".[108] In the context of international organizations, the ILA's definition of accountability provides a tool in overcoming this looming analytical paralysis. The ILA distinguishes three levels of accountability:

> [First level] the extent to which international Organisations, in the fulfillment of their functions as established in their constituent instruments, are and should be subject to, or should exercise, forms of internal and external scrutiny and monitoring, irrespective of potential and subsequent liability and/or responsibility; [Second level] tortuous liability for injurious consequences arising out of acts or omissions not involving a breach of any rule of international and/or institutional law (*e.g.* environmental damage as a result of lawful nuclear or space activities); [Third level] responsibility arising out of acts or omissions which do constitute a breach of a rule of international and/or institutional law (*e.g.* violations of human rights or humanitarian law, breach of contract, gross negligence, or as far as institutional law is concerned acts of organs which are ultra vires or violate the law of employment relations).[109]

The three levels are part of a holistic accountability concept. In this book, emphasis is placed on the legal dimension of accountability *i.e.* the need for ITA missions to be accountable and on the legal mechanisms through which such accountability can be achieved as a means of confining the exercise of public power. In particular, accountability here is understood as the opportunity to uphold basic – predominantly human rights-related – standards when public

judgment; [...] This simple view of the matter suggests several important consequences. It proves incontestably, that the judiciary is beyond comparison the weakest of the three departments of power, that it can never attack with success either of the other two; and that all possible care is requisite to enable it to defend itself against their attacks".

[108] Bovens (2007), pp. 449-454.

[109] ILA 2004, p. 5.

powers are exercised. As the UN Commission on Human Rights pointed out, accountability is a critical factor with regard to the enjoyment of human rights.[110]

A discussion about accountability involves at least the following three questions: who should be accountable, to whom and, finally, for what should an account be given?[111] The capacity of an accountability regime to bring about actual redress and/or compensation has occasionally been considered a fourth constitutive element of accountability.[112] If left unvarnished, however, this proposition would do an injustice to accountability mechanisms, the outcomes of which have no binding effect. Keeping in mind accountability mechanisms whose authority builds upon the power of naming, blaming and shaming, this suggested fourth element is a matter of effectiveness rather than an indispensable element of a particular accountability mechanism or regime.[113]

Firstly, it should be determined which entity is addressed by the call for accountability. The answer is related to the postulation that "power breeds responsibility".[114] Hence, as an entity enjoys more public power, the call for accountability will increase. Whether this entity is an individual or an institution is of subsidiary importance. This book explores accountability demands that target international administering entities once they have assumed overall responsibility for the administration of a particular territory through the exercise of all facets of public power. These accountability demands concern any such part of the administering entity that is engaged in the exercise of public power, including actors in the general decision-making process, individuals or agencies dealing with specific issues such as privatization or housing.[115] It might also relate to the administering entity as a whole, referring to either the UN or particular missions such as UNMIK and UNTAET as subsidiary organs of the UN.[116]

---

[110] *E.g.* UN, Commission on Human Rights (CommHR), *The Role of Good Governance in the Promotion of Human Rights*, Resolution 2000/64, 22 April 2000.

[111] This classification is generally accepted by scholars. *Cf.* Scott C. (2000), 'Accountability in the Regulatory State', (27)(1) *Journal of Law and Society*, pp. 38-60. Additional elements are sometimes added. For example, Bovens adds a fourth element related to the *why* behind account giving, *see* Bovens (2007).

[112] *See e.g.* Bovens (2007), pp. 451-452; Mulgan (2000), p. 556.

[113] Bovens (2007), pp. 451-452. Nevertheless, entities exercising public power might ultimately be perceived as not being accountable if the accountability regime within which they operate is proverbially toothless.

[114] Eagleton C. (1928), *The Responsibility of States in International Law*, New York: New York University Press, p. 208.

[115] For an elaborate report on the lack of independent oversight with respect to the international judiciary, *see e.g.* AI, *Serbia (Kosovo): The challenge to fix a failed UN justice mission*, Doc. EUR 70/001/2008, January 2008.

[116] A cursory overview of complaints filed with a particular oversight body established under the international administration of Kosovo reflects the variety of possible addressees. Besides

Secondly, the question is posed to whom should account be given: that is, who are the relevant beneficiaries? Generally, this is determined by the existence of a principal-agent relationship.[117] In other words, the holders of original authority should ultimately also be the beneficiary of the accountability process. Considered within the context of a state, it is primarily the people, as the original source of authority, to whom accountability should be rendered. To whom then should the international administering entity be accountable, given that the principal-agent relationship between the administered society and the international administration is not regulated by public law and does not rest on any (democratic) election-related process in particular? In this book, the affected entities subjected to international administration – be they individuals, groups of individuals or other entities – are considered to be the ultimate beneficiaries of an ITA-related accountability regime. Other stakeholders exist as well, such as institutions acting as financial donors and states cooperating with the international administering entities. However, though related, an assessment of their demands for accountability falls beyond the scope of this inquiry.

The third component relates to that for which the account-giving entity is held accountable. Throughout this book, emphasis is placed on accountability for the full range of public powers enjoyed by the administering entity and for the exercise thereof, since it is primarily through the exercise of these powers that individuals can be affected adversely. As the parallel is drawn between a state and ITA missions, accountability expectations should conform to what is commonplace in situations where a state exercises public powers within its territory. The accountability demand aims at achieving at least a minimal degree of safeguarding, roughly equivalent to the basic set of safeguards inherent in any government limited by law and subject to scrutiny. Primarily, the demand for accountability relates to the overall exercise of public power, since even when public powers are exercised with the best of intentions, conflicting interests will exist, unintended consequences will occur and affected parties will look for recourse and redress. Regardless of the level of decision-making, accountability demands will be triggered by the process through which public power is exercised as well as by the outcome thereof.[118] Accountability demands might also relate to cases of alleged criminal conduct, mismanagement or corruption

---

UNMIK and the SRSG in general, the complaints referred to acts or omissions of other institutions such as the Kosovo Property Agency, UNMIK police and the Special Chamber of the Supreme Court of Kosovo on Kosovo Trust Agency Related Matters. *See also* Irmscher T. (2001), 'The Legal Framework for the Activities of the United Nations Interim Administration in Kosovo: The Charter, Human Rights and the Law of Occupation', 44 *German Yearbook of International Law*, p. 356.

[117] *See also* Bovens (2007), p. 455 *et seq.*, where Bovens relates the principal-agent relationship predominantly to the process of accountability in the political sense.

[118] *Id.*, p. 460.

involving ITA staff members. In other words, a discriminatory ITA regulation, excessive use of force by ITA police or the infringement of property rights by ITA units can all lead to the violation of certain rights and prompt accountability demands. With respect to all these instances, mechanisms should exist through which accountability can be achieved.

Public law, as discussed in the previous section, provides a legal framework within which an accountability regime in the ITA context can be conceptualized – a regime upheld through different quasi-judicial mechanisms at various levels. Why such an accountability regime is crucial for the legitimacy of ITA missions is discussed in the following section.

1.4.3 LEGITIMACY IN CONTEXT: ACCOUNTABILITY AS A LEGITIMIZING FACTOR

The assumption that institutionalized accountability mechanisms – based on the rule of law, judicial review and independence of judicial oversight bodies – legitimize decision-making processes, and the exercise of public power in general, serves as a point of departure. In this context, legitimacy refers to

> a generalized perception or assumption that the actions of an entity are desirable, proper, or appropriate within some socially constructed system of norms, values, beliefs and definitions.[119]

In other words, legitimacy largely revolves around the acceptance of authority by those governed, and goes beyond the assessment of mere legality.[120] In Habermas' words, "legitimacy means a political order's worthiness to be recognized".[121] Legitimacy has preoccupied bearers of public power for as long as the exercise of such power has existed. In ancient times, legitimacy was almost axiomatic as long as the exercise of authority was perceived to be in accordance with natural or divine law.[122] Later, Hobbes argued that a government based on the principle of absolute sovereignty was the only legitimate form of political authority, since it was the only type of government

---

119 Suchman M. (1995), 'Managing Legitimacy: Strategic and Institutional Approaches', 20 *Academy of Management Review*, p. 574.

120 A legally valid exercise of public powers can be perceived as illegitimate, while in other instances, illegal exercise of authority might at times be recognized as legitimate: for example, on the basis of moral beliefs.

121 Habermas J. (1976), *Communication and the evolution of society*, Boston: Beacon Press, p. 178-179.

122 *See e.g.* Morrow (2005), p. 292; Beatty D.M. (2004), *The ultimate rule of law*, New York: Oxford University Press, p. 2; ButleRitchie (2004), p. 9.

able to avoid the evils of the state of nature.[123] Conversely, according to Locke, the 'Leviathan' could never be legitimate since legitimacy of government depended on the government's willingness to legally anchor the prescriptions of the law of nature.[124] In time, legitimacy turned towards those subjected to the exercise of public power. While legitimacy remained strongly dependent on the source of authority – whether this was considered to be God or the people – the mere source of authority increasingly lost its role as a predominant legitimizing factor.[125] Increasingly, substance and procedure gained importance as elements legitimizing the exercise of public power. The institutionalization of certain public law principles into the decision-making processes became the precondition for any authority to be regarded as legitimate.

Legitimacy deals with subjective social processes, as "nothing is legitimate in itself but only in relation to an audience".[126] Outside the state context, legitimacy concerns vis-à-vis international organizations have increased, since the position of the state as a buffer has faded and the powers of international organizations have expanded. In relation to the exercise of power by international organizations, Ratner argues that though perhaps the aims have become more legitimate, the means have not.[127] This holds equally true in the context of ITA missions, where the international entity in its exercise of public powers acts as a surrogate national authority.

At the outset of deployment, ITA missions arguably enjoy a large degree of legitimacy. In this initial phase, ITA missions embody the will of at least a majority of the local population, albeit a very preliminary and fundamental will, such as for peace or independence. The legitimizing effect thereof is unsustainable. Practice reflects that, save for incidental highs and lows, the legitimacy of ITA missions decreases over time.[128] In trying to reduce this

---

[123] Morrow (2005), p. 36.

[124] *Id.*, p. 80.

[125] Bodansky D., 'Legitimacy' *in* Bodansky D., Brunnee J. & Hey E. (eds.) (2007), *The Oxford Handbook of International Environmental Law*, Oxford: Oxford University Press, p. 710.

[126] Knoll (2007)(1), p. 41.

[127] Ratner (2005), p. 715.

[128] This effectively leads to a loss of normative power, *see* Knoll (2007)(1). Taking Kosovo as an example, the UN Development Programme Early Warning Report No. 26 of November 2009 reflects this decrease. UNMIK's approval ratings dropped from being over 60% in November 2002 to an all-time low in April 2009 of 16% of the respondents being satisfied with the work of UNMIK. It is important to note that even when the political changes of 2008 are taken into account, the decrease is clear. Save for a few peaks, UNMIK's approval remained around 30% as of November 2003. The same holds true for the SRSG, whose support saw a decrease from well over 70% in November 2002 to below 30% in September 2009, at <http://www.ks.undp.org/repository/docs/Fast_Facts_26_English.pdf>. *See also e.g.* Reuters, *UN's Kosovo Rating at Fresh Low as it Readies Exit*, 12 April 2007, at <http://www.reuters.com/article/topNews/idUSL1235427220070412> and The Observer,

legitimacy decrease, ITA missions are inherently barred from invoking two traditionally legitimizing features. Firstly, ITA missions lack democratic underpinning.[129] While this lack does not render them illegitimate *per se* – the legitimacy of hereditary holders of public powers generally relates to output-related factors rather than democracy-related processes – it does recalibrate the standard against which their legitimacy is evaluated. Secondly, ITA missions lack any intrinsic linkage with the local population. The gap between ITA missions and the administered society is wide, as ties – be they historical, cultural, ethnic or linguistic – are lacking.[130] The given situation has led to an increased exploration of other potentially legitimizing factors, related predominantly to the substantive and procedural quality of the exercise of power.[131]

Some argue that the legitimacy of ITA missions is grounded in necessity.[132] According to this argument, the exceptionality of the situation on the ground legitimizes the way in which ITA missions exercise their mandate. The weaknesses of this argument are presented in Section 4.4 below. State consent surfaces as another attempt to a priori legitimize ITA missions: "consent is generally presented as the most powerful source of creating political obligations and hence politically authority".[133] However, consent is given by the 'host state', which is placed outside the decision-making equation as soon as the ITA mission is deployed. In other words, the consent in casu is not expressed through

---

Angry Kosovars call on 'colonial' UN occupying force to leave, 19 October 2003. For a discussion of the issue of legitimacy in the context of UNTAET, *see* Beauvais J.C. (2001), 'Benevolent Despotism, A Critique of U.N. State-Building in East Timor', 33 *NYU Journal of International Law and Politics*, pp. 1101-1178.

[129] *See e.g.* Cogen M. & Brabandere E. (2007), 'Democratic Governance and Post-conflict Reconstruction', 20 *Leiden Journal of International Law*, pp. 669-693 on the role of elections, freedom of association and freedom of expression in the present context; Harland D. (2004), 'Legitimacy and Effectiveness in International Administration', 10 *Global Governance*, p. 15, where Harland, former chief of the UN Peacekeeping Best Practices Unit, argues that to some extent, ITA is inherently illegitimate. *A contrario* Steffek J. (2003), 'The Legitimation of International Governance: A Discourse Approach', 9(2) *European Journal of International Relations*, where Steffek essentially argues that the democratic-deficit critique does not apply to international organizations as it could only relate to state-like entities.

[130] *Cf.* Knoll (2007)(1), p. 40; Steffek (2003), pp. 256 and 271.

[131] *See e.g.* De Wet (2006), pp. 73-74. Mission-specific legitimizing factors have been explored as well. For example, it has been argued that UNTAET, unlike UNMIK, was "legitimized by the obligations of trusteeship that applied to non-self-governing territories". In BiH, the legitimacy of international administration was said to rest with the fact that the exercise of power *in casu* was based on an international treaty, *see* Knoll (2007)(1), p. 42.

[132] *E.g.* Stahn (2005)(3), pp. 40-43 and Zaum (2007), pp. 62-64 where the argument is made that peace and security, and in fact the need for government as such, legitimize international territorial administrations.

[133] Zaum (2007), p. 59. *See* Section 2.3.1.2 below.

a process that links the administered society and ITA missions; hence, its legitimizing effect remains weak.[134]

Rather, the legitimacy of ITA missions will depend predominantly on two factors. Inevitably, ITA legitimacy will first and foremost remain a function of the local population's subjective assessment of the exercise of public power. As long as the results of the exercise of public power are felt to further the main cause of the local population, the ITA mission will be perceived as legitimate. In this respect, legitimacy turns to yardsticks often related to human rights. As is the case with national governments, legitimacy will depend on the administration's ability to provide public goods effectively and to maintain a certain level of public order and security.[135] In other words, success has a crucial legitimizing effect.[136] Considering the divided nature of target populations, achieving legitimacy with respect to the entire population is nearly impossible on the basis of this first factor alone; decisions will be applauded by some, while others will consider them to be biased and in essence illegitimate. Likewise, failure on the side of the international administrations might be defended. Hence, this book postulates that a major legitimizing role is additionally reserved for more procedural features of the exercise of public power. In this sense, accountability is crucial.[137] An effective accountability regime will serve to scrutinize the governing authorities and to uphold substantive benchmarks related to the exercise of public power. In this manner, accountability mechanisms will have a legitimizing effect on the governing authorities.

In summary, it is postulated that accountability and legitimacy are inherently interrelated, even more so in the context of internationally administered territories. Faced with an almost inherent undemocratic underpinning, ITA

---

[134] *See* Stahn (2005)(3), pp. 38-40. Zaum also makes a clear point in stating that consent in this context is given by states rather than individuals, *see* Zaum (2007), p. 60.

[135] Knoll (2007)(1), p. 45; Black J. (2007), 'Constructing and contesting legitimacy and accountability in polycentric regulatory regimes', 2007/12 *IILJ Working Paper*, p. 20.

[136] *See e.g.* Bodansky *in* Bodansky, Brunnée & Hey (eds.) (2007), p. 711. *See also* Friedrich C.J. (1974), *Limited Government: A Comparison*, London: Prentice-Hall; Englewood Cliffs, p. 114. From an international perspective, *i.e.* legitimacy in the eyes of the international community and the financial contributors, legitimacy will also depend on "representativeness", the coherence of an exit strategy and the speed at which this exit strategy is being implemented, thereby minimizing the costs and time spent on the operation, *see* Knoll (2007)(1), p. 43 and Harland (2004).

[137] Bodansky *in* Bodansky, Brunnée & Hey (eds.) (2007), p. 710. *See also* Esty D.C. (2006), 'Good Governance at the Supranational Scale: Globalizing Administrative Law', 115 *The Yale Law Journal*, pp. 1490-1562; Stahn (2005) (3), p. 10; Kumm M. (2004), 'The Legitimacy of International Law: A constitutionalist Framework of Analysis', 15(5) *European Journal of International Law*, pp. 917-927; Caplan R. (2004)(1), 'International Authority and State Building: The Case of Bosnia and Herzegovina', 10 *Global Governance*, pp. 53-65. On the lack of accountability as a cause for decreasing legitimacy, *see also* HRW, *Better Late Than Never – Enhancing the Accountability of International Institutions in Kosovo*, Briefing paper No. 2, 14 June 2007, (HRW *Kosovo 2007* paper).

missions must reach out to alternative legitimizing factors in order to maintain their legitimacy. Accountability, achieved through the institutionalization of certain public law principles aimed at upholding proper substantive safeguards, plays a crucial role in this respect.

1.4.4 INTERNATIONAL DIMENSIONS: A PUBLIC LAW APPROACH TO INTERNATIONAL LAW

Applying the foregoing public law principles in the context of international territorial administrations implies extracting these principles from their traditional state-centered context. Such outside-the-box approaches are warranted – and arguably necessary – in, as Judge Simma referred to it, "a contemporary international legal order which is strongly influenced by ideas of public law".[138] The public law approach to the ITA accountability deficit is embedded in the broader ongoing debate about the emergence of traditionally state-related public law principles at the international legal level, where hierarchy, centralized authority and democratic underpinning are rudimentary. Two related legal discourses dominate the debate: one on international constitutionalism,[139] the other on global administrative law.[140] Both discourses analyze emerging regulatory processes at the international level and their

---

[138] ICJ, *Accordance with International Law of the Unilateral Declaration of Independence in Respect of Kosovo*, Advisory Opinion, 22 July 2010 (not yet published), Declaration Judge Simma, p. 1, § 3 (*Kosovo*).

[139] *See e.g.* Klabbers, Peters & Ulfstein (2009); De Wet E. (2006)(1), 'The International Constitutional Order', 55 *International and Comparative Law Quarterly*, p. 53; De Wet E. (2006)(2), 'The Emergence of International and Regional Value Systems as a Manifestation of the Emerging International Constitutional Order', 19 *Leiden Journal of International Law*, pp. 611-632. *See also* Bogdandy A. (von) (2006), 'Constitutionalism in International Law: Comment on a Proposal from Germany', 47(1) *Harvard International Law Journal*, pp. 223-242; Schilling T. (2005), 'On the Constitutionalization of General International Law', *The Jean Monnet Program Working Paper 06/05*. For a more moderate understanding of the concept, *see* Klabbers J. (2004), 'Constitutionalism Lite', 1 *International Organizations Law Review*, pp. 31-58; Kumm (2004), pp. 907-931.

[140] *See e.g.* the following working papers from the IILJ Global Administrative Law Series: Kingsbury, Krisch & Stewart (2004); Grant R.W. & Keohane R.O. (2004), 'Accountability and Abuses of Power in World Politics', 2004/7 *IILJ Working Paper*; Dyzenhaus D. (2005), 'The Rule of (Administrative) Law in International Law', 2005/1 *IILJ Working Paper*; Battini S. (2005), 'International Organizations and Private Subjects: A Move Toward A Global Administrative Law', 2005/3 *IILJ Working Paper*; Pallis M. (2005), 'The Operation of UNHCR's Accountability Mechanisms' 2005/12 *IILJ Working Paper*. All can be found at <http://www.iilj.org/publications/InternationalLawandJusticeWorkingPapers.asp>. *See also* Esty (2006).

potential structuring.[141] Of particular relevance for this book is the mutually shared emphasis on the unstructured nature of sporadic mechanisms dealing with review and accountability.

The discourse dealing with international constitutionalism refers to an emerging international community composed of various actors, subscribing to and governed by a shared value system. This process of constitutionalization entails the "(re-)organization and (re-)allocation of competence among the subjects of the international legal order".[142] Ultimately, this view draws "on the normative idea of constitutionalism": namely, the restriction of omnipotence.[143] In terms of substance, the shared value system finds its underpinning in accepted human rights norms – some of which enjoy peremptory status and have an *erga omnes* character – and other "common interests of mankind".[144] The global administrative law discourse provides an adjacent platform where the emergence of public law principles at the international level is discussed. This discourse observes a "single [...] multifaceted global administrative space distinct from the domains of international law and domestic administrative law", within which the emergence of a global administrative law aims to "promote greater accountability in decision-making in the rapidly proliferating variety of global regulatory mechanisms".[145] Conceptualizing the developing global regulatory framework in terms of "administration" helps in overcoming – at least in part – critique based on the "democratic deficit" argument.[146]

---

[141] The distinction between the two discourses, it has been argued, lies in the fact that while "constitutional law today remains either national or international in nature [,] administrative law, however, becomes global", Battini (2005), p. 29.

[142] De Wet (2006)(1), p. 51.

[143] Bryde B., 'International Democratic Constitutionalism', *in* MacDonald R. & Johnston D.M. (eds.) (2005), *Towards World Constitutionalism: Issues in the Legal Ordering of the World Community*, Leiden: Martinus Nijhoff Publishers, p. 106. For approaches to the debate with emphasis on the rule of law, *see e.g.* Cannizzaro E. (2005), 'Machiavelli, the UN Security Council and the Rule of Law', *Global Law Working Paper 11/05*. *See also* UN GA Report of the Sixth Committee, *The rule of law at the national and international levels*, UN Doc. A/61/456, 17 November 2006 as well as the related Report of the UN SG, *Uniting our strengths: Enhancing United Nations support for the rule of law*, UN Doc. A/61/636-S/2006/980, 14 December 2006. Finally, on a more substantive note, *see* Chesterman S. (2008), 'An International Rule of Law?' 56(2) *American Journal of Comparative Law*, pp. 1-39. He proposes "a core definition of the rule of law as a political ideal being seen as a means rather than an end, as serving a function rather than defining a status".

[144] Bryde *in* MacDonald & Johnston (eds.) (2005), p. 107. *See also* De Wet (2006)(1), p. 57; Fassbender B., 'The Meaning of International Constitutional Law', *in* MacDonald & Johnston (eds.) (2005), pp. 842-846. Advocates of this model of international law also stress that 'verticalization of international law' is becoming a reality through the acknowledgment of a hierarchy of norms, with *ius cogens* serving as the top of the pyramid.

[145] Kingsbury, Krisch & Stewart (2004), p. 2.

[146] *Id.*, p. 14.

Both discourses have been the subject of critique, the main points of which boil down to the claim that the present shape of the international community, and with that the stage of development of international law, is not such that it can accommodate the application of basic constitutional concepts and mechanisms.[147] Authors such as De Wet reject this critique by emphasizing the

> significance of constitutionalism as a frame of reference for a viable and legitimate regulatory framework for *any* political community, including those [...] constitutional orders that are formed beyond the state.[148]

The suggested contribution of public law with respect to the ITA accountability deficit builds on the underpinning of the discussed legal discourses.[149] However, as was pointed out in the preceding sections of this introduction, the setting that is created by the deployment of ITA missions is distinct. Hence, certain arguments presented in the aforementioned broader discourses play out differently where ITA missions are concerned. Most notably, this includes arguments concerning the stage of development of international law, the relationship between the international legal system and the individual and the position of the state. This atypical context underlies the legal issues discussed in the following chapters of this book.

1.5 OUTLINE OF THE BOOK

Chapter 1 introduced the concept of international territorial administration and sketched the accountability deficit associated with it. The main research question and the methodology were explained, and definitional considerations were provided. Subsequently, Chapter 2 discusses the Mandate and Trusteeship systems, as well as certain *sui generis* cases of ITA, as historical precedents. The ITA concept as it exists today is delineated and positioned between the two

---

147 For an overview, *see e.g.* Johnston D.M., 'World Constitutionalism in the Theory of International Law', *in* MacDonald & Johnston (eds.) (2005), pp. 18-21; Bryde *in* MacDonald & Johnston (eds.) (2005), pp. 104-105 *See* De Wet (2006)(1), p. 52 on how this traditional presumption has increasingly been challenged. *See also* Klabbers (2004), pp. 31-58, on why a limited conception of constitutionalism would perhaps be better suited for the international legal context.

148 De Wet (2006)(1), p. 53, emphasis added. *See also* Fassbender *in* MacDonald & Johnston (eds.) (2005); Walker N. (2003), 'Post-National Constitutionalism and the Problem of Translation', *2003/3 IILJ Working Paper*. Another author also notes that "comparing a realistically drawn international situation with an idealized national one" is not a "legitimate approach" to the issue at stake, *see* Bryde *in* MacDonald & Johnston (eds.) (2005), p. 105.

149 *See also* the special issue of the *German Law Journal* (2008, vol. 9, no. 11) on 'The Exercise of Public Authority by International Organizations: A Research Project of the Max Planck Institute for International Law'.

opposing realms of international organizations and states. Chapter 3 turns to accountability, and addresses the way in which accountability was approached under the Mandate and Trusteeship system. The accountability mechanisms in place were novel at the time, and provide illustrative examples of how the quest for accountability plays out when the national and the international legal contexts have merged. Chapters 4 and 5 address the heart of this book's topic: the accountability deficit within internationally administered territories. In Chapter 4, three determinants of the accountability-conundrum – the all-inclusive mandate of ITA missions, the lack of a clearly applicable legal framework and near-absolute immunity – are assessed and 'translated', as it were, into the language of public law. Subsequently, the accountability regime in practice is dissected in Chapter 5. Accountability mechanisms are assessed based on the findings attained in the preceding chapters. Chapter 6 concludes with final observations regarding the linkage between public law and the ITA accountability deficit. The concluding chapter suggests three areas for further research, and highlights the reasons that public law principles should be considered in addressing the ITA accountability deficit.

2 INTERNATIONAL TERRITORIAL ADMINISTRATION: INTERNATIONAL ENTITIES AS QUASI-STATES

"We have changed the law"

- *Bernard Kouchner*[1]

This chapter expounds the working definition of ITA missions. As the line between the national and the international becomes increasingly indistinct, international territorial administration represents a most revealing case in point. More than with other international engagements – consider, for example, other conflict-related operations or international economic investment programmes – the scope of authority vested in ITA missions includes competences by means of which particular public orders can be shaped. Effectively, ITA missions to all intents and purposes replace the state. This implies that the host state's jurisdiction is temporarily dissolved *i.e.* that exceptionally comprehensive competences are carried out by the international administrator at the 'national' level, without being embedded in the legal framework of a host state. Thus, what defines ITA missions is not only the unprecedented exercise of public power but also the fact that this exercise of public power in almost every aspect amounts to a parallel between the international administrations and a state's governing structures.[2]

In this Chapter, Section 2.1 addresses situations that emerged in the past where the international community assumed temporary authority to govern a certain territory. Examining these precedents adds to a better understanding of the nature of present ITA missions. Section 2.2 outlines the legal contours of present ITA missions by explaining the setting within which they were established and by introducing the three most relevant cases in point. Finally,

[1] Bernard Kouchner, former SRSG in Kosovo, as quoted in Berman N. (2006), 'Intervention in a "Divided World": Axes of Legitimacy', 17(4) *European Journal of International Law*, p. 758.

[2] *Cf.* Handbook on United Nations Multidimensional Peacekeeping Operations, United Nations, Department of Peacekeeping Operations, Peacekeeping Best Practices Unit, December 2003, pp. 2 and 35.

Section 2.3 zooms in on two selected themes: the legal basis of ITA missions and their impact on the sovereignty of the territory within which they operate. An analysis of these areas illustrates the peculiar nature of territorial administration. Moreover, the two themes illustrate that neither legal area – the legal basis or the host state sovereignty – currently provides an adequate legal framework through which accountability can be addressed.

2.1 PRECEDENTS AND PARALLELS

The administration of territory through an internationally organized effort is not unprecedented, although drawing a parallel between historical precedents and contemporary ITA missions requires vigilance.[3] Linkages between ITA missions and previous undertakings are generally avoided due to the association with colonial and exploitative practices in that past.[4] Alternatively, some authors have employed terms such as "neo-colonialism" and "neotrusteeship" in order to characterize certain traits of contemporary ITA missions.[5]

The establishment of the Mandate system under the League of Nations marked the beginning of institutionalized administration of territories in the name of the international community. The interests of the international community and of the inhabitants of the administered territories were endorsed as the primary basis for international engagement. This practice continued to evolve during the UN Trusteeship system and, in a modified fashion, served as the basis of certain *sui generis* missions of territorial administration at the time.

The following sections focus on the legal framework within which the individual mandates and trusteeships were established. Unlike contemporary ITA missions, mandates and trusteeships were anchored explicitly in the Covenant of the League (Covenant) and the UN Charter respectively. At least on paper, these legal frameworks foresaw the establishment of an accountability

[3] For example, Caplan argues that while a "one size fits all" approach would not be warranted, common features do justify a collective analysis. Similarly, Chesterman points out that "constructing templates" for such operations should be avoided, though "some generalizations are possible", *see* Caplan (2006), p. 4; Chesterman (2005), p. 6 respectively.

[4] *See e.g.* Chesterman (2005), pp. 44-47.

[5] *E.g.* Berman (2006); Fearon J.D. & Laitin D.D. (2004), 'Neotrusteeship and the Problem of Weak States', 28(4) *International Securities*, pp. 5-43. *See also* Stahn (2008), p. 19, where he argues that the "underlying tenet" of ITA is not that different from "the ideological heritage of liberal imperialism […] which sought to defend colonial administration". Chesterman even makes the thought-provoking claim that ITA missions are *not colonial enough*, *see* Chesterman (2005), p. 6. Finally, with respect to UNTAET in particular, *see* Chopra J. (2000)(1), 'The UN's Kingdom of East Timor', 42(3) *Survival*, p. 29, where UNTAET is described as a "pre-constitutional monarch in a sovereign kingdom" and Beauvais (2001), where the term "benevolent despotism" is used.

regime, which facilitated a statutory – rather than the present ad hoc – approach to accountability.

2.1.1 THE MANDATE SYSTEM

The introduction of the innovative Mandate system in 1919 through the Covenant marked a turning point in the practice concerning international governance of territories.[6] Until then, territories had occasionally been placed under multilateral administration.[7] After World War I, the need for a more systemic approach to international administration increased, as territorial issues that resulted from the war had to be resolved.[8] At the Versailles Conference of 1919, three main options to address the issue were presented: international administration through states, annexation and direct international administration of the territories.[9] Direct international administration, which would have most closely resembled current ITA missions, was set forth by United Kingdom Prime Minister Lloyd George. He proposed direct international governance by the international community or by the League, but his proposal proved to be ahead of its time and was readily dismissed. South African statesman General Smuts worded the dominant sentiment at the time by stating that any such direct administration would result in "paralysis tempered by intrigue".[10]

Amid these differing views, a compromise was reached.[11] Article 22 of the Covenant declared that "tutelage [...] should be entrusted to advanced nations [...] and that this tutelage should be exercised by them as Mandatories on behalf

---

[6] League of Nations Covenant, Art. 22. Preliminary findings on the comparison between mandates, trusteeships and ITA missions in terms of accountability were published previously in Momirov A. (2007), 'The Individual Right to Petition in Internationalized Territories: From Progressive Thought to an Abandoned Practice', 9(2) *Journal of the History of International Law*, pp. 201-229.

[7] The establishment of the 'Free City of Cracow' and its submission to joint Austrian, Prussian and Russian protection in 1815 and the status of the Island of Crete between 1897 and 1909 are most notable illustrations of this practice, *see e.g.* Ydit M. (1961), *Internationalised Territories*, Leiden: A.W. Sythoff, pp. 95-126; Stahn (2008), pp. 53-56.

[8] As a result of World War I, the future status of fourteen territories with approximately twenty million inhabitants had to be determined.

[9] Annexation was most favoured by Britain's dominions Australia and New Zeeland. Political stability, economic gain and even compensation for the efforts made during the war were all arguments used in favour of annexation, *see* Van Ginneken A.H.M. (1992), *Volkenbondsvoogdij; Het toezicht van de Volkenbond op het Bestuur in Mandaatgebieden 1919-1940* (The League of Nations; The supervision of Mandatories by the League of Nations 1919-1940) (diss. Utrecht), Summary in English, p. 7.

[10] Smuts J.C. (1918), *The League of Nations: A Practical Suggestion*, London: Hodder & Stoughton, p. 18. *See also* Van Ginneken (1992), p. 7. For a further analysis of this rejection, *see* Stahn (2008), pp. 76-78.

[11] For a detailed description of the negotiations, *see* Van Ginneken (1992), pp. 5-25; Hall D. (1948), *Mandates, Dependencies and Trusteeship*, London: Stevens & Sons Limited.

of the League". The Covenant made clear that the "well-being and development of [peoples living in the mandated territories] form a sacred trust of civilization".[12] As United States President Woodrow Wilson, a prominent advocate of the Mandate system, emphasized: "the interests of the populations concerned must have equal weight with the equitable claims of the government whose title is to be determined".[13]

Mandated territories were grouped into three categories, based on their stage of development.[14] The categorization determined the extent of authority of the Mandatories. In some cases, the role of the Mandatory was reduced to rendering "administrative advice and assistance" in a transitional period towards independence.[15] The Mandatory had to guarantee basic freedoms and was in charge of foreign policy. Such mandates are comparable with modern-day capacity building missions, oriented towards assisting local government structures. With respect to some less developed territories, it was considered that the Mandatories were "responsible for the administration of the territory under

[12] League of Nations Covenant, Art. 22.

[13] Unlike during the 1884 Berlin Conference, where essentially the colonization of Africa was endorsed, at the Versailles Conference common interests as well as the interests and well-being of the affected populations were – at least nominally – considered a priority, *see e.g.* Wright Q. (1930), *Mandates under the League of Nations*, Chicago: University of Chicago Press, 1968 reprint, pp. 24-25.

[14] Art. 22 of the Covenant distinguished three categories. Category A referred to parts of the Ottoman Empire, where certain communities "had reached a stage of development where their existence as independent nations can be provisionally recognized, subject to the rendering of administrative advice and assistance by a 'Mandatory' until such time as they are able to stand alone". This category included Iraq, Palestine and Syria. Category B generally included territories in Africa, where certain peoples were "at such a stage that the Mandatory must be responsible for the administration of the territory under conditions which will guarantee freedom of conscience and religion, subject only to the maintenance of public order and morals, the prohibition of abuses such as the slave trade, the arms traffic and the liquor traffic, and the prevention of the establishment of fortifications or military and naval bases and of military training of the natives for other than police purposes and the defense of territory, and will also secure equal opportunities for the trade and commerce of other Members of the League". 'B' mandates included Ruanda-Urundi, Tanganyika and French and British Togoland. Finally, category C referred to certain South Pacific Islands as well as South-West Africa, "which, owing to the sparseness of their population, or their small size, or their remoteness from the centers of civilization, or their geographical contiguity to the territory of the Mandatory, and other circumstances, can be best administered under the laws of the Mandatory as integral portions of its territory, subject to the safeguards above mentioned in the interests of the indigenous population". The most prominent 'C' mandate was South-West Africa while other 'C' mandates included Nauru, New Guinea and Samoa.

[15] League of Nations Covenant, Art. 22. The imminent independence of 'A' mandates was predetermined, while the future status of 'B'and 'C' mandates remained unclear. A clear determination of the future status with respect to the 'B' and 'C' category would have made it impossible to reach a compromise, as states aspiring to annexation would not have accepted the Mandate system, *see e.g.* Chowdhuri R.N. (1955), *International mandates and trusteeship systems: a comparative study* (diss. Amsterdam, UvA), The Hague: Martinus Nijhoff, p. 53.

[certain] conditions".[16] Finally, in some cases, territories were to be administered as an integral part of the judicial system of the Mandatory. The last two categories provided for overall administration of the territories but imposed a set of conditions aimed at preventing abuse such as the prohibition of slave trade, arms traffic and the establishment of military bases.[17]

The outbreak of World War II brought an end to the Mandate system and to the League of Nations *in toto*. In 1946, the League was dissolved at a meeting of the League's Assembly. The Mandate system was terminated and its assets and services were transferred to the newly created United Nations.[18]

2.1.2 THE TRUSTEESHIP SYSTEM

With the creation of the UN, the Trusteeship system was established to replace the Mandate regime. The territories covered by the newly created system were former mandated lands and territories detached from World War II enemies.[19] Territories could also be placed voluntarily under trusteeship, though this was never done in practice. The establishment of the Trusteeship system marked a shift in approach towards international administration of territories. The newly established system amended the mandate system in several ways.

The Trusteeship system was based on the idea that less advanced societies needed assistance in order to develop. This idea was reflected through a complete change of terminology used in the Charter.[20] Contrary to the Mandate system, the Charter was explicit in stating that all trusteeships aimed at guiding the administered societies to some form of self-government.[21] The Charter in fact devotes more attention to the trusteeships than its predecessor did with respect to the Mandate system. Instead of one article, the Charter devotes Chapters XII and XIII to the Trusteeship system and to the particular trusteeship agreements, concluded between concerned states and approved by the UN General Assembly. Chapter XIII is devoted to the Trusteeship Council, the main

[16] League of Nations Covenant, Art. 22.

[17] *Id.*

[18] *See e.g.* Hall D. (1947), 'The Trusteeship System', 24 *British Yearbook of International Law*, p. 33.

[19] UN Charter, Art. 77. Eleven territories in total were subjected to the Trusteeship system: French and British Togoland, Somaliland, French and British Cameroons, Tanganyika, Ruanda-Urundi, Western Samoa, Nauru, New Guinea and a group of Pacific Islands.

[20] *E.g.* UN Charter, Art. 76.

[21] Hall describes the concept of trusteeships as "a conception which is at the forefront of the human advance. It assumes a relatively stable human society in which nations, themselves mature, rational, and governed in their actions and policies by high conceptions of law and justice, undertake to assist less advanced peoples to climb the ladder of self-government", *see* Hall D. (1946), 'The British Commonwealth and Trusteeship', 22 *International Affairs*, p. 199.

body within the Trusteeship system and – defunct since 1994 – a principal organ of the UN. Most relevant to the present context is that the explicit opposition to direct international governance of territories had eroded. Based on a proposal made by China, Article 81 of the Charter allows for "the Organization itself" to assume administering authority.[22] However, the Charter did not envisage any procedural or organizational structure in this respect. In practice, the UN never assumed direct authority over a territory pursuant to Article 81 of the Charter; "[t]he organization displayed an almost natural instinct against the formal exercise of direct administering authority under the Trusteeship system".[23] Over time, all trust territories achieved self-government, either through independence or autonomy within a sovereign state. The last trusteeship was dissolved in 1994, with the independence of the island state of Palau. On 1 October 1994 the Trusteeship Council officially suspended its operations.[24]

2.1.3 *Sui generis* Administrations

During the period of the Mandate and Trusteeship systems, the international community engaged in, or envisaged, several *sui generis* operations in which territories were in fact placed under direct international rule. The Saar Basin and the city of Danzig were placed under direct international administration, while similar plans were envisaged for Trieste and Jerusalem. These operations fell outside the aforementioned systems.

The Saar Basin was the subject of a territorial dispute between Germany and France. In order to prevent complete annexation by France, the League Council appointed a Governing Commission, tasked with the temporary rule of the Saar Basin in the name of the League, consisting of a citizen of the Saar, one French national and three other members. This governing arrangement was based directly on the Treaty of Versailles and lasted from 1922 until 1935.[25] While Germany formally held on to its territorial title, "within the territory of the Saar Basin the Governing Commission [had] all the powers of government hitherto

[22] UN Charter, Art. 81. *See also* Chowdhuri (1995), p. 58.
[23] Stahn (2008), p. 106.
[24] UN Trusteeship Council Res. 2200 (LXI) (1994), on the suspension of the obligation to meet annually. On the termination of the Palau Trusteeship Agreement, *see* SC Res. 956 (1994). At the 61st Regular Session of the UN General Assembly, 22 September 2006, the vice-president of the Republic of Palau, Mr. Elias Camsek Chin, shed light on Palau's view on the role that the trusteeship period played in the country's history: "we were the last country to emerge from the UN Trusteeship System. During the Trusteeship, it was the UN that showed us that every country, regardless of size, has a role to play. The UN provided our nation with a platform from which we could achieve independence and establish our sovereignty and for this we are forever grateful".
[25] Treaty of Versailles, Part III, Section IV, Ann., Art. 16.

belonging to the German Empire [...] including the appointment and dismissal of officials, and the creation of such administrative and representative bodies as it may deem necessary".[26] Existing laws were to stay in place, while the Governing Commission had the obligation to organize the administration of the territory, including the organizing of local elections and the establishment of appeals courts. France retained primary authority regarding economic issues, including the right to exploit mines and to subject the Saar Basin to the French customs system.[27] After international administration, the League was to determine the status of the territory, taking the results of a plebiscite into account. Though the referendum allowed for the continuation of international rule – an option that, if chosen, would have created a unique situation of long-term international administration – the Saar plebiscite resulted in the unification of Saarland with Germany.[28]

Simultaneously, from 1919 untill 1939, the League assumed control over the city of Danzig, which was separated from Germany and Poland and declared a 'Free City'. A High Commissioner was granted considerable powers in order to fulfill his tasks, amongst which was the protection of the Danzig Constitution. The High Commissioner was able to veto treaties that were not in the interest of the city's independence, and amending the constitution was only possible with the consent of the League.[29] While many of the powers remained with the local Free City authorities or with Poland, the High Commissioner had the final word regarding disputes between Danzig and Poland in issues dealing with the demarcation of their respective powers.[30] The League had effectively assumed the position of an arbitrator – an unsustainable position, considering the broader developments in Europe at the time. In 1939, Danzig was overrun and occupied by German troops.[31]

In comparison to the Mandate system, in both cases the League itself administered the territories; the League had assumed "the execution of sovereign rights over a given territory, since in regard to 'Mandated Territories' their sovereignty was *quasi* entirely conferred on the Mandating Powers". [32] Whether

---

[26] *Id.*, Art. 19. On the issue of sovereignty, *see* Section 2.3.2 below.

[27] *Id.*, Art. 32.

[28] *See further* Russel F.M. (1966), *The international government of the Saar*, New York: University of California Publications; Bisschop W.R. (1924), *The Saar controversy*, London: Sweet & Maxwell.

[29] Paris Convention between Danzig and Poland, 9 November 1920, Art. 6; Treaty of Versailles; Part III, Section XI, Ann., Art. 103; Art. 49 of the Constitution of the Free city of Danzig.

[30] Treaty of Versailles, Part III, Section XI, Ann., Artt. 100-108. *See also* Caplan (2006), pp. 28-29.

[31] On the Saar administration, *see e.g.* Stahn (2008), pp. 173-182.

[32] Ydit (1961), p. 224. The formula used for the Saar and Danzig territories was also proposed but never implemented for the territorial disputes over the city of Fiume (Rijeka) and the

the League administered the territories successfully remains a subject of debate amongst authors.[33]

The UN contemplated several operations that did not fall entirely within the Trusteeship system, where the UN would assume administering authority. In the aftermath of World War II, the cities of Trieste and Jerusalem were the subjects of conflicting interests for which solutions were hard to find. In the case of Trieste, the Permanent Statute of the Free Territory of Trieste (Trieste Statute) was annexed to the 1947 Treaty of Peace with Italy. The Trieste Statute was an internationally brokered compromise between rival interests of Italy and Yugoslavia: Italy wanted to assume territorial title over the city while allowing international supervision, and Yugoslavia aspired to hold on to the territory of the city by granting it the status of a republic within the Yugoslav federation. The Trieste Statute envisaged that the territory would fall under the full authority of the UN Security Council. The aims of the international involvement were virtually identical to the objectives of the Danzig administration: namely, the appeasement of two conflicting state interests regarding a strategic port city. Consequently, the structure of the envisaged mission was similar to the solutions implemented in Danzig. Based on the Trieste Statute, the Security Council would assume the responsibility of ensuring the protection of basic human rights of the inhabitants and to maintain public order.[34] Local authorities were envisaged to govern the Free Territory under the limits imposed on them by the Trieste Statute. However, a Security Council-appointed Governor would enjoy extensive authority including the right to review legislation adopted by the Trieste Assembly, to veto Trieste Government decisions and to intervene in the ratification process of international treaties contravening the Trieste Statute.[35] However, Cold War reality derailed the plans. Instead, an agreement was reached, dividing the wider Trieste territory between Italy and Yugoslavia.[36]

Dalmatian coast, *see* Ydit (1961), pp. 53-55. Other isolated operations are sometimes mentioned, such as the League's engagement in the border dispute between Colombia and Peru around the city of Leticia from 1933 to 1934 and the League's attempts to resolve the dispute concerning the Memel Territory (now Lithuania) between 1924 and 1939. *See e.g.* Stahn (2008), pp. 185-187; Caplan (2006), p. 30; Chesterman (2005), pp. 22-25; Ydit (1961), pp. 59-62.

[33] While the Saar Basin endeavour is almost unanimously regarded as a success, the Danzig administration has led to more debate. As has been suggested, some of the contextual reasons contributing to the Danzig failure can be found in the shift of priorities within the League along with the changed attitude of all involved parties (the local population, Germany and Poland) towards the international administration; *see e.g.* Stahn (2008), pp. 163-185; Ratner (1996), p. 95.

[34] Permanent Statute of the Free Territory of Trieste; reprinted in (1947) 1(2) *International Organization*, pp. 410-419.

[35] *Id.*, Artt. 11(1), 11(3), 19(4), 20 and 24(1).

[36] Memorandum of Understanding Regarding the Free Territory of Trieste, Italy/United/Kingdom/United States/Yugoslavia, London, 5 October 1954; Treaty Between

Finally, in another example, a recommendation was made to place the city of Jerusalem under the authority of the UN. Though the Trusteeship Council would have been designated to play a crucial role in the administration of the city, all proposed documents refrained from stating explicitly that the city would fall within the Trusteeship system. Instead, the administration of Jerusalem would have been established not within the confines of the Trusteeship system but on the basis of a General Assembly resolution.[37] The proposal aimed primarily at reconciling conflicting sides and guaranteeing the special character of the city: namely, the protection of religious rights of the three faiths dominant in the city. After an initial period of ten years, the Trusteeship Council would determine the rules concerning a referendum to be held, in which the population of the city would vote on their future status.[38] Again, Cold War animosity and the complex situation in the Middle-East resulted in this plan never being implemented.

In summary, international administrations established under the Mandate and Trusteeship systems were characterized by proxies. While ultimate responsibility over the administered territories was held by the League and the UN, respectively, states were appointed to carry out the actual governing. Save for isolated exceptions, a hesitance on the part of the League and the UN to assume a direct and overall administering authority dominated the scene. This reluctance gradually decreased as UN-led peace missions increasingly incorporated elements of civil administration into their mandates. This development culminated in the 1990s with the establishment of three all-encompassing international civil administrations which are at the focus of this book.

2.2 OUTLINING CONTEMPORARY INTERNATIONAL TERRITORIAL ADMINISTRATION

Territorial administration is a dynamic concept and has been understood to encompass missions with varying mandates, ranging from overall international administration to political assistance. Here, a narrow understanding of the concept is adopted. This understanding implies that by establishing direct territorial administrations, international entities assume all-encompassing authority to exercise public power within a given territory for a temporary

---

the Socialist Federative Republic of Yugoslavia and Italy, Osimo, 10 November 1975. *See also* Ydit (1961), pp. 231-272.

[37] GA Res. 181 (II), 29 November 1947, introduced the concept of an internationalized Jerusalem, and requested the UN Trusteeship Council to work out the proposal, *see in general* Stahn (2008), pp. 99-102 and 195-203; Ydit (1961), pp. 273-315.

[38] UN Trusteeship Council Res. 34 (III) (1948); Statute of Jerusalem, U.N. Doc. T/118 Rev. 2, 21 April 1948.

period of time and that this authority is ultimate in nature: that is, it supersedes all governing institutions possibly existing at the local – that is, the national – level.

Section 2.2.1 describes the context that allowed for ITA missions to be established. Section 2.2.2 then introduces the three most relevant cases in point: the international administration of BiH, Kosovo and East Timor.

2.2.1 ITA MISSIONS: BEYOND THE PEACEKEEPING PARADIGM

As UN peacekeeping missions developed over time, the maintenance of peace was outgrown as the exclusive aim of such engagements. By adding elements of 'nation building', international efforts to restore peace focused on the sustainability of this peace, on the conflict-torn state and the society itself. The expansion of non-military aims and competences is part and parcel of the way in which peacekeeping evolved. Increasingly, this meant that UN missions were equipped with elements of government-like authority. The UN missions in Cambodia and Congo, as well as the UN's approach towards Namibia, illustrate this and are considered by some to belong to the ITA family.[39]

Although the present emergence – or re-emergence, rather – of territorial administration by international bodies fits this evolution of peacekeeping, it cannot be regarded merely as a single consecutive step. Rather, the evolution of peacekeeping should be seen as the context in which ITA was able to re-emerge. Studies of this evolution generally depict a gradual increase of complexity of UN-led missions accompanied by broadening mandates. This has led to a widely accepted classification of first, second and third-generation peacekeeping missions.[40] Attempts have often been made to fit ITA missions into this categorization, at times even describing them as a "fourth-generation" category of missions.[41] The incorporation of ITA missions into this classification, as well as the description of the evolution of peacekeeping as something steady and linearly progressive, is problematic and does not entirely reflect practice.[42]

---

[39] For a general overview of the United Nations Transitional Authority in Cambodia (UNTAC), *see* <http://www.un.org/Depts/dpko/dpko/co_mission/untac.htm>. For a general overview of the United Nations Operation in the Congo (ONUC), *see* <http://www.un.org/Depts/DPKO/Missions/onuc.htm>.

[40] *E.g.* Ratner S. (1996), *The new UN peacekeeping; Building peace in lands of conflict after the cold war*, New York: St. Martin's Press.

[41] White N.D. & Klaasen D., 'An emerging legal regime', *in* Klabbers, Peters & Ulfstein (2009), p. 2; Kondoch B., 'Human rights law and UN peace operations in post-conflict situations', *in* Klabbers, Peters & Ulfstein (2009), pp. 24-25.

[42] *E.g.* Wilde (2003). Wilde makes a compelling argument that complexity as such is not a feature exclusively belonging to contemporary undertakings. In other words, the development of peace-related efforts cannot be regarded as completely linear.

Certain authors have even suggested such a categorization of ITA missions would be misleading, one of the reasons being that by being categorized as 'peacekeeping' missions, ITA missions would tap unjustly into the legitimacy of these peacekeeping operations.[43]

Regardless of possible categorizations, the evolution of the traditional peacekeeping mandate is undisputed. The United Nations Panel on Peace Operations, convened in March 2000 by the UN Secretary-General and chaired by Lakhdar Brahimi, issued a report containing a concise and authoritative review of peace and security-related activities undertaken by the UN.[44] The report, aimed at summarizing the lessons learned from past operations, identifies peacemaking, peacekeeping and peacebuilding as the three cornerstones of UN peace-related efforts.[45] The report indicates that the traditional conflict-related engagement of the UN, peacekeeping, has "evolved rapidly" from a primarily military operation to "incorporate a complex model of many elements, military and civilian, working together to build peace in the dangerous aftermath of civil wars".[46]

Thus far, the UN has addressed ITA in a cursory and fragmented fashion. Indeed, the *Brahimi* Report devotes a separate paragraph to transitional civil administration. Taking the establishment of UNMIK as a turning point, the report notes that "[t]hese operations face challenges and responsibilities which are unique among United Nations field operations".[47] Another UN document, the UN Handbook on Multidimensional Peacekeeping Operations, notes that UN peacekeeping operations have become 'multidimensional', as they increasingly began to include non-military components.[48] This handbook also makes separate reference to ITA by stating that "multidimensional peacekeeping operations [...] may be required to [administer] a territory for a transitional period, thereby carrying out *all the functions that are normally the responsibility of a government*" which creates a situation in which the international presence is

---

[43] Wilde (2004).

[44] Report to the UN SG, *Report of the Panel on United Nations Peace Operations*, UN Doc. A/55/305-S/2000/809, 21 August 2000 (*Brahimi* Report).

[45] *Id.*, § II.A.

[46] *Ibid.* In particular, the report identifies peacebuilding as "activities undertaken on the far side of conflict to reassemble the foundations of peace and provide the tools for building on those foundations something that is more than just the absence of war". Some authors consider missions of territorial administration to be a distinct variant of statebuilding, *see e.g.* Chesterman (2005), p. 5.

[47] *Brahimi* Report, § II.H. The report further criticizes the UN's urge to classify ITA as a peace operation and touches upon the question of whether the UN should be engaged in such missions at all.

[48] Handbook on United Nations Multidimensional Peacekeeping Operations, United Nations, Department of Peacekeeping Operations, Peacekeeping Best Practices Unit, December 2003, p. 1.

"responsible for directly managing all aspects of civilian life while simultaneously working to devolve its responsibilities to local authorities".[49] The handbook strongly emphasizes that "governance mandates are the exception rather than the norm in peacekeeping".[50]

Likewise, it has been widely acknowledged amongst authors that ITA missions, in terms of their extensive mandate, are by far the most comprehensive undertaking amongst all other international peace-related engagements.[51] On a sliding scale indicating the scope of powers enjoyed by UN peace-related missions, ITA missions are located at the end, where the scope of authority is at its maximum. As Ford and Oppenheim remarked,

> Multidimensional peacekeeping forms the conceptual, operational, and political basis for U.N. transitional administration. However, transitional administration stretches beyond even the most complex and expansive peacekeeping arrangements, as it is rooted in a grant of governance authority by a resolution of the Security Council.[52]

In addressing the present accountability deficit, one should keep in mind Brahimi's observation that missions operating under such exceptional mandates face unique challenges.[53] Establishing a coherent accountability mechanism is one such challenge, which justifies – at the very least – the consideration of 'unique' solutions.

2.2.2 ITA MISSIONS: INTRODUCING THE OHR, UNMIK AND UNTAET

In keeping with the definitional parameters set out in the previous section, the international administrations of different parts of the former Yugoslavia – most prominently BiH and the territory of Kosovo – and East Timor are most representative examples of ITA missions.[54] The following paragraphs introduce

---

[49] *Id.*, pp. 2 and 35, emphasis added.
[50] *Id.*, p. 35.
[51] *E.g.* Stahn (2008); Wilde (2008); Caplan (2006), p. 21; Chesterman (2005).
[52] Ford C.E. & Oppenheim B.A. (2008), 'Neotrusteeship or Mistrusteeship? The "Authority Creep" Dilemma in United Nations Transitional Administration', 44(1) *Vanderbilt Journal of Transnational Law*, p. 68, footnote omitted.
[53] *Brahimi* Report, § II.H.
[54] Around the same time as the mission in BiH was set up, the territory of former Yugoslavia gave ground to the establishment of another mission of international territorial administration. During the 1990s, the relatively unknown region of Eastern Slavonia, Baranja and Western Sirmium, further referred to as Eastern Slavonia, was the scene of one of the most devastating chapters in the disintegration of the former Yugoslavia. The territory, falling within the present borders of the Republic of Croatia, had unilaterally declared independence

these missions briefly, as they will be referred to extensively throughout this book.

Bosnia and Herzegovina

The internationalization of BiH in 1995 was an "exceptional response" to a "unique, extraordinary and complex" situation.[55] The Dayton Peace Agreement, which ended the military conflict in BiH in 1995, established the Office of the High Representative (OHR).[56] Under the purview of the established Peace Implementation Council (PIC), a conglomerate of 55 states, the OHR acted as the "chief civilian peace implementation agency" in the country.[57] The OHR was

establishing the de facto independent Republic of Serb Krajina. Grave military losses in 1995 resulted in territorial decapitation of the entity and a nearly complete efflux of the local Serbian population. Consequently, re-absorption of the region into the Croatian constitutional system became inevitable. On 12 November 1995, agreement was reached between the Croatian Government and the local Serb community through the Basic Agreement on the Region of Eastern Slavonia, Baranja and Western Sirmium. The region was to be administered by a UN body during a transitional period, envisaged to last two years, which would lead to the re-integration of the region into the Croatian state. On 15 January 1996, SC Res. 1307 (1996) consequently established the United Nations Transitional Authority in Eastern Slavonia, Baranja and Western Sirmium (UNTAES). A Transitional Administrator was appointed who had "overall authority over the civilian and military components of UNTAES and who will exercise the authority given to the Transitional Administration in the Basic Agreement". Within its envisaged two year period, the mission was completed on 15 January 1998, putting a seal on Croatian territorial reunification. For basic information on UNTAES, *see* <http://www.un.org/Depts/dpko/dpko/co_mission/untaes.htm>.

[55] SC Res. 1031 (1995), § 39.

[56] The General Framework Agreement for Peace in Bosnia and Herzegovina, negotiated in Dayton, Ohio, USA, and signed in Paris on 14 December 1995 (Dayton Peace Agreement), established the OHR. Subsequently, a Peace Implementation Conference (London, 8-9 December 1995) led to the establishment of the Peace Implementation Council (PIC) consisting of 55 states and entities in support of the peace process. Also, a Steering Board was established as the executive arm of the PIC, giving political guidance to the High Representative, at <http://www.ohr.int/ohr-info/gen-info/>. Aiming to streamline the cooperation between all international actors in BiH, a Board of Principals was established in 2002 in order to "serve as the main co-coordinating body for International Community activity in [Bosnia and Herzegovina]", at <http://www.ohr.int/board-of-princip/default.asp?content_id=27551>. The military component of the overall peace endeavor was assumed by the NATO-led Stabilization Force (SFOR) which was operative until December 2004, when the military presence in BiH was replaced by the EU through the establishment of an EU military mission, EUFOR, backed by SC Res. 1575 (2004), at <http://www.euforbih.org/eufor/index.php>.

[57] Within BiH, prior to the Dayton Peace Agreement, a distinct mission of international administration was set up by the EU – formally speaking by the twelve member states individually – in 1994. The EU engaged in the administration of the historical city of Mostar in which the ethnic division between the Croat and Muslim communities had paralyzed public life. The European Union Administration of the City of Mostar (EUAM) was agreed upon and established in 1994 by the EU and was phased out in 1996. Restricted in scale and limited in

set up to represent the international community and oversee the activities of other organizations engaged in the peacebuilding process. Instead of establishing the OHR, the UN endorsed the establishment and confirmed the High Representative's final authority "in theatre regarding interpretation of Annex 10 on the civilian implementation of the Peace Agreement".[58] The fact that the UN does not formally lead this undertaking distinguishes the international presence in BiH from subsequent UN-led ITA missions. Furthermore, the High Representative later took up a second function as the EU Special Representative (HR/EUSR), reflecting the EU's increased role within the international administrative structures of BiH.[59] This increasing EU role in the administration of BiH and Kosovo will not be discussed as such.[60] Open-ended in terms of duration, the OHR assumed vast and effectively ultimate authority within an independent BiH. Caught between praise and criticism alike, the OHR remains the subject of ongoing debate, pending imminent closure.

Kosovo

Simultaneously, tensions in the Federal Republic of Yugoslavia, and its constituent republic of Serbia in particular, were rising as the discriminatory practices against the ethnic Albanian population living in the autonomous province of Kosovo grew more fierce and the Albanian separatist resistance against it became more violent and excessive. State policy backed by police and military operations on the one side and pro-independence aspirations backed by frequent insurgent attacks on the other side culminated in an armed conflict between the Albanian Kosovo Liberation Army and the Serbian military and police forces. Between March and June 1999, NATO intervened by carrying out a bombing campaign against the Federal Republic of Yugoslavia. This conflict resulted in the withdrawal of the Serbian administration and armed forces from

---

duration, EUAM provides a contrast to the vast international administration missions established in the whole of BiH and in other regions. Within the framework of the Common Foreign and Security Policy of the EU, a Memorandum of Understanding on the European Administration of Mostar was signed on 5 July 1994, *see* European Union Council Doc. 7696/94, Annex I, Brussels, 10 June 1994. EUAM was envisaged to administer Mostar for a period of two years. In 1996, EUAM was phased out and power was transferred to the local authorities, *see* Council Joint Action 96/476/CFSP of 26 July 1996, OJL 195, 6 August 1996, pp. 0001-0002. *See also* Pagani F. (1996), 'L'administration de Mostar par l'Union Européenne', *Annuaire français de Droit International*, pp. 234-254. *See also* Section 5.1.3 below.

[58] SC Res. 1031 (1995), §§ 26-27.

[59] "The EU Special Representative is the lynchpin in the European Union's presence in Bosnia and Herzegovina ensuring a coordinated and coherent EU approach to building self-sustaining peace and stability by assisting the country move beyond peace implementation towards European integration", at <http://www.eusrbih.eu/>.

[60] *See* Section 1.2.1 above.

Kosovo and in June 1999, UNMIK was established as an open-ended mission unparalleled in scope and complexity, aimed primarily at the promotion of substantial autonomy and self-government of the territory.[61] The UN together with several other international organizations took responsibility for the overall civilian administration of Kosovo. UNMIK was set up as an interim administration, pending a final political solution to the Kosovo dispute. As of 2005, numerous initiatives have been set in motion to reach an agreement on the final status of the territory. However, up until the time of writing, March 2011, all efforts have remained futile.[62]

---

[61] The Kumanovo Military Technical Agreement between the International Security Force and the Governments of the Federal Republic of Yugoslavia and the Republic of Serbia (Kumanovo Agreement), endorsed on 3 June 1999 by the Serbian Parliament and Yugoslav Federal Government, formalized the withdrawal of the national security forces (though a limited amount of these forces was envisaged to return; SC Res. 1244 (1999), Art. 4, a clause which was never implemented). This agreement paved the way for the establishment of UNMIK. On 10 June 1999, SC Res. 1244 (1999) was adopted, deploying an "international civil and security presence". A Special Representative was to be appointed by the UN SG to "control the implementation of the international civil presence" and to "coordinate closely with the international security presence to ensure that both presences operate towards the same goals and in a mutually supportive manner". UNMIK itself was established as a UN-led joint effort in which the UN cooperates with the Organization for Security and Co-operation in Europe (OSCE) and the European Union (EU). After the unilateral declaration of independence by the local authorities of Kosovo on 17 February 2008 and the initiation of a comprehensive EU led mission, the status of UNMIK remains uncertain. For the essentials on structure and evolvement of UNMIK as well as UNMIK's views on achievements and future prospects, *see* <http://www.unmikonline.org/>.

[62] Such initiatives include, amongst others, the establishment of the United Nations Office of the Special Envoy of the Secretary-General for the Future Status Process for Kosovo (UNOSEK) and the appointment of Martti Ahtisaari as the Special Envoy of the Secretary-General of the United Nations for the Future Status Process for Kosovo. The UN SG's appointment of Martti Ahtisaari was approved by the UN Security Council on 10 November 2005, UN Doc. S/2005/709. The efforts further included internationally supervised negotiations between the Priština and Belgrade representatives and the engagement of the International Contact Group, an informal gathering of influential states with considerable interest in the peace process in the Balkans. The Contact Group emerged in 1994 and was intensively engaged in the BiH peace process. It subsequently re-emerged during the Kosovo status talks. For details on the Contact Group, and especially its role within broader peace-related engagements, *see* Schwegmann C. (2000), *The Contact Group and its Impact on the European Institutional Structure*, EU-ISS Occasional Paper 16, European Union Institute for Security Studies, Paris, at <http://aei.pitt.edu/677/>. These efforts resulted in the Comprehensive Proposal for the Kosovo Status Settlement (Ahtisaari proposal), presented by Ahtisaari to the UN Security Council in March 2007, proposing internationally supervised independence for Kosovo, *see* UN Doc. S/2007/168/Add.1 dated 26 March 2007. This proposal argued for "internationally supervised independence" for Kosovo, referring to the issue as a "unique case that demands a unique solution", *see* Ahtisaari proposal p. 4. Following rejection by Serbia, the Security Council failed to adopt Ahtisaari's proposal regardless of strong support from Western states. *See* "*Резолуција Народне Скупштине Републике Србије поводом 'предлога за свеобухватно решење статуса Косова' Специјалног Изасланика Генералног Секретара УН Мартија Ахтисарија и наставка*

Despite the deadlock at the UN level, after Kosovo's unilateral declaration of independence,[63] UNMIK has been the subject of major restructuring. An International Steering Group (ISG) was created, representing 25 states. Its primary purpose is "to support full implementation of the Comprehensive Proposal for the Kosovo Status Settlement of UN Special Envoy Martti Ahtisaari", despite the non-adoption of the Ahtisaari proposal.[64]

In a shift towards international supervision 'Bosnian style', a dual function was created: the International Civilian Representative & European Special Representative in Kosovo (ICR/EUSR).[65] Amongst other things, the

---

преговора о будућем статусу Косова и Метохије" (Resolution of the National Assembly of the Republic of Serbia following UN Special Envoy Martti Ahtisaari's "Comprehensive Proposal for the Kosovo Status Settlement" and Continuation of Negotiations on the Future of Kosovo-Metohija), adopted by the Parliament of Serbia on 14 February 2007. *See also e.g.* the statement issued by the co-sponsors of the draft-resolution on Kosovo, 20 July 2007 and the Joint Contact Group statement published upon presentation by the Special Envoy of his draft comprehensive proposal, 2 February 2007, at <http://www.unosek.org/unosek/en/docref.html>.

[63] *Deklarata e Pavarësisë së Kosovës* (Kosovo Declaration of Independence), adopted by the Assembly of Kosovo on 17 February 2008.

[64] *See* the press statement of the first meeting of the International Steering Group (ICG) for Kosovo, 28 February 2008, Vienna, Austria, at <http://www.ico-kos.org/?id=3>.

[65] UN Doc. S/2007/168/Add.1 dated 26 March 2007, Ann. IX. For the appointment of the International Civilian Representative, *see* press statement of the First meeting of the International Steering Group (ICG) for Kosovo, 28 February 2008, Vienna, Austria, at <http://www.ico-kos.org/?id=3>. In the context of preparations for a future expanded EU presence in Kosovo, the Council of the European Union adopted two documents: Council Joint Action 2006/304/CFSP of 10 April 2006, OJL 112, 26 April 2006, pp. 19-23 and Council Joint Action 2006/623/CFSP of 15 September 2006, OJL 253, 16 September 2006. The Council Joint Action from April established an EU Planning Team (EUPT). This team was envisaged to "ensure a smooth transition between selected tasks of UNMIK and a possible EU crisis management operation, in the field of rule of law and other areas that might be initiated by the Council in the context of the future status process". This operation was shaped through the adoption of Council Joint Action 2008/124/CFSP of 4 February 2008, OJL 42, 16 February 2008, pp. 92-98, establishing the European Union Rule of Law Mission in Kosovo (EULEX), a mission which "shall assist the Kosovo institutions, judicial authorities and law enforcement agencies in their progress towards sustainability and accountability and in further developing and strengthening an independent multi-ethnic justice system and multi-ethnic police and customs service, ensuring that these institutions are free from political interference and adhering to internationally recognized standards and European best practices". On the other hand, the Council Joint Action from September established an "EU-team to contribute to the preparations of the establishment of a possible international civilian mission in Kosovo, including a European Union Special Representative component" (ICM/EUSR Preparation Team; later renamed ICO/EUSR Preparation Team pursuant to Council Joint Action 2007/517/2007 of 16 July 2007, OJL 190, 21 July 2007, pp. 38-39). Here, all preparation activities were oriented towards the establishment of the political component of the EU operation, the International Civilian Office in order to provide support to an International Civilian Representative/European Union Special Representative (ICR/EUSR), at <http://www.ico-kos.org/?id=1>. The EU appointed the first ICR/EUSR

representative's office coordinates the work of the EU Rule of Law Mission (EULEX).[66] In December 2008, only after endorsement by the UN Security Council, EULEX became operational and to a large extent assumed UNMIK's authority regarding Kosovo's civilian administration. EULEX operates under "overall authority" of the UN and Security Council Resolution 1244 (1999),[67] while UNMIK remains responsible for certain tasks and within certain parts of Kosovo's territory until agreement on UNMIK's further reconfiguration is reached.[68] Complicated by Kosovo's disputed status, a discussion of the nature and scope of authority of the ICR/EUSR and EULEX – especially in relation to UNMIK – requires additional research and will not be dealt with here.

> A report from the UN Secretary-General in 2008 illustrates the developments on the ground and their impact on UNMIK. "As is evident from the developments on the ground, my Special Representative is facing increasing difficulties in exercising his mandate owing to the conflict between Resolution 1244 (1999) and the Kosovo Constitution, which does not take UNMIK into account. The Kosovo authorities frequently question the authority of UNMIK in a Kosovo now being governed under the new Constitution. While my Special Representative is still formally vested with executive authority under Resolution 1244 (1999), he is unable to enforce this authority. In reality, such authority can be exercised only if and when it is accepted as the basis for decisions by my Special Representative. Therefore, very few executive decisions have been issued by my Special Representative since 15 June". Furthermore, the report states that "The Assembly of Kosovo continues to pass legislation, which is now adopted without reference to the powers of my Special Representative under Resolution 1244 (1999) or the Constitutional Framework".
>
> The way in which UNMIK chose to approach this turn of events is for example illustrated by the fact that UNMIK ceased to issue travel documents. Paragraph 9 of the report states: "The decision by the Kosovo authorities to start issuing Kosovo passports following adjustment of the technical equipment at the Civil Registry Central Processing Centre means that it is no longer possible for UNMIK to continue to issue travel documents; as a consequence, their issuance was discontinued". Paragraph 20 provides another example: "the economic reconstruction pillar of UNMIK (pillar IV) ceased all substantive operations on 30 June, pursuant to a decision by the European Commission. As a consequence, UNMIK does not at present possess any technical capacity or budgetary allocation to perform functions formerly carried out by pillar IV, if and when required".
>
> *Report by the UN SG,* UN Doc. S/2008/692, 24 November 2008.

through Council Joint Action 2008/123/CFSP of 4 February 2008, OJL 42, 16 February 2008, pp. 88-91.

[66] As well as EU member states, other countries cooperate with EULEX, such as Norway, Switzerland, Turkey and the United States, *see* <http://www.eulex-kosovo.eu/?id=2#>.

[67] *E.g.* B92, *EU: Euleks pod autoritetom UN* (EU: Eulex under UN authority), 28 November 2008, at <http://www.vesti.rs/Politika/EU-Euleks-pod-autoritetom-UN.html>.

[68] *UN Secretary-General Ban Ki-moon addressed the necessity of the reconfiguration of the UN presence in Kosovo in his report to the Security Council*, UN Doc. S/2008/354, 12 June 2008, especially §§ 30-47.

East Timor

Turning to the third selected ITA mission, on 30 August 1999, in a UN-supervised referendum, the population of the Indonesia-governed territory of East Timor rejected Indonesia's proposal for autonomy within Indonesia, and by an overwhelming majority opted for independence from its internationally never-recognized Indonesian sovereign. Amid violent conflict following the referendum, the UN established the United Nations Transitional Administration in East Timor (UNTAET).[69] As agreed by Indonesia and Portugal, the latter being East Timor's colonial administrator and nominal sovereign, the mission included both military and public administration components and had the clear aim of guiding East Timor towards independence. Two days after East Timor became an independent state on 20 May 2002, the mission was formally terminated, leaving behind a downscaled international presence.

2.3 INTERNATIONAL TERRITORIAL ADMINISTRATION: TWO SELECTED THEMES

The following sections illustrate the elusive legal environment in which ITA missions operate. For this purpose, two themes are selected: the unclear legal basis upon which ITA missions are established (Section 2.3.1) and the extent to which ITA missions can be considered to operate within the ambit of 'host state' sovereignty (Section 2.3.2). These themes further illustrate the peculiar nature of ITA missions. Although their legality is undisputed, the UN Charter does not provide them with for a fit-for-purpose institutional basis. Furthermore, the deployment of ITA missions has an impact on 'host state' sovereignty which exceeds the impact that results from other adjacent undertakings, such as traditional peacekeeping. Furthermore, the following discussion lays the foundation for a more fundamental question: namely, what body of law

[69] On 5 May 1999, the authorities of Indonesia and Portugal agreed for a plebiscite to be held in which the population of East Timor would decide upon the future status of the territory they inhabited. As independence was the overwhelming outcome of the referendum, massive violence broke out. Eventually, Indonesian Armed Forces and the administration moved out of East Timor completely. Based on this situation on the ground, and the agreement between Indonesia and Portugal on the transfer of authority to the UN, on 25 October 1999, SC Res. 1272 (1999) was adopted, establishing UNTAET and empowering it to assume full civil administration of the territory. UNTAET further contained a military component, with reference to the multination force previously deployed pursuant to SC Res. 1264 (1999). UNTAET was formally terminated on 20 May 2002, upon the independence of East Timor. UNTAET was dismantled, leaving behind an ever-decreasing UN presence and a fragile security and economic situation on the ground. *See e.g.* <http://www.un.org/peace/etimor/etimor.htm>.

regulates and confines the exercise of public power by ITA missions, as discussed in Chapter 4.

2.3.1 ITA MISSIONS: AN ELUSIVE LEGAL BASIS

Though their legality is largely undisputed, debate exists on the nature of the legal basis underlying ITA missions.[70] Consequently, the attention of commentators has shifted from whether international entities have the power to engage in the administration of territories to what comprises the nature and boundaries of this power.[71] The ambiguity surrounding the legal basis of ITA missions has a detrimental effect on the accountability – and as a consequence, legitimacy – of ITA missions, as a clear legal framework within which the accountability deficit can be addressed is lacking.

2.3.1.1 The UN Charter

With the establishment of ITA missions, the question of whether the UN Charter allows for territorial administration at all has effectively become moot. However, the Charter does not provide a specific fit-for-purpose legal basis for ITA missions. This is in sharp contrast to the Mandate and Trusteeship systems, both of which systems had an explicit underpinning in the Covenant and the Charter respectively. At present, Chapter VII of the Charter is the primary legal foundation, while the implied powers doctrine and extensive interpretation of certain Charter provisions have also been invoked to place ITA within the ambit of the Charter.

Article 24 and Chapter VII

The competence of the UN to administer a territory was debated during the drafting of the UN Charter. A proposal was made at the time by Norway to include provisions into Chapter VII to that effect. The proposal stated that the Security Council could:

---

[70] *See e.g.* Milano E. (2006), *Unlawful territorial situations in international law: reconciling effectiveness, legality and legitimacy*, Leiden: Nijhoff; Milano E. (2003), 'Security Council Action in the Balkans: Reviewing the Legality of Kosovo's Territorial Status', 14(5) *European Journal of International Law*, pp. 999-1022.

[71] Stahn (2008), p. 414.

> take over on behalf of the Organisation the administration of *any territory* of which the continued administration by the state in possession is found to constitute a threat to the peace.[72]

The reference to "any territory" indicates that the Norwegian delegation envisaged a need for the UN to engage in the administration of territories beyond the scope of the Trusteeship system, since the system could not be applied to "territories which have become Members of the United Nations".[73] The proposal was ultimately rejected. Opposing states argued that if Chapter VII were to include an explicit list of competences, this could be interpreted as an exhaustive list, limiting the powers of the UN under Chapter VII with respect to activities falling outside such a list of competences.[74] Despite the rejection, these negotiations suggested that the power to administer "any territory" indeed falls within the purview of Chapter VII. This view was subsequently reinforced in practice. Chapter VII was found to imply the authority of the Security Council to engage in the administration of the Free Territory of Trieste in the manner envisaged by the Trieste Statute. An inclusive interpretation of Chapter VII was openly defended by the Secretary-General[75] and Chapter VII, in conjunction with Article 24 of the Charter,[76] became the basis for the adoption of the Trieste Statute.[77] In a similar fashion, the UN state-like activities in Namibia were sanctioned when the Secretary-General stated:

> *in the absence of an intervening Sovereign jurisdiction between the General Assembly and the people* of the territory of Namibia [...] no governmental authority exists other than the General Assembly and the Security Council.[78]

[72] As quoted by Stahn (2008), p. 416, emphasis added. *See also* Chesterman (2005), p. 50.
[73] UN Charter, Art. 78.
[74] Stahn (2008), p. 416.
[75] Statement made by the UN SG, 10 January 1947. *See* Repertoire of the Practice of the Security Council, 1946-1951, p. 483.
[76] UN Charter, Art. 24: "1. In order to ensure prompt and effective action by the United Nations, its Members confer on the Security Council primary responsibility for the maintenance of international peace and security, and agree that in carrying out its duties under this responsibility the Security Council acts on their behalf. 2. In discharging these duties the Security Council shall act in accordance with the Purposes and Principles of the United Nations. The specific powers granted to the Security Council for the discharge of these duties are laid down in Chapters VI, VII, VIII, and XII. 3. The Security Council shall submit annual and, when necessary, special reports to the General Assembly for its consideration".
[77] SC Res. 16 (1947).
[78] ICJ, *Legal Consequences for States of the Continued Presence of South Africa in Namibia (South West Africa) notwithstanding Security Council Resolution 276 (1970)*, Written Statement of the Secretary-General of the United Nations, 7 December 1970, p. 85, emphasis

The ICJ upheld this line of reasoning in its advisory opinion regarding the Namibia dispute.[79] The UN General Assembly also adopted the view that the UN could engage "[i]n those areas and on those matters where sovereignty is not rested in a member state".[80] The dispute over Namibia was not the only time that Article 24 of the Charter has been interpreted so as to imply the authority of the UN to administer territories.[81] For example, during the preparation of the Trieste administration, the Secretary-General characterized Article 24 as "a grant of power sufficiently wide to enable the Security Council to approve the documents in question" and thus assume final administrative authority over the Free Territory of Trieste.[82]

On this occasion, the representative of Australia voiced unequivocal opposition during the Security Council debates. Australia argued that although Article 24 indeed gives the Security Council the primary responsibility to maintain international peace and security, it also explicitly refers to Chapters VI, VII, VIII and XII regarding the competences of the Security Council, which chapters fail to include territorial administration. In other words, Australia argued, the powers entrusted to the Security Council that amount to the administration of territory went beyond the necessary means to ensure international peace and security, and hence failed to fall under even the broadest interpretation of Article 24.[83]

Hans Kelsen voiced similar objections at the time, denouncing such an extensive interpretation of Article 24. Even if interpreted extensively, he argued, "it would hardly be possible to justify in this way the assumption of the headship of a state or state-like community".[84] Kelsen adopted a positivist approach: no provision in the Charter could justify the exercise of governmental authority by

added (*Continued Presence of South Africa*). The UN SG did add a caveat in reference to the previous administration of Namibia by the League: "[a] fundamental premise of the actions and responsibilities undertaken by the United Nations and its members in respect of Namibia has been that the United Nations has had, and continues to have special responsibilities towards the people and Territory of Namibia".

[79] ICJ, *Continued Presence of South Africa*, Advisory Opinion, 21 June 1971. References to ICJ judgments and advisory opinions (and particular pages thereof), as published in the ICJ Reports, unless stated otherwise.

[80] Report by the UN SG, *Compliance of Member States with the United Nations Resolutions and Decisions relating to Namibia, taking into account the Advisory Opinion of the International Court of Justice of 21 June 1971*, UN Doc. A/AC.131/37, 12 March 1975.

[81] The line between the implied powers doctrine on the one hand and extensive interpretation of specific articles from the UN Charter on the other hand is amorphous. In effect, the two approaches amount to the same result, *e.g.* Stahn (2008), pp. 424-430; De Wet (2004). *See also* ECtHR, *Behrami and Behrami v. France, Saramati v. France, Germany and Norway*, No. 71412/01 & 78166/01, Grand Chamber, Decision, 31 May 2007, § 130 (*Behrami*).

[82] Stahn (2008), pp. 424-430.

[83] Kelsen H. (1950), *The Law of the United Nations*, London: Stevens & Sons Limited, p. 834, n. 7.

[84] *Id.*, p. 834.

the UN, as "the Organization is not authorized by the Charter to exercise *sovereignty* over a territory" outside the scope of the Trusteeship system.[85] Kelsen did remain realistic, by concluding his critique with the observation that the UN "has not the legal, but it has certainly the actual power to assume [such functions] for the Security Council".[86]

Eventually, the extensive interpretation of Chapter VII, which provides the Security Council with the authority to adopt legally binding resolutions, gained importance. On various occasions, Chapter VII has served as the legal basis for Security Council measures that, as such, are not explicitly mentioned by that chapter.[87] Likewise, consensus exists regarding the use of Chapter VII as the basis for ITA missions as well.[88] ITA missions such as UNTAES, UNMIK and UNTAET were all established pursuant to Chapter VII resolutions.[89] Likewise, the Security Council endorsed the implementation of the Dayton Peace Agreement with reference to Chapter VII of the Charter.[90] In particular, depending on whether the military component of the undertaking is integrated into the UN engagement, Articles 41 and 42 of the UN Charter provide the tools for the UN to engage. While Article 41 is limited to the adoption of non-military measures, Article 42 provides a basis for coercive action involving the use of military force. Although Article 41 would provide a legal basis for the establishment of a civil administration, it would not suffice as a legal foundation for UN missions that incorporate military components, as in the case of UNTAET. For the deployment of military forces, the invocation of Article 42 then provides the outcome.

---

[85] *Id.*, pp. 832-836. *See a contrario* Stahn (2008), p. 422.

[86] Kelsen (1950), p. 835.

[87] *E.g.* the Security Council undertook to establish ad hoc international criminal tribunals in relation to the conflicts in former Yugoslavia and Rwanda, *see* SC Res. 827 (1993) and SC Res. 955 (1994).

[88] ECtHR, *Behrami*, § 130. For an elaborate analysis of the UN Charter, and Chapter VII in particular, as the legal basis for ITA, *see* Stahn (2008), pp. 413-446. *See also* De Wet (2004); Zimmermann A. & Stahn C. (2001), 'Yugoslav Territory, United Nations Trusteeship or Sovereign State? Reflections on the Current and Future Legal Status of Kosovo', 70 *Nordic Journal of International Law*, pp. 423-460.

[89] SC Res. 1037 (1996), p. 2; SC Res. 1244 (1999), p. 2 and SC Res. 1272 (1999), p. 2 respectively.

[90] In the case of BiH, while the establishment of an all-encompassing international presence in BiH was initiated through the Dayton peace talks and the signing of the Dayton Peace Agreement in Paris, the military component of the presence was authorized by the Security Council with reference to Chapter VII. Pursuant to the Dayton Peace Agreement, Ann. 1A, Art. 1a, the UN Security Council adopted Resolution 1031 (1995) through which it authorized the reconfiguration of the international military presence in BiH.

Chapters VI, XII and XIII: Unused Alternatives

At times, alternative legal foundations within the Charter have been suggested. One such alternative is the invocation of Chapter VI, Article 36 in particular, as a possible legal basis. The inclusion of Chapter VI into the debate is justified by the traditional link between UN peacekeeping missions – under which category ITA missions are generally placed – and Chapter VI.[91] Furthermore, if one accepts that ITA missions are based on consent, it would "not seem conceptually accurate" to place the Security Council's ITA-related authority in the ambit of Chapter VII.[92]

It has also been argued that the Trusteeship system in a revived and revised form could provide a legal basis. The Trusteeship system, framed by Chapters XII and XIII, provides the only explicit ground for the UN to engage in the administration of territories. This prompts the question concerning why the trusteeship system was never employed as the legal basis, and whether or not it should have been, since the objectives of the Trusteeship system, as listed in Article 76 of the Charter, do not differ much from the aims underlying ITA.[93]

Along with the termination of the Trusteeship system in 1994, the system's configuration precluded the establishment of ITA missions within the trusteeship framework. Article 77 of the Charter determines the territories that could be placed under the Trusteeship system: mandated lands (77(1)(a)), territories "which may be detached" from Second World War enemy states (77(1)(b)) and "territories voluntarily placed under the system by states responsible for their administration" (77(1)(c)). While the first two options are

[91] Stahn (2008), p. 435; De Wet (2004), p. 317.

[92] De Wet (2004), p. 314.

[93] These aims include, amongst others, furthering international peace and security, promoting advancement of the local population and progressive development towards self-government or independence, encouraging respect for human rights and ensuring equal treatment. *See* Stahn (2008), pp. 440-441, n. 101; Ford & Oppenheim (2008), p. 57, n. 4; Kreijen G. (2004), *State Failure, Sovereignty and Effectiveness: Legal Lessons from the Decolonization of Sub-Saharan Africa*, Leiden: Martinus Nijhoff Publishers, pp. 308-326; Tremper J. M. (2004), 'The Decolonization of Chechnya: Reviving the UN Trusteeship Council", 15(1) *Journal of Public and International Affairs*, pp. 121-141 in reference to a report issued by "The Ministry of Foreign Affairs of the Chechen Republic of Ichkeria" named "*The Russian-Chechen Tragedy: The way to peace and democracy; Conditional independence under an international administration*", *in* (2003) 22(4) *Central Asian Survey*, pp. 481-509; Parker T. (2003), *The Ultimate Intervention: Revitalising the UN Trusteeship Council for the 21st Century*, publication from the Center for European and Asian Studies at Norwegian School of Management, pp. 1-54; Ruffert M. (2001), 'The Administration of Kosovo and East Timor', 50 *International and Comparative Law Quarterly*, pp. 613-631; Helman G.B. & Ratner S.R. (1993), 'Saving failed states', 89 *Foreign Policy*, pp. 3-20. *See also* International Commission on Intervention and State Sovereignty (2001), *Report: The Responsibility to Protect*, Ottawa: International Development Research Center, p. 43.

manifestly archaic, Article 77(1)(c) leaves room for debate. However, Article 78 declares that the Trusteeship system "shall not apply to territories which have become Members of the [UN]".[94] Articles 79, 80 and 81 further determine that the foundation of any potential trust territory will be a trusteeship agreement, thereby anchoring the voluntary nature of the system.[95] Other obstacles also prevented the revival of the Trusteeship system for the purpose of ITA missions. It has been advanced that the extended application of the system might collide with the right to self-determination, although this argument seems to be refuted by the wording of Article 76(b).[96] As well as formal obstacles, "ideological linkage" of the Trusteeship system with decolonization rendered the system inadequate for serving as a legal basis for ITA missions.[97]

2.3.1.2 State Consent

Despite the invocation of Chapter VII, the UN has thus far avoided establishing ITA missions without state consent in order to patch the ambiguity that surrounds the charter-based legal basis.[98] In the case of Kosovo, the Yugoslav Federal Government voted on 3 June 1999 in favour of the "general principles on a political solution to the Kosovo crisis", which include an invitation to establish an international civil administration.[99] Likewise, UNTAET was

[94] Some have argued that Art. 78 is redundant, *see e.g.* Kelsen (1950), p. 574.

[95] Making ITA missions dependent on state consent has been regarded as troublesome by some. *See e.g.* Zimmermann & Stahn (2001), p. 436. State consent was especially regarded as problematic in the event a state had collapsed leaving no state behind to give its consent to be placed under the Trusteeship system, *see* Stahn (2008), p. 440.

[96] Zaum (2007), p. 27; Parker (2003), pp. 41-42.

[97] Stahn (2008), p. 440.

[98] *Cf.* Martti Ahtisaari, who in an interview with a Dutch daily newspaper, when asked to comment on the fact that the UN is still present in Kosovo and that the EU cannot start operating, suggested: "There is always the chance that the Kosovo Government itself says: 'Thank you UN, we do not need you anymore'. It is now an independent state with its own constitution. However, I hope they will not do this", *in* NRC Handelsblad, *Serviërs moeten zich eens gedragen* (Serbs should start behaving themselves), 22 May 2008, at <http://www.nrc.nl/buitenland/article2018048.ece/Serviers_moeten_zich_eens_gedragen>. This view was endorsed by the authorities in Priština. At the time, Kosovo's Prime-minister Hashim Thaçi stated with regard to the deployment of EULEX that "UN Resolution 1244 is absolutely unimportant and without significance for our sovereign country. We, as Kosovo's institutions, will adhere to and realize Kosovo's constitution and other laws adopted by the Kosovo assembly", *in* B92, *K. Albanians still refusing Ban plan*, 25 November 2008, at <www.b92.net/eng/news/politics-article.php?yyyy=2008&mm=11&dd=25&nav_id=55287>.

[99] SC Res. 1244 (1999), preamble and Ann. 1 and 2. The Kumanovo Agreement between KFOR and the Federal Republic of Yugoslavia, dated 9 June 1999, embodies the consent of the Federal Republic of Yugoslavia to the deployment of an international military presence, at <http://www.nato.int/kosovo/docu/a990609a.htm>. The Legal validity of this agreement has been questioned sporadically due to the preceding use of military force. *See* Milano (2003).

established in East Timor after the Indonesian and Portuguese authorities took several steps granting consent to such an undertaking.[100]

The issue of state consent is more significant in the context of BiH, where the international administration is endorsed but not established by the UN. Bear in mind that the international administration of BiH emanates from the Dayton Peace Agreement and is led by a group of states on behalf of the international community.[101] The states, assembled in the Peace Implementation Council, provide guidance to the OHR, itself an "ad hoc international institution".[102] The signing of the Dayton Peace Agreement by the warring sides formally embodies the consent of BiH to the subsequent international deployment.[103] In practice, the expansion of the OHR mandate influenced the way in which emphasis was placed on either UN Security Council resolutions or state consent as the legal basis. The authority initially given to the OHR was limited in nature. During this initial period, between 1995 and 1997, the High Representative emphasized the will of the parties as the source of his authority. After adoption of the extensive Bonn powers in 1997, the High Representative began increasingly to refer to relevant UN Security Council resolutions as the source of his mandate.[104]

In summary, the UN Charter fails to provide a clear legal basis for the establishment of robust ITA missions. Instead, agreement exists on an extensive interpretation of Chapter VII, which allows for the UN to assume the control over a territory outside the Trusteeship system framework. Despite the linkage to Chapter VII, state consent has accompanied the establishment of UNMIK, UNTAET and the OHR.[105] In other words, the UN Charter fails to delineate a

---

[100] Most importantly, a set of political agreements was signed in New York on 5 May 1999 between Indonesia and Portugal. In addition, the referendum results that paved the way for independence were formally accepted by the Indonesian People's Consultative Assembly on 19 October 1999, *see* <http://www.un.org/peace/etimor/UntaetB.htm>. As Indonesia's sovereignty over East Timor was not recognized by the UN, Indonesia's attempt to communicate the Indonesian Assembly's adoption of the referendum results to the UN was discarded as a "formality". Instead, Portugal assured the UN that it would "relinquish its legal ties to East Timor" once a UN Security Council resolution establishing UN administration had been adopted, *see* Chopra J. (2000)(2), 'Introductory Note to UNTAET Regulation 13 (2000)', 39(4) *International Legal Materials*, p. 937.

[101] *See e.g.* the conclusions of the Peace Implementation Conference (London, 8-9 December 1995), at <http://www.ohr.int/pic/default.asp?content_id=5168>. *See further* Section 4.3 below.

[102] SC Res. 1031 (1995), §§ 26-27.

[103] For example, the UN Security Council referred to the "request of the parties" in the context of the establishment of the OHR. The Dayton Peace Agreement, Ann. 10, Art. I(2) states: "In view of the complexities facing them, the Parties request the designation of a High Representative, to be appointed consistent with relevant United Nations Security Council resolutions".

[104] *See* Steiner C. & Ademović N. (eds.) (2010), *Constitution of Bosnia and Herzegovina: Commentary*, Sarajevo: Konrad Adenaur Stiftung e.V, pp. 787-789.

[105] *Cf.* Stahn (2008), p. 47; De Wet (2004), pp. 317-318.

legal playing field within which ITA missions operate. No fit-for-purpose parameters are set concerning the actual configuration of the missions and the manner in which they exercise and expand their mandate.

2.3.2 ITA MISSIONS: BYPASSING THE FRAMEWORK OF SOVEREIGNTY

State sovereignty as an impermeable bar to external interference has become disputed. A changing approach to sovereignty has been prompted by developments such as the increased focus on human rights and the maturing of international criminal law.[106] The inclusive mandate enjoyed by ITA missions generates a debate about how their robust mandate relates to the sovereignty of the internationally administered territory.[107] Questioning whether or not ITA missions operate under the sovereignty of a host state, or even whether ITA missions themselves assume sovereignty over the territory they administer, ties in with the question of a legal framework that may or may not limit the authority of ITA missions. Therefore, the debate about sovereignty is presented in the following paragraphs.

When ultimate authority to exercise public power within a territory has been attributed to a non-state entity, the question is not whether and to what extent this infringes on the local sovereignty: rather, it concerns the question of who exercises sovereign-like powers. Any discussion on the *locus* of sovereignty will be influenced by one's understanding of the concept of sovereignty.[108] The two basic attributes sovereignty can provide its holder are title and power. The legal

---

[106] *See in general* Brownlie I. (2008), *Principles of Public International Law*, New York: Oxford University Press, pp. 105-172; Shaw M.N. (2008), *International Law*, New York: Cambridge University Press, pp. 487-521; Ford & Oppenheim (2008), pp. 75-78; Crawford J.R. (2006), *The Creation of States in International Law*, Oxford: Oxford University Press, in particular pp. 32-33; Slaughter A. (2004), 'Sovereignty and Power in a Networked World Order', 40 *Stanford of International Law*, pp. 283-327. *See also* Steinberg R.H. (2004), 'Who Is Sovereign?', 40 *Stanford Journal of International Law*, pp. 329-345, who argues that while states have remained *legally* sovereign, the degree to which they are *behaviorally* sovereign varies. Finally, *see* the International Commission on Intervention and State Sovereignty (2001), *Report: The Responsibility to Protect*, Ottawa: International Development Research Center.

[107] *E.g.* Knoll (2008); Zaum (2007); Smyrek (2006).

[108] Different definitions of sovereignty have been advanced, *e.g.* international legal sovereignty, domestic sovereignty, Westphalian sovereignty and interdependence sovereignty, *see* Stephen Krasner, as referenced by Slaughter (2004), p. 283. For a view on the emerging concept of earned or conditioned sovereignty, *see e.g.* Williams P.R. & Pecci F.J. (2004), 'Earned Sovereignty: Bridging the Gap Between Sovereignty and Self-Determination', 40 *Stanford Journal of International Law*, pp. 347-386. *See also* Sarooshi D. (2005), *International Organizations and their Exercise of Sovereign Powers*, Oxford: Oxford University Press.

essence of sovereignty is captured by the notion of title.[109] The sovereign ideally has the power to act upon this title through the exercise of jurisdiction within the territory to which it is entitled. The nexus between these two attributes depends on two distinct approaches: the material and the formal.

The material approach to sovereignty argues inseparability of title and actual exercise of power and control. As a "basket of properties", sovereignty must be able to express itself.[110] Internally, a sovereign does so through the exercise of public powers. Externally, sovereignty is, for example, reflected through the authority to decide on foreign policy, treaty-making and membership in international organizations.[111] In other words, the exercise of control is considered constitutive of sovereignty.

In his separate opinion in the PCIJ *Lighthouses in Crete and Samos* case, Judge Manley O. Hudson illustrates succinctly the irrationality of ineffective sovereignty by claiming that holding on to a title without being able to exercise power leads to legal fiction. Hudson recalls, "after 1899 the Ottoman Government exercised no governmental powers in Crete [and that] in its external relations, the Cretan Government acted independently of the Ottoman Government". Hudson therefore concludes as follows:

> If it can be said that a *theoretical sovereignty* remained in the Sultan after 1899, it was a sovereignty shorn of the last vestige of power. [...] A juristic conception must not be stretched to the breaking-point, and a ghost of a *hollow sovereignty* cannot be permitted to obscure the realities of this situation.[112]

Conversely, a formal approach to sovereignty separates the two basic attributes; "administration [is] divorced from sovereignty".[113] In other words, sovereign powers are not equated with sovereign title. The right of disposition is regarded as the essential trait of sovereignty. Only the sovereign can dispose of his powers and, ultimately, of his sovereign title. This dichotomy parallels the relationship between the concepts of ownership and possession, according to which ownership can be separated from the actual use or possession of the subject to which the owner is entitled.[114]

---

[109] Shaw (2008), p. 490.
[110] Zaum (2007), p. 28.
[111] *E.g.* Smyrek (2006), p. 32.
[112] PCIJ, *Lighthouses in Crete and Samos*, Ser. A/B, No. 71, 8 October 1937, Separate Opinion Judge Hudson, p. 127, emphasis added (*Lighthouses in Crete and Samos*).
[113] Brownlie (2008), p. 107.
[114] Shaw (2008), p. 490.

In the *Lighthouses in Crete and Samos* case – contrary to the previously cited separate opinion – the PCIJ embraced the formal approach. In discussing the status of Crete, the Court found that:

> even though the Sultan had been obliged to accept important restrictions on the exercise of his rights of sovereignty in Crete, that sovereignty had not ceased to belong to him, however it might be qualified from a juridical point of view.[115]

The two approaches have also been referred to as 'de facto' and 'de jure' sovereignty. For example, courts in the United States have repeatedly held that the United States' exercise of "administration, legislation and jurisdiction" over the Ryukyu Islands amounted to de facto sovereignty, while Japan's residual title was termed 'de jure sovereignty'. However, although Japan had disposed of all its claims to the actual administration of the territory, it held on to its title as sovereign. As such, Japan remained the sole entity able to dispose of its title, as the final trait of sovereignty.

See e.g. Brownlie (2008), p. 110.

In line with the reasoning of the PCIJ, it is widely accepted that sovereignty remains with its holder, even when reduced to a mere title: a *nudum ius*. This does not mean that the exercise of sovereign rights is irrelevant in determining the holder of sovereignty. Especially when sovereignty is contested, "the actual exercise or display of such [sovereign] authority" should be taken into account.[116] Other factors, such as intent, are also relevant in determining the holder of sovereignty.[117]

The treaties concerning the exercise of control over the Panama Canal Zone during a considerable part of the 20th century are illustrative. With the signing of the *Hay-Bunau Varilla* Treaty in 1903, Panama granted to the United States:

> all the rights, power and authority within the [Panama Canal Zone] which the United States *would* possess and exercise *if* it were the sovereign of the

115 PCIJ, *Lighthouses in Crete and Samos*, Judgment, p. 103. For a critical appraisal of the case, *see* Crawford (2006), pp. 354-357.

116 PCIJ, *Legal status of Eastern Greenland*, Ser. A/B, No. 53, Judgment, 5 April 1933, p. 46 (*Legal status of Eastern Greenland*). Other factors have also been considered as relevant when assessing claims to sovereignty and the sustainability of sovereignty as a *nudum ius* such as the time period during which actual exercise of powers has been separated from the sovereign, the argument here being that the longer a sovereign is unable to exercise his rights, the more likely it becomes that the entity exercising authority will eventually assume sovereignty, *see* Smyrek (2006), p. 45.

117 PCIJ, *Legal status of Eastern Greenland*, p. 46. The subjectivity and limited practical value of intent as an element of sovereignty has prompted criticism, *see* Brownlie (2008), p. 135.

> territory [...] to the entire exclusion of the exercise by the Republic of Panama of any such sovereign rights, power or authority.[118]

This transfer was undertaken for an indefinite period of time. Nevertheless, Panama held on to its title and remained the sole entity that could either dispose of this title or effectuate it again without explicit retrocession.[119] Because the United States did not intend to assume sovereignty, Panama's sovereignty was hibernated, only to regain effect in 1999 pursuant to the second *Torrijos-Carter* Treaty of 1977.[120] In a wholly different setting, the authority of the Allied Forces over Germany after World War II also illustrates the extent to which titular sovereignty and actual administration can be divided. Although occupied, Germany was not annexed and remained sovereign, since the Allied Forces never intended to gain sovereignty over Germany. Indeed, if Germany's sovereignty had ceased to exist (along with the loss of its power to administer), the Allied presence in Germany would not have constituted occupation.[121]

Turning to the ITA context, the accepted formal approach to sovereignty suggests that the assumption of sovereign-like powers by ITA missions does not imply the assumption of sovereign title. However, if sovereignty is reduced to a *nudum ius,* it no longer serves as a limit to the way in which ITA missions administer a particular territory.[122] The following sections zoom in on the nexus between sovereignty on the one hand and ITA missions and their precedents on the other.

2.3.2.1 Sovereignty and the Period of Mandates and Trusteeships

The Mandate and Trusteeship systems were established in a period when sovereignty as a legal principle enjoyed a paramount status.[123] This fueled the debates concerning the relationship between sovereignty and the two systems.[124]

---

[118] Convention between the United States and the Republic of Panama, 18 November 1903, Art. 3, at <http://www.bartleby.com/43/47.html>, emphasis added.

[119] Brownlie (2008), p. 111; Smyrek (2006), pp. 46-51.

[120] *The Panama Canal* Treaty, signed between the United States and Panama, 7 September 1977.

[121] *E.g.* Brownlie (2008), p. 107.

[122] Save for the hypothetical option of an ITA mission wanting to dispose of a territory under its administration.

[123] As argued by the American Secretary of State, Robert Lansing, in 1919, "nine-tenths of all international controversies arise over questions pertaining to the possession of sovereignty and the conflict of sovereign rights", as quoted in Chowdhuri (1955), p. 230.

[124] *See e.g.* Chowdhuri (1955), pp. 229-236; Honig F. (1936), 'International Law and the Transfer of Mandated Territories', 18(4) *Journal of Comparative Legislation and International Law*, pp. 204-211; Wright Q. (1923), 'Sovereignty of the Mandates', 17(4) *American Journal of International Law*, pp. 691-703; Evans L.H. (1932), 'The General

It has been argued that under the Mandate system, the League assumed sovereignty over territories as mandated lands were administered "on behalf of the League".[125] The power of the League with respect to the mandates seems to substantiate this proposition. Certain modifications to the individual mandate regimes were impossible without the League's consent. Broad consensus also exists in support of the opinion that transfer (*i.e.* disposition) of a mandate required unanimous backing by the League.[126] In the event of persistent breaches by a mandatory power of its obligations, the League had the authority to terminate the mandate.[127] In addition, the scope of limitations imposed by the League on the mandatory powers indicated, according to some, that the League held "ultimate sovereignty".[128] Conversely, adversaries argued that the League lacked the essential prerequisites to hold sovereignty. Although the League imposed limitations on the mandatory powers, it had neither established the actual mandates nor was it able to modify or determine their substance unilaterally.[129]

In a similar fashion, it has been debated whether the UN held sovereignty over territories placed under the Trusteeship system. Certain ultimate prerogatives of the UN warranted this claim but opposition was outspoken. As Duncan Hall concluded, "wherever [sovereignty] may be, [it] certainly did not lie in the United Nations".[130]

Alternatively, it has been argued that the mandatory powers and the trust-administering entities assumed sovereignty over the territories they administered. Especially in the context of "C" mandates, where the mandated lands were considered "integral portions of [the mandatory's] territory", this assertion seemed plausible.[131] South Africa, for example, based its claims concerning Namibia on this line of argumentation. This view was rejected. Some dismissed this approach as an expression of colonial thinking.[132] Others pointed to the position of the League with respect to the mandates. The authority

---

Principles Governing the Termination of a Mandate', 26(4) *American Journal of International Law*, pp. 735-758.

[125] League of Nations Covenant, Art. 22

[126] Honig (1936), pp. 210-211.

[127] Wright (1923), p. 702.

[128] *E.g.* Lauterpacht H. (1927), *Private Law Sources and Analogy of International Law*, London: Longmans, Green, pp. 194-196

[129] Chowdhuri (1955), pp. 321-323; Wright (1923), p. 697. However, the argument that the League is not able to unilaterally modify the mandate does not prevent it from holding sovereignty. This limitation is outweighed by the authority of the League to revoke a mandate and by the fact that consent by the League is considered necessary if a mandatory wanted to transfer or dispose of a mandate.

[130] Hall (1948), p. 274.

[131] League of Nations Covenant, Art. 22.

[132] ICJ, *Continued Presence of South Africa*, Separate Opinion Vice-President Ammoun, p. 69, referring to Paul Fauchille's writings from 1922.

of the mandatory powers was subject to limitations imposed by the League and above all, unilateral transfer of the territory was impossible.[133] Furthermore, the League could terminate a mandate.[134] The Mandates Commission also rejected any claim to sovereignty by Mandatories: "sovereignty should not be used to describe the authority of a mandatory over a mandated territory".[135]

The ICJ also denounced the view that Mandatories assumed sovereignty.[136] The argument used by the ICJ is transplantable to the trusteeship context. The UN had authority to terminate trusteeship agreements.[137] Furthermore, the concept of trusteeship was based on the notion that all authority entrusted to the administering powers was confined by the interests of the administered territories and their inhabitants. As such, one could "no more speak of the sovereignty of an administering Power over a Non-Self-Governing Territory than [of] a guardian's ownership of his ward's property".[138]

The connection between the Mandate and Trusteeship regimes and self-determination prompts a third and more population-oriented approach. This approach suggests that while exercise of sovereign rights was temporarily attributed to an administering authority, the sovereignty remained with the people subject to this authority.[139] With regard to the Mandate system, especially in the context of "B" and "C" mandates, the link with self-determination was too weak to support such a theory, leading many authors to oppose it.[140] Conversely, the Trusteeship system as a whole was inseparably linked with the right to self-determination, thus adding strength to the theory. The trusteeship agreement concerning Somaliland was the only agreement to opt explicitly for this view. Article 1 of the attached declaration of constitutional principles stated, "[T]he sovereignty of the Territory is vested in its people and shall be exercised by the Administering Authority on their behalf [...]".[141] However, this approach was not anchored with respect to the Trusteeship system in general.

---

[133] Wright (1923), p. 695.

[134] In the case of Namibia, *see* GA Res. 2145 (XXI), 27 October 1966, SC Res. 264 (1969).

[135] *See* Evans (1933), p. 737.

[136] ICJ, *International Status of South West Africa*, Advisory Opinion, 11 July 1950, pp. 132, 143-144 (*International Status of South West Africa*). Local courts at the time also rejected this view. The Supreme Court of Palestine for example rejected the view that by being the mandatory power, Great Britain had assumed sovereignty over the territory, *see* Bentwich N. (1929), 'Judicial Interpretation of the Mandate for Palestine', 1 *Zeitschrift für ausländisches öffentliches Recht und Völkerrecht*, p. 221.

[137] Stahn (2008), p. 112.

[138] Statement by Mr. Trujillo, Ecuador's representative, at the 9th Session, 485th Plenary Meeting, UN Doc. A/PV. 485, 1 October 1954, § 92.

[139] *E.g.* Stahn (2008), p. 88, arguing that this theory is probably most convincing. *See also* Chowdhuri (1955), pp. 233-234.

[140] Wright (1923), pp. 696-697.

[141] Trusteeship Council, *Trusteeship Agreement for the Territory of Somaliland under Italian Administration*, UN Doc. T/456, 27 January 1950.

Under both systems, little attention was devoted to the theory of 'joint sovereignty': namely, sovereignty divided between multiple entities. Some argued this was the case with regard to the League and the Principle Allied and Associated Powers.[142] Others concluded that sovereignty was held by the Mandatory Powers and the League Council, based on an analysis of the power to amend and alienate the mandates.[143] Joint sovereignty was also advanced by some authors in the context of trusteeship arrangements.[144]

The issue of sovereignty was also debated with respect to the Saar Basin and Danzig, the difference being that in these cases it was the League rather than an assigned state that assumed direct administering authority. The League's administration of the Saar Basin disaggregated the exercise of public power into three parts: Germany remained the nominal sovereign, France was awarded certain sovereign rights and the actual administration of the Saar Basin was entrusted to the League.[145] Germany remained the titular sovereign over the Saar Basin, as it had only ceded to the League – "in the capacity of trustee" – the authority to govern.[146] The provisions dealing with the plebiscite that was to be held in order to determine the future status of the Saar Basin in essence confirm Germany's title. If the *status quo* or a union with France had been the outcome, the Treaty declares that Germany then would respectively "make such renunciation of her sovereignty in favour of the League of Nations as the latter shall deem necessary" or "cede to France [...] all rights and *title* over the territory".[147] These provisions indicate that Germany remained the sovereign as it would otherwise have no rights or title to renounce. This view enjoys broad consensus amongst scholars, reflecting a preference for the formal approach to sovereignty.[148] The Versailles Treaty provisions dealing with the plebiscite did create a paradox as ultimately it was the League that was to decide whether such renunciation or cession was to take place. Combined with the scope of the League's authority, several authors have claimed that in fact sovereignty had already been transferred to the League or that sovereignty was held by the member states of the League, the Governing Commission or the signatories to the Versailles Treaty.[149]

In the case of the Free City of Danzig, the Versailles Treaty went one step further by declaring that Germany renounced all *rights and title* over the

---

[142] Chowdhuri (1955), pp. 234-235.
[143] Wright (1923), p. 698.
[144] Chowdhuri (1955), p. 235.
[145] Chesterman (2005), p. 19.
[146] Treaty of Versailles, Part III, Section IV, Art. 49.
[147] *Id.*, Ann., Chapter III, Art. 35, emphasis added.
[148] *E.g.* Smyrek (2006), pp. 73-75.
[149] Ydit (1961), p. 45, where the Saar Basin is described as an "internationalized territory under the sovereignty of the LON". For other authors and theories, *see* Smyrek (2006), p. 73.

territory to the Principal Allied and Associated Powers.[150] Also in relation to Poland, with which the Free City of Danzig had a *sui generis* bond, Danzig was to be regarded as a foreign state with its own constitution – one guaranteed by the League and explicitly allocating sovereignty to the inhabitants of the Free City of Danzig.[151] While it has been defended that sovereignty remained with the Principal Allied and Associated Powers,[152] authors mainly agree that the sovereignty was held by the Free City of Danzig itself.[153]

2.3.2.2 Sovereignty and International Territorial Administrations

The issue of sovereignty in the present ITA context is subject to similar, predominantly scholarly, debate. A point of departure in the debate is the assumption that the UN and other international organizations are generally regarded as incapable of enjoying sovereignty.[154] The ambiguous status of the internationally administered territories further convolutes the debate. As regards Kosovo, the territory's status is disputed and sovereignty is claimed by two sides. During UNTAET, East Timor was in a transitional phase, heading from decades of annexation towards independence. Finally, BiH's sovereignty remains fragile. The question of sovereignty in these situations can be approached from three perspectives. Firstly, along the lines of the formal approach, it can be argued that the internationalization of a territory leaves sovereign title over the administered territory untouched. In other words, the ITA missions are entitled to govern the respective territories but cannot dispose of them.[155] Secondly and conversely, drawing on the material approach, sovereignty is said to have shifted, leaving room for debate as to which entity

---

[150] Paris Convention between Danzig and Poland, 9 November 1920, Art. 6; Treaty of Versailles, Part III, Section XI, Ann., Art. 100.

[151] PCIJ, *Treatment of Polish Nationals in the Danzig Territory*, Ser. A/B, No. 44, Advisory Opinion, 4 February 1932, p. 24 (*Treatment of Polish Nationals*). *See also* Art. 3 of the Constitution of the Free city of Danzig.

[152] *See e.g.* Crawford (2006), pp. 239-240; Ydit (1961), p. 224.

[153] Smyrek (2006), p. 67; Crawford (2006), pp. 239-240.

[154] Brownlie (2008), p. 167, n. 27 with reference to Kelsen (1950), pp. 195-197 and 684-687 where Kelsen presents his reading of the relevant powers of the UN. Kelsen did point out that as a matter of fact, the Free Territory of Trieste should be seen as a "state-like community under UN sovereignty", Kelsen (1950), pp. 832-835. *A contrario*, Smyrek (2006), p. 37. Recall also that The League did create an opportunity in the Saar Basin-context according to which it could assume sovereignty: namely if the plebiscite had advised the League accordingly. In such a case, Germany would "make such renunciation of her sovereignty in favour of the League of Nations as the latter shall deem necessary", Treaty of Versailles, Part III, Section IV, Ann., Chapter III, Art. 35.

[155] *E.g.* Stahn C. (2001)(1), 'Constitution without a State? Kosovo under the United Nations Constitutional Framework for Self-Government', 14 *Leiden Journal of International Law*, p. 450.

has subsequently assumed sovereign title. Thirdly, as a response to this state of uncertainty, it has been argued that sovereignty as a concept simply does not apply in the present context.[156] The three approaches are briefly set out below in the context of the three ITA missions in order to provide a better understanding of the setting within which the ITA accountability deficit occurs.

In the case of Kosovo, the preamble of Security Council Resolution 1244 (1999) *prima facie* affirms "the commitment of all Member States to the sovereignty and territorial integrity of the Federal Republic of Yugoslavia". Other provisions of the Resolution seem to corroborate Serbia's (as the successor state of the Federal Republic of Yugoslavia) title. For example Paragraph 6 of Annex 2, according to which "an agreed number of Yugoslav and Serbian personnel will be permitted to return [to Kosovo] to [maintain] a presence at key border crossings".[157] Leaving title aside, UN Security Council Resolution 1244 (1999) attributes to UNMIK the authority to perform "basic civilian administrative functions *where and as long as required*".[158] In addition, the Resolution authorizes UN member states to establish an international security presence.[159] According to the formal approach to sovereignty, the inability of Serbia to exercise sovereign rights should not affect Serbia's title during UNMIK's governing of Kosovo. Conversely, a material approach would suggest that sovereignty has shifted. At face value, the demeanour of the SRSG and the way in which UNMIK exercised its mandate seem to support the latter option. In addition, the improbability of Serbia effectuating its sovereignty over Kosovo in the near future has led some authors to assume that it is the UN that exercises sovereignty over Kosovo (albeit on behalf of the people of Kosovo).[160]

That the situation can be interpreted in various ways became obvious during the *Kosovo* advisory proceedings before the ICJ. Kosovo's declaration of

[156] A similar classification has been presented by Chowdhuri in the context of the mandates and Trusteeship systems; Chowdhuri (1955), pp. 230-234. The theory of shared sovereignty has also been advanced. This option seems unlikely and neither of the two main approaches to the concept of sovereignty would be able to fully support it, although a material interpretation of sovereignty does to a certain extent facilitate the concept of joint sovereignty. The 1871 constitution of the German Empire (*Verfassung des Deutschen Reichs)* provides an example, as it declares both the German Empire and the German States holders of sovereignty; Smyrek (2006), p. 38. A formal approach to sovereignty rejects such a possibility. Sovereignty is exclusive and cannot be shared. An entity remains sovereign regardless of any substantial and agreed-upon limitations of its sovereignty, *see* Smyrek (2006), p. 36.

[157] This provision was to be implemented only after withdrawal of Yugoslavia's and Serbia's military and police presence from Kosovo. While this withdrawal was carried out "according to a rapid timetable", the return of some personnel was never effectuated.

[158] SC Res. 1244 (1999), § 11(b), emphasis added. *See also* Section 4.3 below.

[159] SC Res. 1244 (1999), §§ 7 and 9.

[160] *E.g.* Perrit (2004), p. 6.

independence triggered the UN General Assembly to request an advisory opinion regarding the legality of this declaration.[161]

Several states submitted written statements providing their understanding of UN Security Council Resolution 1244 (1999) with respect to Serbia's sovereignty over Kosovo. Some states argued that sovereignty rests with the people, who therefore are allowed to express their sovereign will through a declaration of independence.[162]

Others, such as Poland and Switzerland, argue that UN Security Council Resolution 1244 (1999) does not confirm Serbia's sovereignty, since it touches only upon the issue in the preamble.[163] The Czech Republic and the United States argue that the Resolution attaches the sovereignty over Kosovo to the Federal Republic of Yugoslavia, but that it fails to do so with respect to Serbia.[164]

Other states advocate that UN Security Council Resolution 1244 (1999) determines the relevant legal regime and confirms Serbia's sovereignty over Kosovo. This regime, they maintain, can only be altered by the UN Security Council, and a declaration of independence thus violates the Resolution.[165] Norway adopted a different approach by arguing that the traditional concept of sovereignty is no longer viable and in any event not applicable to the present situation.[166]

The ICJ made no pronouncement on this issue in particular, except for the dictum in paragraph 98, where it seemingly adopted a formal reading of the sovereignty provision: "The interim administration in Kosovo was designed to suspend temporarily Serbia's exercise of its authority flowing from its *continuing sovereignty* over the territory of Kosovo".[167]

---

[161] Request for Advisory Opinion, *Accordance with International Law of the Unilateral Declaration of Independence by the Provisional Institutions of Self-Government of Kosovo*, transmitted to the Court pursuant to GA Res. 63/3, 8 October 2008.

[162] *E.g.* ICJ, *Kosovo*, written statements of Albania, 14 April 2009; Austria, 16 April 2009; Denmark, 17 April 2009; Estonia, 13 April 2009; France, 7 April 2009.

[163] ICJ, *Kosovo*, written statements of Poland, 14 April 2009 and Switzerland, 25 May 2009.

[164] ICJ, *Kosovo*, written statements of the Czech Republic, 14 April 2009 and the United States, 17 April 2009.

[165] *E.g.* ICJ, *Kosovo*, written statements of Argentina, 17 April 2009; Azerbaijan, 17 April 2009; Brazil, 17 April 2009; China, 16 April 2009; Cyprus, 3 April 2009; Libya, 17 April 2009; Slovakia, 16 April 2009; Spain, 14 April 2009.

[166] ICJ, *Kosovo*, written statement of Norway, 16 April 2009.

[167] ICJ, *Kosovo*, Advisory Opinion, 22 July 2010, § 98, emphasis added. Post-2008 Kosovo further illustrates the complexity of the sovereignty-question. Until 2008, the relationship between Serbia's titular sovereignty and UNMIK's all-encompassing exercise of public powers remained to a large extent in balance. While Serbia was incapable of exercising its title over the territory of Kosovo, UNMIK was not in the position to dispose of the territory or to alter its status. Moreover, according to a strict interpretation of UN Security Council Resolution 1244, UNMIK was obliged to prevent any such action that would infringe on

With respect to East Timor, the UN's non-recognition of Indonesia's claim to sovereignty over the territory suggests that the reference to Indonesia's sovereignty in the preamble of UN Security Council Resolution 1272 (1999) does not necessarily confirm Indonesia's alleged title over East Timor.[168] Indeed, no further provisions of the Resolution tie Indonesia's sovereignty to the territory of East Timor. According to the UN, Portugal had remained the nominal sovereign after Indonesia assumed control over the territory. The authorities in Lisbon explicitly renounced this title on 20 October 1999 by recognizing UNTAET as its successor.[169] In other words, Portugal recognized UNTAET as its successor despite the fact that Portugal itself had previously lost the power to effectuate its sovereignty over East Timor. The UN assumed the full authority hitherto belonging to Portugal, and it did so with Portugal's explicit consent while Indonesia's consent was regarded as an unnecessary formality.[170] All facts in conjunction prompted commentators to argue that under these exceptional circumstances, not only sovereign-like powers but also sovereign title during UNTAET rule had been transferred to the UN.[171]

The case of BiH is different, as the independence and sovereignty of BiH, even under international administration, is clearly affirmed and recognized.[172]

Serbia's title. Kosovo's declaration of independence in February 2008 added a new dimension to the situation. The Provisional Institutions of Self-Government bypassed UN Security Council Res. 1244 (1999) and asserted both sovereign title (arguably at the expense of Serbia) as well as power (at the expense of UNMIK).

[168] Especially if one adheres to the idea that sovereignty is held by the people, sovereignty is bound to have remained at the local level regardless of who exercises public authority. As Madison argued: "[the government] must be told that the ultimate authority, wherever the derivative may be found, resides in the people alone, and that it will not depend merely on the comparative ambition or address of the different governments, whether either, or which of them, will be able to enlarge its sphere of jurisdiction at the expense of the other", Federalist Paper No. 46, authored by James Madison, at <www.foundingfathers.info>.

[169] *See* Section 2.2.2 above.

[170] Chopra (2000) (2), p. 937: "In East Timor, Portugal [...] was treated as the lawful administering authority throughout the 24 years of Indonesia's occupation; only Australia had recognized Jakarta's claim. On 20 October 1999, Lisbon's representative in New York, Ambassador Antonio Monteiro, expressed to U.N. officials that Portugal would relinquish its legal ties to East Timor and consider UNTAET its successor with the passage of the Security Council mandate".

[171] *E.g.* Smyrek (2006), pp. 135-136; Linton S. (2001), 'Rising From the Ashes: the Creation of a Viable Criminal Justice System in East Timor', 25 *Melbourne University Law Review*, pp. 135-136; Chopra (2000)(1).

[172] BiH's sovereignty and territorial integrity remain challenged and disputed, predominantly from within. As a reaction hereto, *see e.g.* Declaration by the Steering Board of the Peace Implementation Council, 20 November 2008, stating that "[t]he PIC Steering Board expresses its deep concern about the frequent challenges to the constitutional order of BiH and, in particular, to the sovereignty and territorial integrity of BiH or to the existence of the Republika Srpska as one of two entities under the Constitution of BiH", at <http://www.ohr.int/pic/default.asp?content_id=42667>.

The OHR is defined as an "ad hoc international institution",[173] operating pursuant to Annex 10 to the Dayton Peace Agreement. The same Annex also places the OHR within the ambit of the Vienna Convention on Diplomatic Relations.[174] Moreover, the Dayton Peace Agreement promulgated the Constitution of BiH, contained in Annex 4 to the agreement.[175] The preamble of the constitution reiterates the commitment of the constituent peoples of BiH "to the sovereignty, territorial integrity and political independence of BiH in accordance with international law". Furthermore, Article I of the Constitution emphasizes that BiH "shall continue its legal existence under international law as a state".[176] Accordingly, BiH is considered an equal entity on the international legal level as illustrated by BiH's non-permanent seat in the UN Security Council in 2010/2011.

The theory of suspended sovereignty has evolved as an alternative to the mainstream formal and material approaches. At the time of the Saar Basin administration, it was the League that suggested that sovereignty in the case of the Saar Basin was "in abeyance": the situation typified "a new international legal conception – namely a territory over which there is *no* sovereignty".[177] The Free City of Danzig has also been described by some authors as "a non-sovereign state, to be recognized as a subject of international law with a greatly restricted capacity to act".[178] The theory of suspended sovereignty intends to reconcile the dichotomy between the more traditional formal and material approaches to the concept: sovereignty is either deemed conceptually inapplicable or "effectively suspended, if not terminated".[179] While abhorrent from a traditional perspective, the endorsement of the theory of suspended sovereignty attempts to overcome a theoretical deadlock. Sir McNair's separate opinion in the ICJ's *International Status of South West Africa* advisory opinion is widely cited in this respect and can be transplanted to the present ITA-context:

> The Mandates System (and the "corresponding principles" of the International Trusteeship System) is a new institution – a new relationship

[173] *See* <http://www.ohr.int/ohr-info/gen-info/default.asp?content_id=38519>.
[174] Dayton Peace Agreement, Ann. 10, Art. III(4).
[175] Steiner & Ademović (eds.) (2010).
[176] Constitution of Bosnia and Herzegovina, Art. I(1).
[177] Stahn (2008), p. 172, n. 70, referring to a letter from Eric Drummond, Secretary-General of the League of Nations, to a British diplomat, 15 December 1919, League of Nations Archive No. 11/2474/2432.
[178] Stahn (2008), p. 182, n. 120, referring to Verzijl's taxonomy of the theories advanced with regards to the status of the Free City of Danzig in his International Law in Historic Perspective, part 2 on International Persons.
[179] Smyrek (2006), p. 24, n. 7. *See also* International Commission on Intervention and State Sovereignty (2001), *Report: The Responsibility to Protect*, p. 44.

> between territory and its inhabitants on the one hand and the government which represents them internationally on the other – a new species of international government, which does not fit into the old conception of sovereignty and which is alien to it. The doctrine of sovereignty has no application to this new system. Sovereignty over a Mandated Territory is in abeyance.[180]

In sum, the establishment of ITA missions brings about an anomalous legal situation. The mandate of these missions is inclusive to the extent that it has an unparalleled impact on the sovereignty of the 'host state'. One of the implications thereof is that it becomes virtually impossible for the 'host state' to intervene in the way these missions operate. In other words, in the specific ITA context, sovereignty fails to provide a legal framework within which ITA missions can be considered to operate.

2.4 CONCLUDING REMARKS

In this chapter, contemporary ITA missions were further defined and placed in a historical context. The Mandate and Trusteeship systems were highlighted as precedents while the evolution of UN peace-related efforts was presented as the legal setting within which the concept of internationally administered territories was able to re-emerge.

Furthermore, the chapter expounded two themes that illustrate the *sui generis* nature of these missions. Most previous engagements through which territories were placed under international administration were established under explicit Covenant and Charter-based regimes. The three main ITA missions analyzed in this book lack such a framework. Based on the scope and nature of their mandate, ITA missions have outgrown the sphere of peacekeeping. The implication thereof is that the legal framework that regulates peacekeeping operations is inadequate to deal with the specific public law-related problems that arise in the ITA context. Furthermore, the robust mandate of ITA missions prevents 'host-state' sovereignty from playing any significant role in framing the activities of ITA missions once these missions are deployed.

Getting back to Sir McNair, the second part of the widely quoted paragraph of his separate opinion succinctly places the importance of the issue of sovereignty in a broader context and links it with the subsequent chapters:

---

[180] ICJ, *International Status of South West Africa*, separate opinion Sir Arnold McNair, p. 150.

What matters in considering this new institution is not where sovereignty lies, but what are the rights and duties of the Mandatory in regard to the area of territory being administered by it.[181]

[181] *Id.*

3 Holding International Territorial Administrations to Account: Mandates and Trusteeships as Precedents

"Power tends to corrupt, and absolute power corrupts absolutely"

- *Lord Acton* [1]

With the emergence of the League and the UN as territorial administrators under the Mandate and Trusteeship systems, a new context evolved in which individuals were placed, albeit in most instances indirectly, under the administration of the international community, creating "a new kind of governmental relationship quite foreign to the old ideas of international law".[2] Missions established under these systems faced accountability-related challenges comparable to ones faced by contemporary ITA missions.[3] This chapter provides insight into the ways in which accountability concerns were addressed during the Mandate and Trusteeship systems and emphasis is placed on the institutional aspect of these precedential accountability regimes. In particular, the added value of addressing accountability within a given legal framework, as provided by Article 22 of the Covenant and Chapters XII and XIII of the Charter respectively, is discussed.

---

[1] John Emerich Edward Dalberg Acton, 1st Baron Acton in a letter to Bishop Mandell Creighton, 1887; Hirsch E.D., Kett J.F. & Trefil J. (2002), *The new dictionary of cultural literacy*, New York: Houghton Mifflin, p. 324.

[2] Statement made at the 1929th Session of the Sixth Committee of the Assembly of the League of Nations, as quoted in Evans (1932), p. 737.

[3] To a large extent, thoughts advanced in the following Chapter were discussed previously in Momirov (2007), pp. 201-229.

3.1 ACCOUNTABILITY MECHANISMS AS A FUNCTION OF A STATUTORY FRAMEWORK

The approach to accountability under the Mandate and Trusteeship systems was shaped by the fit-for-purpose legal frameworks, within which the individual mandates and trusteeships were embedded. These legal frameworks functioned as a platform within which accountability could be addressed. Furthermore, the accountability structures were conditioned by the three-pronged relationship between the administered territory, the international organization and the state tasked with the actual administration. Within these legal parameters, accountability regimes were established that were in the vanguard in at least two aspects.

The first aspect essentially relates to the rule of law. Article 22 of the Covenant and Chapters XII and XIII of the Charter, respectively, anchored certain obligations that rested on the Mandatories and the trust-holding states. These obligations were aimed at framing the scope of power of the administering entities. As the following sections illustrate, these obligations were often invoked when misconduct on the part of the administering entities was alleged. Article 22 of the Covenant confirmed that the "well-being and development" of the people placed under the Mandate system "form a sacred trust of civilisation and that securities for the performance of this trust should be embodied in this Covenant". More in particular, the same article prescribes that with regard to "B" and "C" mandates:

> the Mandatory must be responsible for the administration of the territory under conditions which will guarantee freedom of conscience and religion, subject only to the maintenance of public order and morals, the prohibition of abuses such as the slave trade, the arms traffic and the liquor traffic, and the prevention of the establishment of fortifications or military and naval bases and of military training of the natives for other than police purposes and the defence of territory, and will also secure equal opportunities for the trade and commerce of other Members of the League. [4]

In a similar fashion, the Charter clearly sets out the objectives of the Trusteeship system that include, amongst other things, promotion of "the political, economic, social, and educational advancement of the inhabitants of the trust territories".[5]

---

[4] *See* Section 2.1.1 above.
[5] UN Charter, Art. 76(b).

As to the second aspect, in order to uphold these parameters, the legal frameworks expressly provided that a certain degree of review ought to be exercised.[6] The basis for an accountability mechanism was thus not dependent on ad hoc adopted solutions by the administering authority, a trait that characterizes the majority of accountability mechanisms in the present ITA context.

Accountability regimes under the Mandate and Trusteeship systems – as well as under the *sui generis* administrations at the time – were based on three pillars: the obligation to report, the individual right to petition and scrutiny by judicial institutions. Each set of accountability mechanisms is analyzed in the following sections. References to certain articles taken from the archives of the British daily *The Times* illustrate the discussed mechanisms.[7]

3.1.1 REPORTING OBLIGATION

The need for accountability under the Mandate system was primarily fulfilled internally, meaning within the confines of the League. It was acknowledged by the League Council that:

> With regard to the responsibility of the League for securing the observance of the terms of the mandates, the Council interprets its duties in this connection in the widest manner.[8]

The accountability flow was essentially directed towards a supervisory body established by and within the League: the Permanent Mandates Commission (Mandates Commission). Article 22 of the Covenant obliged the Mandatories to render annual reports to the League Council, which would then be examined by the Mandates Commission.[9] The League interpreted the extent of its supervisory role as follows:

[6] League of Nations Covenant, Art. 22 and UN Charter, Art. 87 respectively.
[7] The Times is chosen as an example in the light of Great Britain's colonial past and active engagement in the Mandate and Trusteeship systems, at <http://archive.timesonline.cc.uk/tol/archive/> (last accessed 16 March 2010).
[8] League Assembly, *Responsibilities of the League arising out of Article 22 (Mandates)*, Doc. 20/48/161, 8 December 1920.
[9] League of Nations Covenant, Art. 22 states in pertinent part: "In every case of mandate, the Mandatory shall render to the Council an annual report in reference to the territory committed to its charge. The degree of authority, control, or administration to be exercised by the Mandatory shall, if not previously agreed upon by the Members of the League, be explicitly defined in each case by the Council. A permanent Commission shall be constituted to receive and examine the annual reports of the Mandatories and to advise the Council on all matters relating to the observance of the mandates".

> [It] examines the whole of the administration [...] in light of the principles laid down in the Covenant and of the provisions contained in the Mandates themselves. It does not therefore limit itself to the more or less negative role which would consist in verifying that the Mandatories have not overstepped the powers conferred upon them; it likewise ascertains whether these powers have been put to good use and whether the administration has been in accordance with the interests of the native populations.[10]

The Mandatories were obliged to attach to their annual reports all legislative and administrative decisions that they adopted[11] The examination of these reports could only result in non-binding recommendations made by the Mandates Commission.[12] In practice, these recommendations predominantly addressed the following topics: acts adopted by Mandatories that suggested their sovereignty over the mandated territory, safeguards preventing the Mandatories from profiting from the powers entrusted to them, protection of the interests of the local populations and supervision of the fulfillment of the Mandatory's obligation to develop economically the mandated territories.[13] Thus, the reports actively assessed whether the administering authorities were acting in accordance with their obligations.

Members of the Mandates Commission were appointed in their individual capacity and nationals from Mandatories were required to be in the minority. The members were independent of governmental instructions and were considered to "study and comment on the annual reports and other information presented to them in a quasi-judicial capacity".[14] This striking construction was a compromise between two demands. Firstly, the Mandates Commission had to be acceptable for the Mandatories in order to be able to function. In this respect, recall that under the Mandate system states administered territories on behalf of the League. Consequently, the nature of the oversight system was compromised by the weak position of the League in relation to its member states that acted as mandatory powers.[15] Secondly, a situation in which the Mandatories would be judging their own conduct had to be avoided. Thus, the Mandates Commission was established as a "non-political body [which] would derive its authority from

[10] Series of League of Nations Publications (1945), *The Mandate system: origin, principles, application*, p. 37.

[11] Attaching the full texts of adopted decisions was established as a rule by League Council Resolution dated 29 August 1924.

[12] As Stahn notes, these comments could gain binding force if adopted through a resolution by the League's Council, *see* Stahn (2008) p. 84.

[13] *See* Wright (1968).

[14] Fletcher-Cooke J. (1959), 'Some Reflections on the International Trusteeship System, with Particular Reference to its Impact on the Governments and Peoples of the Trust Territories', 13(3) *International Organization*, p. 422.

[15] *See also* Stahn (2008), pp. 83-86.

impartiality, independence, experience and individual competence of its members".[16]

The Trusteeship system followed suit by obliging the trust-holding powers to submit annual reports to the Trusteeship Council.[17] Though the reporting mechanism in essence did not change, the body dealing with the reports did. The crucial difference between the Mandates Commission and the Trusteeship Council was that the latter consisted of government representatives. Unlike the Mandates Commission, The Trusteeship Council had an equal number of representatives from administering powers and representatives of states not charged with the governing of a trust territory. This situation was defended using the argument that the government representatives of the administering powers were bound to possess in-depth knowledge of the situation in specific trusteeships and, unlike the experts from the Mandates Commission, had closer ties to the respective national authorities and thus had access to more information and data.

In sum, the reporting procedure was essentially an internal oversight mechanism and was the backbone of a broader accountability regime. Reporting provided a chance to assess the overall conduct and achievement of the administering entities, examined against the yardsticks provided by the respective legal frameworks. As an accountability mechanism, however, reporting does not reach out to the individual and is not a procedure that would provide recourse and redress.[18] Another far more remarkable mechanism was considered necessary to fill this gap – individual petition rights.

3.1.2 INDIVIDUAL RIGHT TO PETITION

The avant-garde nature of the individual right to petition warrants a more elaborate assessment of this particular accountability mechanism. The bulk of the discussion relates to the Mandate system as it was under this system that the

[16] Chowdhuri (1955), p. 185.

[17] UN Charter, Art. 87: "The General Assembly and, under its authority, the Trusteeship Council, in carrying out their functions, may: a. consider reports submitted by the administering authority; b. accept petitions and examine them in consultation with the administering authority; c. provide for periodic visits to the respective trust territories at times agreed upon with the administering authority; and d. take these and other actions in conformity with the terms of the trusteeship agreements". Art. 88 of the UN Charter: "The Trusteeship Council shall formulate a questionnaire on the political, economic, social, and educational advancement of the inhabitants of each trust territory, and the administering authority for each trust territory within the competence of the General Assembly shall make an annual report to the General Assembly upon the basis of such questionnaire".

[18] The reporting obligation for ITA missions is discussed in Section 5.1.1 below.

right was shaped; the Trusteeship system followed up on this practice and adapted it where necessary.

Individual petition rights were not envisioned by Article 22 of the Covenant.[19] Furthermore, the constitutive document of the Mandates Commission, adopted by the League Council on 29 November 1920, also makes no mention of such a right. Despite these omissions, debates regarding the right to petition were ongoing from the beginning. Proposals for the introduction of such a right had been made in vain by, *inter alia*, Prime-minister Lloyd George and President Wilson.[20]

While no mention of a right to petition was made on paper, written protests in fact began to reach the League immediately after the establishment of the mandates, concerning by and large the British and French Mandatories. As no procedure had been adopted and the Mandates Commission had not yet been established, it was decided to distribute selected protests to the member states and the League Council.[21] This practice of un-institutionalized blaming and shaming of certain Mandatories was criticized. Winston Churchill, at the time the British Minister of Colonies, stated in 1921 that it is:

> obviously unsuitable that petitions of this nature which are generally *ex parte* statements directed either against His Majesty's Government or against the local Government, should be circulated in this way.[22]

The fact that Great Britain was quick to respond should be understood in the light of Britain's experience with colonial administration and with its extensive engagement under the Mandate system. In addition, a tradition existed of well-

---

[19] Before the right was introduced for individuals to petition the League within the ambit of the Mandate system, an individual right of petition existed in the context of minority rights. These petition procedures were adopted by the League Council in October 1920. Minority group members were allowed to send petitions to the League Council upon which the petitions would be examined by a subcommittee of three League Council members. Both the League Council and the subcommittee were then able to discuss the matter with the government against which the complaints were addressed. This right was notably different from the right of petition in the context of the Mandate system. Although it provided individuals the opportunity to address the League, the merits of their complaints were related to conduct of member states – conduct for which those states were ultimately and exclusively responsible. For further information on the adoption and procedural aspects of the right to petition in the context of minority rights, *see* Herman J. (1994), *Naar de Areopagus: de Volkenbond en het toezicht op de volkenrechtelijke bescherming van nationale minderheden in Oost-Europa: een interdisciplinaire benadering* (Towards the Areopagus: the League of Nations and the supervision of the international protection of national minorities in Eastern Europe: an interdisciplinary approach) (diss. Utrecht).

[20] Hall (1948), p. 199.

[21] Ginneken (1992), p. 174.

[22] Winston Churchill addressing the Premiers of Australia, New Zealand and South Africa on 14 July 1921, *see* Ginneken (1992), p. 205, n. 7.

established rules and principles governing the relationship between the dominions and Great Britain.[23] In terms of petitioning, the right to petition the crown had been provided for by English law ever since the Middle Ages. This right:

> extended automatically to all British subjects in British dependencies and colonies [and was regarded as] one of the immemorial and vital safeguards of individual rights and liberties.[24]

The issue of individual petitioning was brought up during the first gathering of the newly established Mandates Commission in October 1921. Up until that date, the Secretariat of the League had received 71 petitions that were pending consideration.[25] These petitions were predominantly sent by organizations representing the interests of the mandates' populations. The British member of the Mandates Commission advocated:

> [that if the inhabitants of British colonies had the right to petition] the Parliament of the mother-country, the national of a mandated territory might similarly have the right to appeal to the League of Nations, in the name of which the mandate was exercised.[26]

The Mandates Commission declined to take any steps towards regulating the growing flow of petitions. Responding to this lack of initiative, Britain prepared draft rules regarding petition-related procedures.[27] These draft rules set out several main principles. Petitions should go to the Mandatory first, which would then forward them to the Secretary-General accompanied by comments. Conversely, petitions directly sent to the Secretariat were to be sent back. The Mandatory was allowed to deal with inconsequential petitions and the correspondence relating thereto would be sent to the Secretariat. Correctly submitted petitions, along with the mandatory's comments, should be dealt with at the Mandates Commissions gatherings once a year. Regarding dissemination of the petitions, the Mandates Commission would decide which petitions could be distributed amongst members and in which case they should be accompanied by minutes of the sessions related to the particular petitions.

---

[23] *See e.g.* the Balfour Declaration of 1926, as a result of the Imperial Conference of the leaders of the British Empire, London 1926, at <http://www.foundingdocs.gov.au/resources/transcripts/cth11_doc_1926.pdf>.

[24] See Hall (1948), pp. 198-199.

[25] Ginneken (1992), p. 205, n. 9.

[26] As quoted by Ginneken (1992), p. 175.

[27] League of Nations Doc. C.485.1922.VI. C.P.M. XII, 1 August 1922 and C.614.1922.VI.

After being examined by the League Council in September 1922, the British draft proposal was sent to the Mandates Commission for assessment and a compromise was reached. The main amendment was the division that was introduced between petitions coming from inhabitants of the mandated lands and those coming from outside the mandates, such as, for example, a large number of petitions from the United States regarding the situation in Palestine.[28] The latter petitions were to be sent directly to the Secretariat, which would forward them to the chair of the Mandates Commission. This amended proposal was presented to the League Council and was adopted in January 1923.[29]

The procedural rules did not allow for the hearing of petitioners. The issue was discussed at several gatherings of the Mandates Commission.[30] The Mandates Commission argued that in certain instances it had found itself in the position that it could not reach a well-informed decision regarding a petition unless it had the authority to invite the petitioner to be heard *in vivo*. Being aware of the delicacy of this issue, the League Council requested the opinions of the Mandatories. As was to be expected, all Mandatories opposed. The main argument of the Mandatories was that in such a case the Commission would have to engage in a process resembling adversarial in-court proceedings, which was "inconsistent with the very nature of the mandatory system".[31] Reference was also made to national systems in which petition rights were not as a rule accompanied by a hearing.[32] Accordingly, the League Council did not adopt any changes and the option to be heard *in vivo* was not added to the official

[28] Ginneken (1992), pp. 211-218. Many petitions from Arab and Jewish organizations came from North and South America, protesting against the 1937 Division Plan.

[29] League of Nations, *Summary of the procedure to be followed for submitting petitions concerning mandated territories*, Doc. C.545.M.194.1927.VI[A]. *See also* Hall (1948), pp. 314-318. In anticipation of a decision by the League Council on the rules of procedure in respect of petitions, the Mandates Commission had enacted another procedural document, referring to so-called "unofficial and semi-official communications". In this procedure communications were received and considered directly by the Mandates Commission or, if received by the Secretariat, were sent to the chair of the Mandates Commission who would decide on their distribution. *See* Permanent Mandates Commission, *Report on the work of the Second Session of the Permanent Mandates Commission*, submitted to the League Council and Assembly, Doc. C.550.M.332.1922.VI[A], 23 August 1922, p. 8. Once the official rules were adopted, this procedure was abandoned.

[30] *See* Minutes of the 3rd, 8th and 9th Session of the Mandates Commission.

[31] Series of League of Nations Publications (1945), p. 41.

[32] *See e.g.* The Times, *British Mandated Territories. Memorandum to the League*, 20 November 1926, reporting extensively on Great Britain's argument against permitting the hearing of petitioners.

procedure.[33] The Mandates Commission, however, did at times hear and question representatives of the Mandatories.[34]

> The Times reported that during the Mandates Commission's examination of a French government's report, "a delegation of Syrians [...] arrived in Rome with a much-documented petition concerning the interests of the inhabitants of Syria and the Lebanon". The article recalls that the Mandates Commission is not in the position to receive delegations of populations of mandated territories, but notes that "[t]here is nothing, however, to prevent its members from seeing the Arab representatives privately". The article describes the situation in the mandated territory by referring to the (previous) French High Commissioner in Syria as having "rough and ready methods" and adds that "[i]t was characteristic of [the previous French High Commissioner] methods that, when the Druse notables approached him with gifts and with a petition, they were abruptly refused a hearing". The article qualifies the High Commissioner's attitude as "that of an unbending martinet, to whom Maronite patriarch and Druse chieftain were alike subjects of a suzerain Power entitled to an equal and implicit obedience".
>
> The Times, *The French Report on Syria. Mandates Commission Meets,* 17 February 1926 and *The Syrian Mandate*, 18 February 1926.

In practice, the Mandates Commission gained momentum. At a session in October 1925, the Mandates Commission was reminded by its chair that its task "implied *a real limitation of the authority* of the Mandatory Powers".[35] However, subsequent conflicts between the Mandates Commission, the League Council and the Mandatories led to a situation in which the Mandates Commission's competences proved to be limited – the Mandates Commission "kept on balancing between its advisory and supervisory tasks".[36] Overall, 3044 petitions were received by the Mandates Commission.[37] In a large number of

[33] Minutes of the 44th Session of the League Council, p. 438. *See* also Hall (1948), pp. 202-204. *See* however Section 3.1.3.1 below, where it is discussed how oral hearings were allowed with regards to the mandate for South West Africa.

[34] *E.g.* The Times, *S.W. Africa Mandate. Relations with the Natives*, 2 November 1928.

[35] As quoted by Ginneken (1992), p. 183, emphasis added. *See* Ginneken (1992), pp. 180-185 for an elaboration on the development of the Mandates Commission's position regarding petitions.

[36] Ginneken (1992), p. 190; for a detailed review on the actual procedure followed when dealing with petitions, *see* Ginneken (1992), pp. 191-199.

[37] A thorough research carried out by Anique van Ginneken provides a detailed overview of the actual petitions during the Mandate system, with regard to their nature, origin, substance and quantity, *see* Ginneken (1992), pp. 211-218. A total of 3044 petitions were received; 1119 petitions came from inhabitants of the mandates, 1662 from outside the mandates. Most petitions came from, or related to, Palestine and Syria. However, since petitions could be sent from outside of the mandated lands, many petitions from Arab and Jewish organizations came from North and South America. Arab and Jewish petitions from Palestine and abroad protested against the 1937 Division plan and the overall situation. Syria-related petitions condemned the overall French attitude regarding the 'political emancipation' of the territory.

cases the Mandates Commission found that it had no jurisdiction. When petitions were declared admissible and were subsequently granted, the Mandates Commission requested the League Council to approach the Mandatory to try to resolve the issue.[38] At times, this led to a notable effect, such as the initiation of border-dispute settlement talks between French and British Togo, an admonishment directed at France regarding the treatment of minorities in Syria and the League Council's request for Great Britain to assure that the Kurds in Iraq would be protected even after the independence of Iraq.[39] Furthermore, petitions also sparked debates within the particular Mandatories. For example, petitions originating from the mandate of Samoa led to a discussion in the British House of Lords on whether "his Majesty's Government would satisfy themselves that the mandate over Samoa [...] was being administered with due regard to the best interests of the Samoans".[40]

The Trusteeship system not only maintained the right to petition but also made significant improvements as to the way in which the petition system was institutionalized. Unlike the Covenant, the UN Charter explicitly provided a legal basis for the right to petition within the Trusteeship system.[41] The UN Trusteeship division, headed by an Under-Secretary-General, was comprised of four subsections: 1) trusteeship agreements, 2) petitions, 3) territorial analysis

There were also petitions from regions demanding more autonomy, while other regions were requesting direct French governance. Lebanon's petitioners mostly wanted reunification with Syria. Iraq was a source of petitions coming from mainly the Kurds and Assyrians regarding the impending independence of Iraq. African petitions were mainly directed against French run mandates; British and Belgian territories were relatively silent. South Africa as a mandatory power was addressed by 146 petitions from South-West Africa. The petitions mostly regarded political, economical and legal issues such as expropriation, monopolies and court competences. The Mandates Commission found it had no jurisdiction (regarding petitions not coming from mandated lands; the petitions coming directly from the mandated lands were sent back and needed to be sent to the Mandatory. Out of 245 returned petitions, 88 were subsequently returned to the Commission) if the petitions were already dealt with (183), did not fall within the Commissions competence (67), were contrary to the mandate system itself (49), or too general (41), vague (24), trivial (12) or contained 'violent language' (19). Most petitions were either rejected (1638) or undecided (841), while 565 petitions were (partially) granted.

[38] Wright even advocated that in the event a mandatory persisted in violating the mandate or proved incapable of meeting its responsibilities, the mandate could be transferred to another power, basing this on the argument that under general principles of international law, a breach of agreement by one party justifies denunciation by the other; *paraphrased* from Wright (1923), p.702.

[39] *E.g.* The Times, *Plight of Western Abyssinia. Documents at League Council*, 28 September 1936; *The Palestinian Death Sentences. Jewish Petition for Arabs*, 4 May 1930; *Assyrian Levies in Iraq. Discontent Abating*, 7 July 1932.

[40] The Times, *The Samoa mandate*, 9 December 1932.

[41] UN Charter, Art. 87.

and research and 4) reports, questionnaires and visits.[42] The biggest innovation to the petitioning practice was the introduction of oral hearings. This reflected a key shift from the preceding mandate policy.[43] The petition section dealt with incoming petitions as well as requests for oral hearings while a body of rules governed the petition mechanism in terms of procedure.[44] According to these rules, petitioners could be inhabitants of trust territories or other parties, and petitions could be presented in writing or orally. In exceptional cases, no written petition had to precede the oral submission. Based on information received by way of a petition or a report, the UN could also establish a mission that would travel to the trust territory and inquire into the way in which the territory was administered.

In 1954, the Marshall Islands submitted a petition to the UN demanding an "immediate cessation of atom bomb experiments in this atoll area". Generally satisfied with the way in which the United States administered the islands, the petitioners pointed out that the atom bomb experiments had "lethal effect" on the inhabitants. The relocation of many islanders as a result of the experiments was also brought to the attention of the UN. In a preliminary response, the United States' UN delegate stated that his government was "very sorry indeed" and that it was "doing everything humanly possible to take care of everyone who was in the area". Ultimately, the UN Trusteeship Council refused to admit the petition, "thus in effect sanctioning the American Government's latest programme of nuclear bomb tests in the Pacific area". A second petition related to the topic was filed in 1958, not only demanding a halt to the tests but also asking that "an advisory opinion be sought from the [ICJ]. The petition argued that "a binding precedent should be established prohibiting the use of any trusteeship area for any purpose without the consent of the governed".

The Times, *Marshall Islanders' Urgent Plea. "End Atom Bomb Tests"*, 15 May 1954; *U.S. Atom Bomb Tests Sanctioned*, 2 April 1956 and *Petition to Stop U.S. Atom Tests. U.N. Told of Marshall Islanders' Fears*, 25 June 1958.

Another improvement introduced by the Trusteeship system was that the petitions were to be sent directly to the Secretary-General (or transmitted to him through the administrating authority, which was free to choose whether to add its own comments concerning the petition). The same procedure applied for requests for oral hearings. This solved the predicament that existed during the

[42] Report by the UN SG, *Organization of the Secretariat*, UN Doc. A/2731, 21 September 1954, p. 19.

[43] The Charter expanded the options in which the UN could, through the Trusteeship Council, exercise supervisory authority by for example providing for the possibility to conduct periodic visits. The United States had pushed to empower the Trusteeship Council with the right to "institute investigations" but this was rejected by colonial powers, *see* Chowdhuri (1955), p. 59.

[44] *Rules of Procedure for the Trusteeship Council*, approved at the 22nd meeting of its 1st Session; UN Doc. T/1/Rev. I, 23 April 1947 (Rules of Procedure for the Trusteeship Council).

Mandate system, when petitioners had to submit their complaints to the Mandatories: namely, the very authorities they were complaining about.

Petitions concerning issues that were or could be considered by a competent court of the administrating authority were inadmissible. With regard to the merits, petitions could address legislation that was allegedly contrary to the Charter or a particular Trust Agreement. This in effect provided for unlimited subject matter jurisdiction.[45] In terms of outcome, the petition-procedure could only lead to legally non-binding recommendations.[46]

In summary, the right to petition had evolved and petitions were now seen as "a means for ascertaining facts *and* redressing the grievances of the people" compared to the predominant view during the period of the Mandate system when petitions were generally regarded as "additional sources of information".[47] The right to petition bridged the gap between individuals and the League, which ultimately was responsible for their well-being. Furthermore, under the Trusteeship system, the right to petition was anchored in the UN Charter, and thus was not subject to the discretion of the trust-holding powers. From an institutional point of view, the Charter guaranteed a standing mechanism that in the most direct way offered recourse to parties who were adversely affected by the administering entity; the established procedure recognized "that the relationship that exists between individuals or groups and an international organization is a relationship that may also be directly relevant in international law".[48]

3.1.3 JUDICIAL SCRUTINY: THE ROLE OF COURTS

In addition to reporting and petitioning, the third element of the overall accountability framework relates to actual judicial oversight. The Mandate and Trusteeship systems' legal framework in this sense had a twofold function. Firstly, it provided a basic yardstick against which the administrations could be assessed. That way, discussions about which norms governed the administering authorities were bypassed. Secondly, through the framework, the Permanent Court of International Justice (PCIJ) and the ICJ, respectively, were embedded explicitly into the accountability regime.

---

[45] *Id.*, Rules 76-93.

[46] *See e.g.* UN Trusteeship Council Res. 648 (XII), 20 July 1953, UN. Doc. T/1075, 18 August 1953; Report of the UN Visiting Mission to Trust Territories in East Africa, UN. Doc. T/1142, 23 December 1954 and Report on the Trust Territory of Rwanda-Urundi, UN. Doc. T/1141, 8 December 1954.

[47] Chowdhuri (1955), p. 208.

[48] Hey, E. (1997), 'The World Bank Inspection Panel: Towards the Recognition of a New Legally Relevant Relationship in International Law', 2 *Hofstra Law & Policy Symposium 1997*, p. 73.

At this point, a caveat is in place. Engagement of courts – the PCIJ and the ICJ in particular – was facilitated by the fact that territories were administered by states rather than by the international organizations, which enabled international law to treat the administered entities and states as 'equals'. It is argued that the impact of this difference should not be overstated. The issue at hand largely pertains to procedure, and does not diminish the notion that entities that carry out an international mandate to administer territories should be subject to judicial scrutiny. The Mandate and Trusteeship systems' legal frameworks captured this idea, as illustrated by examples from the following sections.

On occasion, domestic courts engaged in the review of particular acts of the international administration. In 1925, the High Commissioner for Palestine (as the highest representative of Great Britain in Palestine) adopted an order aimed at regulating the water supply of the city of Jerusalem. Local inhabitants protested and challenged the order before the Supreme Court of Palestine, alleging that the order contravened the mandate for Palestine *i.e.* that it violated the rights guaranteed by the mandate. The local Court based its jurisdiction on a 1922 Order-in-Council that organized the government structure of Palestine, as the mandate did not vest such jurisdiction in the local Court. The Court held that since it had the power to review legislation, it likewise had jurisdiction *in casu*. On the merits, the Supreme Court of Palestine found the order to be contrary to Article 2 of the Mandate for Palestine and declared it void.[49] On appeal, the Judicial Committee of the Privy Council in Great Britain reversed the judgment in its much-cited *Jerusalem-Jaffa District Governor v. Suleiman Murra* decision.[50] However, the jurisdiction of the Supreme Court of Palestine to hear the case and to review the order was not contested.

The Supreme Court of Palestine did not assume jurisdiction with respect to executive acts of the governing authorities. In 1925, the Court received an application for a writ of Mandamus. Although the arguments presented in the application were based on anti-discrimination provisions of the mandate, the grievances concerned the Postmaster General rather than a piece of legislation. The Court refused to accept the application as it found no jurisdiction in the previously mentioned Order-in-Council.[51]

[49] Art. 2 of the mandate for Palestine read: "The Mandatory shall be responsible for placing the country under such political, administrative and economic conditions as will secure the establishment of the Jewish national home, as laid down in the preamble, and the development of self-governing institutions, and also for safeguarding the civil and religious rights of all the inhabitants of Palestine, irrespective of race and religion".

[50] Judicial Committee of the Privy Council, *Jerusalem-Jaffa District Governor v. Suleiman Murra*, 3 February 1926, English Law Reports 1926, Appeals Cases, p. 321.

[51] Decision of the Supreme Court of Palestine, 24 October 1925, not reported, *see* Bentwich (1929), p. 219.

These examples are worth mentioning for the following two reasons. Firstly, immunity did not prevent the order of Palestine's High Commissioner from being examined by the local Palestinian Court. Immunity was also not the deal-breaker in the second case. Although it might be argued that Palestine's mandate was linked to Great Britain rather than to the League, this is of lesser importance because in both cases immunity could have prevented the courts from engaging. Secondly, although the original decision was overturned, the provisions of the mandate were recognized as being a clear yardstick against which acts of the Mandatory could be reviewed. These two features are in contrast to present ITA-practice, where no explicit fit-for-purpose benchmarks are provided and where immunity is nearly absolute.[52]

Engagement of the local courts was not regulated by the mandate as such. Conversely, under the Mandate system all mandate agreements determined that the PCIJ could hear disputes between League member states and a Mandatory, relating to the interpretation and application of the mandate provisions.[53] All but one mandate agreement included the following provision:[54]

> The Mandatory agrees that, if any dispute whatever should arise between the Mandatory and another Member of the League of Nations relating to the interpretation or the application of the provisions of the mandate, such dispute, if it cannot be settled by negotiation, shall be submitted to the Permanent Court of International Justice provided for by Article 14 of the Covenant of the League of Nations.[55]

Less consistently, some trusteeship agreements explicitly referred to the ICJ while others remained silent on the matter. The Tanganyika Trusteeship Agreement for example stated:

> If any dispute whatever should arise between the Administering Authority and another Member of the United Nations relating to the interpretation or application of the provisions of this Agreement, such dispute, if it cannot be settled by negotiation or other means, shall be submitted to the

---

[52] *See* Sections 4.1, 4.2 and Chapter 5 below.

[53] In general, *see* Feinberg N. (1930), *La Juridiction de la Cour Permanente de Justice Internationale dans let Systeme des Mandats*, Paris: Rousseau. For the relevant articles of the respective mandate agreements, *see* Feinberg (1930), pp. 17-19.

[54] One mandate agreement included a provision having the same gist but with a slightly different wording.

[55] *See* in general Feinberg (1930), pp. 122-137. For the PCIJ's interpretation, *see* PCIJ, *The Mavrommatis Jerusalem Concessions (Greece v. Great Britain in its capacity as Mandatory for Palestine)*, Ser. A, No. 5, Judgment, 26 March 1925, pp. 15-29 (*Mavrommatis Jerusalem Concessions*).

> International Court of Justice provided for in Chapter XIV of the United Nations Charter.[56]

In commenting on the need for judicial oversight with respect to the administration of territories, the ICJ went so far as to say that the whole supervisory system based on the reporting obligation would not be effective if no final and judicial form of scrutiny existed:

> While the faithful discharge of the trust was assigned to the Mandatory Power alone, the duty and the right of ensuring the performance of this trust were given to the League [...] and all its Members within the limits of their respective authority [...]. *The administrative supervision by the League constituted a normal security to ensure full performance by the mandatory of the "sacred trust" toward the inhabitants of the mandated territory, but the specially assigned role of the Court was even more essential, since it was to serve as the final bulwark of protection by recourse to the Court against possible abuse or breaches of the Mandate.* [...] Without this additional security the supervision by the League and its Members could not be effective in the last resort.[57]

It should be restated that a crucial enabling factor for both international Courts to engage was the fact that, under the Mandate and Trusteeship systems, administering powers were assumed by states rather than the League or the UN. In other words, the direct administrator had *locus standi* before the two international Courts. The Courts' general provisions on competence – namely, Article 34 of the PCIJ and ICJ statute, respectively – prevented these judicial bodies from engaging more actively in terms of protection of the local inhabitants. Indeed, this was never the aim of including these Courts into the accountability regime. Nevertheless, the occasional engagement of the respective Courts shows that they could influence the way in which the territories were administered and, to some extent, could protect the rights and interests of the local population and other individuals. The following section illustrates this.

---

[56] Tanganyika Trusteeship Agreement, Art. 19, approved by the UN General Assembly on 13 December 1946.

[57] ICJ, *South-West Africa (Ethiopia v. South Africa; Liberia v. South Africa)*, Preliminary Objections, Judgment, 21 December 1962, pp. 336-338, emphasis added (*South-West Africa*).

3.1.3.1 *From the Mavrommatis Jerusalem Concessions to the Phosphate Lands in Nauru*

The PCIJ exercised its jurisdiction with respect to the Mandate system once through an advisory procedure and, with respect to a particular situation in Palestine, in two contentious cases. The advisory procedure (addressing the British mandate over Mesopotamia and Mosul) touched only indirectly upon issues related to the mandate.[58] The contentious cases (filed by Greece against Great Britain "*in its capacity as Mandatory for Palestine*") are of greater significance.[59] The facts underlying both cases concern an individual claim for reparations, put forth by M. Mavrommatis, a Greek subject and holder of certain rights based on concessionary contracts signed between him and the City of Jerusalem. Thus, Greece was directly exercising diplomatic protection with regard to its subject, who claimed to have incurred losses by acts of the British Government in its capacity as Mandatory power. Leaving aside the merits, the contentious cases reflect several points of interest.

Firstly, prior to the Greek application the parties attempted to settle the case by diplomatic means, as shown by the chronology of events included in the judgment. Despite the fact that the case ended up before the PCIJ, the chronology reflects a *prima facie* bona fides attitude by the British Government in terms of its willingness to settle disputes arising from its obligations as a Mandatory power.

Secondly, due to the facts of the case, the PCIJ grounded its jurisdiction on a previous agreement between the parties rather than on the particular mandate provision that assigns jurisdiction to the PCIJ in cases related to the Palestine mandate.[60] In addressing Great Britain, the PCIJ does emphasize the peculiar position of Great Britain *in casu*. The Court clearly states on several occasions that the claim arises out of acts by "the Government of Palestine and consequently also on the part of His Britannic Majesty's Government, in its capacity as Mandatory Power over Palestine".[61] Because the administering power was a state rather than the League itself, nowhere during the proceedings were immunities invoked. This is distinct from the question of *locus standi,*

[58] PCIJ, *Interpretations of article 3, paragraph 2, of the Treaty of Lausanne*, Ser. B, No. 12, Advisory Opinion, 21 November 1925 (*Interpretations of Treaty of Lausanne*).
[59] PCIJ, *Mavrommatis Jerusalem Concessions*, and PCIJ, *Readaptation of the Mavrommatis Jerusalem Concessions* (*Greece v. Great Britain in its capacity as Mandatory for Palestine*), Ser. A, No. 11, Judgment, 10 October 1927 (*Mavrommatis Readaptation*).
[60] PCIJ, *Mavrommatis Jerusalem Concessions*, Judgment, p. 27 and Art. 26 of the Mandate for Palestine.
[61] *E.g.* PCIJ, *Mavrommatis Jerusalem Concessions*, Judgment, p. 7. Great Britain is also referenced as such on the cover page of the judgment.

where the fact that the respondent was a state also had an enabling effect. Access to justice was thus not a priori obstructed by immunity.

The ICJ touched occasionally upon the Trusteeship system, most prominently so in the series of advisory proceedings relating to South-West Africa (now Namibia). These proceedings addressed the supervisory frameworks imposed on the administering entities under both systems.

Underlying the series of advisory opinions was the persistent reluctance of the Mandatory Power, South Africa, to transfer South-West Africa, the land it administered under the Mandate system, to the Trusteeship system. In its first advisory opinion, the ICJ held that South Africa was not obliged to do so, and decided that Namibia continued to be a mandated territory.[62] This implied that South Africa was still bound by the obligations emanating from its status as Mandatory, including the obligation to submit reports and to transmit petitions from the inhabitants of the territory of South-West Africa. The General Assembly was assigned to assume the supervisory role previously held by the League Council.

Subsequently, the ICJ devoted two advisory opinions to the matter of supervision and the petitioning procedure in particular.[63] Here, the ICJ clarified that the Committee on South-West Africa, as established by the UN General Assembly, had the right to grant oral hearings to petitioners.[64] Recall that the Mandate system did not provide for such hearings.[65] The supervision by the UN of South Africa as a Mandatory Power was not supposed to exceed the supervisory framework, since it existed within the Mandate system. The ICJ nonetheless held that under the Mandate system, the League Council had established the petition procedure and thus would also have had the authority to include in this procedure a right to be heard, although it never used this prerogative. In light of the continuing failure by South Africa to cooperate and adhere to its obligations as a Mandatory, the ICJ held that the Committee on South-West Africa was in a position where it needed to allow oral hearings in order to compensate for the lack of information resulting from South Africa's persistent obstructionism.

---

[62] ICJ, *International Status of South West Africa*, Advisory Opinion.

[63] ICJ, *Voting Procedure on Questions relating to Reports and Petitions concerning the Territory of South West Africa*, Advisory Opinion, 7 June 1955 (*Voting Procedure concerning South West Africa*) and ICJ, *Admissibility of Hearings of Petitioners by the Committee on South West Africa*, Advisory Opinion, 1 June 1956 (*Admissibility of Hearing of Petitioners*).

[64] The Committee on South West Africa was established by GA Res. 749 A (VIII), 28 November 1953. The Committee on South West Africa was established to compensate for the lack of cooperation by the government of South Africa and was, amongst other, tasked to examine and transmit incoming petitions.

[65] *See* Section 3.1.2. above.

> The hearing of petitioners caused uproar within the British government. As The Times reported, "Dr. Malan, the Prime Minister, [...] consulted with all his available Ministers on the position which has arisen as the result of the United Nations Trusteeship Committee's decision to allow tribal representatives from South-West Africa to appear before it". The tumult was sparked by a petition submitted by four native chiefs from South-West Africa. According to The Times, "the Government undoubtedly takes a serious view of this question from the standpoint that the United Nations was never constituted for hearing the claims and complaints of groups within any country through direct representations by individuals".
>
> The Times, *Tribe's Petition to U.N.. S. Africa's Next Move*, 20 November 1951.

As well as these advisory proceedings, contentious cases involved the Northern Cameroons,[66] Nauru[67] as well as the claims brought before the Court by Ethiopia and Liberia concerning South-West Africa.[68] In all three cases, applicants argued that former administering powers had been in breach of the obligations that rested upon them vis-à-vis the territories under their control. However, none of the cases resulted in judgments on the merits.

In *Northern Cameroons,* the ICJ decided that "it cannot adjudicate upon the merits of the claim", as such a judgment would only serve declaratory purposes; the territories under British trusteeship rule had already become part of independent states and the trust was *in casu* already terminated by the UN General Assembly.[69] The Court did note that:

> if during the life of the Trusteeship the Trustee was responsible for some act in violation of the terms of the Trusteeship Agreement which resulted in damage to another member of the United Nations or to one of its nationals, a claim for reparation would not be liquidated by the termination of the Trust.[70]

The *Certain Phosphate Lands* proceedings never went beyond the preliminary objections phase. The application in this case was submitted after the relevant

---

[66] ICJ, *Northern Cameroons* (*Cameroon v. United Kingdom*), Preliminary Objections, Judgment, 2 December 1963, p. 15 (*Northern Cameroons*).

[67] ICJ, *Certain Phosphate Lands in Nauru* (*Nauru v. Australia*), Preliminary Objections, Judgment, 26 June 1992, p. 240 (*Certain Phosphate Lands*).

[68] ICJ, *South-West Africa*, Preliminary Objections, Judgment, p. 319 and ICJ, *South-West Africa*, Judgment, 18 July 1966, p. 6.

[69] GA Res. 1608 (XV), 21 April 1961. During the British administration of the Cameroons, certain issues such as resettlement policies had been brought to the attention of the UN by way of petitioning. *See e.g.* The Times, *Welfare of the Meru Tribe. British Reply to U.N. Critics*, 4 December 1952 and *U.N. Critics of Britain. Motion to Restore Wameru Land*, 3 December 1952.

[70] ICJ, *Northern Cameroons*, Judgment, p. 35.

trusteeship agreement had been terminated. As the former trust territory, Nauru claimed Australia had breached obligations imposed on it by the UN Charter and the relevant trusteeship agreement and demanded reparations.[71] Nauru claimed that jurisdiction of the Court existed on the basis of 'ICJ Statute Article 36, paragraph-2 declarations'. Conversely, Australia argued that, amongst other things, any dispute that had arisen under the trusteeship agreement between the trustee and the indigenous population had been settled by virtue of the trusteeship's termination by the General Assembly on 19 December 1967.[72] In line with its reasoning in *Northern Cameroons,* the Court rejected Australia's argument – as well as most other objections – and ultimately found it had jurisdiction. The case was subsequently discontinued and settled between Nauru and Australia, with Australia agreeing to "assist" Nauru through a financial settlement.[73]

Finally, the *South-West Africa* cases reflect attempts by Ethiopia and Liberia to have the ICJ address South Africa's alleged breaches of obligations under the Mandate system;[74] obligations which, as the Court previously decided, continued to rest upon South Africa.[75] In their applications, Ethiopia and Liberia alleged breaches of various obligations resting upon South Africa in its Mandatory capacity. These ranged from the reporting obligation to more substantive obligations such as the promotion of the "material and moral well-being and the social progress of the inhabitants" of South-West Africa. The applications also alleged a breach of the prohibition to military train the local population and establish military bases.[76] The applicants argued that the Court had jurisdiction based on Article 7 of the Mandate for South-West Africa *i.e.* the jurisdiction-provision common to all but one of the mandates.[77] Although the article confers jurisdiction upon the PCIJ, in line with the ICJ's previous decisions, the article *mutatis mutandis* conferred jurisdiction to the ICJ in the case of South-West Africa.[78] The Court indeed found that it had jurisdiction based on Article 7 of the Mandate.[79] In the second phase of the proceedings, the Court found (by the President's vote) that "the Applicants cannot be considered to have established any legal right or interest appertaining to them [and that] the

---

[71] Nauru Trusteeship Agreement, approved by the UN General Assembly on 1 November 1947.

[72] GA Res. 2347 (XXII), 19 December 1967.

[73] *Agreement for the settlement of the case in the International Court of Justice concerning certain phosphate lands in Nauru*, 10 August 1993, at <http://untreaty.un.org/unts/120001_144071/10/2/00007782.pdf>.

[74] ICJ, *South-West Africa*, Judgment.

[75] ICJ, *International Status of South West Africa*, Advisory Opinion.

[76] ICJ, *South-West Africa*, Judgment, pp. 10-11.

[77] Mandate for South-West Africa, Art. 7, 17 December 1920.

[78] ICJ, *International Status of South West Africa*, Advisory Opinion.

[79] ICJ, *South-West Africa*, Preliminary Objections, Judgment, p. 347.

Court must decline to give effect to them".[80] The Court held that the rights of individual member states of the League with regards to the mandates had been ensured through the member's participation in the organs of the League and through the fact that the League's voting procedures were normally based on unanimity. Thus, the fact that mandates were exercised on the basis of a sacred trust of civilization was not enough to imply interest or right with regard to individual member states so as to enable them to appear before the Court.

More than anything else, the discussed proceedings illustrate how the PCIJ and the ICJ understood and used their jurisdiction with respect to the Mandate and Trusteeship systems. The two Courts were never intended to be the backbone of the relevant accountability regimes or the main oversight body. Nevertheless, their role as the ultimate upholder of the mandate and trusteeship provisions should not be underestimated. By incorporating the Courts explicitly into the accountability regime, the legal frameworks erased all possible doubt regarding the necessity for judicial review, and added *gravitas* to the substantive obligations that were placed on the administering entities by assigning the international Courts a role in the overall accountability system.

3.2 ACCOUNTABILITY MECHANISMS DURING *SUI GENERIS* ADMINISTRATIONS

Section 2.1.3 pointed out that, parallel to the Mandate and Trusteeship systems, several *sui generis* undertakings involving international administration of territories were either planned or carried out. Although these undertakings were not part of the general legal framework provided by the Mandate and Trusteeship systems, similar accountability regimes were established. However, the fact that during the two established administrations the League had become the direct administrator of the territories meant that these accountability mechanisms no longer called upon the League (or the PCIJ) to intervene in instances of malpractice by a Mandatory power. Instead, accountability mechanisms effectively addressed the conduct of the League itself.

In the sections below, the Saar territory and Danzig, as well as the never-realized administrations of Jerusalem and Trieste, will be discussed briefly in terms of the applicable accountability regimes.

---

[80] ICJ, *South-West Africa*, Judgment, p. 51.

3.2.1 THE TERRITORY OF THE SAAR BASIN

When the League established its administration of the Saar territory, it assumed responsibilities beyond the structures provided for by the Mandate system.[81] Considering the vast powers attributed to the League (*i.e.* the Governing Commission) by the Treaty of Versailles, calls for restraint and accountability emerged. As early as in 1924, authors argued:

> Who guarantees to the inhabitants the exercise of their constitutional rights, whatever they are, under the constitution provided in the Treaty of Versailles? Those provisions are silent on the subject. […] to whom have the population to look for the vindication of their constitutional rights and the guarantee that they shall enjoy them? To the Governing Commission? But they may be the aggressors![82]

The Versailles Treaty failed to consider matters of restraint and accountability in this context. The power vested in the Governing Commission was virtually absolute, although the Treaty referred to *rights, well-being* and *welfare* of the population frequently as a normative framework within which the Governing Commission was expected to operate.[83] The organization of government included a basic level of checks and balances accompanied by several more or less couched options for redress.[84]

Similar to the Mandate system, reporting to the League Council was the basis of the supervisory framework. The Governing Commission was under an obligation to report to the League Council, which it did several times a year.[85] This obligation – unlike under the Mandate system – was not explicitly imposed by the Versailles Treaty but was based on directives adopted ad hoc by the League Council.[86]

Unlike the Mandatories, here the League was in a sense reporting to itself, as the Governing Commission was created by and represented the League. The reporting procedure provided the League Council with the necessary information in order to adopt well-informed decisions on the yearly re-election of the Governing Commission's members, the League Council's main weapon

[81] *E.g.* Bisschop (1924), p. 22.
[82] *Id.*, p. 27.
[83] Treaty of Versailles, Part III, Section IV, Saar Ann., Artt. 19, 21, 22 and 33.
[84] For a negative conclusion regarding the overall position of the Saar population in terms of being able to hold their governing authorities to account, *see* Bisschop (1924), p. 30. *See also* Stahn (2008), p. 173: "[t]he main deficit of the Saar model was its unfettered trust in the omnipotence of the Governing Commission".
[85] Ratner (1996), p. 92.
[86] Russel (1926), p. 141.

against potential misconduct and abuse of authority by the Governing Commission.[87]

The Versailles Treaty also did not mention anything about petitioning, though a petitioning procedure did evolve. Petitions could be sent to the Governing Commission which was expected to transmit them to the League Council. Despite the fact that the Governing Commission was bypassed at times, it was the League Council's own view that the "[c]ommission represented the appropriate channel for complaints by Saarlanders to the Council"[88] and that it should not intervene with the Governing Commission's authority "except for reasons of the highest importance".[89]

> A "flow of petitions" was reported by The Times, "alleging infringements of the Treaty and injustices on the part of the Commission" administering the Saar territory. The administration was accused of being biased towards France. The stance of the League Council was also criticized. "The League Council are [sic] responsible for the selection of M. Rault as the first President and chief executive officer. M. Rault does not know a word of German". The newspaper notes that "he has centralized the most important functions in his own hands, and has been in the habit of issuing reports and making decisions without consulting his colleagues".
>
> The Times, *France and the Saar. II. –Grievances of the Populations. A Flow of Petitions*, 11 January 1924.

The necessity of accountability mechanisms is illustrated by the merits of the petitions that, as one author notes, related to the "autocratic attitude and procedure of the Government".[90] The League had no actual means of correcting the wrongdoings of the Governing Commission save for the League's ultimate authority regarding the Governing Commission's composition. Though the reporting obligation as well as the right to petition did establish a basic level of checks and balances with regard to the Saar governing authorities, they failed to bridge the gap between the authorities and the local population.

---

[87] Treaty of Versailles, Part III, Section IV, Saar Ann., Art. 17. *See also* Russel (1926), p. 141; Bisschop (1924), p. 30.

[88] Ratner (1996), p. 92.

[89] *See* Stahn (2008), p. 170, n. 58, citing reports adopted by the League Council. In general, governments could request the Council to examine the Governing Commission's policy and conduct directly. The British Government protested against the criminalization of public criticism of the League and the Versailles Treaty, which according to the relevant decree of the Governing Commission became punishable by five years of imprisonment. The Governing Commission was summoned by the League Council in 1923, which resulted in the review of the decree by the Governing Commission. *See* Russel (1926), p. 210. The German Government has likewise sent protest notes to the League, thereby bypassing the Governing Commission, *see* Russel (1926), p. 200, n. 10.

[90] Russel (1926), p. 177.

In terms of actual judicial scrutiny, records show that at times local courts touched upon the validity of decrees issued by the Governing Commission, since under the Saar administration local courts continued to function.[91] For example, in June 1924 the Governing Commission issued an ordinance prohibiting the display of the German imperial flag. A case against an individual who had displayed the flag was brought before a local court, which acquitted the accused and declared the decree null and void. Upon orders of the Governing Commission, the Public Prosecutor entered an appeal. In second instance, the acquittal was upheld and the flag-display ban was declared *ultra vires* because it had been adopted without the consultation of the local representatives.[92] On appeal, the waving of the flag was "declared to be contrary neither to the laws of the Saar nor to the Treaty of Versailles".[93]

3.2.2 THE FREE CITY OF DANZIG

Pursuant to the Versailles Treaty, the League also assumed authority over the city of Danzig.[94] As was discussed in Section 2.1.3, the Danzig engagement fell

[91] Laws in force on 11 November 1918 in the territory of the Saar continued to apply. Likewise, the existing civil and criminal courts continued to function, though the Governing Commission was tasked to establish appeals courts, *see* Treaty of Versailles, Part III, Section IV, Saar Ann., Artt. 23 and 25.

[92] The Versailles Treaty obliged the governing authorities to include the local population in the decision-making process. The Governing Commission was under the obligation to consult a body of elected representatives of the inhabitants in certain domains of legislative activity, *see* Treaty of Versailles, Part III, Section IV, Saar Ann., Artt. 23 and 26. Participation did not compensate for the lack of accountability mechanisms but, as a procedural virtue, it did contribute to the legitimacy of the governing process. The Saar population was eager to be included in the decision making of the Governing Commission. In response hereto, the Governing Commission established an Advisory Council (*Landesrat*) by issuing a decree on 24 March 1922. This Advisory Council was accompanied by a Technical Committee that enjoyed more or less the same consultative function as the Advisory Council but that was composed of experts and respected citizens. However, the wish of the population was "not granted in a spirit of broad statesmanship", as observed in Bisschop (1924), pp. 43-49. Meetings were scheduled and prepared by the Governing Commission, which also limited the number of topics to be discussed by the Advisory Council. The activities of the Advisory Council in practice added little to the level of participation of the local population. On occasion, the Advisory Council was not consulted at all; *see* for example Bisschop (1924), pp. 71-73, where a petition addressed to the League is discussed in which the local representatives complain that they were not consulted throughout the process of introducing the French Franc as legal tender of the Saar Basin. In fact, the Advisory Council proved futile to the extent that local representatives saw themselves forced to make use of their right to petition in order to address the position in which the Advisory Council had found itself, *see* Petition dated 12 April 1922, reproduced in Bisschop (1924), p. 48, n. (g).

[93] The Times, *German Flag in the Saar. Dispute with the Governing Commission*, 25 June 1925.

[94] Treaty of Versailles, Part III, Section XI, Artt. 100-108.

outside the scope of the Mandate system and differed in certain aspects from the Saar Basin undertaking.

Provisions empowering the League to exercise governmental authority in a proactive manner were few and far between. The Versailles Treaty assigned the League with the task of co-drafting and protecting the Danzig Constitution.[95] As the Danzig Constitution and all its subsequent amendments needed to be approved by the League Council, Danzig and its Constitution were effectively placed under the guarantee of the League.[96] To this end, a High Commissioner was appointed by the League Council.[97] The role of the High Commissioner was one of mediator and arbitrator, much like the role initially envisaged for the High Representative in BiH, being entrusted with the authority to deal:

> in first instance with all differences arising between Poland and the Free City of Danzig in regard to this Treaty or any arrangements or agreements made thereunder.[98]

The arbiter-like nature of the High Commissioner was reiterated by the PCIJ when it held that:

> [t]he functions of the High Commissioner are of a judicial character and limited to deciding questions submitted by one or other of the Parties. The High Commission, therefore, [has] no authority to decide questions which the Parties had not submitted to him.[99]

The High Commissioner's position was anchored in the Constitution, while his authority was interpreted to include matters regarding international treaties that were potentially incompatible with the status of the city.[100] In addition hereto, the High Commissioner could decide on "any matter affecting the relations

[95] *Id.*, Art. 103. The League exercised its constitution-drafting authority by requesting the Constitutive Assembly to alter the draft constitution in line with the League's annotations. *See also* Stahn (2008), p. 183.

[96] *Id.*, Artt. 102-103. On the status of the Danzig constitution vis-à-vis the League of Nations, *see* PCIJ, *Consistency of Certain Danzig Legislative Decrees with the Constitution of the Free City*, Ser. A/B, No. 65, Advisory Opinion, 4 December 1935 (*Consistency of Certain Danzig Legislative Decrees*).

[97] Treaty of Versailles, Part III, Section XI, Art. 103.

[98] *Id.*

[99] PCIJ, *Polish Postal Service in Danzig*, Ser. B, No. 11, Advisory Opinion, 16 May 1925, p. 26 (*Polish Postal Service*).

[100] Paris Convention between Danzig and Poland, Art. 6, 9 November 1920; Constitution of the Free City of Danzig, Art. 49.

between Poland and the Free City" or refer the issue to the League Council.[101] In protecting the Danzig constitution, the High Commissioner could act *proprio motu* or pursuant to petitions. His decisions as well as the incoming petitions were subject to examination by the League Council.[102]

The powers of the High Commissioner should be read in context. Especially in the wake of Nazism's rise to power, instead of demanding constraint, petitions demanded more robust action from the High Commissioner in protecting the Danzig Constitution.

> In 1935, opposition parties in Danzig filed a petition with the League, requesting it "to take immediate steps to empower the High Commissioner to safeguard the liberties and rights prescribed by the Constitution. The populations, states the petition, are not in agreement with the methods of the National-Socialists". In another instance, the League Council heard the High Commissioner and the President of the Danzig Senate with regard to a petition filed on behalf of the Diocese of Danzig. The petition questioned to which extent "the present Government of Danzig could carry out National-Socialism on the German model without infringement of the Constitution guaranteed by the League".
>
> The Times, *More Arrests in Danzig. Opposition's Petition to League*, 10 July 1935 & *A Cloud at Geneva. Voices from the Reich. Saar Reactions*, 19 January 1935.

In practice, over eighty decisions were adopted by the High Commissioner, most of which were indeed appealed before the League Council. In turn, based on Article 14 of the Covenant, the League Council could request advisory opinions from the PCIJ, which it did on six occasions.[103]

---

[101] Paris Convention between Danzig and Poland, Art. 39, 9 November 1920: "Any differences arising between Poland and the Free City of Danzig in regard to the present Treaty or to any other subsequent agreements, arrangements or conventions, or to any matter affecting the relations between Poland and the Free City, shall be submitted by one or the other party to the decision of the High Commissioner, who shall, if he deems it necessary, refer the matter to the Council of the League of Nations. The two parties retain the right of appeal to the Council of the League of Nations".

[102] *Id.*

[103] PCIJ advisory opinions were given in the previously mentioned proceedings *Polish Postal Service in Danzig*; *Treatment of Polish Nationals* and *Consistency of Certain Danzig Legislative Decrees* as well as in PCIJ, *Jurisdiction of the Courts of Danzig*, Ser. B. No. 15, Advisory Opinion, 3 March 1928 (*Jurisdiction of the Courts of Danzig*); PCIJ, *Free City of Danzig and International Labour Organization*, Ser. B, No. 38, Advisory Opinion, 26 August 1930 (*Free City of Danzig and ILO*); PCIJ, *Access to, or Anchorage in, the Port of Danzig, of Polish War Vessels*, Ser. A/B, No. 43, Advisory Opinion, 11 December 1931 (*Port of Danzig*).

3.2.3 THE CITY OF JERUSALEM AND THE FREE TERRITORY OF TRIESTE

Section 2.1.3 pointed out that the UN contemplated direct engagement in the administration of Trieste and Jerusalem. These missions were never fully established. The way in which they were envisaged, "[these missions] relied on robust and authoritarian formulas of international governance".[104] However, the envisaged administrations departed from previous League practice in several ways.

The Trieste Statute awarded the Trieste Governor extensive powers, exceeding the passive authority enjoyed by the Danzig High Commissioner.[105] The Trieste Governor was entrusted with the power to initiate legislative procedures in certain matters and to appoint and remove officials and members of the judiciary.[106] From the perspective of the local population, the Trieste Statute took a clear step towards placing the interests of the population higher up the priority ladder by expressly emphasizing that the Security Council and the Governor had to guarantee the human rights of the inhabitants.[107] The explicit incorporation of human rights into the Trieste Statute was in line with the increasing attention for human rights within international law.[108]

In accordance with the extensive powers of the Trieste Governor, a complex system of checks and balances was envisaged. The primary feature of this system was the central role of the UN Security Council. Similar to the Danzig administration, the status of the Free Territory of Trieste would enjoy international guarantees, *in casu* provided by the UN Security Council. In terms of administration, the Security Council – after consultations with the Italian and Yugoslav governments – would appoint a Trieste Governor.[109] However, the Security Council was to assume a much more prominent role as the designated body to which both the governing authorities of Trieste as well as the Trieste Governor could turn for guidance: namely, the Trieste Governor could request the Security Council to decide in instances in which his proposals for administrative measures were refused by the Trieste Council of Government. Conversely, the Trieste Assembly was allowed to petition the Security Council directly when proposing amendments to the Trieste Statute and could appeal

---

[104] Stahn (2008), pp. 187-188.
[105] *See* inter alia Permanent Statute of the Free Territory of Trieste, Artt. 19(4), 20 and 24(1).
[106] *Id.*, Artt. 19(1), 27 and 16.
[107] *Id.*, Art. 2.
[108] For an overview of how the issue of human rights was dealt with after the failure of the Trieste project, *see* Schwelb E. (1955), 'The Trieste Settlement and Human Rights', 49(2) *American Journal of International Law*, pp. 240-248.
[109] Permanent Statute of the Free Territory of Trieste, Artt. 11 and 25.

decisions taken by the Trieste Governor enacted under his "special powers".[110] However, no mention was made of any individual right to petition the UN. Finally, the Security Council was envisaged to adopt legislation in matters where the local legislative authorities and the Trieste Governor were not able to agree.[111] In such situations, the direct link between individuals and the UN would become even more tangible.

The other undertaking that was never implemented concerns the city of Jerusalem. After several proposals, a Trusteeship Council's final draft of the "Statute for the City of Jerusalem" was submitted to the General Assembly.[112] The Trusteeship Council would assume administrative authority through an appointed Governor, the "representative of the United Nations in the City".[113] The Governor's envisaged powers were extensive and covered all branches of government. Amongst other things, the Governor would have been able to veto legislative acts as well as initiate legislative procedure and even dissolve the local Legislative Council.[114] At the same time, the Trusteeship Council retained the power to appoint and dismiss members of the highest judicial bodies.[115]

No general reporting obligation was included. Instead, instances in which the Governor was obliged to report to the Trusteeship Council were scattered across the Jerusalem Statute and covered only the most excessive use of authority envisaged by the document.[116] In addition, the Jerusalem Statute expressly exempted the Governor "and his official and private property" from the jurisdiction of the local Legislative Council and the courts, effectively granting him immunity from judicial oversight.[117] The Jerusalem Statute did anchor the right of the local population to petition the Trusteeship Council. In fact, rather than empowering a body to receive petitions (and thus indirectly provide for such a right), the Jerusalem Statute listed the right to petition amongst other basic rights which the Statute enshrined:

[110] *Id.*, Art. 22(2): "The popular Assembly may petition the Security Council concerning any exercise by the Governor of his powers under paragraph 1 of this Article" and Art. 37: "This Statute shall constitute the permanent Statute of the Free Territory, subject to any amendment which may hereafter be made by the Security Council. Petitions for the amendment of the Statute may be presented to the Security Council by the popular Assembly upon a vote taken by a two-thirds majority of the votes cast".

[111] *Id.*, Art. 19(6).

[112] *Statute for the City of Jerusalem*, Resolution adopted by the Trusteeship Council at its tenth meeting held on 14 June 1950, GAOR, 5th Session (195), supplement No. 9, UN Doc. A/1286.

[113] *Id.*, Art. 13(1).

[114] *Id.*, Artt. 24(30), 24(2) and 23(3).

[115] *Id.*, Art. 28(1).

[116] *Id.*, Artt. 16(2), 23(3), 24(3), 25(3).

[117] *Id.*, Art. 13(5).

> All persons shall enjoy freedom of conscience and shall, subject only to the requirements of public order, public morals and public health, enjoy all other human rights and fundamental freedoms, including freedom of religion and worship, language, education, speech and Press, assembly and association, petition (*including petition to the Trusteeship Council*), migration and movement.[118]

3.3 CONCLUDING REMARKS

The accountability regimes under the Mandate and Trusteeship systems were characterized by two main features: the fact that the individual missions were setup under pre-existing legal frameworks and that the actual administration of territories was carried out by states, albeit on behalf of the League and the UN respectively.

The fact that territories were administered within a broader legal framework proved beneficial, since the legal frameworks did more than simply enable a more coherent approach to the question of accountability. Bearing in mind the *Zeitgeist* and the institutional particularities of the two systems, the principles of the rule of law and judicial review by an independent body were – at least on paper – embedded in these frameworks. The Mandate and the Trusteeship systems provided basic benchmarks concerning the manner in which territories were to be administered. These benchmarks centred on the well-being of the local population and on the prevention of abuse of power. Furthermore, the systems anchored the supervisory role of the League and the UN, respectively, and prescribed mechanisms through which this supervision took place. This supervision rested on three pillars: the obligation to report, the right to petition and scrutiny by judicial organs, with the PCIJ and the ICJ being included in the supervision regime as a measure of last resort.

The obligation to report served as a fundamental guarantee that the international community would not lose sight of what was happening in the territories that that same community had placed under its indirect jurisdiction. Reporting in terms of accountability was essentially an administrative mechanism, but it served the purpose of monitoring the adherence to the benchmarks set by the respective legal frameworks.[119]

In terms of accountability, a mechanisms more germane to the nature of the discussed undertakings was the individual right to petition. Establishing a direct link between (groups of) individuals and the international community was a *novum*, especially in the context of the general position of individuals in

---

[118] *Id.*, Art. 9(2), emphasis added.

[119] ICJ, *South-West Africa*, Preliminary Objections, Judgment, pp. 336-338.

international law at the time. Its particular importance lies in the fact that it enables other guaranteed rights to be upheld, comparable to the right to access to court. As the UN General Assembly stated, "[t]he right of petition is an essential human right".[120] This right was not guaranteed by the administering state but by the Mandate and Trusteeship systems; the right to petition was detached from the discretion of the administering entity. Furthermore, the right to petition was conceived broadly. Not only could petitions be sent by individuals from the administered territories – they could also be sent from other states.[121] In the case of the League, petitions could also come from non-member states as illustrated by the numerous petitions received from the United States. Finally, the right to petition evolved in such a way as to include a right to be heard. The issue of hearings was discussed occasionally during by the League but was rejected time and again. The fear existed that the Mandates Commission would go far beyond its mandate if it was to invite petitioners to be heard, as this could create a situation in which petitioners and the Mandatory powers would seem equal in standing. Under the Trusteeship system, hearings of petitioners were incorporated into the petitioning procedure. This step further bridged the gap between the administered communities and the international entities. Thus, petitioning provided individuals with an institutionalized opportunity to address the persons they thought were either responsible for or able to resolve their problems.

The PCIJ and the ICJ constituted the final "bulwark of protection" of the rights guaranteed by the League and the UN.[122] The Mandate and Trusteeship systems' legal frameworks incorporated the PCIJ and the ICJ respectively, providing these Courts with an explicit ground for jurisdiction. Advisory proceedings and contentious cases were an *ultimum remedium* through which the administration of territories was scrutinized. States could also initiate proceedings in order to protect their rights or the rights of their nationals as, for example, in the *Mavrommatis Jerusalem Concessions* proceedings.[123]. However,

[120] GA Res. 217 B (III), 10 December 1948.

[121] With regard to the Mandate system, petitions were allowed to come from "communities or sections of the populations of mandated territories" as well as from "any source other than that of the inhabitants of the mandated territories themselves", *see* 'Summary of the Procedure to be followed in the matter of petitions concerning mandated territories', League of Nations Doc. C.P.M.558 (1).

[122] ICJ, *South-West Africa*, Preliminary Objections, Judgment, pp. 336-338.

[123] With respect to advisory proceedings, although such proceedings lacked binding force, the moral authority of advisory opinions was regarded as virtually equal to legally binding effect: "Les fonctions consultatives de la Cour tendent de plus en plus à avoir le meme caractère que son activité tentieuse, et c'est avec raison qu'on considère ajourd'hui la procédure des avis consultatifs comme une << sorte de variante de la procédure contentieuse >>. Bien que n'ayant pas, en théorie, la force obligatoire d'un arrêt, *les avis consultatifs ont acquis l'authorité morale d'une decision judiciaire*; si le Conseil en demandait un à la Cour, il est

defending the rights of the administered population without having further right or interest was dismissed in the *South-West Africa* cases.

The fact remains that the League and the UN attributed the administration of territories to particular states. Thus, it was the proxy state, so to speak, that was responsible for the day-to-day administration of a territory. It might be argued that it would have been difficult for the discussed accountability regimes to operate in the same fashion in a situation of direct international administration. Indeed, the regimes were not envisaged to serve that purpose even though direct international administration was an option within the Trusteeship system. Had the UN exercised this prerogative, the existing accountability mechanisms would have played out differently; one and the same international organization would file and review annual reports, petitions would directly address the conduct of the international organization and judicial scrutiny through contentious cases by the PCIJ and the ICJ would be impossible, as the administrating entity would lack legal standing.[124] Some commentators went a step further in saying that "[t]he machinery of supervision [...] completely breaks down when the administering authority is the Organisation itself".[125]

Section 3.2 shows that under the Saar and Danzig regimes, this proved not to be entirely the case. The Saar Basin and Danzig were administered directly by the League. The accountability regimes were construed in a fashion similar to the ones under the Mandate and Trusteeship systems. Besides the obligation to report, the League requested advisory opinions from the PCIJ on several occasions in order to clarify the status of the administered territories and the role of the international administration. Finally, these particular missions also recognized the right to petition, which under these particular circumstances served as a mechanism through which the local population could voice its discontent directly regarding acts and omissions of the international administration.

In the context of contemporary international administrations, the precedential value of the discussed mechanisms can be summarized as follows. The fact that by and large administration was carried out by states on behalf of the League and the UN does not subtract from the points made throughout this chapter. Firstly, this chapter shows the beneficial effect of embedding international undertakings of such magnitude in a broader legal framework. This holds true with respect to substantive limitations to the power of the administering entity and to ways through which these limits can be upheld. Secondly, in terms of actual accountability mechanisms, the chapter provides insight into the added

certain que cet avis serait, dans tous les cas, observe par la puissance mandataire en cause" *in* Feinberg (1930), p. 196, footnotes omitted and emphasis added.

[124] *See also* Stahn (2008), p. 98.

[125] Charmian Edwards Toussaint, as quoted in Stahn (2008), p. 97, n 29.

value of particular mechanisms, first and foremost the right to petition and judicial oversight by the PCIJ and the ICJ.

In terms of public law, the limitations set by the legal frameworks provided a basis for the rule of law vis-à-vis the international administrations, irrespective of whether this administration was carried out directly or through proxy states. Moreover, the legal frameworks anchored certain accountability mechanisms that pertain to judicial oversight by independent bodies – the existence and mandate of which were not subjected to the discretion of the administering entity.

4 Holding International Territorial Administrations to Account: Determinants of the Accountability Deficit

"The last six months have also made clearer how daunting the task is that the [UN] has undertaken in East Timor. The Organization had never before attempted to build and manage a State. Nor did it have an opportunity to prepare for this assignment; the team in East Timor had to be assembled ad hoc and still lacks important expertise in a number of fields"

- *Report of the Secretary-General on UNTAET, July 2000*[1]

What are the causes that underlie the observation that international entities by and large remain unaccountable for the way in which they administer territories?[2] And how do these causes translate in terms of public law? This chapter posits that the accountability deficit is defined by three interrelated and mutually reinforcing determinants. In short, the following three linkages between features of ITA missions and public law are expounded.

Firstly, a coherent legal framework that would regulate and confine the exercise of sovereign-like powers by ITA missions is lacking. Substantive or procedural limitations are, if at all, mostly self-imposed and developed *en route*. In terms of public law, this uncertainty at least *prima facie* implies an unlimited government and a weak rule of law. No legal framework exists within which ITA missions are expected to operate and, consequently, no clear yardstick against which the administering entity can be scrutinized are at hand (Section 4.1).

Secondly, ITA missions retain a robust conception of immunity. While behaving as states rather than international organizations, the administering entities are shielded by a set of all-encompassing immunities, rooted in functional necessity-related arguments. In terms of public law, these immunities

---

[1] *Report by the UN SG on UNTAET*, UN Doc. S/2000/738, 26 July 2000, § 64.

[2] UN-led missions are taken as the basis of analysis, while the OHR is discussed by way of comparison.

prevent international administrations from being subjected to judicial review (Section 4.2).

Thirdly, ITA missions enjoy an all-inclusive and highly concentrated mandate. With respect to all dimensions of public power, ITA missions are located at the very top of the proverbial food chain. Even after a gradual transfer of power, as the holders of the *Competenz-Competenz,* ITA missions retain ultimate authority, since they hold on to certain prerogatives as well as to the discretionary power to overrule any exercise of public power by the local authorities. In terms of public law, the mandate exercised by ITA missions corresponds to an undesirable accumulation of power. Through the recurring concentrated institutional design, international administrators enjoy the final say in virtually all matters of public concern leaving no space for independent judicial scrutiny or, effectively, any other form of institutional checks and balances (Section 4.3).

Figure 1: The ITA-accountability Deficit in Terms of Public Law

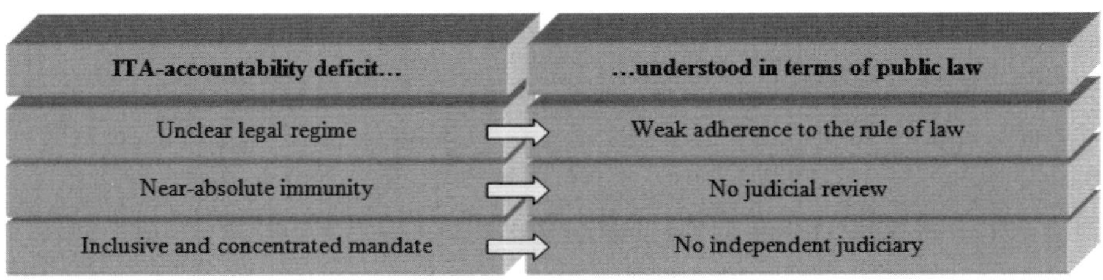

Taken together, these three determinants shape the ITA accountability deficit.[3] In the following sections, these three determinants are discussed in relation to UNMIK's administration of Kosovo, UNTAET's administration of East Timor and, by way of comparison, the OHR's powers in BiH. The situation has often been defended by invoking a state-of-emergency argument; hence, the concluding remarks of this chapter will turn to this defence and the inadequacy thereof.

4.1 LACK OF A CLEARLY APPLICABLE LEGAL FRAMEWORK

In the ITA context, the term 'applicable legal framework' can refer to two distinct matters. The first relates to the body of laws that binds ITA missions and regulate their exercise of public power. The second refers to the law applicable

[3] With respect to all figures in this book: © Momirov.

within the internationally administered territory. The following sections focus on the first – and more relevant for this book – matter.[4]

In order for the rule of law to be upheld, a set of legal norms that bind ITA missions in their exercise of public power need to be identified. As far as internal law of the organization is concerned, the UN Charter does not provide for ITA missions explicitly, and thus fails to provide a tailored set of rules that address the exercise of public power by ITA missions in particular.[5] Turning to international and domestic law, it can be said that neither bodies of law provide a fit-for-purpose legal framework in this respect. The following sections analyze the extent to which international and domestic law can nevertheless serve as a source of legal obligations resting on ITA missions.

4.1.1 INTERNATIONAL LAW: UNPREPARED

International law does not envisage situations in which international organizations exercise sovereign-like powers. Consequently, when such situations do occur, international law fails to provide a coherent legal framework that would regulate the exercise of public powers. Nevertheless, several fields of international law relate to ITA missions in different ways. The bulk of ongoing debate amongst authors has centred on the applicability of international humanitarian law and – considering the overall military control of ITA missions – the law of occupation.[6]

ITA missions are generally categorized as peacekeeping operations. In keeping with this categorization, international humanitarian law is applicable with respect to the military components of ITA missions.[7] The UN confirms this view.[8] International humanitarian law, however, does not cover the extensive mandate of ITA missions and is not suitable to address the overall exercise of state-like public powers by international entities.

[4] The issue of applicable law within an internationally administered territory is touched upon in Section 4.1.2 below.

[5] *See* Section 2.3 above. *See also* Section 5.1.2 below for a discussion on the role of internal oversight procedures.

[6] *See e.g.* Stahn (2008), pp. 115-146; Doyle (2001); Shraga D. (2000), 'UN Peacekeeping Operations: Applicability of International Humanitarian Law and Responsibility for Operations-related Damage', 94(2) *American Journal of International Law*, pp. 406-412. *See also* Aoi C. *et al.* (eds.) (2007), *Unintended consequences of peacekeeping operations*, New York: United Nations University Press.

[7] *Cf.* Reinisch A. (2001)(2), 'Developing Human Rights and Humanitarian Law Accountability of the Security Council for the Imposition of Economic Sanctions', 95(4) *American Journal of International Law*, pp. 851-871.

[8] UN SG's Bulletin, *Observance by United Nations forces of international humanitarian law*, UN Doc. ST/SGB/1999/13, 6 August 1999.

ITA missions are also sometimes mentioned in the same breath as military occupation. This linkage should be rejected based on conceptual differences between the two types of undertakings.[9] Firstly, the raison d'être behind military occupation is incomparable and to some extent incompatible with the aims and purposes of ITA missions. Secondly, while military occupation is unlawful and non-consensual in nature, the legality of the present ITA missions has generally remained undisputed.[10] Moreover, ITA missions to date have been consent-based even though this consent may have resulted from political pressure, as with UNTAET or the use of military force, as was the case prior to the deployment of UNMIK.[11] These conceptual differences are important, since military occupation implies the application of the law of occupation which imposes certain obligations on the occupying power.[12] Some of these obligations are contrary to the very essence of ITA missions. For example, the law of occupation limits the authority of the occupying power to amend local laws, alter the status of judges and engage in other similar activities:[13] "[o]ccupation is

---

[9] *A contrario* Ratner S. (2005), 'Foreign Occupation and International Territorial Administration: The Challenges of Convergence', 16 *European Journal of International Law*, pp. 695-719.

[10] Illustrative is the statement by Kofi Annan, UN SG at the time the occupation of Iraq was established, where he called the occupation an "illegal act that contravened the UN Charter", at <http://news.bbc.co.uk/1/hi/world/middle_east/3661134.stm>. Subsequent to the initial military operation, the US/UK presence in Iraq was acknowledged by the UN Security Council and the "effective administration of the territory" was called upon to "promote the welfare of the Iraqi people". SC Res. 1483 (2003), § 4. AI for example stated in 2003, that "[d]espite appearances, the present situation [in Iraq] is not a "legal vacuum". The forces of the USA and the UK, as occupying forces under international law, have clear obligations to protect the Iraqi population", *see* AI, *Iraq: Responsibilities of the occupying powers*, 16 April 2003, index number MDE 14/089/2003, at <http://www.amnesty.org/en/library/info/MDE14/089/2003>. Populations under military occupation remain protected by the legal framework of international human rights law, which is not excluded by the simultaneous application of international humanitarian law. This has been confirmed by the ICJ in *Legality of the Threat or Use of Nuclear Weapons*, Advisory Opinion, 8 July 1996, p. 18, § 25 and *Legal Consequences of the Construction of a Wall in the Occupied Palestinian Territory*, Advisory Opinion, 8 July 2004, §§ 105-113, 127-134. *See further* De Wet E. (2004), 'The Direct Administration of Territories by the United Nations and its Member States in the Post Cold War Era: Legal Bases and Implications for National Law', 8 *Max Planck Yearbook of United Nations Law*, p. 305.

[11] *A contrario* Stahn (2008), p. 47.

[12] Art. 64(2) of the Fourth Geneva Convention states: "The Occupying Power may, however, subject the population of the occupied territory to provisions which are essential to enable the Occupying Power to fulfill its obligations under the present Convention, to maintain the orderly government of the territory, and to ensure the security of the Occupying Power, of the members and property of the occupying forces or administration, and likewise of the establishments and lines of communication used by them".

[13] Convention (IV) Respecting the Laws and Customs of War on Land and Its Annex: Regulations Concerning the Laws and Customs of War on Land, The Hague, 18 October 1907, Art. 43; Convention Relative to the Protection of Civilian Persons in Time of War,

meant to be [...] minimalist in terms of its impact on the population".[14] This is in sharp contrast to ITA missions, where legislating is one of the main attributes of authority of the international administrator. Thus, because ITA missions cannot be considered to be engaged in belligerent occupation, the law of occupation does not provide an applicable legal framework.[15]

Given the nature of ITA missions – which is predominantly one of civil administration rather than military engagement – a third legal regime proves more relevant: international human rights law.[16] In part, this relates to a broader ongoing discussion about the applicability of international human rights law to international organizations. The ILA concluded in 2004 that the applicability of human rights norms can be construed in various ways, which include applicability through constituent documents, applicability based on the status of the norms (in the case of customary international law, general principles of law or peremptory norms) or, where possible, accession to human rights treaties by international organizations.[17] The ILA report mentions ITA missions separately but fails to go beyond recommending that human rights guarantees should be part of the internal regulatory framework of such missions:

> IO-s should incorporate basic human rights obligations into their operational guidelines, policies and procedures, particularly when exercising governmental authority in the conduct of temporary administration over a particular territory.[18]

Geneva, 12 August 1949, Artt. 54-56 and 64. *See also* Chesterman (2005), p. 7; Boon K. (2005), 'Legislative Reform in Post-Conflict Zones: Jus Post Bellum and the Contemporary Occupant's Law-Making Powers', 50 *McGill Law Journal*, pp. 3-41. *See also* De Wet (2004), pp. 326-329.

[14] Ratner (2005), p. 700.

[15] *E.g.* Irmscher (2001), pp. 374-395.

[16] *E.g.* White N.D. & Klaasen D. (eds.) (2005), *The UN, human rights and post-conflict situations*, Manchester: Manchester University Press.

[17] ILA 2004, p. 22. *Cf.* Mégret F. & Hoffmann F. (2005), 'Fostering Human Rights Accountability: An Ombudsman for the United Nations', 11 *Global Governance*, pp. 317-318. These authors suggest an external, internal and hybrid conception for the applicability of human rights standards to the UN, a three-pronged approach that roughly corresponds to the options for applicability listed by the ILA report.

[18] *Id.*, p. 23. The ILA report also proposes a set of norms, so-called "recommended rules and practices" (RRP) deemed to apply to all international organizations and considered a "vital prerequisite for a well functioning accountability regime". These RRPs include norms that should be applied, irrespective of subsequent liability or responsibility. Arguably, most of the RRPs mirror expectations that are commonplace vis-à-vis the exercise of public powers by states, such as the claims for good governance and procedural regularity. Moreover, the principle of constitutionality and institutional balance is included, referring to the obligation resting on any international organization to act within the confines of its own rules. The RRPs as proposed by the ILA are not discussed here, *but see* Section 6.3 below.

The following sections discuss the three main suggestions made by the ILA, and analyze how they play out in the context of ITA missions. In this analysis, emphasis is placed on the UN as the main actor in the ITA context.

4.1.1.1 Applicability of Human Rights Norms Through Constituent Documents

Norms governing the activities of the UN can be found in the UN Charter: namely, the purposes and principles of the UN.[19] It should be noted that the *protection* of human rights as such is not included amongst the purposes. Despite this omission, the way in which international human rights law as well as the UN itself developed over time confirms the importance of human rights within the UN system. Missions such as UNMIK and UNTAET are subsidiary organs of the UN and are *ipso facto* bound by the same norms that bind the UN.[20] These norms are the most undisputed guidelines for the exercise of ITA-mandates.[21] However, unlike during the Mandate and Trusteeship systems, the UN Charter fails to list specific standards that apply to ITA missions,[22] and as a result, it remains abstract with respect to obligations.

More in particular, the actual constituent documents of UNMIK and UNTAET include the promotion and protection of human rights in the list of responsibilities of the ITA missions. UN Security Council Resolution 1244 (1999) affirms in paragraph 11(j) that "protecting and promoting human rights" is one of the main responsibilities of the international administration in Kosovo. With regard to East Timor, UN Security Council Resolution 1272 (1999) proclaims the same.[23] These provisions, however, do not establish explicitly an obligation for UNMIK and UNTAET to abide by specific human rights norms. In other words, ITA missions promote respect for human rights at the local level, but their constituent documents fail to institutionalize international human

---

[19] UN Charter, Art. 24(2) referring to Chapter 1 of the Charter.

[20] *See e.g.* Irmscher (2001), p. 355. *Cf.* Wilde R. (1998), 'Quis Custodiet Ipsos Custodes?: Why and How UNHCR Governance of "Development" Refugee Camps Should be Subject to International Human Rights Law', 1 *Yale Human Rights & Development Law Journal*, pp. 107-128.

[21] *E.g.* Irmscher (2001), pp. 362-366.

[22] AI has argued that in this respect, UNTAET is different from UNMIK. Since UNTAET was based on an act of self-determination, according to AI, UNTAET should be considered analogous to a trusteeship, which would result in different legal responsibilities resting on UNTAET compared to UNMIK, *see* AI, *East Timor: Building a new country based on human rights*, ASA 57/05/00, August 2000, pp. 3-4. *See also* Wilde (2008), pp. 153-189.

[23] *Report of the UN SG on the situation in East Timor*, UN Doc. S/1999/1024, 4 October 1999, Section IV in general, and § 29(h) in particular.

rights law explicitly as part of the legal framework governing the activities of ITA missions.[24]

4.1.1.2 *Applicability of Human Rights Norms Based on the Legal Status of these Norms*

Regarding the second option through which applicability may be construed, widespread consensus exists that the UN is bound by those human rights standards that have gained the status of customary international law.[25] This consensus is echoed in the context of ITA missions. For example, the UN Secretary-General stated that "[i]n assuming its responsibilities, UNMIK will be guided by internationally recognized standards of human rights as the basis for the exercise of its authority in Kosovo".[26] Leaving aside the modality of effectuating ones guaranteed rights, the exercise of public power based on an ITA-mandate should conform to internationally recognized human rights norms.

UNMIK and UNTAET have been ambiguous in institutionalizing this view. Immediately upon their deployment, UNMIK and UNTAET issued regulations stating "[i]n exercising their functions, all persons undertaking public duties or holding public office in [Kosovo/East Timor] shall observe internationally recognized human rights standards".[27] Exercising all public powers, the international administrator *stricto sensu* ought to be the primary addressee of this provision. However, the wording falls short of determining explicitly whether the referenced human rights standards restrain the decision-making process of the international administrator.[28] For its part, UNMIK has made clear

[24] Marshall D. & Inglis S. (2003), 'The Disempowerment of Human Rights-based Justice in the United Nations Mission in Kosovo', 16 *Harvard Human Rights Journal*, pp. 95-145.

[25] *E.g.* White & Klaasen, in Klabbers, Peters & Ulfstein (2009), p. 7.

[26] *Report of the UN SG on UNMIK*, UN Doc. S/1999/779, 12 July 1999, § 42. *See also* § 75 where it is stated that the laws adopted by UNMIK should be in conformity with human rights standards. For a similar interpretation, *see* Ombudsperson Institution in Kosovo, Special Report No. 2, *On Certain Aspects of UNMIK Regulation No. 2000/59 Amending UNMIK Regulation No. 1999/24 on the Law Applicable in Kosovo (27 October 2000)*, 30 May 2001, § 8. Some commentators point to another way in which international norms could impact or limit the authority of ITA missions. The authors give an account of debates during the transitional period of East Timor, during which it was argued that, based on the right to self-determination, political participation and the emerging principle of democratic governance, UNTAET should conform to policy choices of the local population even if such choices were not in line with other – weaker – international legal norms, *see* Morrow & White (2002), p. 14.

[27] UNTAET Reg. 1999/1, Section 2 and UNMIK Reg. 2000/59, Section 1, § 1.3. The regulations further add that no person holding public office shall discriminate on any ground.

[28] *E.g.* Stahn (2005)(3), p. 35, where this "dichotomy" is addressed. Some authors conclude that these regulations do impose obligations on the international administration. With respect to UNTAET, *see e.g.* Linton (2001), p. 136.

that the relevant regulation does not imply that UNMIK is bound by the human rights treaties applicable in Kosovo.[29] Conversely, UNMIK's partner organization in Kosovo, the OSCE, was explicit in stating that "[a]ll authorities in Kosovo, including SRSG and KFOR, are bound by the applicable law, including international human rights standards".[30] Thus, while ITA missions are eager to determine the human rights norms that limit the exercise of public power by local authorities, they remain vague regarding their own obligations in this respect.

4.1.1.3 Applicability of Human Rights Norms Through Treaties: Three Options

The added value of limits to the exercise of public power being imposed through treaties as opposed to the previously discussed options is twofold. Firstly, treaties encompass a broader range of guarantees than does international customary law, as the number of rights enjoying customary status is limited. Secondly, treaties generally come with enforcement mechanisms through which guaranteed rights could be effectuated. Applicability of human rights treaties could be argued in three distinct ways: accession of ITA missions to human rights treaties (as the ILA report suggested), the continued applicability of previously ratified human rights treaties and extraterritorial application of human rights treaties. The three approaches come with different legal challenges, all of which are discussed below.

Treaties and Accession

With respect to accession, it should be kept in mind that human rights treaties are essentially state-oriented and do not allow for international organizations to become signatories. For example, Article 59(1) ECHR states that the Treaty is only open to Council of Europe member states. Article 4 of the Statute of the Council of Europe reserves such membership for states only.[31] Similar constructions can be found in the American Convention on Human Rights and in

[29] HRCee, *Report Submitted by the United Nations Interim Administration Mission in Kosovo to the Human Rights Committee on the Human Rights Situation in Kosovo Since June 1999, Kosovo (Serbia and Montenegro)*, UN Doc. CCPR/C/UNK/1, 13 March 2006, §§ 123-124. UNMIK's attitude was criticized by NGOs, *see e.g.* AI, *Human rights protection in post-status Kosovo/Kosova: Amnesty International's recommendations relating to talks on the final status of Kosovo/Kosova*, EUR 70/008/2006, 24 July 2006, p. 8.

[30] OSCE Mission in Kosovo, *Review 1: The Criminal Justice System in Kosovo (February-July 2000)*, 10 August 2000, p. 19.

[31] Statute of the CoE, Chapter II, Art. 4.

the core international human rights treaties.[32] This also has an impact in terms of enforcement, as the jurisdiction of accompanying courts or oversight mechanisms is preconditioned by these provisions, making it impossible for entities such as UNMIK to appear before these bodies.

In the context of the ECHR, this obstacle has been solved with respect to the EU by the adoption of Protocol 14, although a similar solution for ITA missions has been considered unlikely, as it would necessitate the amendment of all relevant documents in response to a "transitional problem of limited duration"[33] although Council of Europe Rapporteur Lloyd has stated "extension of the jurisdiction of the Court to include acts and omissions of [UNMIK] remains an important eventual aim".[34]

From the perspective of UNMIK and UNTAET, respective constituent documents grant these entities the power to conclude international agreements and accede to international treaties necessary for the exercise of their mandate.[35] For example, UNMIK has concluded several bilateral trade agreements with, for instance Albania and Croatia, and signed multilateral treaties such as the Treaty establishing the Energy Community between EU and South Eastern Europe in 2005, the Central European Free Trade Agreement in 2006 and the European Common Aviation Area Agreement in 2006.[36] Likewise, UNTAET concluded a bilateral agreement with Australia relating to the demarcation of maritime zones and acted as a national government when it signed agreements with the World Bank.[37] With respect to human rights treaties, actual accession never took place.

Treaties and Automatic Succession

The second approach through which human rights treaties could offer protection to individuals and groups subject to international administration is by arguing

[32] American Convention on Human Rights, Part III, Chapter X, Art. 74(1). *See also* ICCPR, Part VI, Art. 48 and ICESCR, Part V, Art. 26.

[33] Venice Commission Kosovo Report, p. 19. *See also* Protocol No. 14 to the Convention for the Protection of Human Rights and Fundamental Freedoms, which entered into force on 31 May 2010.

[34] CoE, *Protection of human rights in Kosovo*, Report of the Committee on Legal Affairs and Human Rights, Doc. 10393, 6 January 2005, Section C(i), § 38.

[35] *Id.*, § 35. In practice, numerous treaties have been signed by the missions in the name of their respective territories.

[36] UNMIK, *Key agreements driving Kosovo's economic development*, at <http://www.unmikonline.org/archives/euinkosovo/upload/Regional%20integration%20Key%20agreements%20driving%20Kosovos%20economic%20development%20FINAL.pdf>.

[37] An exchange of Notes on 11 December 1989 constituting an Agreement between the Government of Australia and the United Nations Transitional Administration in East Timor – concerning the continued operation of the Treaty between Australia and the Republic of Indonesia on the Zone of Cooperation in an Area between the Indonesian Province of East Timor and Northern Australia – entered into force on 10 February 2000.

the treaties' continued applicability, either through the nominal sovereign or from the perspective of the individuals.

From the perspective of the nominal sovereign, ITA missions would be bound by the same obligations that bind the host state or bound it prior to the establishment of the ITA missions.[38] For example, in practice this would imply that the population of Kosovo enjoys the protection afforded by treaties to which Serbia (and previously the Federal Republic of Yugoslavia and the State Union of Serbia and Montenegro) as the nominal sovereign is a party. Such "automatic succession" is generally rejected.[39]

In this respect, the Venice Commission, for example, reasoned as follows. Serbia is a member of the Council of Europe and has ratified the ECHR. Pursuant to UN Security Council Resolution 1244 (1999), Serbia in principle does not exercise jurisdiction over Kosovo "within the meaning of Article 1 ECHR", making it impossible to hold Serbia accountable for human rights violations that cannot be attributed to it.[40] Instead, with respect to the local authorities in Kosovo, the population is protected by the ECHR by virtue of UNMIK Regulation 2001/9 – which declares the ECHR applicable to Kosovo's local authorities – rather than by Serbia's ratification of the convention.

The Venice Commission rejects along the same line of argumentation the notion that Serbia's ratification could result in obligations resting upon UNMIK.[41] Such a link, the Venice Commission argues, would imply that UN territorial administrations in general are bound by any pre-existing obligation to which the administered territory is subjected. The Venice Commission concluded that Article 103 of the UN Charter prevents such a proposition.[42] As Council of Europe Rapporteur Lloyd observed, this might be an overstatement of the issue as subjection to the ECHR would involve UNMIK rather than the

---

[38] *See also* Wilde (1998), where this type of applicability is considered as a minimum for UNHCR's governance of refugee camps. However, despite UNHCR's effective authority over the camps, the UNHCR undisputedly operates within the confines of the legal and constitutional system of the host-state.

[39] *E.g.* De Wet (2004), pp. 318-320.

[40] Venice Commission Kosovo Report, p. 17. The Venice Commission Kosovo Report adds, however, that Serbia remains responsible for violations committed by its organs which are still operating in the territory of Kosovo, in particular the parallel court system throughout the northern part of Kosovo. *See* on the topic of Kosovo's parallel court system Baylis E.A. (2007), 'Parallel Courts in Post-Conflict Kosovo', 32 *The Yale Journal of International Law*, pp. 1-59.

[41] CoE, *Protection of human rights in Kosovo*, Report of the Committee on Legal Affairs and Human Rights, Doc. 10393, 6 January 2005, Section C(i), § 33.

[42] The Venice Commission notes that this does not mean that action taken under Chapter VII are *legibus solutes*. However, limits should be derived from general international law rather than, for example, regional treaties.

UN.[43] UNMIK has also been persistent in rejecting any obligations emanating from treaties to which Serbia is a party.[44]

Automatic succession might also be argued from the perspective of the individual addressees of human rights treaties; once granted, individuals continue to enjoy human rights guarantees within a state regardless of subsequent governmental/constitutional changes. For example, the Human Rights Committee invoked this argument against UNMIK's refusal to be bound by the ICCPR through automatic succession:

> The rights enshrined in the Covenant belong to the people living in the territory of the State party. [Once] the people are accorded the protection of the rights of the Covenant, such protection devolves with territory and continues to belong to them, notwithstanding change in Government of the State party, including dismemberment in more than one State or State succession or any subsequent action of the State party designed to divest them of the rights guaranteed by the Covenant.[45]

Even if consensus existed in favour of the continued applicability of treaties, the related pitfalls should not be forgotten. Firstly, legal frameworks based on human rights treaties would be highly sensitive to context. For example, this would imply that UNMIK's exercise of public power would be governed by the ICCPR and ICESCR (based on the ratification by the Socialist Federative Republic of Yugoslavia in 1971), while the population of East Timor would be left without such protection (Indonesia only acceded in 2006). Instead, any potential use of pre-existing human rights obligations should be considered as a minimum standard of protection.[46] Secondly, the actual effectuation of guaranteed rights would remain problematic. Enforcement mechanisms, just like the human rights treaties to which they belong, are state-oriented and their application to non-state subjects is difficult. A tailored approach would be required in order to provide means through which guaranteed rights could be effectuated. Examples thereof are provided in Section 5.3.3 below.

---

[43] CoE, *Protection of human rights in Kosovo, Report of the Committee on Legal Affairs and Human Rights,* Doc. 10393, 6 January 2005, Section C (ii) (d), § 56.

[44] HRCee, *Report Submitted by the United Nations Interim Administration Mission in Kosovo to the Human Rights Committee on the Human Rights Situation in Kosovo Since June 1999, Kosovo (Serbia and Montenegro)*, UN Doc. CCPR/C/UNK/1, 13 March 2006, § 124.

[45] *See e.g.* HRCee, *General Comment 26, Continuity of Obligations*, UN Doc. A/53/40, Vol. 1, Ann. VII (1998), § 4.

[46] *See also* Stahn (2005)(3), p. 54, on an origin-neutral application of governance obligations.

Treaties and Extraterritorial Application

Thirdly, human rights protection might be construed through the extraterritorial application of human rights treaties. This type of application has been discussed most prominently in the context of military activities by states beyond their own borders. More in particular, circumstances such as the occupation of Iraq, Turkey's influence in the northern part of Cyprus and the military base in Guantánamo Bay triggered judicial bodies to pronounce on the issue. ECtHR decisions such as *Loizidou, Banković, Öcalan, Ilaşcu* and *Issa* reflect an ambiguous approach of the ECtHR towards extraterritorial applicability of the convention.[47] Decisions adopted under several other legal frameworks, such as the ICCPR and the American Convention on Human Rights, have further shaped the debate.[48] The relevant case law reveals several decisive factors in determining whether and to what extent treaty obligations can be applied beyond the borders of a contracting party. In the following sections, and with an emphasis on the developments under the ECHR-regime, the following factors are assessed from the perspective of ITA missions: attribution, jurisdiction and the issue of *espace juridique*. What becomes clear is that arguing for the extraterritorial applicability of human rights treaties in the ITA-context is *prima facie* appealing, but abounds in pitfalls.

A primary legal issue concerns attribution, as it is difficult to link the acts of the OHR or the SRSG to any particular state. A parallel can be drawn, in terms of attribution, with the situation concerning the detention of former 'deputy Führer' Rudolf Hess in the jointly administered Allied Military Prison in Berlin. A claim was filed against the United Kingdom alleging a violation of Articles 3 and 8 ECHR. In principle, extraterritorial application was accepted in *Hess*:

> there is in principle, from a legal point of view, no reason why acts of the British authorities in Berlin should not entail the liability of the United Kingdom under the Convention.[49]

[47] ECtHR: *Loizidou v. Turkey* (Preliminary Objections), No. 15318/89, 23 March 1995 (*Loizidou*); *Banković et al. v. Belgium and 16 Other Contracting States*, No. 52207/99, Grand Chamber, Decision on Admissibility, 12 December 2001 (*Banković*); *Öcalan v. Turkey*, No. 46221/99, Grand Chamber, 12 May 2005 (*Öcalan*); *Ilaşcu et al. v. Moldova and Russia*, No. 48787/99, 8 July 2004 (*Ilaşcu*); *Issa et al. v. Turkey*, No. 31821/96, 16 November 2004 (*Issa*).

[48] *See e.g.* Coomans F. & Kamminga M. (2004), *Extraterritorial Application of Human Rights Treaties*, Antwerp: Intersentia, pp. 141-183 for views on the extraterritorial application within the inter-American human rights protection system.

[49] European Commission on Human Rights (ECommHR), *Ilse Hess v. United Kingdom*, No. 6231/73, Decision on Admissibility, 28 May 1975 (*Ilse Hess*).

However, in this particular case, it was concluded that the administration of the prison was "at all times quadripartite". It was held that "the United Kingdom acts only as a partner in the joint responsibility" and that "the joint authority cannot be divided into four separate jurisdictions".[50] Also with respect to ITA missions, attribution proved to be the deal-breaker. In *Behrami* and several other ITA-related decisions, discussed in Section 5.3.2.1 below, the ECtHR decidedly channeled attribution towards the UN instead of the participating states, thereby barring itself from hearing this and similar cases *ratione personae.*[51]

This seems to be in contrast to the approach adopted by the Human Rights Committee under the ICCPR. In principle, extraterritorial effect was accepted in *Saldias de López v. Uruguay.*[52] The Human Rights Committee specified that contracting states remain under their obligations even in the context of peacekeeping operations.[53] In *Kurbogaj v. Spain*, this view was later confirmed in the ITA context.[54]

A second point of attention relates to the fact that human rights provide guarantees to people falling under the jurisdiction of the contracting parties. For example, Article 1 ECHR determines that the "High Contracting Parties shall secure to everyone within their jurisdiction the rights and freedoms defined in Section I of this Convention". A similar provision is found in Article 2 of the

[50] *Id.*

[51] ECtHR, *Behrami.*

[52] HRCee, *Delia Saldias de Lopez v. Uruguay*, Communication No. 052/1979, View, UN Doc. CCPR/C/OP/1, p. 88 (1984), 29 July 1981, §§ 12.1 and 12.2: "12. I The Human Rights Committee further observes that although the arrest and initial detention and mistreatment of Lopez Burgos allegedly took place on foreign territory, the Committee is not barred either by virtue of article 1 of the Optional Protocol ("... individuals subject to its jurisdiction ...") or by virtue of article 2 (1) of the Covenant ("... individuals within its territory and subject to its jurisdiction ...") from considering these allegations, together with the claim of subsequent abduction into Uruguayan territory, inasmuch as these acts were perpetrated by Uruguayan agents acting on foreign soil. 12.2 The reference in article 1 of the Optional Protocol to "individuals subject to its jurisdiction" does not affect the above conclusion because the reference in that article is not to the place where the violation occurred, but rather to the relationship between the individual and the State in relation to a violation of any of the rights set forth in the Covenant, wherever they occurred".

[53] The HRCee clarified: "States Parties are required [...] to respect and to ensure the Covenant rights to [...] anyone within the power or effective control of that State Party, even if not situated within the territory of the State Party. [...] This principle also applies to those within the power or effective control of the forces of a State Party acting outside its territory, regardless of the circumstances in which such power or effective control was obtained, *such as forces constituting a national contingent of a State Party assigned to an international peace-keeping or peace-enforcement operation*", *see* HRCee, *General Comment 31 [80] on The Nature of the General Legal Obligation Imposed on States Parties to the Covenant*, UN Doc. CCPR/C/21/Rev.1/Add.13, 29 March 2004, § 10, emphasis added.

[54] HRCee, *Kurbogaj and Kurbogaj v. Spain*, Communication No. 1374/2005, Decision on Admissibility, UN Doc. CCPR/C/87/D/1374/2005, 14 July 2006, discussed further in Section 5.3.2.1 below.

ICCPR, which states, "Each State Party [...] undertakes to respect and to ensure to all individuals within its territory and subject to its jurisdiction the rights recognized in the present Covenant". Whether an act or omission is considered to have taken place under the jurisdiction of a contracting party needs to be determined on a case-by-case basis.

The decisive factor in this respect can be distilled from *Loizidou,* where the Turkish influence in the northern part of Cyprus was addressed. Here, the ECtHR held that there needs to be effective control – whether over a territory or a person – for the applicant to be under the jurisdiction of the contracting party against which a complaint is filed.[55] The territorial dimension of this approach implies that once effective control is found to exist, the party that holds control is not only responsible for its own actions but also for the actions of any subordinated bodies exercising public powers:

> [t]he obligation to secure, in such an area, the rights and freedoms set out in the Convention derives from the fact of such control whether it be exercised directly, through its armed forces, *or through a subordinate local administration.*[56]

How this second factor has played out in the ITA context will be discussed in the subsequent chapter when the particular accountability mechanisms are discussed.[57] Suffice it to say that effective control over administered territories is apparent. Furthermore, applying the previous reasoning implies that international administrations are not only responsible for their own acts but also for the acts of the local administrations. This is important because over time, local administrations established under UNMIK and UNTAET gained considerable authority to exercise public power. However, the effective control of ITA missions has not been attributed to any particular contracting party, at least not by the ECtHR, but to the international organization, rendering the relevant applications inadmissible.[58]

---

[55] ECtHR, *Loizidou*, § 62: "Bearing in mind the object and purpose of the Convention, the responsibility of a Contracting Party may also arise when as a consequence of military action – whether lawful or unlawful – it exercises effective control of an area outside its national territory".

[56] *Id.*, emphasis added. In *Cyprus v. Turkey*, where the court also considered the situation in the northern part of Cyprus, the argument was restated: "Having effective overall control over northern Cyprus, [Turkey's] responsibility cannot be confined to the acts of its own soldiers or officials in northern Cyprus but must also be engaged by virtue of the acts of the local administration which survives by virtue of Turkish military and other support", *see* ECtHR, *Cyprus v. Turkey*, No. 25781/94, 10 May 2001, § 77 (*Cyprus v. Turkey*).

[57] *See* Sections 5.3.2 and 5.3.3 below.

[58] ECtHR, *Behrami*.

Finally, the rationale behind regional human rights treaties has surfaced as a relevant factor in the context of extraterritorial application, despite the fact that case law remains ambiguous in this respect. In *Cyprus v. Turkey,* the ECtHR held that:

> Having regard to [Cyprus'] continuing inability to exercise their Convention obligations in northern Cyprus, any other finding [than extending Turkey's jurisdiction beyond its borders] would result in *a regrettable vacuum* in the system of human-rights protection in the territory in question by removing from individuals there the benefit of the Convention's fundamental safeguards and their right to call a High Contracting Party to account for violation of their rights in proceedings before the Court.[59]

The Court seemingly narrowed the scope of its reasoning in *Banković* by arguing that this rationale relates primarily to territories that previously fell within the ambit *i.e.* within the *espace juridique* of the ECHR. In 1999, NATO forces bombed the main building of Serbia's national broadcaster RTS in Belgrade, killing 16 persons. At the time, the Federal Republic of Yugoslavia was not party to the ECHR. In the admissibility decision, the Court stated:

> It is true that, in its above-cited *Cyprus v. Turkey* judgment (at para. 78), the Court was conscious of the need to avoid "a regrettable vacuum in the system of human-rights protection" in northern Cyprus. However, and as noted by the Governments, that comment related to an entirely different situation to the present: the inhabitants of northern Cyprus would have found themselves excluded from the benefits of the Convention safeguards and system which they had previously enjoyed, by Turkey's "effective control" of the territory and by the accompanying inability of the Cypriot Government, as a Contracting State, to fulfil the obligations it had undertaken under the Convention.[60]

The standalone nature of *Banković* was subsequently illustrated in *Issa* and *Öcalan,* where the *espace juridique* argument was not employed with respect to Turkish activities in Iraq and Kenya.[61] The ECtHR has thus far not employed the *sepace juridique*-argument in cases related to ITA missions, due to the fact that the applications were declared inadmissible on other grounds.

---

[59] ECtHR, *Cyprus v. Turkey*, § 78, emphasis added.
[60] ECtHR, *Banković*, § 80.
[61] ECtHR, *Issa* and *Öcalan*.

In sum, extraterritorial application is accepted in principle by various courts and oversight bodies.[62] Effectuating these rights proves difficult. As ECtHR case law illustrates, attribution is largely channeled towards the UN instead of state parties, rendering incoming application inadmissible. Thereby, the Court effectively anchored the same legal vacuum it had previously pledged to prevent when it considered the situation in the northern part of Cyprus.

To conclude the section on international law, it can be stated that the law on peacekeeping does not regulate the scope of activities of ITA missions while the applicability of the law of occupation should be rejected on the basis of conceptual differences between ITA missions and occupying powers. As it stands, the role of international human rights law in framing the exercise of public power is nominally recognize but weakly institutionalized. Effectuating these rights becomes difficult, as the operative human rights legal frameworks as well as their oversight mechanisms are state-oriented and by and large exclude international organizations from membership. Finally, a problem with alternative ways through which treaty-based human rights law could be applied to ITA situations is the context-sensitive nature of these approaches. On the one hand, if human rights standards were to be imposed on ITA missions through automatic succession, human rights protection would be dependent on the relationship between ITA 'host states' and the human rights treaties. On the other hand, if human rights standards were to apply through extraterritorial application, the applicable human rights framework would depend on the treaties to which each particular ITA-contributing state is a party, thus adding to legal uncertainty and fragmentation.

4.1.2 DOMESTIC LAW: UNEQUIPPED

Domestic law has a weak potential in terms of functioning as a legal framework that would regulate and confine the exercise of public power by ITA missions. The reason for this becomes apparent through a preliminary consideration relating to the prefix 'domestic' in the ITA context. Under international administration, domestic law is a tapestry of various bodies of law, both local and international. The content and structure of domestic law is determined by the international administration: namely, international regulations are part and parcel of the domestic legal order while the international administrator has the prerogative to amend or repeal locally adopted legislation. Indeed, the contrary would lead to a conceptual dilemma: if ITA missions were to be embedded in domestic law, it would be difficult to qualify the missions as international administrations to begin with. The process of deciding on locally applicable law

[62] Coomans & Kamminga (2004), p. 3.

is first briefly assessed in order to explain the peculiar meaning of 'domestic' in the present context. Subsequently, the weaknesses of domestic law as a legal framework are discussed.

4.1.2.1 Decrypting the 'Domestic' in Domestic Law

The (re-)establishment of a local legal order, *i.e.* the (re-)introduction of the rule of law enjoys highest priority amongst the aims of ITA missions.[63] However, no pre-existing set of transitional rules is available that could be declared applicable by an ITA-mission. As ITA missions govern different territories and under different conditions, it is indeed hard to imagine a pre-set body of rules that would suit all circumstances.

The present ad hoc shaping of a legal order has proven to be challenging and at times controversial. ITA missions decide on the applicable law immediately upon their establishment. This body of applicable law consists of ITA regulations and existing local laws as far as these laws are not discriminatory or in any other way inconsistent with specified human rights standards and the ITA regulations.[64] In addition, with regard to the legislative activities subsequently carried out by local authorities, international administrations retain crucial prerogatives. These prerogatives may include the duty to promulgate locally adopted laws and the power to repeal local laws that are deemed incompatible with ITA regulations, human rights standards or relevant UN Security Council resolutions.[65]

The determination of applicable law is crucial for the local judicial system to be able to function properly. In the case of BiH, the Dayton Peace Agreement established the OHR and promulgated the Bosnian Constitution simultaneously. As the supreme law, the constitution included transitional provisions determining the applicable law. In UN-led missions, the process is different. In East Timor, UNTAET decided on the applicable law in its first regulation, while UNMIK reached a final decision on the applicable law in Kosovo in late 2000.[66]

---

[63] Recall that from a conceptual standpoint this prerogative is one of the most notable differences between ITA and military occupation, *see* Section 4.1.1 above.

[64] In *Kosovo*, the ICJ held that UNMIK regulations are part of international law, since they derive their binding force from Chapter VII-based SC Res. 1244 (1999), *see* ICJ, *Kosovo*, §§ 88-93.

[65] *See e.g.* Irmscher (2001), p. 357, where Irmscher qualifies the legislative powers of the SRSG as seemingly "absolute, both with regard to the content and to the law-making process".

[66] For East Timor, *see* UNTAET Reg. 1999/1, Sections 2 and 3. Section 3, § 3.1. reads: "Until replaced by UNTAET regulations or subsequent legislation of democratically established institutions of East Timor, the laws applied in East Timor prior to 25 October 1999 shall apply in East Timor insofar as they do not conflict with the standards referred to in Section 2, the fulfillment of the mandate given to UNTAET under United Nations Security Council

UNMIK's initial attempt to decide on the applicable law revealed a lack of preparation and sparked criticism amongst the local judiciary. UNMIK Reg. 1999/1 acknowledged the continuity of existing laws except for the laws that were deemed discriminatory in nature.[67] This unfortunate choice effectively reaffirmed the legal system as it was shaped under the previous regime.[68] Immediately, the local judiciary announced it would not apply the controversial laws.[69] Consequently, UNMIK amended Regulation 1999/1 by adopting a more context-sensitive legal regime through Regulations 1999/24 and 2000/59. The complexity of domestic law structures in the ITA context is best illustrated by the following scheme, depicting the legal order of Kosovo after the local authorities – Provisional Institutions of Self-Government (PISG) – were established.

resolution 1272 (1999), or the present or any other regulation and directive issued by the Transitional Administrator". In addition, UNTAET Reg. 1999/1, Section 3, § 3.2 explicitly declared several laws void. For Kosovo, *see* UNMIK Reg. 1999/1, Sections 2 and 3, Section 3 as repealed by UNMIK Reg. 1999/25, 12 December 1999 and replaced by UNMIK Reg. 1999/24, 12 December 1999, as amended by UNMIK Reg. 2000/59, 27 October 2000. Section 1, § 1.1 reads: "The law applicable in Kosovo shall be: (a) The regulations promulgated by the Special Representative of the Secretary-General and subsidiary instruments issued thereunder; and (b) The law in force in Kosovo on 22 March 1989. In case of a conflict, the regulations and subsidiary instruments issued thereunder shall take precedence" and § 1.2: "If a court of competent jurisdiction or a body or person required to implement a provision of the law, determines that a subject matter or situation is not covered by the laws set out in Section 1.1 of the present regulation but is covered by another law in force in Kosovo after 22 March 1989 which is not discriminatory and which complies with Section 1.3 of the present regulation, the court, body or person shall, as an exception, apply that law". Despite differences on the ground, the same human rights documents were listed in the regulations. UNTAET Reg. 1999/1, Section 2: "The Universal Declaration on Human Rights of 10 December 1948; The International Covenant on Civil and Political Rights of 16 December 1966 and its Protocols; The International Covenant on Economic, Social and Cultural Rights of 16 December 1966; The Convention on the Elimination of All Forms of Racial Discrimination of 21 December 1965; The Convention on the Elimination of All Forms of Discrimination Against Women of 17 December 1979; The Convention Against Torture and other Cruel, Inhumane or Degrading Treatment or Punishment of 17 December 1984; The International Convention on the Rights of the Child of 20 November 1989". UNMIK Reg. 1999/24 and UNMIK Reg. 2000/59, Section 1, § 1.3(b) adds "The European Convention for the Protection of Human Rights and Fundamental Freedoms of 4 November 1950 and the Protocols thereto".

[67] UNMIK Reg. 1999/1, Section 3.

[68] The initial UNMIK Reg. 1999/1 also omitted to specify explicitly the supreme status of all future UNMIK regulations.

[69] *E.g.* Berman N. (2006), 'Intervention in a 'Divided World': Axes of Legitimacy', 17(4) *European Journal of International Law*, pp. 743-769. *See also* United States Institute of Peace, *International Judges and Prosecutors in Kosovo*, Special Report, October 2003.

Figure 2: Applicable law in Kosovo under UNMIK

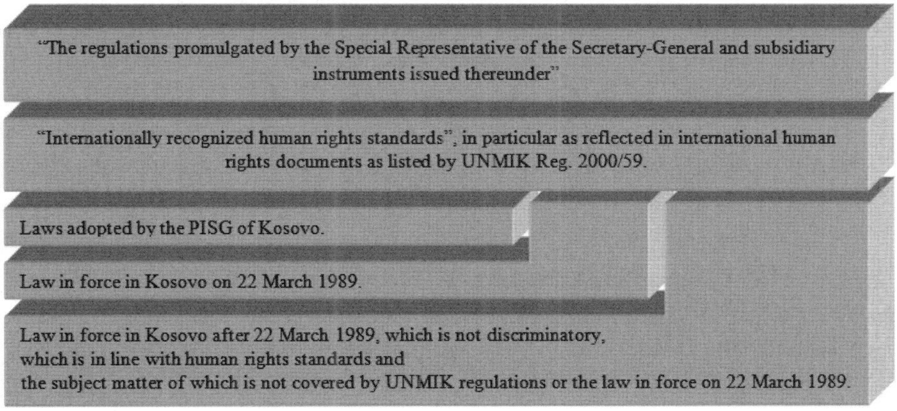

Though UNMIK's amendments showed that the administration was sensitive to public dismay, the established legal order was criticized for being overly complex and impossible for the local judiciary to apply.[70] For example, the Council of Europe's European Commission for Democracy Through Law (Venice Commission) observed in its comprehensive "Opinion on Human Rights in Kosovo: Possible Establishment of Review Mechanisms" (Venice Commission Kosovo Report) that the established system does not always provide "a clear indication of which laws are superseded and which remain in force".[71] With respect to ITA missions in general, the *Brahimi* Report reaches a similar conclusion and observes that an interim legal code would help to overcome at least some of the problems arising from the present method of deciding on the applicable law. A "common United Nations justice package" would be predetermined and could be applied upon establishment of the mission.[72]

[70] *See e.g.* CoE, *Protection of human rights in Kosovo*, Report of the Committee on Legal Affairs and Human Rights, Doc. 10393, 6 January 2005 and HRCee, *Consideration of Reports Submitted by States Parties Under Article 40 of the Covenant, Concluding observation of the Human Rights Committee, Kosovo (Serbia)*, 87th Session, UN Doc. CCPR/C/UNK/CO/1, 14 August 2006, § 8.

[71] Venice Commission Kosovo Report, § 57.

[72] *Brahimi* report, §§ 79-82.

> The supremacy of international administrators generally relates to the whole corpus of domestic law. In Bosnia and Herzegovina, the situation is somewhat exceptional as the constitution itself is an internationally adopted document. The Dayton Peace Agreement created the Bosnian Constitution and established the OHR in one breath. However, it leaves unanswered the question as to whether the Constitution falls within the ambit of the High Representative's authority. In 1996, lawyers discovered a reference mistake in the Constitution. Carl Bildt, at the time High Representative, suggested that he could correct the error based on his powers ex Annex 10 to the Dayton Peace Agreement. This view was rejected by the US Secretary of State, who argued that the Constitution was beyond the reach of the High Representative. The error was nevertheless corrected informally; the Presidency of Bosnia and Herzegovina was informed and a new version of the Constitution was published. Save for this incident, the OHR has consistently maintained the view that the state Constitution does not fall within the purview of the High Representative. Constitutions of the entities in Bosnia and Herzegovina have been amended extensively by the High Representative.
>
> ECtHR, *Sejdić and Finci v. Bosnia and Herzegovina*, No. 27996/06 & 34836/06, Grand Chamber, Judgment, 22 December 2009, §§ 17.

4.1.2.2 The Weakness of 'Domestic' Law as a Legal Framework

Keeping in mind the peculiar nature of the domestic legal order, this section now returns to the question of whether domestic law can serve as a limit to the exercise of public power by ITA missions. The supremacy of international regulations over domestic law allows for the discussion to be brief. Domestic law is decided on and can be amended by ITA missions and can therefore, under the present circumstances, hardly serve as a real limitation to the ITA mandate.

On paper, (pre-existing) domestic law is awarded some guiding value with regard to the way in which the international administration is to exercise its mandate. For example, in a report to the Security Council dealing with the authority of UNMIK, the Secretary-General stated that "UNMIK will respect the laws of [Serbia]" provided they do not conflict with human rights norms or UNMIK regulations.[73] However, ITA practice provides little or no evidence that domestic law of the 'host state' has ever played a significant role in ITA decision-making.[74]

[73] *Report of the UN SG on UNMIK*, UN Doc. S/1999/779, 12 July 1999, § 36.

[74] However, at times local decision-making has influenced the way in which an ITA mandate is carried out. In 2001, the Federal Republic of Yugoslavia and neighbouring Macedonia concluded a border demarcation agreement. The border amendment resulted in the transfer of Kosovo territory to Macedonia. At first, UNMIK dismissed the agreement as immaterial. However, following a positive statement made by the Security Council, the SRSG accepted that "the border agreement between FYROM and the Federal Republic of Yugoslavia, signed in February 2001, must be respected". Although the bilateral agreement is not a local law, it is nevertheless a product of the local decision-making process. *See* Statement of the Security Council, *Condemnation of violence in Former Yugoslav Republic of Macedonia*, UN Doc.

Domestic law does provide a basis for claims made with respect to allegations of misconduct. Such claims are based on the applicability of domestic law to the international presence. For example, pursuant to UNMIK Reg. 2000/47,

> UNMIK personnel shall respect the laws applicable in the territory of Kosovo and regulations issued by the Special Representative of the Secretary-General, in the fulfilment of the mandate given to UNMIK by Security Council resolution 1244 (1999). They shall refrain from any action or activity incompatible therewith.[75]

Recall that with respect to the Roma lead-poisoning drama, criminal complaints were filed at the local level alleging violations of the Provisional Criminal Code of Kosovo.[76] In another example, local lawyers in Priština argued that UNMIK executive orders dealing with individual detentions breach the Yugoslav and Kosovo criminal procedure codes.[77] These attempts were in vain. Jurisdictional immunity makes it impossible to assess the actual effects of domestic law being employed as the basis of criminal complaints against members of ITA missions. Thus, the potential of domestic law in this sense is dependent on the waiver of immunity, discussed in Section 4.2 below. The situation in BiH is similar. Enjoying the status of a diplomatic mission, the OHR is legally bound by the laws of BiH. Nevertheless, jurisdictional immunity prevents the limits provided for by domestic law from actually being effectuated.

Finally, domestic law has on occasion been called upon in order to frame the powers of international administrations in a more robust manner. The 1994 EU Administration of Mostar (EUAM), a confined *sui generis* ITA mission, had to exercise its powers in accordance with the constitution of the Federation of BiH. Pursuant to Articles 2 and 7.2 of the Memorandum governing the EUAM, the administration of Mostar was placed within the ambit of the constitution rather than above it.[78] The fact remains that *in casu,* the EU was administering a city within a state rather than a whole territory, making the EUAM more suitable for such an operational choice.

S/PRST/2001/7, 7 March 2001 and UNMIK, *SRSG Steiner meets FYROM President Trajkovski*, Press Release, 18 March 2002.

[75] UNMIK Reg. 2000/47, 18 August 2000, Section 3.5.

[76] The complaint was filed on 31 August 2005. The local criminal code was adopted by means of UNMIK Reg. 2003/25, 6 July 2003, as amended.

[77] *E.g.* IWPR, *Kosovo: Court Overturns Haekkerup Detention Orders*, 11 January 2002.

[78] *See* Section 5.1.3 below.

4.1.3 SUMMARY

The exercise of public powers by ITA missions is currently neither embedded in nor regulated by a coherent legal framework. Rather, the legal playing field is improvised and determined by the fact that ITA missions continue to be perceived as parts of international organizations rather than state-like entities.

Under these circumstances, it is nearly impossible to uphold the rule of law in a meaningful way. International law currently fails to provide a clear set of obligations that would curb the mandate of ITA missions. Likewise, the UN Charter and the constitutive resolutions of individual ITA missions remain abstract in this respect. Finally, the absolute supremacy of the ITA-regulatory framework over domestic law prevents domestic law from serving as a substantive framework for the exercise of public power by ITA missions. To the extent ITA missions are obliged to respect domestic law, jurisdictional immunity by and large prevents domestic law from being effectuated.

No ITA mission will argue that it does not respect certain legal standards, especially those dealing with human rights. Commitment to these standards is expressed throughout UN reports and press statements, but it amounts to no more than statements of good faith. As the Council of Europe pointedly remarked with respect to UNMIK:

> UN Security Council Resolution 1244 is, in fact, the only text which binds UNMIK, and it sets out the latter's role in very broad terms which concentrate on political and administrative responsibilities. Human rights are mentioned only once in this document, where one of the "main responsibilities" of UNMIK is stated to be "protecting and promoting human rights".[79]

The question is posed as to whether such a nominal adherence to basic human rights norms is sufficient. It is argued that it is not. Rather, a state-parallel should be made. More precisely, this state-parallel already exists in terms of mandate and should be extended to the issue of applicable law. With respect to states, adherence to human rights norms by governing authorities is no longer acceptable in name only. At the international level, states by and large commit themselves through various treaties and auxiliary mechanisms. Explicit commitments to basic human rights standards, and the institutionalization of these commitments by ITA missions, are currently lacking. Without clearly applicable standards and institutionalized compliance mechanisms, upholding the rule of law remains problematic.

---

[79] CoE, *Protection of human rights in Kosovo,* Report of the Committee on Legal Affairs and Human Rights, Doc. 10393, 6 January 2005, Section B(i), § 5.

4.2 EXTENSIVE IMMUNITY

In addition to an unclear legal framework, the second determinant of the ITA accountability deficit is grounded in the fact that ITA missions enjoy virtually absolute immunity. More in particular, while exercising state-like powers, ITA missions hold on to a notion of immunity conceived through an international organizations-oriented mindset. In terms of public law, the main consequence thereof is that judicial review is made virtually impossible. Firstly, Section 4.2.1 introduces in brief the uneasy relationship between immunity of international organizations and human rights. Section 4.2.2 then explores to what extent this friction can be mitigated. The possibility for immunity to be waived is discussed, together with the increased engagement of courts in assessing the validity of immunities. Finally, Section 4.2.3 addresses how immunity translates to the ITA-context and consequently adds to the accountability deficit.

4.2.1 IMMUNITY AND HUMAN RIGHTS: FRICTION

Focusing on the UN, immunity is primarily governed by the Convention on Privileges and Immunities of the United Nations (General Convention), which builds on the immunity provided to the UN by Article 105 of the Charter. Article II, Section 2 of the General Convention grants the UN "immunity from every form of legal process".[80] The convention is generally considered to be directly applicable within domestic legal orders and is sometimes refined through the adoption of national legislation.[81] In terms of rationale, immunity is considered to be an indispensable shield against "unilateral interference by individual governments".[82] This jurisdictional immunity of the UN is grounded in functional necessity, granting the organization "such privileges and immunities as are necessary for the fulfillment of its purposes".[83] However, the provisions in the General Convention are interpreted widely so as to confer absolute immunity on the UN and its subsidiary bodies.[84]

This extensive conception of immunity gives rise to friction from the perspective of human rights law. This friction essentially occurs along the

---

[80] General Convention, Art. II, Section 2.

[81] *E.g.* International Organizations Immunities Act, 29 December 1945, 59 Stat. 669.

[82] ECtHR, *Waite and Kennedy v. Germany*, No. 26083/94, 18 February 1999, § 63 (*Waite and Kennedy*).

[83] General Convention, preamble.

[84] Reinisch A. & Weber U.A. (2004), 'In the Shadow of Waite and Kennedy. The Jurisdictional Immunity of International Organizations, the Individual's Right of access to the Courts and Administrative Tribunals as Alternative Means of Dispute Settlement', 1 *International Organizations Law Review*, p. 60, n. 5, quoting the UN Office of Legal Affairs.

following lines. In the exercise of their mandate, international organizations affect individuals. Occasionally, this leads to allegations of human rights violations. Because of the jurisdictional immunity, individuals in search of recourse and redress are prevented from having their claims heard before a court or tribunal.

The human rights implications of this conundrum are twofold. Firstly, an absolute conception of jurisdictional immunity arguably leads to a breach of the right to an effective remedy (guaranteed by, for example, Article 2(3) ICCPR and Article 13 ECHR).[85] Secondly, by denying individuals the opportunity to seek recourse and redress, alleged breaches of human rights norms are left unsanctioned. In other words, effectuating guaranteed rights becomes impossible. In order to mitigate this situation, immunity can be waived. Furthermore, courts are increasingly adopting a human rights approach in dealing with the immunity of international organizations. Both implications are discussed below.

4.2.2 IMMUNITY AND HUMAN RIGHTS: WAIVER AND THE *SOLANGE* APPROACH

The General Convention provides for immunity to be waived.[86] The decision on whether immunity should be waived is taken, on a case-by-case basis, by the Secretary-General who has the "right and the duty to waive immunity of any official in any case where, in his opinion, the immunity would impede the course of justice".[87] As immunity is functional in nature, the decision is twofold. Firstly, does immunity apply in a given case? In the *Difference Relating to Immunity from Legal Process of a Special Rapporteur of the Commission on Human Rights* (*Cumaraswamy*) opinion, the ICJ confirmed that the Secretary-General holds the "primary" role in deciding whether an act falls within the

[85] Here, the right to an effective remedy should be understood in a broad sense, related to such adjacent rights dealing with the access to court and fair trial. *See e.g.* the Universal Declaration on Human Rights (Art. 10), the ICCPR (Art. 14) as well as regional documents such as the American Convention on Human Rights (Art. 8) and the ECHR (Art. 6). The right to access to court is implied in these documents and has been recognized by the ECtHR as implicit to Art. 6 ECHR in *Waite and Kennedy*, § 50 in reference to the court's previous case law. Although ECtHR case law recognizes that these rights can be restricted by immunity, this restriction needs to pursue a legitimate aim and has to be proportionate, *see* ECtHR, *Al-Adsani v. the United Kingdom*, No. 35763/97, 21 November 2001, §§ 52-67 (*Al-Adsani*). *See also e.g.* Francesco F. (ed.) (2007), *Access to justice as a human right*, Oxford: Oxford University Press; Koopmans (2003), pp. 233-239.

[86] General Convention, Art. II, Section 2.

[87] *Id.*, Sections 20 and 23.

scope of the performance of a mandate.[88] A local court, faced with a case involving immunity, can reverse the Secretary-General's decision on this matter. According to the ICJ, setting aside the Secretary-General's decision is only justified "for the most compelling reasons".[89] Secondly, if immunity applies, should it be waived? With respect to this decision, the responsibility lies solely with the Secretary-General.

A network of internal investigation mechanisms assists the Secretary-General in reaching a well-informed decision on whether to waive immunity.[90] Although internal oversight procedures focus primarily on traditional peacekeeping, they apply to UN personnel in general. Allegations of misconduct are investigated under the auspices of the UN Office of Internal Oversight (OIOS), usually by way of ad hoc and locally established boards of inquiry.[91] When it comes to UN missions, the boards make a recommendation with regard to waiver and possible repatriation to the head of mission, usually the SRSG, which recommendation is then passed on to the Secretary-General for consideration.[92] If immunity is waived, disciplinary measures can then be taken by the Office of Human Resources Management while additional judicial steps can be taken by the sending state upon repatriation.

With regard to the military components of peacekeeping missions, the OIOS holds a complementary position as military personnel remains under the primary jurisdiction of the troop-contributing country. Cooperation in investigations is regulated through memoranda of understanding between the OIOS and particular troop-contributing states. Immunity of military personnel with regard to local jurisdictions is furthermore governed by Status of Forces agreements.[93]

If a waiver is not granted, the General Convention calls for alternative dispute settlement mechanisms to be established.[94] At the UN level, various options have been considered in order to establish an organization-wide alternative mechanism, amongst others the establishment of a UN

[88] ICJ, *Difference Relating to Immunity from Legal Process of a Special Rapporteur of the Commission on Human Rights*, Advisory Opinion, 29 April 1999, §§ 50-61 (*Cumaraswamy*).
[89] *Id.*
[90] Internal oversight mechanisms are discussed in paragraph 5.1.2 below. *See also e.g.* Report of the Sixth Committee, *Criminal accountability of United Nations officials and experts on mission*, 64th Session, UN Doc. A/64/446, 12 November 2009 and also older documents such as Report of the UN SG, *Implementation of the recommendations of the Special Committee on Peacekeeping Operations*, 54th Session, UN Doc. A/54/670, 6 January 2000.
[91] *See* OIOS Investigations Manual, 2009, at <http://www.un.org/depts/oios/pages/id_manual_mar2009.pdf>.
[92] Report of the UN SG, *Implementation of the recommendations of the Special Committee on Peacekeeping Operations*, 54th Session, UN Doc. A/54/670, 6 January 2000, § 16.
[93] *See* further Section 5.1.2 below.
[94] General Convention, Art. VIII, Section 29.

Ombudsperson.[95] The requirement to establish alternative dispute settlement procedures has not only sparked calls for reform within the UN. In general, the existence of alternative mechanisms – or lack thereof – has been the driving force behind a developing line of reasoning used by courts and tribunals to deal with the immunity of international organizations. According to this approach, courts have jurisdiction over international organizations in the field of human rights protection as long as these organizations do not provide for a level of human rights protection equivalent to that of the legal order within which the court dealing with the case operates. This means that the validity of the immunity-defence will depend on the availability of alternative mechanisms through which disputes can be resolved *i.e.* human rights can be protected.[96]

The German *Bundesverfassungsgericht* developed the approach in its famed *Solange*-judgments.[97] In the last of three judgments, the *Bundesverfassungsgericht* restated in relation to the European Community that:

> Acts done under a special power, separate from national powers of Member States, exercised by a *supra*-national organization also affect the holders of basic rights in Germany. They therefore affect the guarantees of the Constitution and the duties of the Constitutional Court, the object of which is the protection of constitutional rights in Germany – in this respect not merely as against German state bodies.[98]

National courts from various jurisdictions took up this approach.[99] This reasoning was also upheld at the international level. The ECtHR held in *Waite and Kennedy* that:

95 *E.g.* Mégret & Hoffmann (2005), pp. 43-63.

96 Reinisch & Weber, in assessing several such alternative mechanisms provided by international organizations, conclude that in general they fall short of respecting many of the standards generally associated with fair trial, *see* Reinisch and Weber (2004), pp. 109-110.

97 Germany, Federal Constitutional Court, *Internationale Handelsgesellschaft mbH v. Einfuhr- und Vorratsstelle für Getreide und Futtermittel*, 37 BVerfGE 271, 29 May 1974 in 2 *Common Market Law Review* 540 (*Solange I*); *Re application of Wünsche Handelsgesellschaft*, 73 BVerfGE 339, 22 October 1986 in 3 *Common Market Law Review 225* (*Solange II*) and *Brunner et al. v. The European Union Treaty*, 89 BVerfGE 155, 12 October 1993 in 1 *Common Market Law Review* 57 (*Solange III*). The same approach was adopted at the international level, *e.g.* ECommHR, *Melchers & Co. v. Federal Republic of Germany*, No. 13258/77, 9 February 1990, 64 Decisions and Reports, p. 138. 12 October 1993 (*Melchers*).

98 Germany, Federal Constitutional Court, *Solange III*, in 1 *Common Market Law Review* 57, p. 253.

99 A cursory analysis of the case law provided by the Oxford Reports on International Law shows that courts from different jurisdictions have been balancing the immunity of international organizations against the right to access to court. For example, In Denmark, the

> a material factor in determining whether granting [the European Space Agency] immunity from German jurisdiction is permissible under the [ECHR] is whether the applicants had available to them reasonable alternative means to protect effectively their rights under the Convention.[100]

In two other decisions, *Bosphorus* and *Kadi I,* the ECtHR and the European Court of Justice, respectively, embraced similar lines of reasoning.[101] In *Bosphorus,* the ECtHR anchored the 'equivalent protection' approach to situations where immunity from jurisdiction of international organizations might prevent cases from being heard. The European Court of Justice took a similar approach in *Kadi I.* Here the Court had to pronounce on a Council (of the European Union) Regulation which gave effect to 'smart sanctions' imposed by the Security Council.[102] The Court considered that the existing review mechanism at Security Council level was insufficient, as the re-examination procedure of the Sanctions Committee "clearly [...] does not offer the guarantees of judicial protection". [103] For this reason, the Court held that "in principle the full review" of lawfulness (of Community acts) should be ensured by the Court.[104]

In sum, courts increasingly engage in a balancing act in which they consider whether upholding the jurisdictional immunity of an international organization

---

alternative dispute settlement requirement from the General Convention was referred to when, *ex officio,* the Danish court engaged in an assessment of the immunity of UNICEF, *see* Denmark, Court of Second Instance for the Eastern Circuit (Østre Landsret), sitting as a court of first instance, Case No U 2000 478 Ø, *Investerings- & Finansieringsselskabet af 11/1 1984 ApS v. UNICEF*, ILDC 64 (DK 1999), 26 August 1999. A Belgian court also decided that the balancing act applied to the immunity from execution, *see* Belgium, Brussels Court of Appeal, *Lutchmaya v. Secrétariat général du Groupe des États d'Afrique, des Caraïbes et du Pacifique*, Journal des Tribunaux 2003, 684, ILDC 1363 (BE 2003), 4 March 2003. This line of argument was subsequently mirrored by *e.g.* Switzerland, Federal Supreme Court, *Consortium X v. Switzerland*, BGE 130 I 312, 2 July 2004, ILDC 344 (CH 2004), and France, Court of Cassation, *La Banque Africaine de Développement v. Mr X*, 04-41012, ILDC 778 (FR 2005), 25 January 2005.

[100] ECtHR, *Waite and Kennedy*, § 68. In Reinisch & Weber (2004), the ECtHR was criticized for not going 'all the way' in carrying out the test it adopted.

[101] ECtHR, *Bosphorus Hava Yollari Turizm ve Ticaret Anonim Sirketi v. Ireland*, No. 45036/98, 30 June 2005 (*Bosphorus*) and European Court of Justice (ECJ), Joined Cases C-402 and 415/05P, *Kadi & Al Barakaat International Found. v. Council of the European Union & Commission of the European Communities*, E.C.R I-6351, 3 September 2008 (*Kadi I*). While the piercing of absolute immunity was by and large welcomed, critical notes were placed as well, *see e.g.* De Búrca G. (2010), 'The European Court of Justice and the International Legal Order after Kadi', 51(1) *Harvard International Law Journal*, pp. 1-50.

[102] Council Reg. 881/2002. 27 May 2002.

[103] European Court of Justice, *Kadi I*, § 322.

[104] *Id.*, §§ 326-327. This was restated in the *Kadi II* decision, General Court, Case T-85/09, *Yassin Abdullah Kadi v. European Commission*, 2010/C 317/52, 30 September 2010, §§ 126-128.

is proportionate from the perspective of human rights, in particular with respect to the right to access to court. In so doing, the existence of effective alternative human rights protection mechanisms proves to be decisive.

> In the 2010 case of the Association of Citizens *"Mothers of Srebrenica" v. State of the Netherlands and the United Nations*, the Court of Appeal in The Hague applied the *Waite and Kennedy* reasoning. In dismissing various erroneous holdings of the District Court, the Court of Appeal first states that the right to a fair trial and access to court enjoy the status of customary international law. Nevertheless, the Court holds that the General Convention provisions on immunity should be "defined as broadly as possible" (§ 4.2). Considering the facts in the given case, the Court ruled that the UN's immunity serves a legitimate goal, that in this case the immunity is proportionate and, finally, that alternative mechanisms are provided. Here, the Court refers to the possibility to initiate proceedings against "the perpetrators" and against the state of The Netherlands which enjoys no immunity before Dutch courts. In the judgment, the Court of Appeal thus upheld the UN's immunity from prosecution.
>
> Netherlands, The Hague Court of Appeal, *Mothers of Srebrenica v. The Netherlands and the United Nations*, 200.022.151/01, Case No. 07-2973, 30 March 2010.

4.2.3 IMMUNITY IN THE CONTEXT OF INTERNATIONAL TERRITORIAL ADMINISTRATION

When assessing the transplantation of broad immunities to the ITA context, it is crucial to keep in mind the nature of ITA missions.[105] In essence, the problem is that indiscriminate transplantation leads to a situation in which a state-like entity is protected by immunities that are traditionally awarded to international organizations. The following paragraphs map this conflicting situation and discuss how it contravenes the principle of judicial review.

With ITA missions, immunity covers both the mission *in toto* as well as individual officials. As well as the applicable General Convention, in Kosovo, the international administration was quick to adopt Regulation 2000/47 in which the scope of UNMIK's and KFOR's immunity is defined.[106] This regulation declares "UNMIK, its property, funds and assets [...] immune from any legal process".[107] Senior UNIMK officials are granted immunity "from local jurisdiction in respect of any civil or criminal act performed or committed by

[105] For an elaborate analysis of the inadequacy of absolute immunity in the ITA context, *see* Rawski F. (2003), 'To Waive or Not to Waive: Immunity and Accountability in U.N. Peacekeeping Operations', 103 *Connecticut Journal of International Law*, pp. 103-132.

[106] UNMIK Reg. 2000/47, 18 August 2000. This regulation defines UNMIK to be the "international civil presence [...] integrating the Interim Civil Administration (United Nations), Humanitarian Affairs (UNHCR), Institution-building (OSCE), and Reconstruction (EU) components".

[107] *Id.*, Section 3.1.

them in the territory of Kosovo".[108] Other UNMIK personnel, including local staff, are covered by immunity "from legal process in respect of words spoken and all acts performed by them in their official capacity".[109] Moreover, comparable immunities are granted to KFOR[110] and to UNMIK contractors.[111] Provisions regarding the waiver of immunity are also included in the UNMIK Regulation.[112] In 2002, UNMIK adopted Administrative Direction 2002/18, fine-tuning the applicable immunity provisions. Article 1.1 stipulates that:

> Nothing in UNMIK Regulation No. 2000/47 shall be interpreted as preventing UNMIK personnel from being held in provisional detention when a request for a waiver of immunity is to be decided upon by the Secretary-General of the United Nations, if there is a grounded suspicion that the person concerned committed a criminal offence and circumstances indicate a risk of flight.[113]

Conversely, UNTAET never adopted a similar resolution. Rather, its immunities were governed by the General Convention.[114] In BiH, the situation is slightly different as the OHR is not a UN subsidiary as such. The OHR, the High Representative and staff members enjoy immunities in line with the Vienna Convention on Diplomatic Relations, as provided by the Dayton Peace Agreement.[115] The immunity provision only applies to the territories of the Dayton Peace Agreement signatories: namely, BiH, Croatia, Serbia and,

---

[108] *Id.*, Section 3.2.
[109] *Id.*, Section 3.3.
[110] *Id.*, Section 2.
[111] *Id.*, Section 4.1: "UNMIK and KFOR contractors, their employees and sub-contractors shall not be subject to local laws or regulations in matters relating to the terms and conditions of their contracts. UNMIK and KFOR contractors other than local contractors shall not be subject to local laws or regulations in respect of licensing and registration of employees, business and corporations". *See also* Hampson F. & Kihara-Hunt A., *in* Aio C. *et al.* (eds.) (2007), *Unintended consequences of peacekeeping operations*, New York: United Nations University Press, pp. 195-220.
[112] UNMIK Reg. 2000/47, 18 August 2000, Section 6.1: "The immunity from legal process of KFOR and UNMIK personnel and KFOR contractors is in the interests of KFOR and UNMIK and not for the benefit of the individuals themselves. The Secretary-General shall have the right and the duty to waive the immunity of any UNMIK personnel in any case where, in his opinion, the immunity would impede the course of justice and can be waived without prejudice to the interest of UNMIK. In relation to personnel of the Institution-building and Reconstruction components, any waiver of immunity shall be carried out in consultation with the heads of those components". Section 6.2 adds with respect to KFOR that "[r]equests to waive jurisdiction over KFOR personnel shall be referred to the respective commander of the national element of such personnel for consideration".
[113] UNMIK Administrative Direction 2002/18, 9 September 2002, Art. 1.1.
[114] *E.g.* Stahn 2005)(3), p. 34, arguing that the lack of an explicit UNTAET resolution resulted in ambiguity.
[115] Dayton Peace Agreement, Ann. 10, Art. III(4).

arguably, Montenegro (the last two being successor states). With respect to other jurisdictions, the immunity of the OHR should in principle be regulated through national law, as is the case in Belgium and the United States.[116]

All three immunity regimes play out in the same way, and in principle they provide international administrations a thick shield against legal proceedings. From a conceptual point of view, this conception of immunity does not fit the ITA context as its main purpose is to prevent interference by local authorities. Such protection becomes redundant when the international organization has become the local authority.[117] This results in a situation comparable to one in which a state enjoys absolute immunity vis-à-vis its own judicial system, its exercise of public power not being subjected to any form of judicial review. Two dimensions of the impact of immunity can be distinguished.

The first point relates to the resulting institutional absence of judicial review of the exercise of public power by ITA missions. International administrators govern by decree. They can promulgate a law, adopt an executive decision, order the detention of an individual or alter the outcome of judicial proceedings by adopting a single regulation.[118] In terms of immunity, this means in principle that all SRSG decisions, regardless of the substance, are covered by immunity and in principle remain barred from judicial review.[119] Their contents cannot be assessed by a judicial body, adding to the weak adherence to the rule of law principle. This is not simply an imperfection or a collateral effect of immunity.

---

[116] Extending Immunities to the Office of High Representative in Bosnia and Herzegovina and the International Civilian Office in Kosovo Act of 2010, 22 U.S.C.A. § 288f-7 (West 2010) and Wet Betreffende het Statuut van Belgie van de 'Hoge Vertegenwoordiger' die Belast is met de Uitvoering op Burgerlijk Gebied van het Vredesakkoord voor Bosnië-Herzegovina (Belgium) 1998 (Belgian High Representative of Bosnia-Herzegovina Act 1998). Applicability of the General Convention could also be argued taking into account the test adopted in ICJ, *Applicability of Article VI, Section 22 of the Convention on the Privileges and Immunities of the U.N.*, Advisory Opinion, 15 December 1989 (*Convention on the Privileges and Immunities of the U.N.*).

[117] *E.g.* Ombudsperson Institution in Kosovo, Special Report No. 1 *on the compatibility with recognized international standards of UNMIK Regulation No. 2000/47 on the Status, Privileges and Immunities of KFOR and UNMIK and Their Personnel in Kosovo*, 18 August 2000, § 23 and Report by Mr. Alvaro Gil-Robles, Commissioner for Human Rights, *Kosovo: The Human Rights Situation and the Fate of Persons Displaced from their Homes*, 16 October 2002, Doc. CommDH(2002)11, p. 11. Stahn argues to the same effect: "Absolute immunity is a contradiction in itself in cases where international actors act as part and parcel of an (internationally supervised) municipal order", *see* Stahn (2005)(3), p. 51.

[118] *See* Section 4.3 below.

[119] In BiH, the Constitutional Court developed the "functional duality" approach by which it distinguishes legislative and executive acts adopted by the OHR. The Court assumed the jurisdiction to review the former, though with tacit approval of the OHR, *see* Section 5.3.1.2 below.

The review-preventing purpose of immunity is sometimes explicitly restated in decisions of the international administration.[120]

While it might be argued that states, in their exercise of public power, also enjoy a certain degree of immunity, the situations are different. In general, legal systems of states provide for different types of acts (*e.g.* laws, administrative acts, executive measures or judicial decisions) to be adopted through different procedures and by different state organs. Depending on the legal system, these acts can be subjected to varying degrees of review, while some of them can enjoy immunity. Due to the decision-making structure of ITA missions, such nuances in the ITA context are non-existent.

From a human rights angle, this institutional lack of judicial review has been criticized by many, as it arguably amounts to a breach of the right to remedy and of related rights pertaining to access to court and fair trial. The Ombudsperson Institution in Kosovo devoted its first special report to this matter.[121] The special report was sparked by mounting individual claims related to damage and occupation of property as well as to personal injuries, all as a consequence of UNMIK and KFOR activities. Using the ECHR as a framework for assessment, the Ombudsperson institution concludes that the immunity enjoyed by UNMIK is incompatible with Articles 6, 8 (in part) and 15 ECHR as well as Article 1 of Optional Protocol 1 to the ECHR. Similar concerns are also voiced by, for example, the Council of Europe, Amnesty International and various commentators.[122] Occasionally, this situation has been mitigated through the establishment of different review mechanisms with respect to particular ITA decisions. For example, in response to a public outcry UNMIK established the "Detention Review Commission [...] for the purpose of reviewing extra-judicial detentions based on executive orders", which is further discussed below.[123] In

[120] *E.g.* OHR, Order of 9 February 2004 *Blocking All Bank Accounts of, held by and/or in the name of Milovan Marijanović*, where the OHR explicitly reminded the local judiciary of their lack of jurisdiction: "[f]or the avoidance of doubt, it is hereby specifically declared and provided that the provisions of the Order contained herein are, as to each and every one of them, laid down by the High Representative pursuant to his international mandate and are not therefore justiciable by the Courts of Bosnia and Herzegovina or its Entities or elsewhere whether in respect of the Banking Agencies or otherwise, and no proceedings may be brought in respect of duties carried out thereunder before any court whatsoever at any time hereafter".

[121] Ombudsperson Institution in Kosovo, Special Report No. 1 *on the compatibility with recognized international standards of UNMIK Regulation No. 2000/47 on the Status, Privileges and Immunities of KFOR and UNMIK and Their Personnel in Kosovo*, 18 August 2000, in particular § 28.

[122] Venice Commission Kosovo Report, Section V and CoE, Parliamentary Assembly, Resolution 1417 (2005), Art. 5(ix); AI, *Briefing to the Human Rights Committee during the 87th Session in July 2006*, AI Index: Eur 70/007/2006, p. 7. *See also e.g.* Werzer (2008), pp. 123-125; Zaum (2007), p. 69.

[123] UNMIK Reg. 2001/18, 25 August 2001, Section 1. Also, UNMIK Regulation 2002/13, 13 June 2002, as amended by UNMIK Reg. 2008/4, 5 February 2008 and UNMIK Reg.

other examples, the local judiciary was assigned temporary jurisdiction to review decisions (adopted either by the local or international administration) that directly gave effect to ITA regulations. This was done, for example, with regard to public procurement procedures for the civil administration in East Timor and to decisions based on the prohibition of logging operations and the export of wood.[124] Several UNMIK regulations likewise established a link between semi-international decision-making procedures and the local judiciary.[125] These and other review mechanisms are discussed in detail in the following chapter.

The second dimension of immunity's impact relates to criminal and civil law proceedings, dealing with individual criminal allegations as well as civil and commercial claims.[126] Immunity shields individuals from being prosecuted, most notably before the local judiciary, since immunity is granted both to individuals as well as to the administration *in toto*. The ECtHR stated in *Al-Adsani*:

> It would not be consistent with the rule of law in a democratic society or with the basic principle underlying Article 6(1) – namely that civil claims must be capable of being submitted to a judge for adjudication – if, for example, a State could, without restraint or control by the Convention enforcement bodies, remove from the jurisdiction of the courts a whole range of civil claims or confer immunities from civil liability on large groups or categories of persons.[127]

The undesirable situation sketched in *Al-Adsani* mirrors the scope the immunity of ITA missions. In other words, ITA immunity leads to a situation that the ECtHR describes as inconsistent with the rule of law. The UN also reflected on this issue in the context of criminal acts of UN staff members. A 2006 UN report highlights situations where the UN asserts executive authority in a territory. The report argues that under such circumstances, where the UN holds control over the judicial system and is expected to uphold human rights standards, "the

---

2008/19, 31 March 2008, mandated the establishment of a Special Chamber of the Supreme Court of Kosovo with the exclusive jurisdiction to review decisions adopted by the Kosovo Trust Agency (the predecessor of the Privatization Agency of Kosovo) in relation to property and privatization issues. The Kosovo Trust Agency was established by UNMIK Reg. 2002/12, 13 June 2002, as amended by UNMIK Reg. 2005/18, 22 April 2005, UNMIK Reg. 2008/16, 20 March 2008 and UNMIK Reg. 2008/27, 27 May 2008. *See* also OSCE, *Privatization in Kosovo: Judicial Review of Kosovo Trust Agency Matters by the Special Chamber of the Supreme Court of Kosovo*, May 2008. *See* further Section 5.2.4 below.

[124] UNTAET Reg. 2000/10, 6 March 2000, Section 42 and UNTAET Reg. 2000/17, 10 May 2000, Section 6.4 which mandates the local judiciary to engage in review of particular decisions adopted by the International Administration. *See* further Section 5.2.4 below.

[125] *E.g.* UNMIK Reg. 2000/20, 12 April 2000; UNMIK Reg. 2000/52, 2 September 2000.

[126] *See also* Stahn (2008), Chapter 14.

[127] ECtHR, *Al-Adsani*, § 47, referring to ECtHR, *Fayed v. the United Kingdom*, No. 17101/90, 12 July 1994.

Secretary-General should have less difficulty waiving any applicable immunity".[128]

In practice immunity continues to be invoked during criminal proceedings against ITA staff members before local and sending-state courts and has been waived only in exceptional cases.[129]

> UNMIK has argued that having a judicial body issue binding decisions vis-à-vis UNMIK would be "problematic" because of the immunities in place, thus explicitly linking immunity with the lack of review mechanisms. UNMIK argues this in light of "possible exposure to liability and the importance of not compromising the discretion of the institutions of the United Nations to interpret the mandate of UNMIK under UNSCR 1244".
>
> HRCee, *Report Submitted by the United Nations Interim Administration Mission in Kosovo to the Human Rights Committee on the Human Rights Situation in Kosovo Since June 1999, Kosovo (Serbia and Montenegro)*, UN Doc. CCPR/C/UNK/1, 13 March 2006, §§ 132.

4.2.4 SUMMARY

The scope of immunities enjoyed by ITA missions is near-absolute. Immunity covers the missions *in toto* as well as individual staff members and runs along the lines of immunity generally enjoyed by international organizations. In the present context, this leads to the following dichotomy: while ITA missions enjoy state-like powers, they retain a conception of immunity common to international organizations.

Under international administrations, all facets of the exercise of public power are in principle covered by an equally extensive immunity. From an institutional perspective, review of the exercise of public power is thus prevented. Moreover, the SRSG occasionally adopts decisions that are judicial in nature, such as individual detention orders or orders that in other ways directly restrict certain rights of particular individuals. In principle, these decisions are likewise not

[128] UN GA, *Report of the Group of Legal Experts on ensuring the accountability of United Nations staff and experts on mission with respect to criminal acts committed in peacekeeping operations*, 16 August 2006, §§ 31-32. NGOs have reported that relevant UNMIK offices have been reluctant to provide information on whether requests for waiver have been made or granted, *see* HRW *Kosovo 2007* paper, p. 19, n. 47 and Venice Commission Kosovo Report, § 65

[129] *See* Section 5.1.3 below for several examples of cases where immunity has been waived. *See also* CoE, *Kosovo: The Human Rights Situation and the Fate of Persons Displaced from their Homes,* Report by Mr. Alvaro Gil-Robles, Commissioner for Human Rights, Doc. CommDH(2002)11, 16 October 2002, p. 12. *See* also AI, *Kosovo (Serbia): The UN in Kosovo – A Legacy of Impunity*, EUR 70/015/2006, November 2006. In East Timor, immunity was waived or was not considered to apply in several cases, *see* Morrow & White (2002), p. 24.

open to appeal. With respect to the acts of individuals, criminal and civil cases are possible only after immunity is waived. In practice, save for certain exceptions discussed in the following chapter, this amounts to a veil of immunity that can hardly be pierced. In summary, immunity in the present context prevents the principle of judicial review from being institutionalized and upheld and, from a human rights perspective, amounts to an infringement of the right to access to court.

These immunities are defended by the functionality-argument: the immunities are deemed indispensable for the functioning of ITA missions. A public law approach to accountability does not reject a certain degree of immunities. Rather, it questions the necessity and above all the proportionality of near-absolute immunity. The functional necessity of overall immunity could also be claimed by states. Nowadays, however, the rule of law-based approach to government would reject such a claim.[130] Overall immunity of ITA missions and the excessive interpretation of the 'functional necessity-rationale' should be rejected on the same grounds.

On a final note, immunity in its present shape is contrary to the message ITA missions want to convey to the local population, which is one of accountability and the rule of law. Moreover, the reliance on immunity arguably affects the way in which power is actually exercised by the international administration. For example, during negotiations concerning possible airlifting of the inhabitants of the lead-contaminated IDP camps in 2005, UNMIK personnel reportedly told the Roma representatives that UNMIK is not concerned about potential lawsuits since the mission is protected by immunity.[131] If nothing else, such an approach by UNMIK to its responsibility vis-à-vis the society governed by it has a negative impact on the way UNMIK is perceived by the public.

---

[130] Reinisch makes a similar argument with regard to state immunity being limited when the state enters the commercial playing field: if states chose to enter the marketplace they should do so under the same conditions as other market participants. By limiting state immunity to their sovereign (*iure imperii*) activities and denying it for their commercial (*iure gestionis*) activities, private parties entering into (commercial) dealings with states no longer faced the risk of being deprived of judicial remedies", Reinisch and Weber (2004), p. 65. In a similar fashion, the immunity of international organizations should adapt to the activities carried out by these organizations.

[131] European Roma Rights Center, *Press Kit on Lead Poisoning in UN Camps in Kosovo*, 8 August 2005, p. 6. During interviews held in Priština in September 2007, a CoE expert in Kosovo and members of the Ombudsperson office in Kosovo all shared the view that near-absolute immunity has had a negative impact on the behaviour of UNMIK personnel and the manner in which they exercise their mandate.

4.3 INCLUSIVE AND CONCENTRATED MANDATE

The third determinant of the accountability deficit relates to the inclusive and concentrated mandate of ITA missions. These missions, and ultimately the international administrator, are granted the authority to exercise all public powers necessary for territorial administration. This one-headed structure might be warranted from an operational perspective, as ITA missions are comprised of numerous components and the centralized coordination of all peace-related efforts is necessary. However, from a public law perspective, this structure amounts to a concentration of powers and prevents the establishment of independent (judicial) bodies necessary in terms of checks and balances. The following sections set out to assess the nature of ITA mandates, while Chapter 5 will illustrate their detrimental effect on the functioning of accountability mechanisms.

The life of an ITA mandate can be described as a three-tiered process.[132] Firstly, through an initial attribution of power, the mission is established with an inclusive yet vaguely specified mandate (Section 4.3.1). Secondly, the ITA mission adopts regulations through which it delineates its authority and ultimately shapes its mandate (Section 4.3.2). Finally, the mission engages in a gradual devolution of its day-to-day authority while holding on to its final say (Section 4.3.3). The first leg of the process is essentially a point in time, whereas the second and the third leg should be understood as a continuum. Both the self-interpretation of the mandate as well as the gradual dispersion of authority commence immediately after the initial attribution and continue at a varying pace all throughout the ITA mission's exercise of its mandate.

4.3.1 MANDATE: INITIAL ATTRIBUTION

At the core of each respective ITA-mandate lies the initial attribution of power. In Kosovo and East Timor, the powers initially attributed to the ITA missions were robust yet vague, while in BiH the initial authority vested in the OHR was weak and supervisory in nature.

Acting under Chapter VII, the UN Security Council established UNMIK and UNTAET and entrusted them with a robust mandate.[133] UN Security Council Resolution 1244 (1999) established UNMIK. Headed by a Special Representative for the Secretary-General (SRSG), UNMIK was mandated to

---

[132] UN-led missions are taken as the basis of analysis, while the OHR is discussed by way of comparison.

[133] SC Res. 1244 (1999) and SC Res. 1272 (1999). *See* in detail Section 2.2.2 above. The delegation of the authority to adopt binding decisions is legally backed by Art. 98 of the UN Charter.

perform "basic civilian administrative functions where and as long as required".[134] No details were provided as to how the mandate should be exercised, and above all, the Resolution makes no mention of any areas that fall outside the scope of UNMIK's authority.[135]

In a more explicit manner, UN Security Council Res. 1727 (1999) endowed UNTAET with "overall responsibility for the administration of East Timor" to be achieved through the exercise of "all legislative and executive authority, including the administration of justice".[136] The Resolution specified the extensive nature of the mandate by stating that the SRSG in East Timor (also referred to as the Transitional Administrator) has the power to, amongst other things, "enact new laws and regulations and to amend, suspend or repeal existing ones".[137] Unlike with UNMIK, UNTAET's founding Resolution included certain vignettes concerning the structure, composition and *modus operandi* of the mission.[138] The only explicit limitation that the Resolution imposed on UNTAET's authority is a temporal one, as it established UNTAET for an initial period of one year.[139] The different approaches adopted in this respect with regard to UNMIK and UNTAET should be read in the light of the different status of the territories: East Timor's imminent independence was agreed upon at the time while Kosovo's status was left undetermined.

The establishment of the OHR in BiH differs in certain respects from what later became UN practice. The OHR was established on the basis of the Dayton Peace Agreement. Acting under Chapter VII, the UN Security Council endorsed the establishment of the OHR as well as the appointment of the first High Representative.[140] The Dayton Peace Agreement designated the OHR as "final authority in theater regarding interpretation of [the Dayton Peace Agreement] on the civilian implementation of the peace settlement".[141] The High

---

[134] SC Res. 1244 (1999), § 11(b). § 19 states that the international civil presence is established for an initial period of 12 months, "to continue thereafter unless the Security Council decides otherwise".

[135] Details on what kind of activities were included in the exercise of "basic civilian administrative functions" were, for example, provided in the UN SG's first report dealing with the situation in Kosovo in 1999, *see Report by the UN SG on UNMIK*, UN Doc. S/1999/779, 12 July 1999.

[136] SC Res. 1272 (1999), § 1. UNTAET also included a military component, unlike in the case of Kosovo where the military presence, KFOR, was not part of UNMIK as such. Compare SC Res. 1727 (1999), § 3(c) with SC Res. 1244 (1999), §§ 5, 6, 7 and 9 where the relationship between the civil and military presences in Kosovo is described.

[137] SC Res. 1272 (1999), § 6.

[138] *Id.*, § 3 on the structure of UNTAET, § 8 on the need for UNTAET to consult and cooperate with the local population and § 15 on the necessity of appropriate training of UNTAET personnel with regard to areas such as human rights law and cultural awareness.

[139] SC Res. 1272 (1999), § 17. Conversely, *see* SC Res. 1244 (1999), § 19.

[140] SC Res. 1031 (1995), § 26.

[141] Dayton Peace Agreement, Ann. 10, Art. V.

Representative's final say in the implementation of the peace agreement was also confirmed by the UN Security Council.[142]

Much like the Danzig administration, the OHR was initially conceived more as a guarantor than as a pro-active administrator.[143] Correspondingly, Article II of Annex 10 to the Dayton Peace Agreement phrases the mandate of the High Representative in mild terms such as "monitoring", "coordinating", "facilitating" and "participating".[144] As the former principal deputy of the High Representative described it, "I remember that creating the Office of the High Representative was almost an afterthought".[145]

The nature of the OHR's initial mandate fits into the broader aim of the Dayton Peace Agreement, which was amongst other things to guarantee the sustainability of BiH as a state. To achieve this, the OHR is guided by the "domestic responsibility" principle.[146] The primary responsibility for administering the country is thus placed at the local level. This local legal order was shaped by the Constitution of Bosnia and Herzegovina, a document attached to the Dayton Peace Agreement.[147] This constitution did not incorporate the OHR into the BiH's constitutional system, leaving the OHR *i.e.* the High Representative as the superimposed guarantor of the peace accord. Soon, as will be discussed below, this weak approach to the OHR's mandate soon proved to be inadequate and unsustainable.

[142] SC Res. 1031 (1995), § 27.

[143] Compare with the administration of Danzig, Section 2.1.3 above.

[144] Dayton Peace Agreement, Ann. 10, Art. II(1) states that the High Representative shall: "a. Monitor the implementation of the peace settlement; b. Maintain close contact with the Parties to promote their full compliance with all civilian aspects of the peace settlement and a high level of cooperation between them and the organizations and agencies participating in those aspects; c. Coordinate the activities of the civilian organizations and agencies in Bosnia and Herzegovina to ensure the efficient implementation of the civilian aspects of the peace settlement. The High Representative shall respect their autonomy within their spheres of operation while as necessary giving general guidance to them about the impact of their activities on the implementation of the peace settlement. The civilian organizations and agencies are requested to assist the High Representative in the execution of his or her responsibilities by providing all information relevant to their operations in Bosnia-Herzegovina; d. Facilitate, as the High Representative judges necessary, the resolution of any difficulties arising in connection with civilian implementation; [...] g. Provide guidance to, and receive reports from, the Commissioner of the International Police Task Force established in Annex 11 to the General Framework Agreement." In terms of method and structure, Art II of Ann. 10 to the Dayton Peace Agreement establishes basic preconditions as to how the High Representative should carry out the mandate.

[145] London School of Economics and Political Science, Centre for the Study of Global Governance, Michael Steiner, *For Example Kosovo: Seven Principles for Peace Building*, Discussion Paper 22, January 2003.

[146] *See* <http://www.ohr.int/ohr-info/gen-info/default.asp?content_id=38612>.

[147] Dayton Peace Agreement, Ann. 4.

In summary, the initial mandates attribute inclusive but insufficiently defined authority to the ITA missions. Unlike the Mandate and Trusteeship systems, no subject matters are excluded from the ITA mission's purview: "[T]he mandate is the floor (but not the ceiling) for everything the Mission does".[148] These words of Jacques Paul Klein, former principal deputy High Representative, encapsulate the essence of the ITA mandates discussed. In addition to a failure to provide clear benchmarks, the constituent documents also institutionalize a highly concentrated decision-making structure and in so doing, prevent the establishment of independent review mechanisms whose jurisdictions would respond to the inclusive mandate of ITA missions.[149]

4.3.2 MANDATE: SELF-INTERPRETATION

Building upon such broad foundations, ITA missions engage in a process of self-delineation of their mandate.[150] It is at this point that the proverbial Pandora's box is opened as missions are seemingly unleashed to freely interpret the scope of their mandate and the way in which it should be exercised.[151] Through regulations adopted at the outset of the missions, the vast scope and concentrated nature of authority is reaffirmed.[152]

UNMIK and UNTAET promulgated regulations in confirmation of their overall authority right at the outset of their deployment.[153] It is at this stage that the methods of administration are anchored: administration by means of regulations and subsidiary acts such as administrative directions.[154] Subsequently, self-interpretation of authority continues throughout the whole

---

[148] Jacques Paul Klein, former SRSG for UNTAES and Principal Deputy High Representative with the OHR in BiH, as quoted *in* Chesterman S. (2003), *You, the People: The United Nations, Transitional Administration, and State-Building*, Final Report, Project on Transitional Administration, International Peace Academy.

[149] *See* Chapter 5 below.

[150] Ford and Oppenheim label this development as "authority creep", referring to excessive and ultimately counterproductive use of authority facilitated by a vague initial mandate, *see* Ford & Oppenheim (2008).

[151] For criticism against "self interpretation" of the mandate, *see e.g.* Stahn (2005)(3), p. 19.

[152] *See* for a similar description with regards to ITA precedents Stahn (2008), p. 54 (regarding the administration of Cracow as a partial yet pioneering experiments in this context); p. 86 (with regards to League of Nations mandates in general); p. 95 (in relation to UN trusteeships), pp. 167-168 and 173; Stahn describes the scope of authority as "omnipotence with unfettered trust in it".

[153] UNMIK Reg. 1999/1, 25 July 1999, as amended by UNMIK Reg. 1999/25, 12 December 1999 and UNMIK Reg. 2000/54, 27 September 2000 (UNMIK Reg. 1999/1, as amended) and UNTAET Reg. 1999/1, 27 November 1999.

[154] UNMIK Reg. 1999/1, as amended, Sections 4 and 5; UNTAET Reg. 1999/1, Sections 4, 5 and 6.

period of administration as the SRSG in effect interprets his or her mandate through every subsequently adopted regulation.

The scope and structure of an ITA mandate have by and large been determined at this point. In order to achieve the main purpose of ITA missions, which is the establishing and maintaining of a transitional administration,[155] "[a]ll legislative and executive authority with respect to [Kosovo/East Timor], including the administration of the judiciary, is vested in [UNMIK/UNTAET] and is exercised by the [SRSG/Transitional Administrator]".[156] The regulations specify that "The [SRSG/Transitional Administrator] may appoint any person to perform functions in the civil administration in [Kosovo/East Timor], including the judiciary, or remove such person".[157] Finally, specific attention is devoted to the administration of property because of UNMIK's and UNTAET's responsibilities in the area of economic reconstruction.[158] Especially in Kosovo, this provision would later serve as a basis for regulations concerning controversial privatization processes.[159]

The mandate of the OHR in BiH developed differently due to the specific nature of the international civil presence.[160] Despite the fact that the OHR had

---

[155] UNMIK Reg. 1999/1, as amended, Preamble: "Acting [...] for the purpose of establishing and maintaining the interim administration in the territory of Kosovo". UNTAET Reg. 1999/1, Preamble: "Acting [...] after consultation with representatives of the East Timorese people, and for the purpose of establishing and maintaining an effective transitional administration in East Timor". *See e.g.* Bongiorno C. (2002), 'A culture of Impunity: Applying International Human Rights Law to the United Nations in East Timor', 33 *Columbia Human Rights Law Review*, pp. 623-692.

[156] *Cf.* UNMIK Reg. 1999/1, as amended, Section 1, Art. 1.1 and UNTAET Reg. 1999/1, Section 1, Art. 1.1. UNTAET Reg. 1999/1 follows SC Res. 1272 (1999) § 8, which adds "the need for UNTAET to consult and cooperate closely with the East Timorese people in order to carry out its mandate effectively".

[157] *Cf.* UNMIK Reg. 1999/1, as amended, Section 1, Art. 1.2 and UNTAET Reg. 1999/1, Section 1, Art. 1.2.

[158] UNMIK Reg. 1999/1, Section 6: "UNMIK shall administer movable or immovable property, including monies, bank accounts, and other property of, or registered in the name of the Federal Republic of Yugoslavia or the Republic of Serbia or any of its organs, which is in the territory of Kosovo", amended by UNMIK Reg. 2000/54, 27 September 2000 to read: "6.1 UNMIK shall administer movable or immovable property which is in the territory of Kosovo, including monies, bank accounts and other assets, where UNMIK has reasonable and objective grounds to conclude that such property is: (a) Property of, or registered in the name of, the Federal Republic of Yugoslavia or the Republic of Serbia or any of their organs; or (b) Socially owned property. 6.2 Administration by UNMIK of property pursuant to Section 6.1 above shall be without prejudice to the right of any person or entity to assert ownership or other rights in the property in a competent court in Kosovo, or in a judicial mechanism to be established by regulation" and UNTAET Reg. 1999/1, Section 7, Art. 7.1: "UNTAET shall administer immovable or movable property, including monies, bank accounts, and other property of, or registered in the name of the Republic of Indonesia, or any of its subsidiary organs and agencies, which is in the territory of East Timor."

[159] *See e.g.* Section 5.2.4 below.

[160] *See* Section 2.2.2 above.

the final say in the peace implementation process from the outset, the High Representative remained initially true to his supervisory mandate. Reports filed to the UN Secretary-General by the High Representative in the period between 1996 and 1997 reflect that the High Representative refrained from issuing legally binding decisions.[161] These reports also reflect the frustration of the High Representative concerning the fact that local institutions had come to a deadlock. On a variety of issues, ranging from the Law on Citizenship to the Law on the Flag of Bosnia and Herzegovina, local decision-makers were not able to reach an agreement. This situation led to a turning point with respect to the way in which the High Representative exercised his mandate. At a meeting in Bonn in 1997, the Peace Implementation Council – the backbone of the OHR and the BiH peace process – effectively changed the role of the High Representative by entrusting him with the Bonn powers.[162] Formally staying within the confines of Annex 10 to the Dayton Peace Agreement, the PIC interpreted the OHR's final authority extensively. The High Representative was empowered to make decisions *i.e.* adopt laws in situations where the local parties are unable to do so, take actions against "persons holding public office" who were deemed to be in violation of the Dayton Peace Agreement and take other measures to ensure the Dayton Peace Agreement's implementation.[163] This change in policy was reported to the UN Secretary-General, and the High Representative immediately engaged in extensive decision-making.[164] It was with the introduction of the Bonn powers that the OHR anchored his supreme position vis-à-vis the BiH local authorities.[165]

---

[161] *See* <http://www.ohr.int/decisions/archive.asp?so=d&sa=on>. *See also* 1st (14 March 1996), 2nd (10 July 1996), 3rd (1 October 1996), 4th (10 December 1996), 5th (16 April 1997), 6th (11 July 1997) and 7th (17 October 1997) *Report of the High Representative for Implementation of the Bosnian Peace Agreement to the Secretary-General of the United Nations*, at <http://www.ohr.int/other-doc/hr-reports/archive.asp?sa=on>.

[162] PIC Conference in Bonn, *PIC Bonn Conclusions*, 10 December 1997, at <http://www.ohr.int/pic/default.asp?content_id=5182#11>. For OHR's own take on this development, *see* <http://www.ohr.int/ohr-info/gen-info/default.asp?content_id=38612 >.

[163] PIC Conference in Bonn, PIC Bonn Conclusions, § XI, Art. 2, 10 December 1997, at <http://www.ohr.int/pic/default.asp?content_id=5182#11>.

[164] *8th Report of the High Representative for Implementation of the Bosnian Peace Agreement to the Secretary-General of the United Nations*, 16 January 1998, at <http://www.ohr.int/other-doc/hr-reports/default.asp?content_id=3671>.

[165] The supreme nature of the OHR's authority has sparked concern amongst many, *see e.g.* CoE, Venice Commission, *Opinion on the Constitutional Situation in Bosnia and Herzegovina and the Powers of the High Representative*, 11 March 2005, Doc. CDL-AD(2005)004 (Venice Commission OHR Report).

4.3.3 MANDATE: GRADUAL DEVOLUTION

Finally, the mandate of the ITA mission is shaped by a process of gradual devolution of power in accordance with the temporary character of international administrations and their aim to establish a functioning government apparatus. This process includes institution building and the institutionalization of participatory decision-making processes. It is, however, crucial to keep in mind that throughout this whole process, ultimate authority is held on to by the international administration.[166]

The responsibility to transfer power to local authorities lies at the core of the ITA mandate. Resolution 1244 (1999) states that UNMIK is responsible for "organizing and overseeing the development of provisional institutions for democratic and autonomous self-government" by "transferring, as these institutions are established, its administrative responsibilities while overseeing and supporting the consolidation of Kosovo's local provisional institutions".[167] In a similar fashion, UNTAET was tasked to "establish an effective administration" and to exercise its authority "with a view to [...] the transfer to these institutions of its administrative and public service functions".[168] In the case of the OHR, the situation was different, as the Dayton Peace Agreement established the OHR and at the same time adopted the Bosnian Constitution, which shaped the constitutional system of BiH. The OHR's initial arbiter-like authority implied that administration of the country was placed in the hands of the local institutions *ab initio*.

Throughout the duration of the ITA mandate, the process of power-sharing remains a balancing act with a potentially delegitimizing effect. For decision-making to be shared, the international administrators need to know with whom to share their authority. In the absence of a system of popular and free elections, determining the appropriate local representatives is potentially arbitrary.[169] Furthermore, though armed conflicts may have come to an end, tensions remain and the local society is bound to be divided. The inability of one ethnic group to feel adequately represented by members of an opposite ethnic or religious community inevitably complicates the establishment of power-sharing arrangements. This concern was echoed by the UN Handbook on Multidimensional Peacekeeping Operations, stressing that SRSGs should "be

[166] Reason for Ford and Oppenheim, for example, to label the power-sharing arrangements as "illusory", *see* Ford & Oppenheim (2008), p. 88.
[167] SC Res. 1244 (1999), Artt. 11(c) and (d).
[168] SC Res. 1272 (1999), Artt. 2(b) and 8.
[169] *See also* Stahn (2005) (3), p. 26.

sensitive to any identification with partisan positions".[170] As late UNTAET SRSG Sergio Vieira de Mello noted:

> The involvement of local leaders is a prerequisite for stability and sustainability of the UN administration. But in the absence of elections, on what basis are leaders to be chosen? Difficulties arose not only in the choice of local representatives but also in the delegation of authority to them. The more powers conferred on local representatives, the closer power is to the people and thus the more legitimate the nature of the administration. But conferring power on non-elected local representatives can also have the undesired effect of furthering a particular party.[171]

As local authorities were granted power in an increasing number of fields, UNMIK and UNTAET held on to their authority to ultimately overrule decisions taken at the local level:

> In any area where a competency has been transferred to the PISG, indeed we always like the PISG to be in the lead. At the same time, you should not forget that under Resolution 1244 the SRSG has the ultimate authority to make any corrective intervention…, even if it is a transferred area.[172]

How does this division of power play out in practice from an institutional point of view? More particularly, does the gradual division of powers provide space for the establishment of institutions that – save for the obstacles discussed in Sections 4.1 and 4.2 – could function as an independent judicial body? The answer is 'no'. The power-transfer process leads to a complex decision-making environment composed of international and local bodies. These decision-making environments are characterized by the supremacy of international actors in Kosovo, BiH and East Timor alike. Under such circumstances, little space for checks and balances through the diffusion of powers exists as all local authorities, whether legislative, executive or judicial, are hierarchically subordinated to the international administrator. In order to illustrate this, essential traits of the power-sharing arrangements under UNMIK, UNTAET and the OHR are discussed below.

---

[170] Handbook on United Nations Multidimensional Peacekeeping Operations, United Nations, Department of Peacekeeping Operations, Peacekeeping Best Practices Unit, December 2003, p. 21.

[171] Sergio Vieira de Mello, *How Not to Run a Country: Lessons for the UN from Kosovo and East Timor* (Unpublished manuscript), quoted in Beauvais (2001), p. 1120.

[172] UNMIK Spokesperson at a UNMIK Press Briefing, 8 March 2006, on the annulment of a decision of Kosovo's Prime-Minister, as quoted in Knoll (2008), p. 305. *See also* Section 5.3.1 below.

4.3.3.1 *Local Authorities under UNMIK*

The process of establishing power-sharing structures in UNMIK-administered Kosovo can be divided in three phases: the interim phase, the provisional phase and the post-2008 phase, the first two of which will be discussed below.[173]

Between February 2000 and May 2001, UNMIK administered Kosovo through the so-called Joint Interim Administrative Structure (JIAS).[174] As UNMIK was being deployed, the complete Serb-dominated Kosovo administration was abandoning Kosovo, leaving behind parallel structures of public administration previously set up by the Kosovo Albanian leaders. These institutions were dismantled and UNMIK established interim structures which functioned until the provisional Kosovo authorities were chosen.

All structures set up under the JIAS operated in accordance with Resolution 1244 (1999), in conformity with the applicable law in Kosovo and the SRSG's legislative and executive acts.[175] In executing his mandate at the central level, the SRSG was assisted by representatives of the local population, which was organized in three bodies: the Interim Administrative Council (IAC), the Kosovo Transitional Council (KTC) and several Interim Administrative Departments (IAD).[176]

---

[173] *See e.g.* Brand M. (2003), '*The Development of Kosovo Institutions and the Transition of Authority from UNMIK to Local Self-Government*', Geneva: Centre for Applied Studies in International Negotiations; Irmscher (2001), pp. 359-362. Kosovo's unilateral declaration of independence and the increase of EU involvement in Kosovo as of 2008 changed the balance of powers on the ground. As was pointed out previously, this period is not covered by the present analysis. In this respect, a UNMIK representative pointed out: "Following the declaration of independence by the Kosovo authorities, a new constitution had been enacted in June 2008 which had undermined the mandated authority of UNMIK. Although UNMIK remained nominally in control, it was no longer able to implement its mandate in full in some areas where other players, including international players, had assumed control. The Mission continued to monitor and report on the situation, in addition to exercising control in a limited area of its mandate", *see* Committee on Economic, Social and Cultural Rights (CESCR), *Summary Record of the 37th Meeting*, 41st Session, UN Doc. E/C.12/2008/SR.37, 20 November 2008, § 44.

[174] UNMIK Reg. 2000/1, 14 January 2000.

[175] *Id.*, Sections 1(a) and (b).

[176] *Id.*, Sections 2, 3 and 7.

Figure 3: Relationship between SRSG and relevant JIAS structures (February 2000-May 2001)

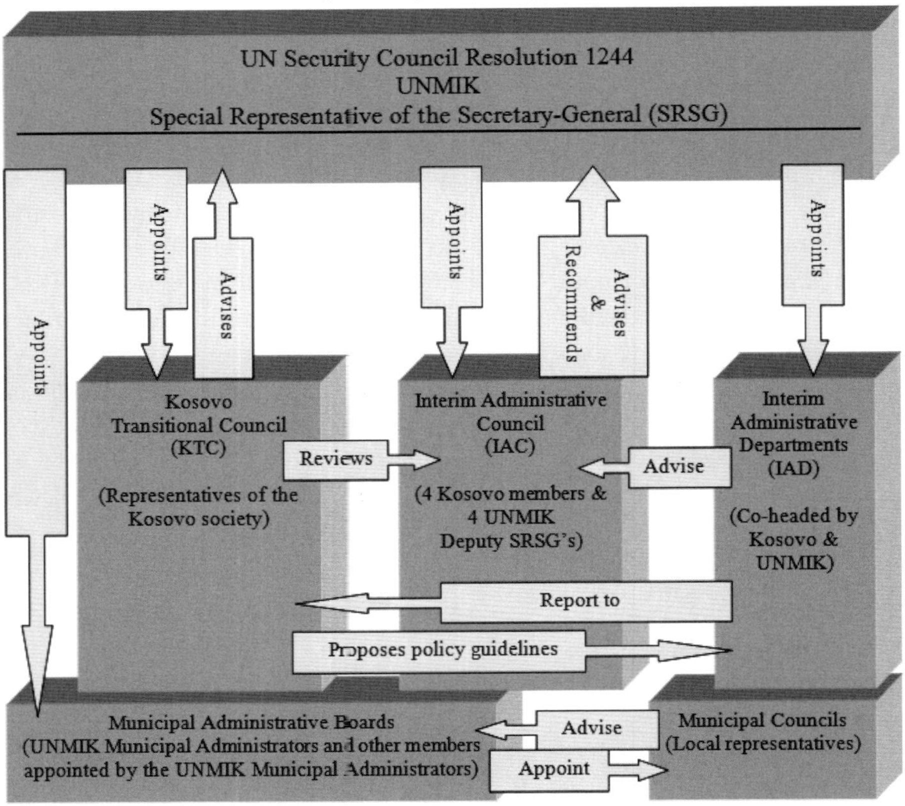

Rather than being a full-fledged state structure, the JIAS was established as a transitional consultative regime. The IAC made recommendations to the SRSG regarding amendments to existing laws and newly adopted UNMIK regulations.[177] Appointed by the SRSG, the IAC was composed of four Kosovo and four UNMIK representatives.[178] As the executive board of the JIAS, the IAC met frequently to discuss daily issues and the SRSG chaired these meetings, albeit without the right to vote.[179] The constituent regulation prescribed that the SRSG should adopt decisions which the IAC had reached by consensus or by a three quarters majority, "unless he advises the [IAC] otherwise in writing".[180]

[177] *Id.*, Section 3, § 3.1. *See e.g.* Brand (2003).

[178] *Id.*, Section 4, § 4.1. The Kosovo representatives included three political representatives of the Albanian population and one representative – with an observer status – of the Serbian local minority. UNMIK was represented by the deputy SRSG's for Civil Administration, Democratization and Institution-Building and Economic Reconstruction.

[179] *Id.*, Section 5, § 5.1.

[180] *Id.*, Section 6, § 6.2.

The KTC was an assembly type of body, established to bridge the gap between the SRSG and the local population. Representing the Kosovo society, the KTC advised the SRSG on all relevant issues and had the right to comment on and suggest alternatives to decisions adopted by the IAC.[181] Finally, several IADs were established to "implement the policy guidelines formulated by the [IAC]" and "make policy recommendations to the [IAC]".[182] Established according to policy-fields, all departments were co-headed by a local and an UNMIK representative, both of which were appointed by the SRSG.[183] If decisions could not be reached by agreement, the UNMIK representative had the final say.[184]

During this interim period, vertical decentralization was achieved through the establishment of municipal organs. Each municipality was administered by a Municipal Administrative Board, headed by a UNMIK Municipal Administrator and composed of other members appointed by him.[185] In the exercise of his mandate, the UNMIK Municipal Administrator was guided by local representatives gathered in Municipal Councils. The local representatives were likewise appointed by the UNMIK Municipal Administrator and had the right to make policy recommendations.[186]

Initiating the second phase of power-sharing arrangements, in May 2001 UNMIK "promulgated" the Constitutional Framework for Provisional Self-Government (Constitutional Framework), thereby establishing the PISG, which replaced the previous interim structures.[187] In essence, the Constitutional Framework established a local constitutional structure and auxiliary institutions. In certain crucial areas, UNMIK retained full authority. For example, no defence or foreign affairs ministry was established. These sovereign-like tasks remained within the sole UNMIK ambit. Other competences were gradually transferred to the PISG, shaping UNMIK increasingly into a monitoring institution.

---

181 *Id.*, Section 2, § 2.5. The KTC consisted of members of the IAC and other political, religious and minority representatives as well as representatives of civil society. *See e.g.* Brand (2003).

182 *Id.*, Section 7, §§ 7.2, 7.3 and Section 9, § 9.2.

183 *Id.*, Section 7, §§ 7.5 and 7.6.

184 *Id.*, Section 7, § 7.9.

185 *Id.*, Section 8, §§ 8.1 and 8.2.

186 *Id.*, Section 8, §§ 8.5 and 8.6.

187 UNMIK Reg. 2001/9, 15 May 2001, as amended by UNMIK Reg. 2002/9, 3 May 2002, UNMIK Reg. 2007/29, 4 October 2007, UNMIK Reg. 2008/1, 8 January 2008 and UNMIK Reg. 2008/9, 8 February 2008 (Constitutional Framework).

Figure 4: Relationship between the SRSG and PISG (May 2001-effectively February 2008)

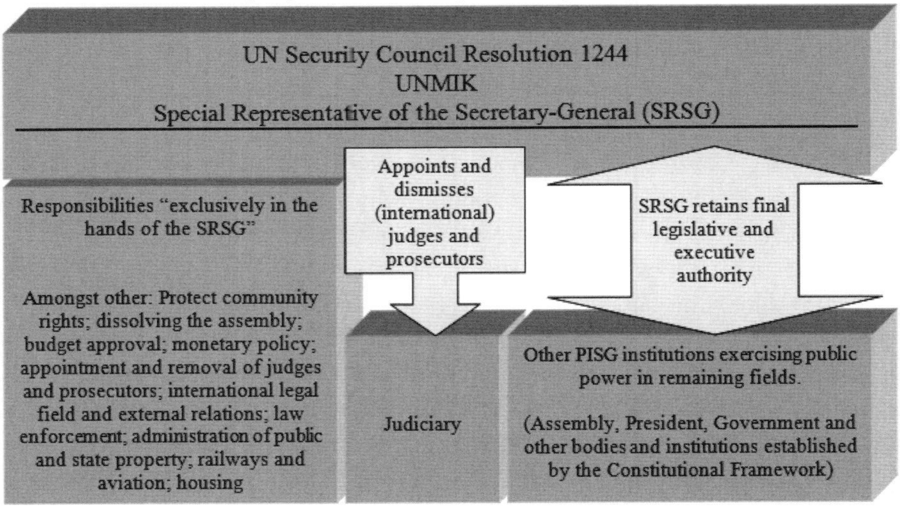

The PISG included institutions such as the Kosovo President, Government and Assembly as well as a new court structure. Examining the institutional structure of the PISG as such is less relevant for the analysis conducted in this book. The way in which the PISG is permeated by the final authority of the SRSG is, however, crucial as it reflects the persisting supremacy of the international presence over local authorities despite the extensive power-sharing arrangements. In the words of the UN Secretary-General, the Constitutional Framework contained:

> broad authority for [the] Special Representative to intervene and correct any actions of the provisional institutions of self-government that are inconsistent with Security Council resolution 1244 (1999), including the power to veto Assembly legislation, where necessary.[188]

The SRSG's supremacy is anchored throughout the Constitutional Framework. The preamble and Chapter 12 of the Constitutional Framework confirm explicitly that neither the Constitutional Framework nor the exercise of powers by the PISG affect the ultimate authority of the SRSG, which includes the power to dismiss public officials.[189] The PISG are empowered to exercise public power

[188] *Report of the UN SG on UNMIK*, UN Doc. S/2001/565, 7 June 2001, § 23.

[189] Constitutional Framework, preamble: "Affirming that the exercise of the responsibilities of the Provisional Institutions of Self-Government in Kosovo shall not in any way affect or diminish the ultimate authority of the SRSG for the implementation of UNSCR 1244 (1999)" and Chapter 12: "The exercise of the responsibilities of the Provisional Institutions of Self-

in various fields, enumerated by the Constitutional Framework.[190] Chapter 8 of the Constitutional Framework lists the areas that remained "exclusively in the hands of the SRSG". Amongst the most robust ones, the SRSG retained exclusive competencies with respect to dissolving the assembly and calling elections;[191] the appointment and dismissal of (international) judges and prosecutors;[192] the administration of "public, state and socially-owned property";[193] the appointment of board members of various financial and banking institutions;[194] the approval of Kosovo's budget[195] and the control of UNMIK Customs Service.[196] Moreover, laws adopted by the assembly enter into force only after promulgation by the SRSG.[197] Similarly, the Constitutional Framework itself could only be amended by the SRSG, either *proprio motu* or upon a request of the assembly.[198] Furthermore, powers remained reserved for the SRSG in the field of international law and external relations;[199] law enforcement;[200] infrastructure;[201] housing[202] and vertical decentralization.[203] Finally, in the area of defense, the SRSG was to "coordinate closely" with the international security presence.[204]

Government under this Constitutional Framework shall not affect or diminish the authority of the SRSG to ensure full implementation of UNSCR 1244 (1999), including overseeing the Provisional Institutions of Self-Government, its officials and its agencies, and taking appropriate measures whenever their actions are inconsistent with UNSCR 1244 (1999) or this Constitutional Framework".

190 Constitutional Framework, Chapter 5.

191 *Id.*, Chapter 8, Art. 8.1(b). The SRSG has to consult with the President of Kosovo before exercising this power.

192 *Id.*, Chapter 8, Artt. 8.1(g) and (h).

193 *Id.*, Chapter 8, Art. 8.1(q).

194 *Id.*, Chapter 8, Art. 8.1(x).

195 *Id.*, Chapter 8, Art. 8.1(c). In exercising this particular power, the SRSG acts on the advice of the Economic and Fiscal Council.

196 *Id.*, Chapter 8, Art. 8.1(f).

197 *Id.*, Chapter 9, Art. 9.1.45. In the words of the Venice Commission: "It needs to be underlined that laws adopted by the Assembly are promulgated by the SRSG. In practice, it is not uncommon that, when the SRSG refuses to promulgate a law, instead of sending it back before the Assembly, he proceeds himself with the necessary amendments. This practice – about which the Commission has certain reservations – raises the question of whether the thus-amended laws can still be considered as 'Assembly laws'", *see* CoE, European Commission For Democracy Through Law (Venice Commission), *Opinion on Human Rights in Kosovo: Possible Establishment of Review Mechanisms*, 8-9 October 2004, § 138 (Venice Commission Kosovo Report).

198 Constitutional Framework., Chapter 14, Art. 14.3.

199 *Id.*, Chapter 8, Art. 8.1(i), (m), (n) and (o).

200 *Id.*, Chapter 8, Art. 8.1(j) and (k).

201 *Id.*, Chapter 8, Art. 8.1(s).

202 *Id.*, Chapter 8, Art. 8.1(t).

203 *Id.*, Chapter 8, Art. 8.1(u).

204 *Id.*, Chapter 8, Art. 8.2. Throughout the Constitutional Framework, the SRSG's authority is further confirmed and specified, *e.g.* Chapter 9, Artt. 9.1.3(e), 9.2.4(a), 9.4.7 and 9.4.8.

In summary, Kosovo's institutions undisputedly received ample space to exercise public power, as participation and consultation on the part of local stakeholders were gradually institutionalized. Despite all power-sharing arrangements, the overall final say remained unequivocally with the SRSG. The SRSG's power with respect to local authorities is best illustrated by a variety of executive decisions, ranging from setting aside decisions of municipal assemblies to interference with decisions adopted by boards of directors of public enterprises.[205]

In terms of public law, the bundling of power in a single entity resulted in the absence of an independent judiciary: namely, the absence of independent oversight bodies within Kosovo's internationalized legal order. In particular, the interrelationship between the judiciary and the executive branch, both of which are ultimately embodied in the SRSG, is troublesome as it facilitates interference with the judicial process. Examples thereof are given in Sections 5.2.3, 5.2.4 and 5.3.1.2. The concentration of power combined with short-term contracts for international judges, the executive allocation of cases and a lack of transparency have a detrimental effect on the establishment of independent judicial or quasi-judicial oversight and, when occasionally oversight mechanisms are established, creates an unacceptable semblance of bias.[206] In a 2005 report, the Council of Europe recalled that despite all power-sharing arrangements,

> [a]ll legal texts directly applicable in Kosovo, with the sole exception of UN Security Council Resolution 1244, may equally be revised or revoked by an SRSG without the need for consultation with any local body or the possibility of any parliamentary or judicial review.[207]

4.3.3.2 Local Authorities under UNTAET

Notwithstanding their conceptual similarity, UNTAET and UNMIK were set up under two decidedly different conditions. From the outset, it was clear that UNTAET's mandate would not last long. UNTAET knew from the beginning it needed to set up institutions that would soon become the governing apparatus of an independent state. Contrary to UNMIK, UNTAET did not adopt an all-encompassing document similar to Kosovo's Constitutional Framework.

---

[205] *E.g.* UNMIK Executive Decision 2002/10, 11 September 2002; UNMIK Executive Decision 2002/16, 18 December 2002; UNMIK Executive Decision 2003/11, 27 August 2003; UNMIK Executive Decision 2004/1, 18 February 2004; UNMIK Executive Decision 2004/22, 7 October 2004.

[206] *See e.g.* AI, *Serbia (Kosovo): The challenge to fix a failed UN justice mission*, EUR 70/001/2008, January 2008.

[207] CoE, *Protection of human rights in Kosovo,* Report of the Committee on Legal Affairs and Human Rights, Doc. 10393, 6 January 2005, Section B(i), § 7.

Instead, UNTAET gradually developed East Timor's transitional administration through three phases: the period right after the establishment of UNTAET, the first transitional administration and the second transitional administration.[208]

Figure 5: Relationship between SRSG and the East Timor Transitional Administration (October 1999-May 2002)

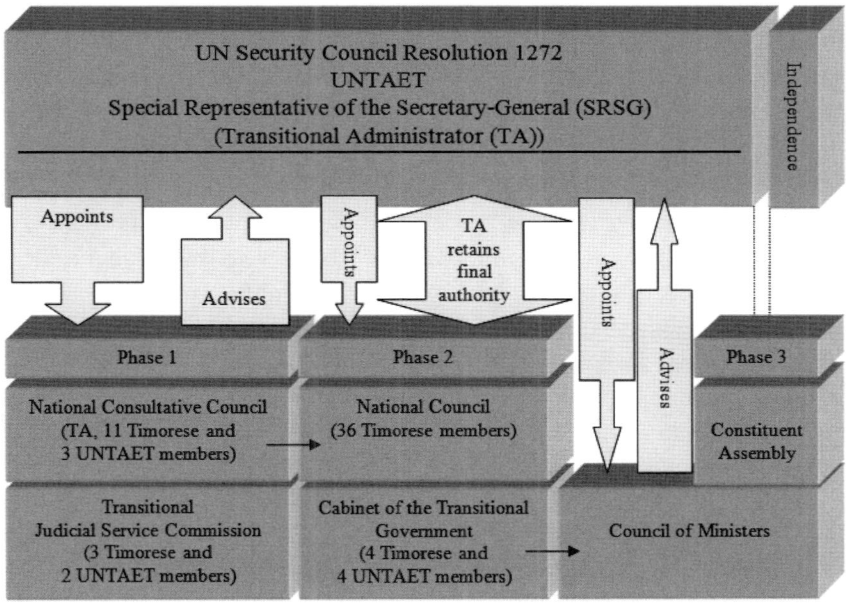

Immediately after deployment, UNTAET established two principal consultative bodies: the National Consultative Council (NCC) and the Transitional Judicial Service Commission.[209] The NCC made policy recommendations to the Transitional Administrator while the Transitional Judicial Service Commission solely had a consultative status in the appointment procedures of judges and prosecutors. Members of both bodies were appointed by the Transitional Administrator.[210] Furthermore, the constituent regulations reiterated that none of the powers vested in the institutions prejudiced the final authority of the

[208] *See also* Morrow J. & White R. (2002), 'The United Nations in Transitional East Timor: International Standards and the Reality of Governance', 22 *Australian Yearbook of International Law*, pp. 1-45.

[209] UNTAET Reg. 1999/2, 2 December 1999 and UNTAET Reg. 1999/3, 3 December 1999. *See* in general Beauvais (2001).

[210] UNTAET Reg. 1999/2, 2 December 1999, Section 2, Art. 2.5 and UNTAET Reg. 1999/3, 3 December 1999, Art. 2.5.

Transitional Administrator, which also included the power to dismiss public officials.[211]

In July 2000, UNTAET took a further step towards the establishment of sustainable East Timorese institutions. The new phase of the relationship between UNTAET and local institutions was characterized by UNTAET as a commitment to "co-government".[212] The NCC was reformed into the National Council and the Cabinet of the Transitional Government was established.[213] Composed of 36 Timorese representatives, the National Council had now outgrown a mere consultative status and was empowered to initiate, modify, draft and amend regulations. All members were appointed by the Transitional Administrator while the exercise of these newly delegated powers remained subject to approval of the Transitional Administrator.[214]

Finally, in the final phase towards East Timorese independence, the Transitional Administrator set in motion processes necessary for the election of a constituent assembly which was to draft the future constitution of East Timor.[215] The elected members of the assembly were empowered to consider regulations "as may be referred to [them] by the Transitional Administrator".[216] Though the preamble of the relevant regulation refers to the authority of the Transitional Administrator, the regulation itself does not reiterate this explicitly and does not state that the Transitional Administrator can remove members of this constituent assembly from power. In this final stage, the Transitional Administrator also established a Council of Ministers – replacing the Cabinet – and appointed its members.[217] This executive body was established as the final consultative body to the Transitional Administrator before Timorese independence in May 2002. As Morrow & White conclude:

> As a matter of practical reality, by August 2001, the Transitional Administrator had relinquished a large measure of his executive authority, as well as his responsibility for legislative review. As a matter of law, however, final legislative and executive authority remained in the

---

[211] UNTAET Reg. 1999/2, 2 December 1999, Section 1, Art. 1.3 and UNTAET Reg. 1999/3, 3 December 1999, Artt. 11.2, 13.2 and 14.2.

[212] UNTAET, *UN Mission in East Timor Suggests Power Sharing Arrangements*, 30 May 2000, at <http://www.un.org/en/peacekeeping/missions/past/etimor/news/N300500>.

[213] UNTAET Reg. 2000/24, 14 July 2000, as amended by UNTAET Reg. 2000/33, 26 October 2000, and UNTAET Reg. 2000/23, 14 July 2000.

[214] UNTAET Reg. 2000/24, 14 July 2000, as amended, Section 2, Artt. 2.1 and 2.3 and Section 3, Art. 3.3.

[215] UNTAET Reg. 2001/2, 16 March 2001.

[216] *Id.*, Section 2, Art, 2.5.

[217] UNTAET Reg. 2001/28, 19 September 2001.

> Transitional Administrator's hands, not delegable to any other institution during the period of UNTAET's mandate".[218]

In sum, the development of the local administration in East Timor differed from its Kosovo-counterpart due to inevitable variables. Unlike UNMIK, UNTAET enjoyed a pre-set timeframe and a clearly defined long-term aim. However, these contextual differences did not have a major impact on the mandate of the international administration. The SRSG's ultimate authority vis-à-vis the local institutions of East Timor was not derogated by the establishment of local governing structures. In East Timor, the concentration of authority in the person of the SRSG also barred the establishment of independent judicial review bodies and prevented the local judiciary from filling this gap.[219]

4.3.3.3 Local Authorities under the OHR

The relationship between local authorities in BiH and the OHR differs from the previously analyzed missions as the OHR was initially set up as monitoring institution. The Dayton Peace Agreement established a full-fledged constitutional system in confirmation of the sovereignty of BiH. However, the complexity of this constitutional system is of limited relevance for the present topic.[220] Unlike UNMIK and UNTAET, the OHR was initially not set up as an integral component of the decision-making processes at all levels, hence no diagram is provided. The OHR's authority was embodied by an extra-constitutional network of joint institutions, which brought the international presence and the local authorities together.[221] With the adoption of the Bonn powers in 1997, the nature of the OHR's authority changed as assessed in Section 4.3.2 above. As a state, BiH continued to operate independently, albeit with the High Representative having the power to exercise his prerogatives as he sees fit.

---

[218] Morrow & White (2002), p. 19.

[219] *See* Section 5.3.1 below.

[220] The internal structure of BiH was further convoluted in March 1999 by the establishment of a third territorial unit, the Brčko District. Pursuant to an arbitral award, this unit is governed by its own laws and authorities. The district is also placed under international oversight embodied in the institution of the Supervisor of the Brčko District. Initially established as the Regional Office North of the Office of the High Representative, in 2002 the institution was renamed Brčko Final Award Office. The structure and international administration of Brčko will not be discussed in this book. However, *see e.g.* Steiner & Ademović (eds.) (2010); Karnavas M. (2003), 'Creating the Legal Framework of the Brčko District of Bosnia and Herzegovina: A Model for the Region and Other Post conflict Countries', 97(1) *American Journal of International Law*, pp. 111-131. *See also* <http://www.ohr.int/ohr-offices/brcko/>.

[221] *E.g.* Dayton Peace Agreement, Ann. 10, Artt. II(2), (3), (5) and (8).

The actual use of the Bonn powers varies in terms of frequency. While some High Representatives have used their powers extensively, others have reduced the use of the Bonn powers to a minimum. In terms of legitimacy, the acceptance of such international authority within BiH generally runs along ethnic fault lines.[222] From a public law perspective, however, the introduction of the Bonn powers created a situation similar to the one described in relation to UNMIK and UNTAET. Critique has been steady as the decisions adopted by the OHR relate to all spheres of public power and remain uncontrolled.[223] No independent judicial or quasi-judicial oversight bodies have been established to control the overall exercise of Bonn powers. Furthermore, the accumulation of power has made it possible for the OHR to intervene and prevent local courts from assuming the role of judicial watchdog, as will be discussed in Section 5.3.1 below.

4.3.4 SUMMARY

The aim of Section 4.3 was to set out the nature and structure of ITA mandates. In the light of the public law argument, several points are of interest. First, ITA missions operate under a very broad mandate. The mandate provides for the exercise of essentially all public power usually vested in a state, which warrants the comparison between ITA missions and a state's governing structures in terms of competences and effect. Second, as they are initially drawn up, ITA-mandates provide little or no guidance as to how the exercise of attributed public power ought to be structured and exercised. The mandate is left open for self-interpretation by the ITA missions. This has resulted in a situation where the international legislative and executive authority is vested in a single institution *i.e.* a single officeholder, the SRSG and the High Representative respectively. As the same officeholder is ultimately responsible for the administration of the judiciary, all three branches of government are effectively merged, leaving no space for an independent judiciary *i.e.* independent (judicial) oversight.

A former international judge in Kosovo was quoted saying: "You can't have one man responsible for all arms of government – that's nonsense".[224] As Hobbes admitted, "he that is bound to himself only, is not bound".[225] Thirdly, the present section illustrated that despite all power-sharing arrangements between the international and local authorities, the ultimate decision-making

---

[222] Venice Commission OHR Report, pp. 5-6.

[223] *E.g.* Venice Commission OHR Report.

[224] AI, *Serbia (Kosovo): The challenge to fix a failed UN justice mission*, EUR 70/001/2008, 29 January 2008, p. 39.

[225] Hobbes T. (1996), *Leviathan*, in J.C.A. Gaskin (ed.), Oxford: Oxford University Press, pp. 176-177.

prerogative remains with the international actors. In other words, when it comes to accountability, the diffusion of authority through the discussed power-sharing arrangements does not necessarily imply a diffusion of responsibility.

Briefly looking ahead at Chapter 5, it is at this point proposed that the situation analyzed above impacts the ITA accountability regime in a twofold way. First, the supremacy of the SRSG and the High Representative over all local branches of government, especially the judiciary, effectively incapacitates these institutions from establishing any meaningful relationship vis-à-vis the international administration in terms of the latter's accountability. Secondly, the concentration of all power in one single officeholder makes it difficult for the international presence to establish independent accountability mechanisms from within. In other words, the structure adopted by ITA missions leaves scant opportunity for adequate internal checks and balances.

4.4 CONCLUDING REMARKS AND THE INADEQUACY OF THE '*STATE-OF-EMERGENCY*' DEFENCE

This chapter assessed how three recurring features of ITA missions translate in terms of public law.[226] Because each section concluded with a summary, instead of a repetition thereof, the present concluding remarks address the three determinants in conjunction from the perspective of the state-of-emergency defence. Namely, the initial emergency situation on the ground in the administered territories has been invoked in order to justify all three determinants of the accountability deficit. The following paragraphs address this defence, and the inadequacy thereof.

ITA missions are established as a response to exceptional circumstances on the ground. The mere fact that their establishment is based on Chapter VII of the Charter implies there is a threat to international peace and security. Indeed, initially some degree of "management by shouting" is inevitable; priority on the ground is justifiably given to humanitarian relief, peace and security.[227] The former principal legal adviser to UNTAET described the situation of the judiciary in East Timor as follows:

> The preexisting judicial infrastructure in East Timor was virtually destroyed. Most court buildings had been torched and looted, and all court

[226] Firstly, the lack of a clearly applicable legal framework leads to a weak adherence to the rule of law in terms of substantive standards. Secondly, near-absolute immunity prevents, amongst other things, the exercise of judicial review by foreign and domestic courts. Thirdly, the concentration of public power in a single entity frustrates the establishment of an independent judiciary, and checks and balances in more general terms.

[227] Bert Maan, CoE Expert, Interview, Priština, 13 September 2007.

> equipment, furniture, registers, records, archives, and-indispensable to legal practice-law books, case files, and other legal resources dislocated or burned. In addition, all judges, prosecutors, lawyers, and many judicial support staff who were perceived as being members de facto of the administrative and intellectual privileged classes, or who had been publicly sympathetic to the Indonesian regime, had fled East Timor after the results of the popular consultation were announced. Fewer than ten lawyers were estimated to have remained, and these were believed to be so inexperienced as to be unequal to the task of serving in a new East Timorese justice system.[228]

During a state of emergency, expectations vis-à-vis the authorities change in order to facilitate a solution to the situation. ITA missions have used the exceptional situation on the ground to defend the institutional features discussed in the previous sections. In reports and during press conferences, the emergency situation is often invoked to justify various measures as well as related procedural issues.[229] As Marshall and Inglis reported based on interviews conducted in Kosovo, "many inside [UNMIK] argued that adherence to [human rights] standards was not possible in the light of the obstacles UNMIK faced".[230] A former legal officer of the UNTAET Human Rights Unit observed the same sentiment:

> [T]here is often the reply when inconsistencies with human rights standards are pointed out that [East Timor] cannot "afford" policies respecting human rights. Often, I think the problem relates to ignorance of the ways in which those standards can be met.[231]

Here it is argued that invoking the state-of-emergency defence to justify the present archetypal institutional design of ITA missions is flawed. The flaws can be found by assessing the way main human rights treaties deal with the issue of

---

[228] Strohmeyer H. (2001), 'Collapse and Reconstruction of a Judicial System: The United Nations missions in Kosovo and East Timor', 95 *American Journal of International Law*, p. 50, footnotes omitted.

[229] *E.g.* UNMIK, Press Briefing, 2 July 2001 regarding the OIK's report on UNMIK detentions. Two years into the mission, UNMIK still categorized Kosovo as an "internationally-recognized emergency". Hence, it was argued, international human rights standards accept the need for special measures that, in the wider interests of security, and under prescribed legal conditions, allow authorities to respond to the findings of intelligence that are not able to be presented to the court system", *see* UNMIK News, *UNMIK Refutes Allegations of Judicial Bias and Lack of Strategy*, News No. 98, 25 June 2001.

[230] Marshall & Inglis (2003), p. 105.

[231] Former Legal Officer of the UNTAET Human Rights Unit Anne-Marie Devereux, as quoted in Bongiorno C. (2002), 'A culture of Impunity: Applying International Human Rights Law to the United Nations in East Timor', 33 *Columbia Human Rights Law Review*, p. 652.

derogation. This treaty-based legal framework is considered to be authoritative *in casu* despite the fact that ITA missions are not party to human rights treaties, and are therefore bound neither by the treaty provisions nor by the way these treaties deal with derogations. Most human rights treaties allow for states to derogate from certain obligations under exceptional circumstances.[232] The 'law on derogations' provides various parameters, some of which are presented below in light of the present topic.

Firstly, the treaties are unequivocal in stating that the emergency situation must be severe to the extent that it "threatens the life of the nation".[233] The ECtHR, for example, leaves states a wide margin of appreciation in terms of deciding whether a situation can be characterized as a threat to the life of the nation.[234] An assessment of the facts as to whether this is generally the case during ITA missions falls outside the scope of this inquiry.

Secondly, assuming the existence of the state of emergency, some rights remain non-derogable. These rights are listed in the relevant treaty provisions and differ depending on the treaty. The ICCPR and the ECHR explicitly prohibit the derogation from certain rights, including the right to life as well as the prohibition of torture.[235] In the ITA-context, the status of several other principles is also relevant. For example, the American Convention on Human Rights treats the right to participate in government as a non-derogable right.[236] This is noteworthy since international administrators have extensively used their prerogatives to bar individuals from running for office.[237] Also, the Human Rights Committee has

---

[232] *E.g.* Art. 4 ICCPR, Art. 15 ECHR, Art. 27 American Convention on Human Rights. The African Charter on Human and Peoples' Rights is an exception, as it allows for no derogations at all, *see* African Commission on Human and Peoples' Rights, *Commission Nationale des Droits de l'Homme et des Libertes v. Chad*, Comm. 74/92, § 21, adopted at the 18th Ordinary Session, October 1995, at <http://www.achpr.org/english/Decison_Communication/Chad/Comm.%2074-92.pdf>.

[233] Art. 4(1) of the ICCPR. *See also* Art. 15(1) ECHR: "In time of war or other public emergency threatening the life of the nation" and Art. 27(1) of the American Convention on Human rights: "In time of war, public danger, or other emergency that threatens the independence or security of a State Party". The African Charter on Human and Peoples' Rights is an exception, as it allows for no derogations at all, *see* African Commission on Human and Peoples' Rights, *Commission Nationale des Droits de l'Homme et des Libertes v. Chad*, Comm. 74/92, § 21, adopted at the 18th Ordinary Session, October 1995, at <http://www.achpr.org/english/Decison_Communication/Chad/Comm.%2074-92.pdf>.

[234] Over time, the ECtHR shifted from a strict interpretation in *Lawless v. Ireland*, No. 332/57, 1 July 1961, § 28 (*Lawless*) to a more 'margin-of-appreciation-based' approach in *Ireland v. the United Kingdom*, No. 5310/71, 18 January 1978, § 207 (*Ireland v. the United Kingdom*).

[235] Derogation under the ICCPR is prohibited with regard to Artt. 6, 7, 8(in part), 11, 15, 16 and 18, *see* ICCPR, Art. 4.2. Under Art. 15(2) ECHR, derogation is prohibited from rights enshrined in Artt. 2 (in part), 3, 4 (in part) and 7.

[236] Art. 23 in conjunction with Art. 27(2) of the American Convention on Human Rights.

[237] *See e.g.* Section 5.3.1.2 below.

qualified the right to an effective remedy as a non-derogable right.[238] Emphasis is placed on this right as extraordinary powers to arrest and detain are amongst the most common measures adopted in times of emergency. UNMIK and UNTAET practice reflect this.[239] Moreover, international administrators have used their prerogatives to override decisions of local courts and detain previously released individuals. This finding is also of particular importance in the present context, where emphasis is placed on the lack of accountability mechanisms. Few or no review mechanisms were put in place by UNMIK and UNTAET to oversee the use of extraordinary powers.

In this respect, the ECtHR has taken a somewhat more lenient approach, compared to the way the American Convention on Human Rights has been interpreted, in recognizing that it cannot be expected that judicial guarantees will be provided immediately in times of emergency. The Court, however, reaffirmed the necessity of adequate safeguards during a state of emergency.[240] Based on these and other limitations, the Ombudsperson Institution in Kosovo has illustrated how certain steps taken by UNMIK would constitute a breach of the ECHR even if a state of emergency were considered to exist.[241]

---

[238] HRCee, *General Comment 29*, UN Doc. CCPR/C/21/Rev.1/Add.11, 31 August 2001, § 14: "Article 2, paragraph 3, of the Covenant requires a State party to the Covenant to provide remedies for any violation of the provisions of the Covenant. This clause is not mentioned in the list of non-derogable provisions in article 4, paragraph 2, but it constitutes a treaty obligation inherent in the Covenant as a whole. Even if a State party, during a state of emergency, and to the extent that such measures are strictly required by the exigencies of the situation, may introduce adjustments to the practical functioning of its procedures governing judicial or other remedies, the State party must comply with the fundamental obligation, under article 2, paragraph 3, of the Covenant to provide a remedy that is effective".

[239] *See e.g.* 5.2.4 below.

[240] ECtHR, *Ireland v. the United Kingdom*, § 220: "The incorporation right from the start of more satisfactory judicial, or at least administrative, guarantees would certainly have been desirable […] but it would be unrealistic to isolate the first from the later phases. When a State is struggling against a public emergency threatening the life of the nation, it would be rendered defenceless if it were required to accomplish everything at once, to furnish from the outset each of its chosen means of action with each of the safeguards reconcilable with the priority requirements for the proper functioning of the authorities and for restoring peace within the community. The interpretation of Article 15 must leave a place for progressive adaptations." *See also* ECtHR, *Marshall v. the United Kingdom*, No. 41571/98, Decision on Admissibility, 10 July 2001 (*Marshall*) and *Aksoy v. Turkey*, No. 21987/93, 18 December 1996 (*Aksoy*).

[241] *E.g.* Ombudsperson Institution in Kosovo, Special Report No. 1 *on the compatibility with recognized international standards of UNMIK Regulation No. 2000/47 on the Status, Privileges and Immunities of KFOR and UNMIK and Their Personnel in Kosovo*, 18 August 2000, where the Ombudsperson repeatedly builds his argument regarding breaches of international human rights law in the following way: "The Ombudsperson also considers that even if the current situation in Kosovo may be considered to constitute a 'public emergency' in the sense of article 15 of the European Convention on Human Rights".

Thirdly, conventions generally require the state of emergency to be proclaimed *i.e.* that the derogations are reported. The American Convention on Human Rights and the ICCPR contain this explicit requirement.[242] It is considered that the ECHR, while it does not require proclamation of the state of emergency explicitly, likewise implies that the invocation of the state of emergency should be subject to scrutiny by national parliaments (and the ECtHR).[243] While this might be a procedural rather than a substantive condition, the underlying rationale relates directly to the rule of law:

> [Official proclamation] is essential for the maintenance of the principles of legality and the rule of law at times when they are most needed. When proclaiming a state of emergency with consequences that could entail derogation from any provision of the Covenant, States must act within their constitutional and other provisions of law that govern such proclamation and the exercise of emergency powers [...][244]

The main tenet underlying this requirement is that derogations should be regulated by law and subjected to scrutiny. In the present ITA context, this is not the case. Indeed, the exceptional powers of the international administrator are in accordance with an extensive interpretation of the founding documents. However, while the constituent documents in general deal with an exceptional situation, the powers attributed to the ITA missions are not treated accordingly. Rather, the extensive prerogatives are part and parcel of the ITA mandate. Furthermore, as powers are concentrated in the SRSG and the High Representative, respectively, no standing judicial body can scrutinize the exercise of exceptional measures, while at the same time acts of local parliaments are subordinated to regulations adopted by the international administrations.[245]

Finally, a fourth and overarching point concerns the temporal dimension of derogations. Besides requirements of proportionality, the relevant treaty provisions demand that 'emergency powers' shall only be in place as long as the emergency situation necessitates such measures. For example, the Human Rights Committee urged Israel to "review the necessity for the continued state of emergency [in place since 1948] with a view to limiting as far as possible its

---

[242] Art. 27(3) of the American Convention on Human Rights and Art. 4(3) ICCPR.

[243] CoE, *Opinion of the Council of Europe Commissioner for Human Rights on certain aspects of the United Kingdom 2001 derogation from Art. 5 para. 1 of the [ECHR]*, Opinion 1/2002, CommDH(2007), 28 August 2002.

[244] HRCee, *General Comment 29*, UN Doc. CCPR/C/21/Rev.1/Add.11, 31 August 2001, § 2.

[245] *See* Section 5.2.4 and 5.3.1 below.

scope and territorial applicability".[246] Similar observations were adopted by the committee with respect to Syria (where the state of emergency has remained in force since 1963, only to be abolished in 2011) and the United Kingdom (where emergency measures have been in place since 1976).[247] In the ITA context, the situation is quite contrary to the observations made by the Human Rights Committee. The anatomy of ITA missions is coined through a state-of-emergency mindset. However, ITA missions are set up to last for a longer period of time which, at least in the cases of BiH and Kosovo, exceeds the period during which these territories can actually be considered to be in a state of emergency. At some point, despite dysfunctional local authorities and economic hardship, the situation on the ground will simply cease to qualify as an emergency situation, while the structures and procedures of ITA missions remain unchanged.[248]

In summary, the initial emergency on the ground in internationally administered territories is undisputed. Moreover, individual instances that necessitate extraordinary measures might occur in the period thereafter. However, these derogatory measures must be regulated by law and do not abate the need for (judicial) review procedures. As the Human Rights Committee has argued, "[m]easures derogating from the provisions of the [ICCPR] must be of an exceptional and temporary nature".[249] Conversely, under ITA missions, derogatory measures are institutionalized and systemic rather than exceptional and temporary.[250] The following and final chapter analyzes the accountability regimes that apply to ITA missions and illustrates, from a public law

---

[246] HRCee, *Consideration of Reports Submitted by States Parties Under Article 40 of the Covenant, Concluding observation of the Human Rights Committee, Israel,* 63rd Session, UN Doc. CCPR/C/79/Add.93, 18 August 1998, § 11. *See also* HRCee, *Consideration of Reports Submitted by States Parties Under Article 40 of the Covenant, Concluding observation of the Human Rights Committee, Israel,* 99th Session, UN Doc. CCPR/C/ISR/CO/3, 29 July 2010, § 7.

[247] HRCee, *Consideration of Reports Submitted by States Parties Under Article 40 of the Covenant, Concluding observation of the Human Rights Committee, Syrian Arab Republic,* 84th Session, UN Doc. CCPR/CO/84/SYR, 9 August 2005, §§ 6 and 12; HRCee, *Consideration of Reports Submitted by States Parties Under Article 40 of the Covenant, Comments of the Human Rights Committee, United Kingdom of Great Britain and Northern Ireland,* UN Doc. CCPR/C/79/Add.55, 27 July 1995,§ 5. *See also* HRCee, *Consideration of Reports Submitted by States Parties Under Article 40 of the Covenant, Concluding Observations of the Human Rights Committee, United Kingdom of Great Britain and Northern Ireland and Overseas Territories of the United Kingdom of Great Britain and Northern Ireland*, UN Docs. CCPR/CO/73/UK & CCPR/CO/73/UKOT, 6 December 2001, §§ 6 and 18.

[248] *See e.g.* Venice Commission OHR Report, pp. 21-22.

[249] *Id.*, § 2.

[250] *See also* Werzer J. (2008), 'The UN Human Rights Obligations and Immunity: an Oxymoron Casting a Shadow on the Transitional Administrations in Kosovo and East Timor', 77 *Nordic Journal of International Law*, p. 115; Zimmermann & Stahn (2001), pp. 434-435.

perspective, how the determinants of the accountability deficit play out in practice with regards to accountability mechanisms.

5 Holding International Territorial Administrations to Account: The Accountability Deficit in Practice

"UNMIK generally adhered to international human rights standards"

- *U.S. Department of State, Country Report 2000, Yugoslavia*

"UNTAET generally respected the human rights of East Timorese"

- *U.S. Department of State, Country Report 2000, East Timor*

In this chapter, the accountability regime as it exists in practice is analyzed in the light of the three determinants presented in Chapter 4. The accountability mechanisms discussed in this chapter illustrate, so to speak, the incapacitating effect of the fact that the three public law principles – the rule of law, judicial review and an independent (judicial) oversight body – are currently not embraced and institutionalized by ITA missions.

The chapter is divided into three segments. Section 5.1 addresses the accountability mechanisms which accompany ITA missions from the moment these missions are deployed. Subsequently, Section 5.2 addresses accountability mechanisms that are established in time, often ad hoc and as a response to external criticism. Finally, Section 5.3 considers how existing institutions have engaged in shaping the accountability framework of ITA missions. In other words, what type of interaction has evolved between ITA missions and existing institutions and oversight procedures, such as courts or the UN human rights mechanisms, in terms of improving accountability and ensuring human rights protection?

The aim of this chapter is not to provide a comprehensive overview of mechanisms and their effectiveness.[1] In this respect, conventional categorizations fail. For example, when local courts are staffed by international judges operating pursuant to regulations adopted by the international administration, it is debatable whether such courts can still be qualified as local.[2] Hence, a sharp distinction between domestic and international mechanisms fails. Likewise, the question of whether or not the outcome of an accountability process is binding or not may not always provide a clear ground for categorization. For example, a binding judgment rendered by a judicial body loses its effect when the legal system in place allows the international administrator to overturn or simply disregard the judgment.

Instead, the overall accountability regime is addressed from an institutional perspective and certain illustrative mechanisms are highlighted in order to show how ITA missions have dealt with their own accountability. More in particular, an analysis is provided as to how the determinants of the accountability deficit, discussed in Chapter 4 in terms of public law, impact the ITA accountability mechanisms on the ground.

5.1 INITIAL ACCOUNTABILITY FRAMEWORK: THE PREVALENCE OF A PEACEKEEPING MINDSET

The legal frameworks under which ITA missions are established – the UN Charter, UN Security Council resolutions and, in the case of BiH, the Dayton Peace Agreement – provide for a rudimentary accountability regime, primarily focused on overall monitoring and internal oversight. The backbone of this regime is comprised of the obligation to report (Section 5.1.1) and internal oversight procedures that include UN-level and mission-specific mechanisms (Section 5.1.2). These mechanisms are supplemented by compensatory claims procedures (Section 5.1.4) and by national judiciaries (Section 5.1.3) where, subsequent to a waiver of immunity, ITA-mission staff members can be held to account.

---

[1] *Cf. e.g.*, OSCE Mission in Kosovo Human Rights and Rule of Law, *Remedies Catalogue*, 2 September 2004, at <http://www.osce.org/documents/mik/2004/09/3457_en.pdf> (OSCE Kosovo Remedies Catalogue 1). An updated version of this catalogue was issued on 27 October 2010 (OSCE Kosovo Remedies Catalogue 2). Reference will mostly be made to the first version of this catalogue as it addresses the period during full UNMIK administration.

[2] *See* Section 4.1.2 above.

5.1.1 THE REPORTING OBLIGATION

The reporting obligation flows from the principal-agent relationship between the UN and particular ITA missions and serves as a basic monitoring device. The obligation to report is regulated by the constituent resolutions.[3] The Dayton Peace Agreement likewise placed the OHR under an obligation to report to the UN as well as the EU and the PIC.[4] The UN subsequently confirmed this obligation by requesting the Secretary-General to transmit the OHR's reports to the Security Council.[5]

The Secretary-General is expected to report to the Security Council on the progress of the missions on a regular basis, which in practice amounted to three to four reports per year. The ITA reports deal with the overall situation on the ground by informing the principals on structural developments within the ITA missions, on the political situation in the administered territories and on various topics such as the rule of law and capacity-building. The reports further provide statistical data related to crime figures, composition of the ITA missions as well as financial data such as copies of the consolidated budgets of the administered territories.

Recall that the obligation to report was incorporated into the Mandate and Trusteeship systems.[6] As a consequence of a lacking fit-for-purpose legal framework, the contemporary reporting obligations differ most notably in two aspects. Firstly, under the previous systems the Mandates Commission and the Trusteeship Council had the primary responsibility to consider the reports. Nowadays, ITA-related reports are handled by the Security Council. The difference is noteworthy, as the Mandates Commission and the Trusteeship Council were specialized bodies devoted solely to the internationally administered territories.[7] Secondly, in reviewing the incoming reports, the Security Council has no tailored benchmarks against which the reports can be assessed. A cursory assessment of the substance of the reports shows that the reports score low in terms of introspection. The reports inform the Security Council on the situation on the ground and on the obstacles that the missions face, but contain little or no critical assessment of the missions as such.[8] In addition, the practice according to which the Mandatories were obliged to attach all legislative and executive decisions to their annual reports has been

[3] With respect to UNTAET: SC Res. 1272 (1999), § 18 and with respect to UNMIK: SC Res. 1244 (1999), § 20.
[4] Dayton Peace Agreement, Ann. 10, Art. II(1) (f).
[5] SC Res. 1031 (1995), § 32.
[6] *See* Section 3.1.1 above.
[7] Moreover, members of the Mandates Commission were appointed in their individual capacity, *see* Section 3.1.1 above.
[8] More particularly, the ITA accountability deficit has rarely been discussed in the reports.

discontinued.[9] Whereas, for example, the second UNMIK report had all SRSG regulations attached to it, other ITA-mission reports do not to go beyond describing legislative and executive decisions of the SRSG in general terms.[10] This may be warranted by the increased accessibility of regulations through the internet. However, subsidiary acts such as executive orders remain unpublished.

In sum, the reporting procedure is by its very nature a political rather than a judicial accountability mechanism, not intended to provide recourse or redress. The aim of these reports is to provide a comprehensive insight into the situation on the ground and into the achievements of the ITA missions. However, in the light of lacking parameters, it is difficult to use the reports as a tool through which the exercise of power by ITA missions can be assessed in more detail.

5.1.2 INTERNAL OVERSIGHT PROCEDURES

Internal oversight mechanisms provide a more hands-on approach to the actual exercise of the ITA-mandate and alleged misconduct. At the UN level as well as within individual missions, procedures exist which deal with allegations of abuse of power by staff members *ex post*. As part of the internal law of the organization, the procedures depend on which organization is engaged in the exercise of an ITA mandate. The following paragraphs address the role of internal oversight within overall ITA accountability regimes, focusing on the institutionalized oversight framework of the UN.

As the UN Office of Internal Oversight Services (OIOS) describes: "[t]he [oversight] process is generally part of the internal justice system designed to ensure employee accountability and is, therefore, *strictly administrative*".[11] The predominant purpose of internal oversight is to uphold internal standards that, when breached, can trigger disciplinary measures. For conduct falling beyond the disciplinary realm, such as criminal conduct, internal oversight serves as a steppingstone for further measures which fall under the responsibility of domestic jurisdictions, discussed in Section 5.1.3 below. Also, the jurisdiction of the OIOS with regard to military personnel is little or none. Troop-contributing countries retain primary jurisdiction over their nationals. They have the authority to conduct investigations through ad hoc Boards of Inquiry and to initiate disciplinary and judicial proceedings upon repatriation. Here, the role of the OIOS is restricted to preliminary fact-finding and is further determined through agreements between the UN and the sending states.[12]

---

[9] League Council Resolution dated 29 August 1924.

[10] *Report of the UN SG on UNMIK*, UN Doc. S/1999/987, 16 September 1999.

[11] OIOS Investigations Manual, March 2009, § 2.1, emphasis added.

[12] *Id.*,§§ 1.2 and 6.6.5.

At the UN level, relevant internal oversight procedures are structured in the following way. Allegations of abuse of power by UN staff – both in terms of mismanagement and misconduct – are investigated by the OIOS under the auspices of the UN Conduct and Discipline Unit (CDU).[13] The OIOS oversees and develops policy guidelines related to conduct and discipline. In every individual peacekeeping mission, subsidiary Conduct and Discipline Teams assist in maintaining a level of internal accountability through prevention, enforcement and remedial action.

OIOS has the authority to investigate a broad range of allegations concerning "violations of rules or regulations, mismanagement, misconduct, waste of resources or abuse of authority".[14] This broad mandate makes it possible for the OIOS to investigate activities carried out under the civil administration-part of an ITA-mission.[15] OIOS also issues audit reports and investigates finance-related issues. Findings of OIOS investigations can prompt the UN Office of Human Resources Management to adopt disciplinary measures.

In the ITA context, the multilateral exercise of public power and the complexity of power-sharing arrangements with local entities make it difficult at times to locate the precise culprit behind certain types of misconduct. This holds especially true with regards to allegations of financial mismanagement and corruption, which often relate to institutions at the local level which are managed jointly by international and local actors. In East Timor, for example, the Office of the Inspector General was established in 2000 and was responsible for "developing a culture of accountability and transparency" within the East Timor Transitional Administration.[16] Also more specific oversight units were established, such as the Judicial Inspection Unit in Kosovo, falling under the UNMIK Department of Justice. The unit investigates allegations of misconduct

[13] The CDU was established within the Department of Peacekeeping Operations. The CDU considers misconduct to be "failure by a staff member to comply with his or her obligations under the Charter of the United Nations, the Staff Regulations and Staff Rules or other relevant administrative issuances or to observe the standards of conduct expected of an international civil servant. Misconduct may lead to the institution of a disciplinary process and the imposition of disciplinary measures. Similar provisions apply to all other categories of UN peacekeeping personnel", at <http://cdu.unlb.org/FAQ2.aspx> (last visited 24 March 2010).

[14] OIOS website, at <http://www.un.org/depts/oios/pages/id.html>.

[15] *E.g.* Koyama S. & Myrttinen H., 'Unintended consequences of peace operations in Timor Leste from a gender perspective' and Kent V., 'Protecting civilians from UN Peacekeepers and humanitarian workers: Sexual exploitation and abuse', in Aoi *et al.* (eds). (2007), pp. 23-66. *See also* Charlesworth H. & Wood M. (2001), ''Mainstreaming Gender' in International Peace and Security: The case of East Timor', *26 Yale Journal of International Law*, pp. 313-317.

[16] *Report of the UN SG on UNTAET (for the period 27 July 2000 to 16 January 2001)*, UN Doc. S/2001/42, 16 January 2001, § 38. Reports on various issues related to mismanagement were issued.

of, both local and international, prosecutors and judges. Findings of misconduct are handed over to the Kosovo Judicial and Prosecutorial Council where disciplinary proceedings can be initiated.

> The well-reported case of the fraudulent senior UNMIK official Jo Hans Dieter Trutschler illustrates the functioning of internal oversight mechanisms. Three points from the case are highlighted here.
>
> 1. In 2000, Mr. Trutschler was appointed international co-head of UNMIK Public Utilities Department and Chairman of the Supervisory Board of the Kosovo Energy Company (KEK). Under the pillar structure of UNMIK, this department fell under the EU-administered fourth department dealing with reconstruction. Hence, Mr. Trutschler held an EU letter of appointment. In terms of internal oversight mechanisms, a multitude of actors results in a multitude of procedures. In the present case, Mr. Trutschler was under the investigation of two bodies: the OIOS and the European Anti-Fraud Office of the European Commission. The latter claimed jurisdiction "based on the consideration that the reconstruction function of UNMIK, including significant parts of its funding and management, is executed by the European Union under the overall responsibility of the United Nations and the [SRSG]", while the former assumed jurisdiction based on the UN's overall responsibility for the mission. With both bodies being engaged, a joint investigation was carried out.
> 2. In at least three separate instances, the OIOS found Mr. Trutschler, a German national, had abused his power. The established facts constituted furthermore a criminal offence under Kosovo and German law. In total, $4.3 million belonging to KEK had been transferred by Mr. Trutschler to his private bank accounts. Furthermore, Mr. Trutschler had been appointed to a senior position without any background check; all academic degrees and studies listed on his CV were false. Moreover, he lacked experience in the field he was supposed to manage. Based on these findings, OIOS made recommendations regarding further legal action and internal institutional improvements.
> 3. Mr. Trutschler was prosecuted and sentenced to 3.5 years of imprisonment by the competent court in the German city of Bochum. OIOS findings were used during the trial and an OIOS investigator testified Thus, the internal oversight mechanism opened the door for further legal proceedings.
>
> UN GA, *Report of the Office of Internal Oversight Services on the investigation into the fraudulent diversion of $4.3 million by a senior staff member of the reconstruction pillar of the United Nations Interim Administration Mission in Kosovo (UNMIK),* UN Doc. A/58/592, 13 November 2003.

It should be kept in mind that internal oversight procedures are essentially disciplinary in nature. Moreover, these procedures generally address the conduct of individuals and do not engage in the overall review of the ITA mission decision-making processes. Indispensable as it might be, internal oversight is neither intended nor equipped to uphold a broad range of standards during the full-fledged administration of a territory, and even more so because internal oversight is not conducted within a specific ITA-oriented legal framework. Results of internal investigations can, however, trigger a waiver of immunity.

Consequently, the door is open for judicial proceedings in the sending-states or by the local judiciary, as is discussed in the following section.

5.1.3 DOMESTIC JURISDICTIONS

Constituent resolutions of ITA missions do not reserve a role for domestic jurisdictions in terms of review of the international administration, in line with the ITA missions' supremacy over all local institutions. The UN in general relies on domestic jurisdictions for attaching legal consequences to misconduct or criminal acts committed by UN staff. The UN has encouraged domestic jurisdictions to adopt the necessary measures in order to facilitate trials – in particular criminal – against UN staff members.[17] After it is determined that immunity either does not apply or should be waived in a given case, proceedings can be initiated before the local judiciary. Otherwise, if repatriation were one of the disciplinary measures adopted, it would be up to the judiciary of the mission-contributing state rather than the local courts to decide whether to take further steps.

In practice, cases have been rare with respect to members of the civilian components of ITA missions. In Kosovo, for example, UNMIK personnel has been prosecuted and sentenced by the local judiciary only in exceptional cases.[18] Statistical data reflecting the actual number of immunity waivers is difficult to find; NGO reports indicate that relevant offices have been reluctant to provide such information.[19] With respect to sending-state jurisdictions, the previously discussed case of Mr. Trutschler is illustrative.[20] After being indicted by the German authorities, the former senior UNMIK staff member surrendered and admitted guilt before the Bochum District Court, where he was sentenced.

Conversely, case law grew steadily with respect to misconduct by members of military and police contingents; some instructive examples deserve mentioning. In 2001, two UN Civilian Police officers, who were off duty and thus did not enjoy immunity, were detained in East Timor on allegations of rape. SRSG Sergio Vieira de Mello added that "this proves that in East Timor no one is above the law".[21] In another instance, the United States Army Court of Criminal Appeal sentenced a Staff Sergeant to lifelong imprisonment without

[17] UN GA, *Report of the Group of Legal Experts on ensuring the accountability of United Nations staff and experts on mission with respect to criminal acts committed in peacekeeping operations*, 16 August 2006, § 44.

[18] Venice Commission Kosovo Report, p. 15; AI, *Kosovo (Serbia): The UN in Kosovo – A Legacy of Impunity*, Doc. EUR 70/015/2006, November 2006.

[19] HRW *Kosovo 2007* paper, p. 19, n. 47. For examples of abuse of immunity by UNMIK, *see e.g.* Nilsson (2004), pp. 401-404

[20] *See* Section 5.1.2 above.

[21] UNTAET, press item, at <www.un.org/peace/etimor/DB/Db060701.htm>.

parole for raping and murdering an 11-year-old girl while on KFOR-duty in Kosovo.[22] The OSCE Kosovo Remedies Catalogue also provides several examples; in one case a KFOR soldier was court-martialed in Germany and sentenced to 15 years of imprisonment, while in another case, for a far lesser offence, a KFOR soldier lost a rank but was not prosecuted.[23]

Moreover, the conduct of military personnel has led to civil claims before national courts. In the 2004 UK landmark case *Bici v. Ministry of Defence,* a British Court found the British Ministry of Defence was liable for negligence and trespass after British military personnel in Kosovo shot and killed two men while injuring two other persons. The claims were made by Mohamet and Skender Bici, one of whom suffered physical injury, while the other suffered psychiatric illness as a consequence of the events. It was the first time that claims for compensation had been made with regard to British peacekeepers. The Ministry of Defence argued, amongst other things, combat immunity. The Court dismissed the defence and awarded damages to the claimants.[24]

Turning to BiH, the Dayton Peace Agreement did not entrust the local judicial bodies with oversight-authority vis-à-vis the OHR. Not only does this correspond to the final authority vested in the OHR, it is also in line with the initial supervisory role of the OHR. The Dayton Peace Agreement did establish *ab initio* a complex framework of checks and balances, albeit as part of the BiH domestic legal order. This framework consisted of local institutions, some of which were semi-internationalized through international members or international appointment procedures. Although no oversight function was ever envisaged for the local judiciary, some of the established institutions attempted to assume jurisdiction over the OHR at a later stage, as the powers of the OHR increased. This development is discussed in Section 5.3.1 below, together with other situations in which various institutions tried to expand their jurisdiction so as to cover the activities of international administrators.[25]

---

[22] The United States Army Court of Criminal Appeal, Crim. App. No. 20000635, *United States v. Ronghi*, 27 May 2003. This decision was confirmed by the United States Court of Appeals for the Armed Forces, No. 03-0520, *United States v. Frank J. Ronghi,* 30 June 2004.

[23] OSCE Kosovo Remedies Catalogue 1, p. 36. International organizations have urged KFOR to establish "transparent and independent mechanisms dealing with complaints against KFOR troops in Kosovo" since the beginning of KFOR's deployment, AI, *Kosovo: Amnesty urges accountability in KFOR*, News Service, AI Index: EUR 70/01/00.

[24] The United Kingdom, Court of Appeal - Queen's Bench Division, *Bici & Anor v. Ministry of Defence*, [2004] EWHC 786 (QB), 7 April 2004.

[25] *See* Section 5.3.1.2 below.

Much attention was devoted to accountability as the EU assumed temporary administration of the city of Mostar (EUAM). Three options were discussed in this respect as the founding 1994 Memorandum of Understanding was drafted. The first option was to leave review mechanisms out of the document and to regulate the issue afterward, similar to the way in which UNMIK and UNTAET approached accountability in 1999. A second option was to appoint an EU Ombudsman for Mostar, able to issue recommendations and forward them to the Council of the EU. The Ombudsman would be appointed by the Council of the EU rather than the EU Administrator of Mostar; thus the establishment of the institution as well as appointment would not depend on the discretion of the administrator. A third and most progressive option discussed was the establishment of a special court. This court would have the power to repeal or revise decisions of the EU Administrator. Moreover, the members of the court would potentially be appointed "by the Council of the EU, acting on a proposal from the EU Administrator". This is at odds with UN practice in Kosovo, where such appointments were made by the SRSG himself.

The adopted memorandum opted for option two and established an Ombudsman (Article 7a), subsequently appointed by Council decision 94/776/EC on 28 November 1994. Together with the obligation to report (Article 7.3) and the fact that the EU Administrator had to act within the confines of the constitution of the Federation of Bosnia and Herzegovina (Articles 2 and 7.2), the accountability regime within which EUAM operated reached beyond the accountability frameworks of the OHR, UNMIK and UNTAET.

General Secretariat of the Council, *NOTE re Former Yugoslavia, second round of negotiations with Croats and Muslims of Mostar, Brussels, 8 to 10 June 1994,* No. 7696, 10 June 1994.

5.1.4 COMPENSATORY CLAIMS PROCEDURES

An additional and final element of the accountability regime that governs ITA missions from the outset of their deployments is comprised of compensatory claims procedures. These procedures deal with private law claims that arise from peacekeeping operations. Usually, claims brought to the UN under these procedures generally relate to the usurpation of real estate by UN missions or other torts. Considering the nature of these procedures, it can be argued that they do not constitute a part of the accountability regime as such. However, given the extensive immunity enjoyed by ITA missions, civil law claims cannot be dealt with by the local judiciary, as would have been the case if such immunity had not been afforded. Thus, claims commissions supplement the existing internal oversight procedures from a civil law perspective.

Two UN documents in particular deserve mention with respect to claims commissions. Firstly, consider that the General Convention calls for the establishment of alternative dispute settlement mechanisms, most notably with regard to cases where immunity is not waived.[26] Claims commissions are

[26] General Convention, Art. VIII, Section 29.

considered to be just such an alternative dispute settlement mechanism. Secondly, the 1990 UN Model Status-of-Forces Agreement envisages the establishment of a "standing claims commission".[27] The prefix "standing" is misleading, as the document is generally understood to connote the establishment of a claims commission under each individual UN mission.[28] These standing commissions were intended to structure the then existing situation in which "local claims review boards" were established. The difference was that while such review boards were fully integrated into the UN-missions, a "standing claims commission" was to include a member of the host-state government.[29] Seven years after the proposals to modify the situation were made, the Secretary-General assessed them and concluded that no standing claims commissions had been established.[30] The Secretary-General nevertheless upheld the principles underlying the claims procedures envisaged by the UN. These procedures, framed by temporal-, financial- and "operational necessity"-related limitations, allow for:

> third-party claims against the Organization for personal injury, illness or death, and for property loss or damage (including non-consensual use of premises) resulting from or attributable to the activities of members of peacekeeping operations in the performance of their official duties[31]

Although the founding documents of the particular ITA missions do not mandate the establishment of claims commissions, these bodies have been set up by the individual ITA missions. In the case of UNTAET, based on the 'alternative dispute settlement' provision of the General Convention, East Timor's international administration had the authority to receive compensation claims. Conversely, UNMIK established a claims commission by the same regulation which deals with UNMIK's immunities.[32] The Council of Europe,

---

[27] Report of the UN SG, *Model status-of-forces agreement for peace-keeping operations*, UN Doc. A/45/594, 9 October 1990, Art. 51.

[28] *Cf.* Zwanenburg M. (2005), *Accountability of peace support operations*, Leiden: Nijhoff, p. 288; Shraga D. (2000), 'UN Peacekeeping Operations: Applicability of International Humanitarian Law and Responsibility for Operations-related Damage', 94 *American Journal of International Law*, pp. 406-412.

[29] Report of the UN SG, *Model status-of-forces agreement for peace-keeping operations*, UN Doc. A/45/594, 9 October 1990, Art. 51.

[30] Report of the UN SG, *Administrative and budgetary aspects of the financing of the United Nations peacekeeping operations: financing of the United Nations peacekeeping operations*, UN Doc. A/51/903, 21 May 1997, § 7.

[31] GA Res. 52/247, 17 July 1998, §§ 5-13.

[32] UNMIK Reg. 2000/47, 18 August 2000, Section 7. The claims commission was set up to deal with "third party claims for property loss or damage and for personal injury, illness or death arising from or directly attributed to KFOR, UNMIK or their respective personnel and which do not arise from 'operational necessity' of either international presence".

siding with concerns raised by the Ombudsperson Institution in Kosovo, criticized UNMIK's claims commission, arguing that it provided neither a right for the claimants to be heard nor incorporated an institutionalized opportunity to appeal.[33] In a 2007 report, Human Rights Watch characterized the same claims commission as weak, adding that few of its interviewees, including "the majority of the UNMIK staff", even knew of the claims commission's existence.[34] This was corroborated through interviews held in Priština and Prizren in 2007 with lawyers from the local Ombudsperson offices.[35]

In summary, claims commissions do not counter the concentrated authority vested in the SRSG or in any other decision-making authority, nor do they impose substantive limits to the exercise thereof. Rather, claims commissions in the ITA context supplement the existing accountability regime in terms of civil law claims.[36]

[33] Venice Commission Kosovo Report, pp. 13-14. This was in contrast to the claims commission established by KFOR, under which *e.g.* "the appeals process incorporates many elements of proper judicial proceedings, including an opportunity for individuals to be heard or legally represented", The KFOR claims commission was also criticized, as subjection of individual KFOR contingents was not compulsory.

[34] HRW *Kosovo 2007* paper, p. 18.

[35] Interviews held in Priština and Prizren with staff of the local Ombudsperson offices as well as with prominent members of the local communities, 16 and 17 October 2007.

[36] *See* Section 5.2.3 below.

The following incident illustrates how the different elements of the initial accountability regime can play out in practice. On 10 February 2007, Priština was the stage of protests organized by the pro-independence Vetëvendosje movement. As a security measure, UNMIK police were deployed to control the demonstration. The protest turned violent and UNMIK police units from the Romanian contingent used tear gas and fired rubber bullets to contain the crowd. Two persons, Mon Balaj and Arben Xheladini, were killed and over 80 others wounded.

The conduct of UNMIK police officers is governed by procedures assessed previously in Section 5.1.2, and particularly by the internal Policy and Procedures Manual, which regulates disciplinary procedures in case of alleged violations of the code of conduct. This manual deals with investigations of alleged criminal misconduct and implicitly allows for individual complaints to be submitted. The manual recognizes that UNMIK police officers may be placed in provisional custody for the purpose of an investigation. Depending on the outcome, the case can then be referred to international prosecutors for subsequent prosecution before Kosovo courts. Prosecution, however, is conditioned by a waiver of immunity by the UN Head Quarters in New York (or the national government if the officers are part of a national contingent), upon request by the international prosecutor submitted through the legal advisor of the SRSG. Until immunity is waived, the investigation team cannot formally approach the UNMIK police officers in question.

The use of force by UNMIK police *in casu* was the subject of various proceedings. UNMIK promptly instructed a special prosecutor to set up an investigation and submit findings to the SRSG. In two separate reports published in 2007, the special prosecutor found that the deaths were unnecessary and that they could have been avoided. He criticized the manner in which the UNMIK police operated and recommended that UNMIK, the UN and the Romanian government find ways to compensate the families. Compensation claims were filed in December 2007. UNMIK released a press statement on 10 February 2010 according to which a compensation offer was made by the UN at the end of 2009.

Before the reports were made public and a decision on waiver of immunity could be taken, members of the Romanian unit had been pulled back by the Government of Romania. Despite UNMIK's request to extend the stay of the implicated officers, all 75 Romanian officers left the mission on 21 March 2007. Consequently, no investigation was conducted by local Kosovo authorities while a subsequent investigation by military prosecutors in Romania failed to identify the perpetrators.

As the report of UN Special Representative Hina Jilani concludes: "legal inconsistencies, together with other factors including ammunition which was long past its expiry date, ambiguities in operational orders and imprecision in authorizing the deployment of rubber bullets, and a breakdown in the chain of command and supervision, indicate the responsibilities of the international police in the deaths of two persons and the injury of many others, and are illustrative of the problem of accountability of the actions of UNMIK".

See UNMIK Police Policy and Procedures Manual, UNMIK Dir. 2002/18, 9 September 2002; HRC, *Report of the Special Representative of the Secretary-General on the situation of human rights defenders*, Hina Jilani, Mission to Serbia, including Kosovo, 7th session, UN Doc. A/HRC/7/28/Add.3, 4 March 2008; OIK Ex Officio Report No. 008/2007. *See also* UNMIK Press Release, *Departure of Romanian FPU from Kosovo,* 23 March 2007; HRW *Kosovo 2007* paper, p. 19, n. 46; AI, *Kosovo: No justice for the February 2007 killings,* Public Statement, 9 February 2009, AI Index: EUR 70/001/2009.

5.2 ADDRESSING THE ACCOUNTABILITY DEFICIT: AD HOC RESPONSES

ITA missions establish auxiliary accountability mechanisms over time. These mechanisms are not mandated by the founding documents of the respective ITA missions. Rather, they are established ad hoc and are often a response to external criticism. Their added value for the accountability framework rests in the fact that these mechanisms typically address the extraordinary powers enjoyed by ITA missions. In other words, they are set up as an acknowledgment of the vast impact of civil administration and in recognition of the fact that the traditional accountability regime, analyzed in the previous section, does not suffice.

More than the previously analyzed procedures, these mechanisms are devised as an expression of public law principles. They aim at upholding certain (predominantly human rights-related) standards by reviewing particular categories of decisions of the international administrations. The following sections analyze these mechanisms, their added value in terms of public law and the reasons that prevent them from gaining momentum.

Two categories of mechanisms can be distinguished. The first category includes safeguards that are built into the decision-making processes of ITA missions. These *ex ante* safeguards aim at guaranteeing that ITA decisions and policies are in line with internal and human rights standards (Section 5.2.1). The second category reflects the evolving practice of ad hoc established quasi-independent review institutions. They take the shape of ombudsperson institutions, review panels and specialized bodies dealing specifically with certain types of decisions adopted by ITA missions, such as for example detentions based on decree. From an institutional perspective, the mechanisms generally lack independence and enjoy a weak mandate.[37] Practice also reflects that the establishment of such mechanisms has not been a priority for the international presence. Nevertheless, these institutions are the backbone of the way in which ITA accountability is currently addressed, as they constitute an antipode, so to speak, to the governing structures of the ITA missions (Sections 5.2.2 through 5.2.4).

5.2.1 SAFEGUARDS AS PART OF THE DECISION-MAKING PROCESS

This section focuses on procedural safeguards built into the decision making process of ITA missions rather than review mechanisms. With respect to UN-led missions, UN Headquarters plays a supervisory role during the ITA decision-

[37] *See also* HRW *Kosovo 2007* paper, p. 2

making process, although its role is not anchored or well defined.[38] The Office of Legal Affairs reviews draft ITA-regulations in terms of conformity with the ITA mandate in general rather than with specific standards.

In addition to this centralized assistance from the UN Headquarters, in practice a more mission-specific approach evolved with human rights units being integrated into the decision-making structures of each particular ITA mission. The aim of these units is to maintain a level of adherence to human rights standards, in line with the overall mainstreaming of human rights within the UN *i.e.* the recognition of a human rights dimension within all the activities of the UN.[39] Safeguard units were incorporated into all three ITA missions in a similar fashion. In BiH, for example, in the light of the multitude of international actors exercising public power, the coordination of human rights-related issues is managed through a framework of institutions and a Human Rights Coordination Center.[40] The UNTAET Human Rights Unit served a similar purpose in East Timor.[41] Safeguards were also institutionalized in the case of UNMIK, and will be assessed in more detail.

In cooperation with the OSCE, UNMIK established the Human Rights Oversight Committee (HROC) and its operative arm, the Inter-Pillar Working Group on Human Rights (IPWG), the name of the latter referring to the then existing pillar structure of UNMIK.[42] The HROC was tasked with "ensuring that the actions and policies of all UNMIK Pillars and Offices are in compliance with international human rights standards".[43] Furthermore, the HROC dealt with "individual cases of high importance that have not been resolved at a lower level". Finally, the HROC was responsible for responding to external human rights-related criticism directed at UNMIK.[44] The HROC was composed of the Principal Deputy SRSG, the heads of various UNMIK components, the Director of the UNMIK Office of Returns and Communities, the Head of Office of the

[38] *See* Morrow & White (2002), pp 27-28.

[39] *See e.g.* Report of the UN SG, *The Rule of Law and Transitional Justice in Conflict and Post-conflict Societies*, UN. Doc. S/2004/616, 23 August 2004. *See also* Chesterman (2005), pp. 128-145; Kumm (2004), pp. 907-927.

[40] For an overview, *see further* <http://www.ohr.int/ohr-dept/hr-rol/thedept/hr-coord-cent/default.asp?content_id=3523>.

[41] *See e.g.* AI, *East Timor: Building a new country based on human rights*, ASA 57/05/00, August 2000, pp. 28-29.

[42] OSCE, Annual Report on OSCE Activities 2002, p. 20. *See also* OSCE mission in Kosovo fact sheet, May 2005, p. 4 and HRW *Kosovo 2007* paper, p. 17.

[43] Venice Commission Kosovo Report, p. 22.

[44] *Id.* At times, other components of UNMIK took a proactive approach to upholding human rights standards vis-à-vis their UN partner and engaged by issuing comments on UNMIK regulations, *see e.g.* OSCE Mission in Kosovo, Department of Human Rights and Rule of law, *Observations and Recommendations of the OSCE Legal System Monitoring Section: Report No. 6, Extension of Custody Time Limits and the Right of detainees: The Unlawfulness of Regulation 1999/26*, 29 April 2000.

UN High Commissioner on Human Rights and – as an observer – the Deputy Commander of KFOR.[45] The HROC's deliberations were held behind closed doors, remained confidential and were not allowed to be the "subject of public reporting".[46] Based on the deliberations, the HROC could make recommendations to the SRSG.[47]

To conclude, safeguards that are institutionalized under the human rights mainstreaming umbrella add to the quality and coherence of the exercise of public power in the ITA context. These safeguards play a role in upholding the rule of law in terms of respect for human rights standards. The establishment of such safeguard units, however, does not diffuse the power of international administrators by providing independent review. Furthermore, these units do not compensate for the lack of institutionalized mechanisms through which decisions of the ITA missions can be challenged in retrospect by adversely affected individuals or groups.

5.2.2 OMBUDSPERSON INSTITUTIONS

Amongst the ad hoc established ITA accountability mechanisms, the creation of ombudsperson offices has received the most attention. Well established under many national legal regimes, these institutions scrutinize the activities of public bodies within their jurisdiction. Likewise, ombudsperson offices under ITA missions are established to deal primarily with complaints against the local authorities. The ombudsperson offices are established as sustainable bodies, *i.e.* they are intended to continue scrutinizing local authorities once the international administrations have been terminated. The added value of these institutions in the present context lies in the fact that in the case of UNMIK and UNTAET, the institutions' mandates covered the exercise of public powers by the international authorities. Being the only institutions with such broad jurisdiction vis-à-vis the international administration, the ombudsperson offices gained a crucial spot in the overall accountability regime despite the non-binding nature of their mandate.

An ombudsperson office was established in East Timor, albeit no UNTAET regulation was ever adopted to that effect. Rather than an independent body, a report of the Secretary-General envisaged the institution as part of the office of

[45] Venice Commission Kosovo Report, p. 22.

[46] *Id.*

[47] *Id.* Reports on the establishment and functioning of the HROC have been ambiguous and contradictory. According to the Venice Commission Kosovo Report, the IPWG met every other week and the recommendations of this body were usually followed. However, that same report claims that the HROC had met only three times up until 2004, and that it has been dormant since, *see also* HRW *Kosovo 2007* paper, p. 17, n. 40.

the SRSG – a red flag in terms of independence of the Ombudsperson's office.[48] The mandate of the office was described as one of monitoring "the fairness of the mission's implementation of its public administration and governance mandate and address complaints by the local population".[49] The powers of the Ombudsperson office to carry out this mandate were limited. The Secretary-General's report provided for a weak mandate to "inquire into UNTAET activities" and conduct interviews, follow up on individual cases, prepare investigative reports" and provide recommendations for remedies.[50] Appointed in September 2000, the Ombudsperson only became operational in May 2001.[51]

While the powers of the East Timorese ombudsman were limited to the extent of being almost ineffectual, this did not spark widespread criticism. As Chesterman suggests, the need for a robust ombudsman was less than in the case of Kosovo and BiH.[52] Indeed, several features of the UNTAET mission warrant such a claim, including the limited timeframe of the mission, a clear political goal, a high level of local ownership and a state of emergency that arguably lasted throughout the duration of the mission.

Contrary to the limited amount of information concerning the Ombudsperson office in East Timor, the work of its counterpart in Kosovo has been well-documented and merits a detailed assessment. The Ombudsperson Institution in Kosovo (OIK) established itself as the most outspoken defender of human rights when it comes to violations as a result UNMIK and other bodies exercising the ITA-mandate in Kosovo.[53] The OIK was established by UNMIK in 2000, under the umbrella of the OSCE.[54] According to its initial mandate, it could receive

---

[48] *E.g.* Report of the UN SG, *Financing of the United Nations Transitional Administration in East-Timor*, UN Doc. A/55/443, 3 October 2000, § 42 and Report of the Advisory Committee on Administrative and Budgetary Questions, *Financing of the United Nations Transitional Administration in East Timor*, UN Doc. A/55/531, 30 October 2000.

[49] UN, Report of the UN Advisory Committee on Administrative and Budgetary Questions, *Financing of the United Nations Transitional Administration in East Timor*, UN Doc. A/55/531, 30 October 2000, § 33.

[50] Report of the UN SG, *Financing of the United Nations Transitional Administration in East-Timor*, UN Doc. A/55/443, 3 October 2000, § 42.

[51] AI reported in August 2000 that no Ombudsperson's office had been established yet in East Timor, though discussions regarding the issue were ongoing, *see* AI, *East Timor: Building a new country based on human rights*, ASA 57/05/00, August 2000, p. 8. In 2001, AI reported that an Ombudsperson office was established. Citing UNTAET's daily briefing of 1 June 2001, AI reported that the Ombudsperson office was examining some 20 cases, *see* AI, *East Timor: Justice past, present and future*, ASA 57/001/00, July 2001, pp. 29-30.

[52] Chesterman S. (2002), *The United Nations as Government: Accountability Mechanisms for Territories Under UN Administration*, Fighting Corruption in Kosovo: Lessons from the Region Conference, Priština, 4-5 March 2002.

[53] *See* in general <http://www.ombudspersonkosovo.org/>.

[54] UNMIK Reg. 2000/38, 30 June 2000, replaced by UNMIK Reg. 2006/6, 16 February 2006, as amended. Some authors refer in this respect to the Rambouillet accords from 1999, in

complaints related to alleged human rights violations and the abuse of authority by the local as well as the international civil administration.[55] Besides dealing with individual complaints, the OIK could engage in *ex officio* investigations concerning particular events or acts adopted by the international administration.[56] At the time of its establishment and throughout most of its mandate, OIK's authority to hear and investigate complaints regarding *inter alia* UNMIK made it the only stand-alone institution explicitly tasked to engage in such oversight. The ECHR, its protocols and the ICCPR shaped the main standard against which the exercise of public power was investigated.[57] The OIK, furthermore, grew to become a leading partner in policy-making and often enjoyed a consultative status in various decision-making processes.

Certain limitations framed the OIK's mandate. For example, KFOR did not fall under the purview of the OIK. The constituent regulation mandated the OIK to enter into an agreement through which KFOR would subject itself to the scrutiny of the OIK.[58] Though numerous complaints against KFOR were received by the OIK, such an agreement was never reached and complaints were forwarded to KFOR's internal oversight mechanisms. The power of the OIK was further limited as it could only make recommendations.[59] Another issue of concern was the fact that the OIK's independence was weakly guaranteed. Nominally, Section 2 of UNMIK Regulation 2000/38 emphasized the institution's independence. However, Sections 6 and 8 determined that it was the SRSG who held the right to appoint the Ombudsperson and remove him or her from office. The weak institutional position of the OIK – being established by a UNMIK regulation rather than Security Council 1244 (1999) – is probably best reflected in the fact that the SRSG repealed the OIK's jurisdiction over UNMIK in 2006, as analyzed in the following paragraphs.[60]

In 2006, UNMIK curtailed the jurisdiction of the OIK. Despite recommendations to the contrary made by, amongst others, the Council of Europe, the institution was "Kosovanized" and the Kosovo Assembly was tasked to nominate and elect a new ombudsman.[61] As the responsibilities for the

---

which an independent ombudsperson was envisaged, *see* Waters C. (2007), 'Nationalising Kosovo's Ombudsperson', 12(1) *Journal of Conflict and Security Law*, pp. 139-148.

[55] UNMIK Reg. 2000/38, 30 June 2000, Art. 3.1.

[56] *Id.*, Artt. 4.1 and 4.4.

[57] *Id.*, Art. 1.1.

[58] *Id.*, Art. 3.4.

[59] *Id.*, Artt. 4.9 and 4.10.

[60] UNMIK Reg. 2006/6, 16 February 2006, as amended.

[61] CoE, Parliamentary Assembly, Resolution 1417 (2005), Art. 5 (iv) (c) recommended that the OIK should maintain its international status until the end of international administration, regardless of the establishment of other institutions. *See also* Waters C. (2008), ''Kosovanizing' the Ombudsperson: Implications for Kosovo Peacekeeping', 15(5) *International Peacekeeping*, pp. 648-662.

Ombudsperson institution were transferred from the international to the local authorities, the OIK's jurisdiction was limited so as to exclude complaints relating to UNMIK. The OIK's new mandate was to "provide accessible and timely mechanisms for the review of actions constituting an abuse of authority *by the Kosovo Institutions*".[62]

The transfer of the institution to local authorities led to confusion. The transitional provisions under Section 19 of UNMIK Reg. 2006/6 provided for the acting ombudsperson to continue to exercise his mandate under the original regulation until the appointment of a new ombudsperson by the Assembly. A few days after the adoption of UNMIK Reg. 2006/6, the acting ombudsperson sent a letter to then SRSG, Søren Jessen-Petersen, in which he regretted the fact that the OIK had learned about the actual adoption of the regulation by chance, and in which he asked for a clarification of the transitional provisions, especially with respect to the numerous cases pending against UNMIK.[63] In response, UNMIK pointed to the establishment of a new body, the Human Rights Advisory Panel, and in seeming disregard of the transitional provisions it had previously adopted dismissed the concerns raised by the OIK:

> Rather than duplicating the work of the [HRAP], and since the Ombudsperson Institution is now a local institution, it is UNMIK's position that the focus of the Institution must now be on PISG structures.[64]

The OIK began to reject complaints directed against UNMIK, while pending complaints were prepared for transfer to the soon-to-be established Human Rights Advisory Panel.[65] However, the election of a new ombudsperson was not high on the priority list of the Kosovo Assembly. For months, no ombudsperson had been appointed, and OIK's inquiries on what to do with the incoming complaints against UNMIK remained unanswered.[66] Though complaints were not accepted officially, the acting ombudsman would at time publicly call UNMIK to account, as was done in relation to the 2007 riots and the shooting of two protesters by UNMIK police.[67]

---

62 UNMIK Reg. 2006/6, 16 February 2006, Art. 3.1, emphasis added.

63 OIK, Letter to the Special Representative of the Secretary-General, 22 February 2006.

64 UNMIK, Steven P. Schook, Principal Deputy Special Representative of the Secretary-General, letter to the OIK, 1 August 2006. The Human Rights Advisory Panel is discussed extensively in Section 5.2.3 below.

65 OIK, Press Release, 22 January 2008 and interviews with OIK senior staff in 2007.

66 *Id.*

67 OIK Press Release, *Acting Ombudsperson calls for Swift, Thorough and Independent Investigation into Protest Deaths*, 11 February 2007. *See also* HRW *Kosovo 2007* paper, p. 15.

This legal uncertainty prompted concerns amongst organizations such as Human Rights Watch, calling on UNMIK to restore the OIK's old mandate.[68] UNMIK's response remained ambiguous. In some reports, UNMIK labeled the vacuum – and the related closing of several cases pending against UNMIK at the time – as an "unfortunate consequence" of the new mandate.[69] In other instances, UNMIK was unequivocal: no gap existed, since transitional provisions provided for an extension of the initial mandate.[70] Ultimately, it was agreed that the transitional provisions did apply.[71] Thus, OIK continued to act on the basis of its protracted 2000 mandate until June 2009 when the Kosovo Assembly – in its fifth attempt – elected a new ombudsperson, more than three years after the OIK was placed under the ambit of the local authorities.

Overall, and according to some, the inherently limited powers of an ombudsperson office disqualify the institution from being considered a meaningful accountability mechanism.[72] Notwithstanding the non-binding nature of the ombudsperson's reports, the role of these institutions should not be underestimated. The achievements of the OIK between 2000 and 2009 corroborate this best.

The OIK was a pioneer in voicing concerns over the near absolute authority of the SRSG as well as the manner in which the SRSG exercised it. In doing so, the OIK pierced the veil of assumed goodwill with respect to the SRSG, challenging the international administration to pay more attention to the way it administered the territory of Kosovo.[73] The OIK based the bulk of its criticism on the assumption that UNMIK had taken up the role of a surrogate state; a role that triggers certain obligations and imposes limitations. Time and again, the institution repeated the point of departure of its reasoning:

---

68 HRW, *Not on the Agenda. The Continuing Failure to Address Accountability in Kosovo Post-March 2004*, Vol. 18, No. 4(D), May 2006, p. 66. *See also* AI, *Briefing to the Human Rights Committee during the 87th Session in July 2006*, AI Index: Eur 70/007/2006, pp. 7-8; AI, *Human rights protection in post-status Kosovo/Kosova: Amnesty International's recommendations relating to talks on the final status of Kosovo/Kosova*, EUR 70/008/2006, 24 July 2006, pp. 9-10.

69 UNMIK, *Progress Report on the implementation of the Framework Convention for the Protection of National Minorities in Kosovo submitted by the United Nations Interim Administration Mission in Kosovo*, 21 July 2008, CoE Doc. ACFC(2008)001, p. 16.

70 CESCR, *Implementation of the International Covenant on Economic, Social and Cultural Rights, Replies by United Nations Interim Administration Mission in Kosovo (UNMIK) to the list of issues (E/C.12/UNK/Q/1) to be taken up in connection with the consideration of the document submitted by UNMIK (E/C.12/UNK/1)*, 41st Session, UN Doc. E/C.12/UNK/Q/1/Add.1, 6 October 2008, § 5.

71 OIK, Press Release, 22 January 2008.

72 *E.g.* OSCE Kosovo Remedies Catalogue 1, p. 5.

73 *E.g.* Nilsson (2004), pp. 389-411.

> Resolution 1244 establishes UNMIK as a surrogate state, one of whose main responsibilities is to protect and promote human rights. [...] [t]he SRSG, as the head of this surrogate state, has an affirmative obligation to exercise his legislative and executive authority to ensure that international human rights standards are fully integrated and respected in Kosovo.[74]

In pursuing that line of argumentation, the OIK emphasized that at times UNMIK proved to be less than cooperative.[75] Research focused specifically on the OIK corroborates this and reflects a deep miscomprehension on the side of UNMIK with regard to the function of the Ombudsperson institution.[76] The OIK was nevertheless able to position itself as the leading human rights defender vis-à-vis UNMIK. During the period when UNMIK's authority was at a maximum, the OIK was headed by the internationally appointed human rights lawyer, Marek Nowicki, and staffed by local lawyers. The institution assessed all aspects of the exercise of public power by UNMIK against recognized international legal standards, with an emphasis on the human rights standards enshrined by the ECHR. On a general level, the institution did so by adopting a proactive approach to *ex officio* investigations and its authority to issue special reports. On a more individual level, with a main office in Priština and branches throughout the territory of Kosovo, the OIK increased its accessibility for the local population. All these factors together earned the institution bipartisan trust amongst the otherwise deeply divided society of Kosovo.

---

[74] Ombudsperson Institution in Kosovo, *First Annual Report 2000-2001*, 18 July 2001, p. 11 in reference to Ombudsperson Institution in Kosovo, Special Report No. 2, *On Certain Aspects of UNMIK Regulation No. 2000/59 Amending UNMIK Regulation No. 1999/24 on the Law Applicable in Kosovo (27 October 2000)*, 30 May 2001.

[75] *E.g.* OIK, Fourth Annual Report 2003-2004, 12 July 2004, pp. 16-17. *See also* Mr. Marek Nowicki's statement made at his speech to the CoE Parliamentary Assembly on 25 January 2005 and his remarks made during the Meeting of the Committee on Legal Affairs and Human rights of the Parliamentary Assembly of the CoE on The Human Rights Situation in Kosovo, Paris, 16 March 2004.

[76] Waters (2007), p. 144: "many UNMIK officials saw the need to respond to the Ombudsperson's requests as a diversion of resources and found the criticisms stinging when faced with an impossible mandate and insufficient resources. The Ombudsperson was reportedly even accused by a former Special Representative of the Secretary-General of not playing 'team ball', which if true reveals a fundamental misunderstanding of the Ombudsperson's role by UNMIK leadership", footnotes omitted.

A cursory overview of statistical data listed in the OIK annual reports covering the period between 2000 and mid-2009 reflects the following points.

Approximately 1396 complaints were received against UNMIK, with complaint numbers dropping to zero after 2007 due to the new OIK mandate and the increased power transfer to local authorities after 2006. Some 1960 complaints were received against the local authorities, including municipalities, courts, ministries and the Kosovo police. A steady number of annual complaints were received against specialized institutions such as the Housing and Property Directorate, totaling around 380. Despite the OIK's lack of jurisdiction with respect to KFOR, some 180 complaints were received addressing KFOR conduct. The number of non-admissible complaints received against other parties numbers around 470, including several complaints against NGO's, Serbia and other states such as Germany.

In dealing with individual complaints, the OIK addressed various issues such as the practice of barring individuals from running for election (*e.g.* Ex Officio investigation No. 19/1), the UNMIK detentions with respect to the Niš Express bus-bombing (Report Reg. No. 256/01, Report Reg. No. 257/01, Report Reg. No. 258/01), ill-treatment by UNMIK police (*e.g.* Report Reg. No. 361/01) and the two killings by UNMIK police during the 2007 Priština demonstrations (Report Ex Officio No. 008/2007).

In special reports, besides dealing with acts of the local authorities, the OIK criticized various aspects of UNMIK's exercise of power, arguing incompatibility with international law and the ECHR in particular. Most notably, the special reports addressed the immunities enjoyed by UNIMK (Special Report No. 1), detentions based on UNMIK executive orders as well as the setup of the Detention Review Commission for Extra-judicial Detentions Based on Executive Orders (OIK Special Reports No. 3 and 4), UNMIK's registration policy with respect to real-estate sales contracts (Special Report No. 5) and the situation in the led-contaminated IDP camps in the north of Kosovo (Report Ex Officio 50/2010).

See OIK annual reports between 2000 and 2009.

5.2.3 HUMAN RIGHTS PANELS

Calls for strengthening the ITA accountability framework at times also include proposals for the establishment of institutions specifically mandated to scrutinize the ITA missions. Unlike in Kosovo, in East Timor and in BiH no such institutions were established. The Council of Europe early on suggested the establishment of an oversight body for the UN in Kosovo.[77] This body would

[77] Venice Commission Kosovo Report, p. 25. The suggested panel was to be composed of SRSG-appointed judges who would review the conformity of UNMIK regulations with human rights standards. The body would also consider appeals to decisions of the UNMIK claims commission, analyzed in Section 5.1.4 below, *see* CoE, Parliamentary Assembly, Resolution 1417 (2005), § 5(v). The panel would not hear individual complaints; a limitation that should be read in conjunction with other proposals made by the CoE at the time that included the establishment of a Human Rights Court for Kosovo and the strengthening of the OIK. The findings of the advisory panel would not be binding, though according to the

complement safeguard mechanisms such as the HROC. While the suggested panel was never established, in 2006 UNIMK established a *sui generis* institution much like the proposed body: the Human Rights Advisory Panel (HRAP).[78] Established in February 2006, the three members of the HRAP convened their first meeting only in November 2007, due to "logistical difficulties" such as budget shortages and lack of office space.[79] Due to the changed circumstances in Kosovo, or, in UNMIK's words, due to its "diminished ability to effectively exercise executive authority", UNMIK decided that the HRAP shall stop accepting new complaints as of March 2010.[80] The rise and fall of the HRAP, as discussed below, pointedly illustrates three things: the hesitance of UNMIK to establish a meaningful oversight body; the struggle of the HRAP to achieve and retain its independence; and finally, the detrimental effect of the HRAP's ad hoc nature in terms of its independence and authority to review UNMIK's decisions.

The HRAP was established at a time when the OIK's jurisdiction had just been curtailed. The HRAP had the jurisdiction to hear complaints concerning UNMIK. The HRAP further interpreted its mandate when it held that acts of the PISG are attributable to UNMIK as a consequence of UNMIK's continuing ultimate authority.[81] Complaints against institutions whose acts are not attributable to UNMIK, such as KFOR and the OSCE (as far as internal OSCE matters are concerned), remained inadmissible.[82] In particular, the HRAP was

---

proposal, UNMIK was expected to commit itself to accept the findings in general and where necessary provide redress. Furthermore, it was suggested by the Venice Commission that such an advisory panel would consider cases where UNMIK failed to respond to recommendations made by the OIK. Although the Venice Commission was committed to the strengthening of the OIK, the report made the striking suggestion that UNMIK might be more willing to accept findings coming from "its own panel" rather than coming from the OIK.

[78] UNMIK Reg. 2006/12, 23 March 2006, as amended. The CoE labeled the HRAP as a "first complaints mechanisms of its kind", *see Report of the Council of Europe Commissioner for Human Rights' Special Mission to Kosovo(1)*, Doc. CommDH(2009)23, 2 July 2009, p. 13. The unique position of the HRAP is also recognized by the institution itself: the HRAP proudly claims on the homepage of its website that it is "the only human rights mechanism in existence that deals specifically with human rights violations allegedly committed by or attributable to a United Nations field mission", at <www.unmikonline.org/human_rights/index.htm>. Arguably, this exclamation calls for praise and criticism alike. The drafting process of the HRAP constituent regulation is illustrated in detail in Knoll B. & Uhl R. (2007), 'Too Little, Too Late: The Human Rights Advisory Panel in Kosovo', 5 *European Human Rights Law Review*, pp. 535-549.

[79] HRW *Kosovo 2007* paper, p. 16. The lack of resources was also noted in *e.g.* CoE Advisory Committee on the Framework Convention for the Protection of National Minorities, *Second Opinion on Kosovo(1)*, Doc. ACFC/OP.II(2009)004, 05 November 2009, pp. 10-11.

[80] UNMIK Administrative Direction 2009/1, 17 October 2009, Section 5.

[81] HRAP, *Nexhmedin Spahiu v. UNMIK*, Case No. 02/08, 20 March 2009, Opinion.

[82] HRAP, *Brahim Sahiti v. UNMIK*, Case No. 03/08, 10 April 2008, Decision on admissibility and HRAP, *Dejan Jovanović v. UNMIK*, Case No. 39/08, 17 October 2008, Decision on admissibility.

intended to fill the structural gap with respect to the inability of individuals from Kosovo to have access to the ECtHR.[83] This is reflected in the HRAP's institutional design and mandate, which strengthen the ties with the ECHR and the ECtHR.[84] In comparison to the OIK, a slight improvement was made in terms of independence by including the President of the ECtHR into the appointment procedure of the HRAP members. Although the President of the ECtHR nominates the members, the actual appointment for a renewable period of one year is carried out by the SRSG.[85] The Human Rights Committee voiced concerns regarding the HRAP's weak independence while Human Rights Watch went one step further in its criticism by arguing that:

> since the panel is created by UNMIK regulation [and] its procedures [are] subject to amendment by UNMIK, it is hard to see how the panel can be considered independent.[86]

When this issue was raised in writing by the Committee on Economic, Social and Cultural Rights (CESCR), UNMIK failed to respond and to elaborate on how the independence of the panel was guaranteed.[87] The issue was discussed

---

[83] UNMIK Reg. 2006/12, 23 March 2006, Section 2, as amended. *See also* HRW *Kosovo 2007* paper, p. 16. *See also* HRCee, Report Submitted by the United Nations Interim Administration Mission in Kosovo to the Human Rights Committee on the Human Rights Situation in Kosovo Since June 1999, Kosovo (Serbia and Montenegro), UN Doc. CCPR/C/UNK/1, 13 March 2006, § 131. *See further* HRAP, Annual Report 2008, pp. 3 and 8.

[84] UNMIK Reg. 2006/12, 23 March 2006, Section 1, Art. 1.2. The HRAP's temporal jurisdiction was limited to cases concerning UNMIK conduct or decisions from 23 April 2005 onwards. However, complaints regarding acts which gave rise to a continuing human rights violation are admissible, as confirmed in HRAP, *Olga Lajović v. UNMIK*, Case No. 09/08, 16 July 2008, Decision on admissibility. The limited temporal jurisdiction prevented the HRAP from admitting a complaint from Agim Behrami, whose case was also declared inadmissible by the ECtHR, *see* Section 5.3.2.1 below. In terms of material jurisdiction, the HRAP has been criticized, as it would not "address the lack of a judicial remedy against administrative decisions by UNMIK", *see* OSCE Mission in Kosovo, Monitoring Department/Rule of Law Division, Legal System Monitoring Section; *Privatization in Kosovo: Judicial Review of Kosovo Trust Agency Matters by the Special Chamber of the Supreme Court of Kosovo*, 21 May 2008, at <http://www.osce.org/kosovo/32012>, p. 23.

[85] UNMIK Reg. 2006/12, 23 March 2006, Section 5, as amended.

[86] HRCee, *Consideration of Reports Submitted by States Parties Under Article 40 of the Covenant, Concluding observation of the Human Rights Committee, Kosovo (Serbia)*, 87th Session, UN Doc. CCPR/C/UNK/CO/1, 14 August 2006, § 10. *See* also UNMIK, *Comments to the 2nd Opinion on Kosovo (1) of the Advisory Committee on the Framework Convention for the Protection of National Minorities*, 31 May 2010; HRW *Kosovo 2007* paper, p. 16. *See also* AI, *Briefing to the Human Rights Committee during the 87th Session in July 2006*, AI Index: Eur 70/007/2006, p. 9.

[87] CESCR, *Implementation of the International Covenant on Economic, Social and Cultural Rights, Replies by United Nations Interim Administration Mission in Kosovo (UNMIK) to the list of issues (E/C.12/UNK/Q/1) to be taken up in connection with the consideration of the*

again during a session of the CESCR, where UNMIK stated that there was no problem with the HRAP's independence, inaccurately claiming that the panel members were *not* appointed by UNMIK.[88]

The power of the HRAP is limited. As an advisory organ, the panel's findings and recommendations have no binding effect; "the [SRSG] shall have exclusive authority and discretion to decide whether to act on the findings of the [HRAP]".[89] The final authority of the SRSG is further reflected in the mandate of the HRAP, as the panel cannot compel UNMIK to submit necessary documents or to cooperate with investigations.[90] Despite these predicaments, the HRAP mirrored the proactive approach adopted by the OIK, not least due to the fact that one of the newly appointed HRAP members was Marek Nowicki, former head of the OIK. This proactive approach led to a strained relationship between UNMIK and the HRAP, which culminated in 2009 with the promulgation of UNMIK Administrative Direction 2009/1 by which UNMIK, once again, limited the powers of an oversight body and effectively discontinued it.[91]

Up until March 2010, the HRAP had received approximately 516 complaints, 53 of which have been closed leaving 463 cases pending at the time of writing. Of the 53 closed cases, a human rights violation was found in 10 cases, while no violation was established in 2 instances. The remaining cases were declared (partially) inadmissible or were taken from the list.

Based on data from the HRAP 2008 and 2009 annual reports, the bulk of complaints concern the right to life (including the corollary issue of ineffective investigations into murder cases), fair trial, enjoyment of property and the right to an effective remedy.

See <http://www.unmikonline.org/human_rights/index.htm>. *See also* HRAP, *Brahim Sahiti v. UNMIK*, Case No. 03/08, Decision on admissibility, 10 April 2008 and *Dejan Jovanović v. UNMIK*, Case No. 39/08, Decision on admissibility, 17 October 2008.

---

document submitted by UNMIK (E/C.12/UNK/1), 41st Session, UN Doc. E/C.12/UNK/Q/1/Add.1, 6 October 2008, § 6.

88 CESCR, *Summary Record of the 37th meeting*, 41st Session, UN Doc. E/C.12/2008/SR.37, 20 November 2008, § 35.

89 UNMIK Reg. 2006/12, 23 March 2006, Section 17, Art. 17.3, as amended.

90 The wording of the pertinent sections is confusing. Though the regulation determines that the SRSG "shall" cooperate with the HRAP, it continues by saying that "requests for the appearance of UNMIK personnel or for the submission of United Nations documents shall be submitted to the Special Representative of the Secretary-General. In deciding whether to comply with such requests, the Special Representative of the Secretary-General shall take into account the interests of justice, the promotion of human rights and the interests of UNMIK and the United Nations as a whole", UNMIK Reg. 2006/12, 23 March 2006, Sections 15 and 17, as amended.

91 UNMIK Administrative Direction 2009/1, 17 October 2009.

5.2.3.1 *Avoiding Accountability Through Executive Interference: The Demise of the HRAP*

In 2009, UNMIK Administrative Direction 2009/1 imposed several measures that drastically affected the HRAP's *modus operandi.* It was decided that "[p]ublic hearings of the [HRAP] shall be conducted in such manner and settings that allow a clear sense of non-adversarial proceedings to be conveyed to all participants and to the public at large".[92] Quite to the contrary, the OSCE had previously argued with respect to other review mechanisms in Kosovo that they should be adversarial in nature.[93]

UNMIK also tightened the admissibility criteria with a retroactive effect. As an *ultimum remedium,* the HRAP only accepted complaints once all other avenues for review had been exhausted. In line with Article 13 ECHR, these mechanisms need to be available and effective.[94] While normally it would be up to the HRAP to determine whether a mechanism falls under this category, the Administrative Direction declared explicitly that the UN Third Party Claims Process shall be recognized as an "available avenue": that is, an alternative remedy.[95] The Administrative Direction also determined that admissibility issues could from now on be addressed at any time during the HRAP proceedings. Finally, by that same Administrative Direction, UNMIK decided that no new complaints shall be accepted by the HRAP after 31 March 2010, thus effectively discontinuing the institution.[96]

The fundamental modifications of the HRAP's mandate and their retroactive effect fall nothing short of executive interference (in the ITA context, one might add 'by the legislator') into the realm of the judiciary. This interference is facilitated by the institutional design of UNMIK and the ad hoc nature of the

[92] *Id.*, Section 1, Artt. 1.1. and 1.3. The Administrative Direction went so far as to determine that "[t]he venue and seating arrangements for public hearings conducted by the Advisory Panel shall be consistent with the non-adversarial nature of the proceedings", *see* HRAP, Annual Report 2009 for the HRAP's dismay with regard to the Administrative Direction.

[93] OSCE Mission in Kosovo, Department of Human Rights and Rule of law, *Observations and Recommendations of the OSCE Legal System Monitoring Section: Report No. 6, Extension of Custody Time Limits and the Right of detainees: The Unlawfulness of Regulation 1999/26*, 29 April 2000, p. 4.

[94] HRAP, *Shaip Canhasi v. UNMIK*, Case No. 04/08, 12 November 2008, Opinion.

[95] UNMIK Administrative Direction 2009/1, 17 October 2009, Section 1, Art. 1.3. *See also* HRAP, Annual Report 2009, Section 2.2: "Any complaint that is or may become in the future the subject of the UN Third Party Claims process or proceedings under Section 7 of UNMIK Regulation No. 2000/47 on the Status, Privileges and Immunities of KFOR and UNMIK and their personnel in Kosovo of 18 August 2000, as amended, shall be deemed inadmissible for reasons that the UN Third Party Claims Process and the procedure under Section 7 of Regulation No. 2000/47 are available avenues pursuant to Section 3.1 of (Regulation No. 2006/12)".

[96] UNMIK Administrative Direction 2009/1, 17 October 2009, Section 5.

HRAP, as the existence and nature of the HRAP was solely dependent on UNMIK's discretion. In practice, the modification of the HRAP's mandate prevented the panel from deciding on the merits with regard to two high-profile cases pending before it, concerning the toxic IDP camps and the shooting of two demonstrators by UNMIK police during the 2007 Priština protests. The factual backdrops of these cases have already been discussed; what follows is a recount of the proceedings before the HRAP in order to illustrate the effect of executive interference.[97]

The internally displaced persons living in the lead-contaminated camps near Mitrovica filed a complaint with the HRAP in 2008, alleging various human rights violations, most prominently relating to the right to life, fair trial and effective remedy.[98] The complaint was initially declared admissible in part.[99] Several months later, UNMIK issued Administrative Direction 2009/01. As the IDPs had previously filed a compensation claim under the UN Third Party Claims system, UNMIK re-opened the admissibility issue before the HRAP based on the new rules UNMIK itself had imposed.[100] The plaintiffs responded by arguing that:

> the promulgation of UNMIK Administrative Direction No. 2009/1 itself is a collateral attack on the Panel's decision on admissibility of 5 June 2009, which violates fundamental principles of international administrative law and the rule of law, including due process, non-retroactivity, and fundamental fairness. The complainants attack a number of provisions of the Administrative Direction as being internally inconsistent, overbroad and in violation of the rule of law.[101]

The HRAP noted that normally it would be within the discretion of the panel to determine the availability of alternative avenues for redress, *i.e.* to assess whether a particular mechanism qualifies as one. The disputed administrative direction makes this determination instead. Consequently, the HRAP found itself obliged to declare the complaint inadmissible *in toto.*[102]

---

[97] *See* Sections 1.1 and 5.1.4 above.

[98] The plaintiffs claimed violations under various human rights documents, such as the ECHR, the ICCPR, ICESCR, CEDAW, CERD and the CRC. For the facts of the case, *see* Section 1.1 above.

[99] HRAP, *N.M. et al. v. UNMIK*, Case No. 26/08, 5 June 2009, Decision on admissibility.

[100] On behalf of the IDPs, the European Roma Rights Centre had filed a compensation claim on 10 February 2006.

[101] HRAP, *N.M. et al. v. UNMIK*, Case No. 26/08, 31 March 2010, Second Decision on admissibility, § 26.

[102] HRAP, *N.M. et al. v. UNMIK*, Case No. 26/08, 31 March 2010, Second Decision on admissibility, §§ 43-51. The HRAP did emphasize that in the light of its discontinuation, an

The controversial administrative direction had an identical effect on the pending *Balaj et al.* case concerning the excessive use of force by UNMIK police in Priština in 2007. The injured parties filed a complaint in October 2007, alleging violations of the right to life (including both the substantive and the procedural aspect thereof), the right to peaceful assembly and the prohibition of torture. The plaintiffs also claimed that their right to a fair trial and effective remedy had been violated.[103] Initially, the case was declared admissible.[104] Despite timely invitations sent to UNMIK to comment on the issue of admissibility, UNMIK objected to the admissibility (on the basis of non-exhaustion of available remedies) only after the admissibility decision had been adopted.[105] Furthermore, after an intensive written exchange between the HRAP and both parties, UNMIK refused to attend a public hearing scheduled by the HRAP due to the looming semblance of an adversarial process. UNMIK subsequently issued the disputed Administrative Direction that in part directly addressed the issue of public hearings. Consequently, on the basis of the new rules of procedure, the HRAP had to revise its previous decision and – in the words of the HRAP – "regrettably" declare the initial complaint inadmissible.[106]

alternative avenue must be made available to the claimants after the UN Third Party Claims procedure has been terminated.

[103] The plaintiffs invoked, amongst others, the ECHR, the ICCPR and the CAT.

[104] HRAP, *Balaj et al. v. UNMIK*, Case No. 04/07, 6 June 2008, Decision on admissibility.

[105] AI refers to this as one of UNMIK's methods to derail the process, *see* AI, *Hearing into deaths in Kosovo could find UN accountable*, Press Release, 23 March 2009.

[106] HRAP, *Balaj et al. v. UNMIK*, Case No. 04/07, 31 March 2010, Second Decision on admissibility. This decision also contains an elaborate overview of the procedural history of the proceedings.

In the *Balaj et al.* case, UNMIK Administrative Direction 2009/1 was also addressed by the plaintiffs through a separate complaint. Kadri Balaj, complainant in the case previously declared admissible by the HRAP and pending final decision, filed this second complaint with the HRAP. In what resembles an interlocutory appeal, the plaintiffs argue the following:

Para. 8: The complainants allege a violation of their right to a fair trial as guaranteed by Article 6(1) of the European Convention on Human Rights (ECHR). According to the complainants, Administrative Direction 2009/1 "purports to have the effect of (1) reopening the issue of admissibility, (2) determining the live issue of admissibility, (3) preventing the Panel from considering the merits of the complaint, (4) prevent[ing] adversarial proceedings, in application no. 04/07, and (5) undermining the independence and impartiality of the Panel". They state that the Administrative Direction constitutes "an obvious attempt by the executive, in this case the SRSG, to provide a binding interpretation of the relevant law", and as such amounts to "a very serious breach" of the right to a fair hearing. Para. 9: The complainants explicitly state that they "reserve their right to argue that the provisions of Administrative Direction 2009/1 are *ultra vires* and contrary to the requirements of [Regulation No. 2006/12 of 23 March 2006 on the establishment of the Human Rights Advisory Panel".

As it is "within the discretion of the SRSG to determine the regulatory scheme of the complaint system", the HRAP decided that it "therefore regretfully concludes that it has no jurisdiction to examine the complaint".

HRAP, *Kadri Balaj et al. II v. UNMIK*, Case No. 320/09, Decision on admissibility, 12 February 2010.

In summary, the assessment of the OIK and the HRAP makes an ambivalent impression at best. On the one hand, the added value of these institutions is undisputed. Especially in a legal environment where other check and balances are scarce, these institutions reduce the existing gap in terms of recourse and oversight. On the other hand, the assessment illustrates pointedly how the three determinants of the accountability deficit affect the functioning of these institutions and, consequently, the accountability regime as such. Established at the discretion of the SRSG rather than on the basis of a broader legal framework, it was possible for the international administrations to modify the mandates of the oversight institutions when and to the extent that it saw fit. This weak foundation was further compromised by a weak institutional independence, which led to the ultimate demise of both institutions in terms of their jurisdiction vis-à-vis the international administration.

5.2.4 REVIEW PROCEDURES WITH SPECIALIZED JURISDICTION

Review mechanisms such as the OIK and the HRAP could only lead to non-binding recommendations. None of these mechanisms imposed actual limits on the SRSG's authority, nor could decisions of the SRSG be repealed; whether they could bring about change ultimately depended on the SRSG's discretion. In a few exceptional cases, the SRSG established review mechanisms with specialized jurisdiction that had the authority to review, but above all override, decisions adopted by the SRSG and by supporting agencies to which decision-making authority had been delegated.

Occasionally, local courts were mandated to engage in such review procedures. For example, this was the case with regard to public procurement procedures for the civil administration in East Timor[107] and to decisions based on the prohibition of logging operations and the export of wood.[108] A similar procedure was set up in the context of the protection of endangered species, biodiversity and biological resources.[109] Other examples include the ad hoc establishment of procedures and specialized bodies. Two main examples from Kosovo are discussed below.

The Special Chamber of the Kosovo Supreme Court on Kosovo Trust Agency Related Matters

One example concerns the review procedure established in the highly sensitive context of privatization in Kosovo. In 2002, UNMIK established the Kosovo Trust Agency (KTA).[110] In short, the KTA was responsible for the privatization process in Kosovo until 2008, when the KTA was replaced by the Privatisation Agency of Kosovo (PAK).[111] The KTA was set up as an administrative rather than a commercial entity, entrusted with the administration of publicly owned enterprises such as the Kosovo Electricity Corporation, Kosovo Railways, Priština International Airport and the Post and Telecommunication of Kosovo.[112]

---

[107] UNTAET Reg. 2000/10, 6 March 2000, Section 42.

[108] UNTAET Reg. 2000/17, 10 May 2000, Section 6.4 which mandates the local judiciary to engage in review of decisions by the International Administration. The local judiciary in effect functioned as a court of second instance as applications for review were first sent to the Deputy Transitional Administrator for review, *see* Section 6.1.

[109] UNTAET Reg. 2000/19, 30 June 2000, Section 8.4.

[110] UNMIK Reg. 2002/12, 13 June 2002, as amended.

[111] On 21 May 2008, the Assembly of Kosovo adopted Law No. 03/L-067, *On the Privatization Agency of Kosovo*, replacing the Kosovo Trust Agency. Pursuant to this law, UNMIK Reg. 2002/12, 13 June 2002 ceased to have legal effect. The present paragraphs discuss the situation as it existed prior to the establishment of the PAK.

[112] UNMIK Reg. 2002/12, 13 June 2002, Chapter II, Section 5, Art. 5.5, as amended.

In order to do so, the authority of the KTA encompassed "any action that the Agency considers appropriate to preserve and enhance the value, viability or governance of the enterprise".[113] Most notably, pursuant to UNMIK Regulation 2005/18, the KTA was not required to determine ownership of enterprises and assets prior to privatization, thus allowing for privatization of assets owned by third parties.[114] This effectively opened the door for expropriation in contravention of Article 1 of Protocol 1 to the ECHR.

KTA decisions were expected to trigger many claims because of the complexity of the privatization process in Kosovo, which involved a multiplicity of stakeholders and several preceding waves of "confiscation, nationalization and socialization" that occurred during the Socialist Federative Republic of Yugoslavia.[115] Hence, UNMIK established the Special Chamber of the Kosovo Supreme Court on Kosovo Trust Agency Related Matters (Kosovo Special Chamber) as a judicial body exclusively empowered to adjudicate claims concerning the KTA and the PAK.[116]

Two features of the Kosovo Special Chamber deserve mentioning. Firstly, rather than reviewing decisions of the SRSG as such, the Kosovo Special Chamber scrutinizes the KTA, an agency within the Kosovo administration. The link between the KTA and the SRSG, however, is close because "[the SRSG] holds exclusive power to administer enterprises and property. The privatization process has been delegated to the Trust Agency".[117] Secondly, as part of the Supreme Court of Kosovo, the Kosovo Special Chamber was established as a durable mechanism rather than a temporary body, envisaged to continue operating beyond the period of international administration. The following paragraphs primarily discuss the relationship between the Kosovo Special

---

[113] *Id.*, Chapter II, Section 6, Art. 6.1, as amended.
[114] OSCE Kosovo Privatization Report, p. 10.
[115] *Id.*, p. 6. The range of stakeholders includes various entities such as the Republic of Serbia, Kosovo, municipal organs and workers councils.
[116] UNMIK Reg. 2002/13, 13 June 2002. This regulation was amended in 2008 and since then reads UNMIK Reg. 2008/4, 5 February 2008, as amended. References made to the constituent regulation of the Kosovo Special Chamber relate to the amended regulation, unless otherwise indicated. For a detailed survey of the privatization process and the work of the Kosovo Special Chamber, *see* OSCE Mission in Kosovo, Monitoring Department/Rule of Law Division, Legal System Monitoring Section, *Privatization in Kosovo: Judicial Review of Kosovo Trust Agency Matters by the Special Chamber of the Supreme Court of Kosovo*, 21 May 2008 (OSCE Kosovo Privatization Report). The present paragraphs are based largely on the findings of fact published in this report. *See also* International Center for Transitional Justice, *Property Rights in Kosovo: A Haunting Legacy of a Society in Transition*, Occasional Paper Series, February 2009. Law No. 03/L-067, *On the Privatization Agency of Kosovo* in Art. 24.8 provides that all decisions of the PAK shall be subject to review by the Kosovo Special Chamber.
[117] OSCE Kosovo Privatization Report, p. 5.

Chamber and the KTA as it existed between 2002 and 2008 due to the de facto changed role of UNMIK in Kosovo after this period.

Throughout the bulk of its operational history, decisions of the Kosovo Special Chamber were final and binding, with no possibility of appeal.[118] Although initial drafts for the setup of the procedure did include a second instance procedure, this proposal was never effectuated due to financial constraints.[119] Amendments in 2008 introduced a limited possibility to appeal by establishing an appellate panel within the Kosovo Special Chamber.[120] In terms of composition, the Kosovo Special Chamber initially had five judges. The amendments of 2008 expanded the number of judges to 20.[121] The amendments did not change the fact that a majority of judges (including the presiding judge) were international (3 and 13 respectively) and all judges were appointed by the SRSG, after consultations with the President of the Supreme Court.[122]

Certain aforementioned institutional features are emblematic of the way ITA accountability mechanisms are set up and are problematic in terms of the public law principles. The appointment procedure raises questions regarding the Kosovo Special Chamber's independence. The situation becomes even more complicated, as the Chairman of the KTA Board is also the Deputy SRSG. Consequently, "both the judiciary and the [KTA] report to the same individual – the [SRSG] (who is also the legislator)".[123] Additional critique has been voiced with regard to the *modus operandi* of the Kosovo Special Chamber, concerning the multiple functions often enjoyed by the judges of the chamber, procedural delays and the fact that decisions are rarely published.[124]

---

118 *See also* UNMIK Administrative Direction 2006/17, 6 December 2006, Art. 45.6. However, informal appeal was possible. Cases assigned to three-judge panels could be reviewed upon request by a judge or party by the full Kosovo Special Chamber. This occurred in 10 to 20 percent of the cases, *see* OSCE Kosovo Privatization Report, p. 36, n. 199. In 2010, Art. 21 of the Kosovo draft Law on Courts envisaged that "[t]he Supreme Court [of Kosovo] includes the Appeals Panel of the Kosovo Property Agency and the Special Chamber of the Supreme Court, the judges of which are part of the Supreme [Court]", Kosovo draft Law on Courts, Art. 21.

119 OSCE Kosovo Privatization Report p. 35, n. 193. The authority of the Kosovo Special Chamber is far reaching, at times triggering criticism regarding its own procedures and legitimacy, *see e.g.* the OSCE Kosovo Privatization Report.

120 UNMIK Reg. 2008/4, 5 February 2008, Artt. 3.3, 4.4 and 9.5.

121 *Id.*, Section 3.

122 *Id.*, Section 3, Art. 3.1.

123 OSCE Kosovo Privatization Report, p. 38.

124 *Id.*, pp. 38-47.

> The Kosovo Special Chamber pronounced itself on, amongst other things, the relationship between UNMIK regulations and international human rights standards in the following two landmark cases. In its decision of 9 June 2004, in the case *Vahdet Kollari et al. v. KTA,* the Kosovo Special Chamber set a precedent by refusing to apply a provision of UNMIK Reg. 2003/13, arguing inconsistency with international human rights standards. In the case of *Aleksandar Hadžijević and Vera Frtunić v. KTA and SOE Trepča Hotels,* 20 November 2007, the Kosovo Special Chamber ruled against a KTA decision in favour of the claimant's claims to ownership. It held that certain provisions of UNMIK Regulations 2005/18 and 2002/13 were contrary to Article 1 of Protocol 1 to the ECHR and Article 6 ECHR respectively. The Kosovo Special Chamber ruled that the ECHR "supersedes the provisions of the relevant UNMIK Regulations".
>
> International Center for Transitional Justice, *Property Rights in Kosovo: A Haunting Legacy of a Society in Transition,* Occasional Paper Series, February 2009.

Despite the fact that the actual decisions subjected to review were not UNMIK regulations as such, the review mechanism stands out as it scrutinized decisions adopted in a field which at the time fell exclusively under the competence of the SRSG. Overall, the establishment of the Kosovo Special Chamber provides a rare example of including (semi-)domestic legal bodies as an overview organ into the decision-making process of the international administration.

Detention Review Commission for Extra-Judicial Detentions Based on Executive Orders

A second example of a specialized review body was established in Kosovo in the context of one of the most controversial powers of the SRSG: the right to issue executive orders based on which individuals were detained despite being previously released by the local judiciary. No mechanism existed within the ITA legal framework through which such executive orders could be reviewed, thus contravening the *habeas corpus* principle and the rights guaranteed by Article 5 ECHR, Article 9(4) ICCPR as well as Article 286(2) of the Provisional Criminal Procedure Code of Kosovo. This situation led to widespread criticism voiced by Amnesty International as well as local institutions.[125] Moreover, the Human Rights Committee denounced such practice and requested the revocation of this particular prerogative based on its incompatibility with the ICCPR.[126]

---

[125] OIK Special Report 3, 29 June 2001, *On the Conformity of Deprivations of Liberty Under 'Executive Orders' with Recognised International Standards*; AI, *Briefing to the Human Rights Committee during the 87th Session in July 2006*, AI Index: Eur 70/007/2006, pp. 37-39.

[126] HRCee, *Consideration of Reports Submitted by States Parties Under Article 40 of the Covenant, Concluding observation of the Human Rights Committee, Kosovo (Serbia)*, 87th Session, UN Doc. CCPR/C/UNK/CO/1, 14 August 2006, § 17.

The SRSG established the Detention Review Commission for Extra-Judicial Detentions based on Executive Orders (DRC) in August 2001, for the specific purpose of reviewing the controversial executive detention orders.[127] It was established for a period of only three months, within which period it could engage in review *ex officio* or upon receiving a petition by persons whose detention was based on such orders.[128] The decisions of the DRC were binding and not subject to appeal.[129] Section 6 of UNMIK Regulation 2001/18 states:

> If the Commission decides that an extra-judicial detention based on an executive order is not justified, the executive order shall cease to have effect and the detained person shall be immediately released.[130]

Conversely, in the event that the DRC confirmed a particular executive order, such a decision was to be "treated as a decision of a panel of the Supreme Court to order detention within the meaning of Article 197(2) of the applicable Law on Criminal Procedure".[131] By establishing the DRC, the SRSG in part subjected his decision-making authority to review, thereby weakening the finality of his overall authority.

However, the DRC is illustrative of the deficiencies in the UN's ad hoc approach to accountability. Established for a period of three months, the DRC's mandate was never renewed. Consequently, the founding regulation ceased to be applicable by the end of October 2001, while the SRSG's authority to issue executive orders for detention remained in place. In terms of staffing, the DRC was composed of three members – a judge from Germany, the UK and the United States – appointed by the SRSG.[132] As with other SRSG-established bodies, the appointment procedure raised concerns in terms of independence.[133] Another concern surfaced with the UN-drafted initial rules of procedure, which envisaged the process to be closed to the public and to the media. Only after intervention of the newly appointed DRC members were these rules amended

---

[127] UNMIK Reg. 2001/18, 25 August 2001, Section 1. Extra judicial detentions under the responsibility of KFOR did not fall under this regulation. According to the OSCE Kosovo Remedies Catalogue 1, Art. 7(k) of KFOR Detention Directive 42 provided a right to petition for detainees, but no further mechanisms or procedures were set up.

[128] UNMIK Reg. 2001/18, 25 August 2001, Section 4, Art. 4.1 and Section 10.

[129] UNMIK Reg. 2001/18, 25 August 2001, Sections 6 and 7.

[130] *Id.*, Section 6, Art. 6.2.

[131] *Id.*, Section 6, Art. 6.3.

[132] *Id.*, Section 2, Art. 2.1. The SRSG appointed the members on the basis of his authority to appoint and remove from office international judges pursuant to UNMIK Reg. 2000/6, 15 February 2000, as amended.

[133] *See also* AI, *Briefing to the Human Rights Committee during the 87th Session in July 2006*, AI Index: Eur 70/007/2006, pp. 38-39.

and finalized to allow for public hearings.[134] Based on these concerns and certain other procedural features, the OIK concluded that the DRC could not be considered a "court" in the sense of Paragraph 4, Article 5 ECHR, and therefore did not address the apparent breach of Article 5 ECHR.[135]

In practice, the DRC only dealt with one particular case, in which three suspects were detained for their alleged connection to the February 2001 bombing of a Serbian bus, killing more than nine passengers.[136] In its sole decision, the DRC found that the detentions were justified and prolonged them for a maximum of 90 days.[137] The procedural chronology of the case against Florim Ejupi, the main suspect in the bus-bombing incident, is discussed briefly below, as it pointedly captures the determinants of the accountability deficit and the interaction between the various actors within Kosovo's semi-international judicial system over the past decade.

5.2.4.1 The Case of Florim Ejupi and Kosovo's Judicial System

In March 2001, after more than nine people were killed and dozens wounded in the February 2001 Niš Express bus-bombing, British KFOR soldiers arrested Florim Ejupi, the main suspect, together with three other suspects. On 27 March 2001, an international panel of judges of the Priština District Court upheld the detention of Ejupi based on DNA evidence, and released the remaining three suspects. On 28 March 2001, SRSG Hans Haekkerup overruled the decision of the Court by issuing executive orders prolonging the detentions of the three released suspects for a period of 30 days. These orders were renewed repeatedly. While the three suspects remained in detention, on 14 May 2001, Ejupi escaped from the Unites States' detention centre at Camp Bondsteel in Kosovo where he had been detained.

[134] Account of Judge Jack F. Nervin, former presiding judge of the DRC, published as a news item for the Washington State Bar Association in July 2002, at <http://www.wsba.org/media/publications/barnews/archives/2002/jul-02-kosovo.htm>.

[135] OIK, Special Report 4, 12 September 2001, *On Certain Aspects of UNMIK Regulation No. 2001/18 on the Establishment of a Detention Review Commission for Extra-judicial Detentions Based on Executive Orders (25 August 2001)*, § 26. The OSCE also insisted that review of such executive orders must take place in an adversarial procedure before a court, *see* OSCE Mission in Kosovo, Department of Human Rights and Rule of law, *Observations and Recommendations of the OSCE Legal System Monitoring Section: Report No. 6, Extension of Custody Time Limits and the Right of detainees: The Unlawfulness of Regulation 1999/26*, 29 April 2000, p. 4.

[136] OSCE Kosovo Remedies Catalogue 1, p. 16. Accounts on the number of casualties are conflicting and range between 9 and 11. For several other cases of extra-judicial detentions, *see* AI, *Briefing to the Human Rights Committee during the 87th Session in July 2006*, AI Index: Eur 70/007/2006, pp. 35-36.

[137] UN News, *Kosovo's Detention Review Commission supports detention of bus bombing suspects*, 21 September 2001, at <http://www.un.org/peace/kosovo/news/kosovo2.htm>.

After criticism against the continued renewal of the executive orders, the DRC was established by UNMIK Regulation 2001/18 in August 2001.[138] The DRC became operational in September and reviewed the relevant executive orders, finding that the detentions were justified. The DRC decided that the three suspects should be tried and that their detention should be extended until the commencement of the trial, but no longer than 90 days: namely, until 19 December 2001.[139] The DRC was set up for a period of only three months and the three international members left Kosovo after their mandate had expired. As no trial had yet commenced, the members were called by the UN on 13 December 2001 – six days before the three-month deadline was to expire – to return to Kosovo in order to renew their decisions and to extend the detention period. The members refused.[140]

Once the pretrial detention period expired, requests were filed with the Kosovo Supreme Court to extend the detention further. These requests were rejected, and the three suspects were released from custody. Some commentators mistakenly claimed that by this decision, the Kosovo Supreme Court overruled the SRSG's executive order for detention of the three individuals.[141] By virtue of Article 6.3 of UNMIK Regulation 2001/18, decisions adopted by the DRC upholding an executive order were to be treated as decisions of the Supreme Court of Kosovo. Hence, the Kosovo Supreme Court de jure merely decided not to renew its own decision.

Several years later, on 7 June 2004, Albanian police arrested Ejupi in Tirana pursuant to an international arrest warrant issued by UNMIK. The International Public Prosecutor filed an indictment against Ejupi on 17 May 2006 with the Priština District Court.[142] The indictment charged Ejupi *inter alia* with 12 murders based on both the Criminal Law of Kosovo as well as the Criminal Code of the Socialist Federal Republic of Yugoslavia. Ejupi was tried, and on 6 June 2008, the trial panel of the Priština District Court – composed of three international judges – found Ejupi guilty, sentencing him to a maximum sentence of 40 years of imprisonment.[143]

Appeal was filed with the Kosovo Supreme Court on 4 September 2008. As the political situation on the ground had changed, a mixed panel of judges was this time composed pursuant to the "Law on Jurisdiction, Case Selection and

[138] UNMIK Reg. 2001/18, 25 August 2001.

[139] IWPR, *Kosovo: Court Overturns Haekkerup Detention Orders*, 11 January 2002.

[140] Account of Judge Jack F. Nervin, former presiding judge of the DRC, published as a news item for the Washington State Bar Association in July 2002, at <http://www.wsba.org/media/publications/barnews/archives/2002/jul-02-kosovo.htm>.

[141] IWPR, *Kosovo: Court Overturns Haekkerup Detention Orders*, 10 January 2002.

[142] PP. Nr. 57/2001, 17 May 2006, as amended on 25 September 2007, 02 October 2007, 18 October 2007 and 24 December 2007.

[143] District Court of Priština, C. Nr. 202/2005, Judgment, 6 June 2008.

Case Allocation of EULEX Judges and Prosecutors in Kosovo", consisting of three EULEX judges and two local Kosovo Supreme Court judges. In a controversial decision dismissing the previously used DNA evidence as insufficient, the Kosovo Supreme Court repealed the first-instance verdict and acquitted Ejupi of all charges on 12 March 2009.[144]

> The final judgment of the Supreme Court of Kosovo was received with ambivalence. Representatives of the Serbian population in Kosovo as well as the Republic of Serbia condemned the judgment. Ejupi in his turn stated he had been "a victim of a scheme arranged against him by the British KFOR, Serbia and UNMIK" but concluded by saying that he believed "in EULEX justice".
>
> Economist Media Group, *A controversial decision on the "Nis Express" case announced*, 16 March 2009, at < http://www.emg.rs/en/news/serbia/82247.html>.

5.3 EXISTING INSTITUTIONS: ACCOUNTABILITY THROUGH IMPROVISATION

A third category of accountability processes relates to the interaction between preexisting institutions and ITA missions which evolves in practice as missions continue to administer particular territories. In some cases, this interaction amounts to an outright power struggle as local courts and institutions attempt to assume jurisdiction over international administrations despite existing statutory limitations in that respect (Section 5.3.1). In addition, founding documents of ITA missions do not assign any explicit role to existing international courts and tribunals, which leaves the relationship between these judicial institutions and ITA-mission undefined (Section 5.3.2). Finally, the interaction relates to the manner in which ITA missions position themselves vis-à-vis various international human rights supervisory mechanisms. Most notably, interaction has developed between UNMIK and human rights mechanisms within the UN and Council of Europe systems (Section 5.3.3).

---

144 Supreme Court of Kosovo, Ap-Kž. No. 409/2008, 12 March 2009, Judgment. This judgment was confirmed by the Kosovo Supreme Court on 10 November 2009 – by a panel composed of 1 EULEX Judge and 4 local Judges – after a Request for Protection of Legality was filed by the Office of the State Prosecutor of Kosovo on 28 May 2009, *see* Supreme Court of Kosovo, Pkl-Kzz 71/09, 10 November 2009, Judgment. However, even if granted, a Request for Protection of Legality could not have led to an annulment of the March 2009 Judgment. In another case, the SRSG adopted UNMIK Reg. 2001/2 for the sole purpose of reopening the case of Afrim Zeqiri. This regulation was only applicable 30 days after its promulgation. The Kosovo Supreme Court was expected to review the SRSG's detention order but refrained from assuming jurisdiction as it argued that Zeqiri was detained based on an administrative act and should thus be reviewed through administrative procedures, despite the fact that no such procedures existed, *see e.g.* Marshall & Inglis (2003), p. 120.

5.3.1 LOCAL COURTS AND INSTITUTIONS

The reasons local courts cannot review the exercise of public power by the international administrators of the territory of their jurisdiction are multifold. Some reasons relate to the relationship between domestic courts and international organizations in general (as discussed for example in Section 4 2), while others are linked specifically to the institutional design of ITA missions (discussed in Section 4.3). How does this shape the relationship between local institutions and ITA missions and is there room for change?

From a public law perspective, it seems unacceptable as a matter of principle that an entity holding such vast public powers as the SRSG is exempted from the scrutiny of courts belonging to the legal system in which these powers are exercised. This line of reasoning is also reflected in the UN's recommendation – in the context of UN peacekeeping and criminal responsibility – that "UN staff should be tried as much as possible before local courts due to their proximity to the affected society".[145]

As regards ITA missions, it is crucial to bear in mind that international actors are not merely international organizations operating within a local order; to all intents and purposes they are the supreme authority within that legal order. Exempting them from the jurisdiction of local courts places them outside the reach of the legal order they themselves design and control, and is in principle irreconcilable with the very essence of the rule of law and the need for independent judicial review.[146]

However, the nature of ITA missions *prima facie* precludes their appearance before national courts. Any lawsuit against an organ of the international administration will in fact result in a lawsuit against an international organization – a lawsuit for which national courts in principle lack jurisdiction.[147] If a local court were to assume jurisdiction, immunity would render such a step futile.

Besides the practical feasibility of a local court assuming a supervisory role, the added value of such a development is debatable. First of all, one should

---

[145] UN GA, *Report of the Group of Legal Experts on ensuring the accountability of United nations staff and experts on mission with respect to criminal acts committed in peacekeeping operations*, 16 August 2006, § 44.

[146] Venice Commission Kosovo Report, p. 21: "it must be recalled that in Kosovo UNMIK and KFOR carry out tasks which are *certainly more similar to those of a State administration* [than] *those of an international organization proper*. It is unconceivable and incompatible with the principles of democracy, the rule of law and respect for human rights that they could act as State authorities and be exempted from any independent legal review", emphasis added.

[147] *See also* Venice Commission Kosovo Report, p. 20, where the fact that UNMIK is an international organization is regarded as the main obstacle preventing local courts from assuming the power to engage in judicial review.

consider the nature of local courts within the context of ITA. The local judiciary is managed and supervised by the international authorities. Local courts are internationalized or semi-internationalized in terms of staff. Either directly or indirectly, judges of the local courts are appointed and dismissed by the SRSG through a system that lacks basic checks and balances. Hence, their independence is compromised and their position unsuitable for the job of reviewing acts of the SRSG. It is also doubtful whether it is at all desirable to have local courts assume such an authority under the given circumstances. Various crucial issues need to be regulated in advance in order to prevent such a development from becoming counterproductive. For example, the question arises concerning against which benchmarks a local court would review the acts of ITA missions, as they in principle enjoy the status of supreme law and are not embedded in a broader legal framework.[148] Other issues include determining which courts should have this jurisdiction, the scope of such a jurisdiction and the question of *locus standi*. In particular cases, it has been suggested that local courts could assume the authority to review. For example, the OSCE recommended that UNMIK should allow the Kosovo Supreme Court to review executive orders extending pre-trial detention.[149] However, if left unregulated,

---

[148] *See also* Stahn (2005)(3), p. 23.

[149] OSCE Mission in Kosovo, Department of Human Rights and Rule of law, *Observations and Recommendations of the OSCE Legal System Monitoring Section: Report No. 6, Extension of Custody Time Limits and the Right of detainees: The Unlawfulness of Regulation 1999/26*, 29 April 2000, p. 4. Back in 2004, the CoE proposed the establishment of a Human Rights Court for Kosovo, *see* Venice Commission Kosovo Report, pp. 22-24, echoed by CoE, Parliamentary Assembly, Resolution 1417 (2005), pursuant to CoE, *Protection of human rights in Kosovo,* Report of the Committee on Legal Affairs and Human Rights, Doc. 10393, 6 January 2005. According to § 4 (i) (b) of the Resolution, unlike the Bosnian Human Rights Chamber, the court would be empowered to hear complaints regarding alleged violations of the ECHR and its Protocols by UNMIK and the PISG. The suggested Human Rights Court would differ from existing mechanisms, as the five international and four local judges would be appointed by the President of the ECtHR, to emphasize the link between the ECHR and the Kosovo Human Rights Court, and the obligation of the latter to be guided by the ECHR's case law, *see* Venice Commission Kosovo Report, p. 24. In dealing with cases against UNMIK and KFOR, the court would have an international-members-only composition. Interestingly, the proposal emphasized that the nomination of one of the international judges would be made in agreement with the SRSG, in order to achieve the effect of a national judge. In terms of *locus standi*, applications were to be lodged either by individuals or by the Ombudsperson on their behalf. As for the authority to adopt binding decisions, the Kosovo Human Rights Court was envisaged to have the power to annul decisions of UNMIK that it declared in breach of the ECHR, *see* Venice Commission Kosovo Report, p. 24 and CoE, Parliamentary Assembly, Resolution 1417 (2005), § 4 (i) (g). Proposals had also been made with regard to the post-UNMIK international presence. HRW has recommended that the future Constitutional Court of Kosovo have jurisdiction to deal with complaints against these international authorities for alleged human rights violations. This jurisdiction would be civil rather than criminal in nature and would "not involve personal liability of individuals", *see* HRW *Kosovo 2007* paper, pp. 28-31.

judicial activism in this direction could obstruct the otherwise undisputed authority of the ITA-mission to exercise public powers. In particular, it could lead to legal fragmentation, compromise legal certainty and potentially paralyze the international governing authorities.[150]

Despite these predicaments, yet without much success, local courts have at times challenged the exercise of public powers by the SRSG and relevant subsidiaries. Incidentally, courts have overruled decisions of international administrators or have refused to apply them.[151] In one such example, the SRSG annulled the result of a tender procedure according to which a Kosovo company, Mobikos, was awarded a contract to establish Kosovo's second mobile phone network.[152] The SRSG had intervened after reported allegations of corruption with regard to the tender process.[153] Despite the intervention, the Priština Municipal Court ordered the execution of the contract.[154] UNMIK was swift to declare that the decision of the court disregarded applicable law and was not enforceable.

[150] *See* Perrit (2004), pp. 14-36.

[151] *See* Everly R. (2007), 'Reviewing Governmental Acts of the United Nations in Kosovo', 8(1) *German Law Journal*, pp. 21-38 for a review of several instances where local Kosovo courts refused to apply UNMIK decisions.

[152] UNMIK Executive Decision 2004/25, 20 October 2004.

[153] SETimes, *UNMIK Asks for Suspension of Kosovo's Second Mobile Phone Licence*, 30 June 2004, at <http://www.setimes.com/cocoon/setimes/xhtml/bs/document/setimes/features/2004/06/040630-SVETLA-001>.

[154] Priština Municipal Court, Case No. P. 3044/04, 16 March 2005.

The exchange between the press and a UNMIK spokesperson on 23 March 2005 with respect to the *Mobikos* case illustrates UNMIK's view on interventions by the local judiciary.

"KTV: A question for UNMIK. Following the municipal court order on the second mobile phone operator contract granted to MOBIKOS, what is the stance of UNMIK? Will you refuse or accept this decision of the court?

Neeraj [UNMIK spokesperson]: The SRSG, by an Executive Decision 2004/25 of 20 October 2004, cancelled the tender process for the second mobile phone operator that was carried out by the TRA. This decision was made after a lengthy process of dialogue with relevant members of the Government and the Chairman of the TRA. Through this process of dialogue, and according to the findings of an independent panel of experts established by the Auditor General, it became evident that the tender process for the second mobile operator had been seriously flawed. As indicated in the Executive Decision, action to cancel the process was necessary in the best interests of Kosovo and its economic development, in particular its ability to attract investment. Regrettably, the Chairman of the TRA went ahead with the signing of a contract for the second mobile telephone operator in Kosovo on the morning of October 21 without prior notice to UNMIK or to the Government. By virtue of the SRSG's Executive Decision of October 20, which invalidates all actions, agreements and decisions based on the annulled tender procedure, the agreement between the TRA and the Mobitel-Mobikos Consortium is null and void. The decision of the Municipal Court of Pristina, requiring the TRA to execute the agreement between Mobikos-Mobitel and the TRA is therefore without legal basis and not enforceable. Accordingly, and based on the SRSG's Executive Decision 2004/25 of 20 October 2004, the TRA is required to disregard the court's decision and to abstain from any action that could be seen in any way as implementation of the court's decision.

RTK: Well in relation to what you said it is not very clear to me. So you will disregard the decision of the court or you will allow this to continue to other instances? You said that this decision is null and void, but the court took a decision. Now can the decision of the court be disregarded or the case will continue to other instances? Does UNMIK have the right to declare null and void a decision issued by the court?

Neeraj [UNMIK spokesperson]: You see, while arriving at its decision the court disregarded the applicable law in Kosovo as established by the Executive Decision of the SRSG. Therefore the court's decision is clearly not enforceable. In issuing the Executive Decision the SRSG was acting under the authority vested in him pursuant to the UN Security Council mandate under resolution 1244. In making such a determination the SRSG has full authority to issue an Executive Decision which has the force of law and is not subject to any challenges".

UNMIK, unofficial transcript of Press Briefing Notes, 23 March 2005, at <http://www.unmikonline.org/press/2005/trans/tr230305.pdf>.

In other examples, the Kačanik Municipal Court in Kosovo annulled a decision of the UNMIK Municipal Department of Education.[155] Similarly the Gnjilane District Court found that the detention of Shaban Beqiri and Xhemajl Sejdiu,

[155] Kačanik Municipal Court, Case No. C.nr.2/2001, Judgment, 12 March 2001. For the facts of the case and the subsequent complaint procedure before the OIK, *see* OIK, Report, *Elife Murseli v. UNMIK*, Reg. No. 122/01, 10 December 2001.

based on executive orders of the SRSG, was in contravention of the ECHR and ordered their immediate release.[156] In both cases, the courts ignored UNMIK's immunity. Consequently, UNMIK ignored the judgments. In the *Bota Sot* case, the Priština District Court refused to apply UNMIK Administrative Direction 2003/8 after being petitioned by a UNMIK official to enforce a fine based on that act.[157] After an internal UNMIK memo objected to the Court's decision, the case was appealed before the Kosovo Supreme Court where a re-trial was ordered.[158] The re-trial resulted in a Priština District Court order to enforce the fine.[159]

Similar examples exist with respect to East Timor; three well-reported cases are discussed to illustrate the pitfalls of uncontrolled judicial activism by local courts vis-à-vis international administrations. Furthermore, two of these cases illustrate executive interference with the judiciary on the part of UNTAET, similar to UNMIK's previously described interference in HRAP proceedings.[160] The rebellious East Timorese judgments illustrate how uncontrolled judicial activism fails to contribute to the development of a sustainable legal system. At times, the courts furthered legal uncertainty instead, prompting interventions from the legislator and the president of East Timor.

In its first hearing under UNTAET, the Dili District Court had to decide on allegations of unlawful detention of Victor Alves. Charged with murder, Alves had been arrested in December 1999, and claimed, amongst other things, that pre-trial detention time limits had been exceeded. One day before the hearing, UNTAET Reg. 2000/14 was issued.[161] This regulation had extended relevant detention limits and retroactively validated certain types of arrests and detentions. In addition, it had barred cases such as the present one from being heard by a single judge.[162] Nevertheless, the judge in this case went on to deliver his judgment the following day, in which the Dili District Court refused to apply UNTAET Reg. 2000/14, holding that it was discriminatory and in violation of the legality principle and fundamental human rights standards.[163] As no appeal was possible at the time (the Court of Appeal had not yet been staffed), Alves

---

[156] Gnjilane District Court, *Prosecutor v. Shaban Beqiri and Xhemajl Sediu*, 25 July 2000. *See* further OSCE Mission in Kosovo, *Review 2: The Criminal Justice System in Kosovo (September 2000-February 2001)*, 28 July 2001, p. 81.
[157] Priština District Court, Case No. E 1/04, 16 July 2004.
[158] Supreme Court of Kosovo, Case No. AC/37/2004, 20 August 2004.
[159] Priština District Court, Case No. E 2/04, 14 January 2005.
[160] *See* Section 5.2.3.1 above.
[161] UNTAET Reg. 2000/14, 10 May 2000, Sections 4 and 5.
[162] *Id.*, Section 3.
[163] Dili District Court, *Prosecutor v. Victor Alves*, Case No. 01/Pen.Pra/2000/PD DIL, Decision, 17 May 2000. *See* further Linton (2001), pp. 140-143 for a critical analysis of the judgment.

was released.[164] Reports indicate that the reasoning applied in *Alves* was by and large ignored in similar subsequent proceedings and failed to serve as a precedent.[165]

In another example, freelance journalist Takeshi Kashiwagi had been detained in East Timor by UN police, pursuant to Dili District Court instructions, on accusations of defamation penalized under the Indonesian Criminal Code. On 7 September 2000, the SRSG intervened by issuing an executive order decriminalizing defamation. Consequently, Kashiwagi was released from custody a few days later. The Japanese national brought a claim for compensation for unlawful detention before the Dili District Court in 2001 against various Timorese officials and the SRSG, Sergio Vieira de Mello.[166] The Dili District Court upheld the claim for compensation and declared the SRSG's executive order to be unlawful.[167] This judgment was overruled on appeal by the Dili Court of Appeal.[168]

In a third and final example, after the termination of UNTAET, a series of local judgments contested retroactively the applicable law in East Timor *i.e.* the interpretation of UNTAET Reg. 1999/1. Recall that both UNMIK and UNTAET had declared previously applicable laws to be valid under certain conditions.[169] In July 2003, the Dili Court of Appeal rendered a watershed judgment in the *Armando dos Santos* case. The Court – by a majority of two Portuguese judges with the East Timorese judge dissenting – held that since the Indonesian occupation of East Timor had been illegal, Indonesian law could never have been the valid law in East Timor. Therefore, Section 3.1 of UNTAET Reg. 1999/1, which refers to "laws applied in East Timor prior to 25 October 1999", should be interpreted, the Court held, as referring to Portuguese law.

---

[164] Ultimately, Alves was indicted again in January 2002 before the Special Panels for Serious Crimes of the District Court of Dili, which convicted Alves for murder in 2004 and sentenced him to one year of imprisonment, *see* Dili District Court, The Special Panels for Serious Crimes, Case No. 1/2002, *The Deputy General Prosecutor for Serious Crimes v. Victor Manuel Alves*, Decision, 18 June 2004. Alves' sentence was increased to two years on appeal, *see* Dili Court of Appeal, Case No. 60/2004 TR, Decision, 26 April 2005. On 19 May 2005, the President of Timor Leste issued decree No. 16/2005 commuting Alves' sentence, pursuant to which the Special Panel for Serious Crimes ordered Alves' immediate release a day later, *see* Dili District Court, The Special Panels for Serious Crimes, Case No. 01/2002 (No. 60/2004 TR), *The Deputy General Prosecutor for Serious Crimes v. Victor Manuel Alves*, Order for the Immediate Release of Defendant Victor Manuel Alves Pursuant to Decree No. 16/2005 of the President of the Republic, 20 May 2005.

[165] *See* Judicial System Monitoring Programme, *Report on The General Prosecutor v. Joni Marques and 9 Others (The Los Palos Case)*, March 2002, Dili, East Timor.

[166] *See e.g. Bongiorno (2002)*, pp. 623-692.

[167] AI, *East Timor: Justice past, present and future*, ASA 57/001/00, July 2001, pp. 23-25.

[168] 'Article 19 and Internews', *Freedom of Expression and the Media in Timor-Leste*, December 2005, p. 78.

[169] *See* Section 4.1.2 above.

Furthermore, the Court held that applying UNTAET Reg. 2000/15 to crimes committed before 1999 – the practice thus far in numerous criminal proceedings before the Special Panels for Serious Crimes in East Timor – is unconstitutional.[170] Sentenced for murder pursuant to Indonesian law in first instance, on appeal Dos Santos was found guilty of genocide based on Portuguese law – a crime for which he was not charged – and was sentenced to 22 years imprisonment.[171] The judgment was criticized, as it created legal uncertainty and undermined the basis of numerous previous criminal proceedings and legal transactions that were carried out based on the two disputed UNTAET regulations and Indonesian law.[172] The district courts in East Timor ignored *Dos Santos* and continued to apply Indonesian Law.[173] Likewise, the aforementioned Special Panels for Serious Crimes in East Timor were quick to decide they would not follow *Armando Dos Santos*.[174] Ultimately, the legislator resolved the ambiguity in October 2003 by passing a law that reaffirmed the application of Indonesian law in the absence of other legislation or UNTAET regulations.[175]

The strained relationship between local institutions and international administrators is best illustrated by the situation in BiH. Here, the attempts of local courts and institutions to expand their jurisdiction occurred in a more systematic way, and are therefore indicative of the manner in which international administrations might respond to earnest activism on the part of local bodies. Two examples are discussed below. Section 5.3.1.1 reflects on the relationship between the Government of BiH and the OHR through a particular example whereby the Government tried to establish a specialized review mechanism. Section 5.3.1.2 turns to the relationship between the Constitutional

[170] The Special Panel for Serious Crimes was established by UNTAET in June 2000 as part of the Dili District Court, with the exclusive jurisdiction over serious criminal offences. *See* UNTAET Reg. 2001/15, Section 9.

[171] Dili Court of Appeal, Case No. 16/PID.C.G./2001/PD.DIL, *Prosecutor v. Armando dos Santos*, Decision, 15 July 2003. *See also* AI, *Indonesia: Justice for Timor-Leste: The Way Forward*, ASA 21/006/2004, p. 21, where it is stated that Dos Santos was sentenced to 25 years imprisonment.

[172] For an analysis of the controversial judgment, *see* Judicial System Monitoring Programme, *Report on the Court of Appeal Decision in the Case of Armando dos Santos*, August 2003, Dili, East Timor. The issue was also raised before the UN Security Council, *see Report of the Secretary-General on the United Nations Mission of Support in East Timor*, UN Doc. S/2003/994, 6 October 2003.

[173] Judicial System Monitoring Programme, *Dili District Court Final Report 2003*, November 2003, Dili, East Timor, pp. 15-16.

[174] Dili District Court, The Special Panels for Serious Crimes, Case No. 18a/2001, *Prosecutor v. Domingos Mendonca*, Decision on the Defence Motion for the Court to order the Public Prosecutor to amend the indictment, 24 July 2003, § 49(b).

[175] East Timor, *Law No. 10/2003*, 20 November 2003.

Court of Bosnia and Herzegovina (CCBH) and the OHR and expands on the protracted power struggle between the two bodies.

5.3.1.1 *The Government of Bosnia and Herzegovina and the OHR*

The International Police Task Force (IPTF) operated as a police mission in BiH between 1996 and 2002. Amongst other duties, the IPTF was responsible for the assessment of BiH's police force: that is, the re-certification of BiH's police officers. Some 18000 officers were subjected to this procedure, 793 of them ultimately being banned from serving as a police officer.[176] Initially, officers were barred for life from serving, until the UN Security Council softened the effect of the measure in 2007.[177] Decisions were taken behind closed doors with few or no reasons being communicated to officers who failed to be recertified. In May 2002, after criticism and internal debate, the IPTF made it possible to challenge re-certification decisions through an internal administrative procedure.[178] The mandate of the IPTF was terminated on 31 December 2002, thus creating a problem, as complaints were still pending. Consequently, numerous complaints were filed with various BiH institutions instead, challenging the certification refusals. The BiH courts generally acknowledged they lacked jurisdiction to review IPTF decisions. Some courts, however, adopted a *Kadi*-like line of argumentation.[179] Instead of invalidating the decisions of the IPTF, the courts annulled the dismissals of police officers by the BiH authorities – based on the relevant IPTF decisions – as "domestic law did not list an IPTF decision among the reasons allowing for termination of a police officer's employment contract".[180] The Human Rights Commission within the

[176] *See* in general ESI, *On Mount Olympus. How the UN violated human rights in Bosnia and Herzegovina, and why nothing has been done to correct it*, 10 February 2007.
[177] Only in 2008 did the UN Security Council allowed de-certified police officers to re-apply for jobs within the police force, *see* Letter of the President of the UN Security Council, Emyr Jones Parry, to the Permanent Representative of Bosnia and Herzegovina to the United Nations, 30 April 2007. *See also* CoE, *Report by the Commissioner for Human Rights MR Thomas Hammarberg on his Visit to Bosnia and Herzegovina, 4-11 July 2007*, CommDH(2008)1, 20 February 2008, § 25.
[178] UNMBIH, IPTF Policy P-10/2002 on Removal of Provisional Authorization and Disqualification of Law Enforcement Agency Personnel in BiH, 24 May 2002, § 10, at <http://www.esiweb.org/pdf/mountolympus/IPTF-P10.pdf>.
[179] *See* Section 4.2.2 above.
[180] ESI, *On Mount Olympus. How the UN violated human rights in Bosnia and Herzegovina, and why nothing has been done to correct it*, 10 February 2007, p. 13, referring to a decision by the Sarajevo Municipal Court, *Azmir Omerović v. the Ministry of Interior of the Sarajevo Canton*, No. PR-29/03, 6 May 2004. The ESI report states that this decision is representative of other decisions taken by the court in similar cases.

Constitutional Court of Bosnia and Herzegovina went a step further and, in its dictum, hinted at a violation of Article 6 ECHR by the international administration UN directly.[181]

The OHR reacted immediately to this evolving line of judicial argumentation, warning local authorities not to "challenge the entire restructuring process [of the police]".[182] The OHR received backing from the UN Under-Secretary-General for Peacekeeping Operations, Jean-Marie Guehenno, who wrote to the Presidency of BiH:

> Attempts to reinstate those individuals deemed ineligible for certification threaten the basis for the rule of law in Bosnia and Herzegovina. [...] I would therefore be grateful if you could take the necessary steps to set aside the judgements challenging the validity of the certification process and to ensure that no similar decisions are taken in the future.[183]

Local appeals and third-instance courts in BiH were by and large sensitive to the OHR's warning and quashed the insubordinate judgments while human rights organizations criticized the OHR's interference with the judiciary. In response, the OHR considered solutions such as legislative amendments in order to allow for dismissals based on IPTF decisions; solutions that included the establishment of local or independent review mechanisms remained out of the question.[184]

The situation culminated when, under pressure from local stakeholders, the Government of BiH in December 2006 moved to establish a review commission.[185] Pressure of the international administration proved stronger and the commission was never established.[186] Instead, the UN allowed for the

---

[181] Human Rights Commission within the Constitutional Court of Bosnia and Herzegovina, Decision, *Džaferović v. The Federation of Bosnia and Herzegovina*, CH/03/12932, 7 May 2004, §§ 70-72.

[182] The OHR informed the UN about the development and received the requested backing, *see* ESI, *On Mount Olympus. How the UN violated human rights in Bosnia and Herzegovina, and why nothing has been done to correct it*, 10 February 2007, p. 16.

[183] Letter from Guehenno to the Presidency of BiH, 10 October 2003, as cited in ESI, 'On Mount Olympus. How the UN violated human rights in Bosnia and Herzegovina, and why nothing has been done to correct it', 10 February 2007, p. 18.

[184] ESI, 'On Mount Olympus. How the UN violated human rights in Bosnia and Herzegovina, and why nothing has been done to correct it', 10 February 2007, pp. 18-28. *See* also Venice Commission, *Opinion on a possible solution to the issue of decertification of police officers in Bosnia and Herzegovina*, No. 326/2004, 24 October 2005.

[185] BiH, Council of Ministers, *Draft Decision on the establishment of a commission to review individual cases of decertified police officers who have initiated court proceedings before the courts of Bosnia and Herzegovina, no. 01-37-3498-2/06*, 14 December 2006.

[186] For the OHR's disapproval of the move by the Council of Ministers of BiH, *see* OHR, *OHR's Statement at the International Agencies' Joint Press Conference*, HR-EUSR Calls on Council of Ministers To Agree Review Process With UN, 19 December 2006, at <http://www.ohr.int/ohr-dept/presso/pressb/default.asp?content_id=38730>.

decertified policemen to re-apply, under the condition that they undergo all necessary police training and fulfill all criteria prescribed by domestic law.[187] Attempts by the Government of BiH to monitor the process of re-employment of police officers were dismissed by the OHR.[188]

Extensive use of the Bonn powers by the OHR has also been challenged by local authorities at entity level. For example, the authorities of Republika Srpska in BiH have occasionally challenged the legality of OHR's Bonn power decisions. This has been done through statements made by high officials,[189] acts of the local parliament[190] and announcements by the local Government that a referendum should be held through which the people could give their opinion on the continued exercise of Bonn powers.[191] The OHR has labeled such steps "anti-Dayton and illegal", stating,"rejecting the authority given to the High Representative would represent a grievous breach of both the Dayton Peace Agreement and UN Security Council Resolutions". [192]

5.3.1.2 The Constitutional Court of Bosnia and Herzegovina and the OHR

Before the following paragraphs expound upon the power struggle between judicial bodies in BiH and the OHR, first the relevant BiH judicial organs are first briefly introduced.

The Dayton Peace Agreement established the Commission on Human Rights, which consisted of the office of the Ombudsman and a Human Rights

[187] *See* Letter of the President of the UN Security Council, Emyr Jones Parry, to the Permanent Representative of BiH to the United Nations, 30 April 2007.

[188] ESI, *One year on: the injustice continues*, 26 June 2008.

[189] Beta, *RS: Inckove odluke nelegalne (RS: Inzko's decisions illegal)*, 22 January 2010.

[190] *Cf.* Regional Representation of Republika Srpska in Brussels, *High Representative Must Adhere to Rule of Law*, at <http://www.rep-srpska.eu/rule_of_law.php?lng=en&section=2&page=5> and OHR, Press release, *RS Referendum on Dayton Risks Going Beyond Rule of Law*, 6 January 2010, at <http://www.ohr.int/ohr-dept/presso/pressr/default.asp?content_id=44402>.

[191] Nezavisne Novine, interview with Raffi Gregorian, Principal Deputy High Representative, *The Bonn powers will remain also after February*, 2 February 2010.

[192] OHR, Press release, *RS National Assembly Conclusions in Violation of Dayton*, 29 December 2009, at <http://www.ohr.int/ohr-dept/presso/pressr/default.asp?content_id=44358> stating: "The Office of the High Representative would like to clarify and confirm that the RS Government's positions of 14th December 2009 and the RS National Assembly Conclusions of 28 December 2009 - rejecting the implementation of the laws of Bosnia and Herzegovina enacted by the High Representative - are in violation of the Dayton Peace Agreement". *See also* OHR, Press release, *HR/EUSR Inzko: RS Must Not Put Itself In Breach Of Dayton and UN Resolutions*, 23 December 2009, at <http://www.ohr.int/ohr-dept/presso/pressr/default.asp?content_id=44347>.

Chamber.[193] Save for a reference in Article II of the Constitution of Bosnia and Herzegovina, the Commission on Human Rights was not regulated by the Constitution but fell under Annex 6 to the Dayton Peace Agreement. Established as a judicial institution concerned with upholding the standards set forth in the ECHR, the Human Rights Chamber's decisions were binding and, save for exceptional cases, not subject to appeal.[194] The Ombudsman was also granted substantial powers.[195] The two bodies had complementary jurisdiction to consider alleged human rights violations "committed by the Parties, including by any official or organ of the Parties, Cantons, Municipalities, or any individual acting under the authority of such official or organ".[196] However, no jurisdiction was conferred with respect to decisions adopted by the High Representative.

The regime was established for an initial period of 5 years.[197] During this period, both components of the Commission on Human Rights contained international elements: a majority of judges of the Human Rights Chamber was international (the ECtHR held that still, the chamber constitutes a domestic court),[198] while the OSCE was responsible for the appointment of the ombudsman, who could not be a citizen of BiH. In 2000, the High Representative adopted the Law on the Human Rights Ombudsman of Bosnia and Herzegovina, transferring the institution to the local authorities.[199] The mandate of the Human Rights Chamber was extended to last until the end of 2003.[200] At the end of this extended mandate, in 2003, a transitional body within the CCBH – the Human Rights Commission – was established to deal with almost 9000 remaining applications.[201] The transitional body functioned until the end of 2006, when all remaining cases were transferred to the CCBH.[202]

Turning to the CCBH, the constitutional Court is established by Article VI of the Constitution of Bosnia and Herzegovina.[203] Amongst other functions, the Court upholds the constitution through constitutional review of legislative acts.[204] The Court is composed of local and international judges. The majority,

[193] Dayton Peace Agreement, Ann. 6, Chapter 2, Part A, Artt. II-XII.
[194] *Id.*, Part B, Art. XI(3).
[195] *Id.*, Artt. V-VI.
[196] *Id.*, Part A, Art. II(2) (b).
[197] *Id.*, Chapter 3, Art. XIV.
[198] ECtHR, *Jeličić v. Bosnia and Herzegovina*, No. No. 41183/02, Decision on Admissibility, 15 November 2005 (*Jeličić*).
[199] OHR, *Decision imposing the Law on the Human Rights Ombudsman of Bosnia and Herzegovina*, 14 December 2000.
[200] *Agreement pursuant to Art. XIV of Ann. 6 to the General Framework Agreement for Peace in Bosnia and Herzegovina*, September 2003, at <http://www.hrc.ba/ENGLISH/agreement.pdf>.
[201] Steiner & Ademović (eds.) (2010), pp. 134-135.
[202] *Id.*, pp. 671-680.
[203] Constitution of Bosnia and Herzegovina, Art. VI.
[204] Steiner & Ademović (eds.) (2010), pp. 681-701.

composed of local judges, is appointed by the BiH entities while the international judges are selected by the president of the ECtHR.[205] No document grants explicit jurisdiction to the CCBH to review the OHR – that is the exercise of public power by the High Representative – rather, there is a fundamental clash between the two institutions. In a nutshell, the Court is the designated ultimate upholder of the constitutional system of BiH. However, this system was established by an international peace agreement and the OHR, in turn, is the ultimate defender of this agreement. This uneasy relationship forms the basis of a remarkable line of jurisprudence developed by the CCBH and the former Human Rights Chamber. The relevant cases are discussed at some length below.

Local Courts Claim Limited Jurisdiction

The CCBH early on accepted a fundamental limitation to its authority – the Court lacked jurisdiction to review the documents that are the source of the OHR's authority: namely, the Dayton Peace Agreement, relevant UN Security Council resolutions and the 1997 Bonn declaration.[206] However, with respect to the powers of the OHR, the CCBH held in 2000, in the landmark *U 9/00 re The Law on State Border Service* (*U 9/00*) decision, that the OHR's mandate is characterized by functional duality.[207] On the one hand, the CCBH held that the High Representative exercises powers exclusively attributed to him by the international community. Due to the merits of the case, the Court did not expand on this issue. On the other hand, the High Representative has the power to act instead of local authorities, as he did in the facts underlying the present case. In its decision, dubbed as BiH's *Marbury v. Madison,* the Court held that the latter category of acts falls within the purview of the Court.[208] Seven decades earlier, a similar reasoning had led to the decision in the *Jerusalem-Jaffa District Governor v. Suleiman Murra* case.[209] Although the Court *in casu* found that the challenged law, adopted by the High Representative, was in accordance with the Constitution, the importance of the decision lies in the admissibility of the case.

---

[205] *Id.*, pp. 671-678.

[206] CCBH, *Decision U 7/97*, 22 December 1997 and *Decision U 9/00*, 3 November 2000.

[207] CCBH, *Decision U 9/00*, 3 November 2000.

[208] *See also* CCBH, *Decision U 26/01*, 28 September 2001.

[209] Judicial Committee of the Privy Council, *Jerusalem-Jaffa District Governor v. Suleiman Murra*, 3 February 1926, English Law Reports 1926, Appeals Cases, p. 321, *see* Section 3.1.3 above.

The *U 9/00*-decision holds: "1. [...] On 7 February 2000, eleven members of the House of Representatives of the Parliamentary Assembly initiated proceedings before the Constitutional Court of Bosnia and Herzegovina (hereinafter: the Constitutional Court) according to Article VI.3 (a) of the Constitution of Bosnia and Herzegovina for the evaluation of the constitutionality of the Law on State Border Service."

"5. The Law on State Border Service was enacted by the High Representative on 13 January 2000 following the failure of the Parliamentary Assembly to adopt a draft law proposed by the Presidency of Bosnia and Herzegovina on 24 November 1999. [...] Such a situation amounts to a sort of functional duality: an authority of one legal system intervenes in another legal system, thus making its functions dual. The same holds true for the High Representative: he has been vested with special powers by the international community and his mandate is of an international character. In the present case, the High Representative – whose powers under Annex 10 to the General Framework Agreement, the relevant resolutions of the Security Council and the Bonn Declaration as well as his exercise of those powers are not subject to review by the Constitutional Court – intervened in the legal order of Bosnia and Herzegovina substituting himself for the national authorities. In this respect, he therefore acted as an authority of Bosnia and Herzegovina and the law which he enacted is in the nature of a national law and must be regarded as a law of Bosnia and Herzegovina."

"7. The competence given to the Constitutional Court to "uphold the Constitution" according to the first paragraph of Article VI.3 of the Constitution of Bosnia and Herzegovina, [...] confers on the Constitutional Court the control of the conformity with the Constitution of Bosnia and Herzegovina of all acts, regardless of the author, as long as this control is based on one of the competences enumerated in Article VI.3 of the Constitution of Bosnia and Herzegovina."

CCBH, *Decision U 9/00 re The Law on State Border Service,* 3 November 2000.

The CCBH refined its argument in several subsequent cases. In *U 16/00,* the Court held that along with laws adopted by the OHR *in toto,* it also had jurisdiction to review the High Representative's legislative supplements and amendments.[210] While in most cases the CCBH came to the conclusion that the disputed laws and decisions were in conformity with the constitution, the Court in some instances quashed the challenged acts of the OHR, as it did in case *U 6/06.*[211] The developing functional-duality approach had a spillover effect and the Human Rights Chamber for Bosnia and Herzegovina adopted the same line of argumentation in the *CH/97/60 et al.* decision.[212]

The reasoning of the CCBH builds on all three elements from the public law argument. Firstly, the Court reshapes the hierarchy of legal norms in BiH by declaring that acts adopted by the High Representative – at least when he is acting instead of a national institution – need to be in conformity with the

[210] CCBH, *Decisions U 16/00*, 2 February 2001 and *Decision U 25/00*, 23 March 2001 respectively.

[211] CCBH, *Decision U 6/06*, 29 March 2008.

[212] Human Rights Chamber for Bosnia and Herzegovina, Decision, *CH/97/60 et al.*, 9 November 2001, §§ 122-133.

Constitution of Bosnia and Herzegovina, thereby establishing a legal framework within which the OHR is expected to operate. Secondly, as the upholder of the constitution, the Court positions itself as a review mechanism. Thereby, constitutional guarantees can be effectuated through the CCBH and allegedly unconstitutional legislative acts adopted by the OHR can be challenged. Thirdly, by assuming the right to scrutinize the High Representative's exercise of public power, the authority of the OHR is *prima facie* diffused. In other words, the CCBH subjected the international administration to judicial oversight.

By deciding on the *U 9/00* case, the CCBH did not assume jurisdiction over acts adopted by the OHR in the capacity of international administrator, mostly relating to the removal of individuals from public office.[213] The CCBH was confronted with a request to review a removal order for the first time in a case brought to the Court by former Prime Minister of the Federation of Bosnia and Herzegovina Edhem Bičakčić and 37 members of the House of Representatives of the Parliament of the Federation of Bosnia and Herzegovina. In *U 37/01,* the Court rejected the claim that the OHR's decision to remove Bičakčić from office could be regarded as a judgment rendered by a local BiH Court.[214] Instead, the Court held that such decisions must be considered in the light of the High Representative's special powers. The Court confirmed it has no jurisdiction with respect to such decisions and declared the appeal inadmissible. This aspect of the functional-duality approach was also mirrored by the Human Rights Chamber for Bosnia and Herzegovina.[215]

---

[213] The SRSG in Kosovo also issued executive orders to the same effect, *see e.g.* OIK, Ex officio investigation No. 19/01 *Regarding the Removal of Emrush Xhemajli, Gafurr Elshani and Sabit Gashi from the List of Candidates for the November 2001 Elections*, 29 October 2001, where the OIK found that such orders lack legal basis.

[214] CCBH, *Decision U 37/01*, 2 November 2001. The applicants challenged, *inter alia*, the constitutionality of the High Representative's decision No. 86/01, *Decision removing Edhem Bicakcic from his position as Director of Elektroprivreda for actions during his term as Prime Minister of the Federation of Bosnia and Herzegovina*, 23 February 2001: "For the reasons hereinafter set out I hereby issue the following: DECISION To remove Mr. Edhem Bicakcic from his position of General Manager of the company 'Elektroprivreda', and to bar him from holding any official, elective or appointive public office unless or until such time as I may, by further Decision, expressly authorise him to hold the same. This Decision has immediate effect and will not require any further procedural steps. Mr. Bicakcic must vacate his office immediately".

[215] Human Rights Chamber for Bosnia and Herzegovina, Decision, *CH/98/1266*, 18 December 1998, §§ 14-22 and Human Rights Chamber for Bosnia and Herzegovina, Decision, *CH/00/4027* and *CH/00/4074*, 9 March 2000, §§ 9-10. Both cases refer to Human Rights Chamber for Bosnia and Herzegovina, Decision, *CH/98/230*, 14 May 1998, where the judicial body had already determined it had no jurisdiction with respect to OSCE decisions.

> While some High Representatives have been eager to exercise this prerogative, others were more reluctant. This particular authority of the OHR includes amongst other the power to dismiss (elected) individuals from office, to ban individuals from running for election and to declare actual election results in individual cases null and void. Overall, approximately 188 such decisions were issued predominantly between 1998 and 2004. Conversely, approximately 69 decisions to lift or partially suspend said restrictions were issued in mostly between 2005 and 2010.
>
> Individuals holding a variety of positions within the constitutional legal order of Bosnia and Herzegovina have been subjected to the High Representative's prerogative, including mayors, members of municipal assemblies and executive boards, members of the National Assembly of Republika Srpska, Ministers, Governors, judges, the President of Republika Srpska and members of the Presidency of Bosnia and Herzegovina. Also, individuals have been banned from holding positions within various agencies, enterprises and political parties.
>
> OHR and EU Special Representative website, at <http://www.ohr.int/decisions/removalssdec/archive.asp>.

The OHR Reaffirms his Authority

A caveat must be added when it comes to interpreting the decisions of the judicial bodies as a unilateral development. Two points deserve attention. Firstly, this development fits into the general stance of the OHR, which developed over time, and according to which the OHR should act within the limits of the Constitution of Bosnia and Herzegovina. Statements by the High Representative such as "most people will recognize it would be illegal for me to do things that were unconstitutional or contrary to the Dayton agreement" reflect this.[216] Secondly, the High Representative made clear that the application of the functional-duality doctrine was due to his own consent and waiver of immunity:

> Recalling that the High Representative has, based on his powers deriving from Annex 10 of the General Framework Agreement for Peace in Bosnia and Herzegovina, *agreed* to waive the immunity he enjoys under the said Annex and consented to the review of certain of his acts within the framework of the above mentioned domestic theory of functional duality.[217]

The High Representative not only allowed for the development to take place, he also steered it. In orders aimed at blocking the bank accounts of individuals, the

[216] BBC, *Bosnia Envoy Stands by Sacking*, 19 December 2004, at <http://news.bbc.co.uk/2/hi/europe/4108633.stm>.

[217] OHR, *Order on the Implementation of the Decision of the Constitutional Court of Bosnia and Herzegovina in the Appeal of Milorad Bilbija et al, No. AP-953/05*, 23 March 2007, emphasis added.

OHR made clear that the functional-duality doctrine should not be misapplied or expanded by including the following provision:

> For the avoidance of doubt, it is hereby specifically declared and provided that the provisions of the Order contained herein are, as to each and every one of them, laid down by the High Representative pursuant to his international mandate and are not therefore justiciable by the Courts of Bosnia and Herzegovina or its Entities or elsewhere whether in respect of the Banking Agencies or otherwise, and no proceedings may be brought in respect of duties carried out thereunder before any court whatsoever at any time hereafter.[218]

The CCBH Strikes Back

The power struggle did not end here. In 2004, the CCBH signaled a turn in its approach. Instead of following the line of reasoning it had previously adopted, the CCBH declared several applications – related to removal-orders – inadmissible because they had been filed directly with the CCBH.[219] Since this new basis for inadmissibility relied on the exhaustion of alternative remedies rather than lack of jurisdiction, the Court was soon enough placed before a new application. In case *AP 953/05*, applicants Bilbija and Kalinić – former high ranking officials in Republika Srpska's governmental and political structures – filed appeals with the CCBH challenging their removals from office by the High Representative. Their applications before the CCBH also challenged the preceding decisions of the Court of Bosnia and Herzegovina, the Banja Luka County Court and the Supreme Court of Republika Srpska.[220] The CCBH declared the appeal to be admissible, holding that the applicants had no other

[218] OHR, *Order of 9 February 2004 Blocking All Bank Accounts of, held by and/or in the name of Dragan Bašević*, 10 February 2004. More or less identical provisions were included in other OHR orders with the same effect, including the OHR, *Decision Reviewing the orders Blocking All Bank Accounts of, held by, and/or in the name of certain individuals*, 5 September 2008.

[219] CCBH, *Decision AP 777/04*, 29 September 2004, § 10. Here, the court states that "the appellant did not attempt to challenge the Decision of the High Representative before the competent courts which, in accordance with the Constitution of Bosnia and Herzegovina must apply the European Convention directly and provide protection of the guaranteed rights and freedoms. He, in fact, appealed directly to the Constitutional Court". The CCBH did the same in *e.g. Decision AP 759/04, AP 784/04* and *AP 766/04*, all decisions dated 29 September 2004.

[220] CCBH, *Decision AP 953/05*, 8 July 2006, §§ 1-2.

effective remedies at their disposal.[221] On the merits, the CCBH recalled with respect to removal decisions of the High Representative that:

> the Constitutional Court holds that such decisions have seriously raised issues of the existence of violations of some rights and fundamental freedoms safeguarded by the Constitution of Bosnia and Herzegovina and the European Convention. Among others, the Constitutional Court notes that impossibility to challenge the said decisions of the High Representative leaves such persons without any protection of their rights and fundamental freedoms. Such an approach leaves individuals without any legal remedy by which the observance of Article 13 of the European Convention is brought in question.[222]

The CCBH came to the preliminary conclusion that because of his immunity it cannot review individual decisions of the High Representative. However, the CCBH then turns its attention to BiH. Citing the ECtHR in *Matthews*, the CCBH finds that BiH remains under the positive obligation to secure the implementation of the ECHR regardless of the authority of the OHR:

> the obligations of Bosnia and Herzegovina in public international law to co-operate with the High Representative and to act in conformity with decisions of the UN Security Council cannot determine the constitutional rights of people who are within the jurisdiction of Bosnia and Herzegovina.[223]

Based on this approach, the Court established a breach of the right to an effective remedy by BiH, as it failed to secure legal remedies through which decisions of the High Representative could be challenged.

The OHR Reaffirms Supremacy

Although the CCBH refrained from direct review of the High Representative's decisions, the Court's expansion of its jurisdiction sparked a fierce response from the PIC and the OHR. The PIC expressed concerns by stating:

> The PIC Steering Board noted with concern that domestic actors in Bosnia and Herzegovina have challenged actions undertaken on the basis of

[221] *Id.*, § 32.
[222] *Id.*, § 36.
[223] CCBH, *Decision AP 953/05*, 8 July 2006, § 68. *See also* ECtHR, *Matthews v. United Kingdom*, No. 24833/94, 18 February 1999, §§ 29 and 32 (*Matthews*).

> Dayton and UN Security Council Resolutions under Chapter VII. The Steering Board reminds all institutions that Bosnia and Herzegovina's international obligations under the General Framework Agreement for Peace and the United Nations Charter must be respected. It calls upon the High Representative, in close coordination with the Steering Board Ambassadors, to take appropriate actions to ensure that Bosnia and Herzegovina fulfils these international obligations.[224]

The High Representative followed suit by issuing an unambiguous order in March 2007.[225] The High representative recalled that while he is willing to tolerate the functional-duality doctrine, any further expansion of the CCBH's jurisdiction is impermissible. The High Representative ordered that the CCBH decision shall only be implemented through the OHR, in effect overruling the decision of the CCBH and anchoring his supremacy.

[224] PIC, Communiqué by the Steering Board, 27 February 2007, at <http://www.ohr.int/pic/default.asp?content_id=39236>.

[225] OHR, *Order on the Implementation of the Decision of the Constitutional Court of Bosnia and Herzegovina in the Appeal of Milorad Bilbija et al, No. AP-953/05*, 23 March 2007. *See also* Knoll B. (2007)(2), 'Bosnia: Reclaiming Local power from International Authority', 3 *European Constitutional Law Review*, pp. 357-366.

The order of the OHR further cautions the local institutions:

"Article 2: Any step taken by any institution or authority in Bosnia and Herzegovina in order to establish any domestic mechanism to review the Decisions of the High Representative issued pursuant to his international mandate shall be considered by the High Representative as an attempt to undermine the implementation of the civilian aspects of the General Framework Agreement for Peace in Bosnia and Herzegovina and shall be treated in itself as conduct undermining such implementation.

Article 3: Notwithstanding any contrary provision in any legislation in Bosnia and Herzegovina, any proceeding instituted before any court in Bosnia and Herzegovina, which challenges or takes issue in any way whatsoever with one or more decisions of the High Representative, shall be declared inadmissible unless the High Representative expressly gives his prior consent. [...] For the avoidance of any doubt or ambiguity, and taking into account the totality of the matters aforesaid, it is hereby specifically ordered and determined, in the exercise of the said international mandate of the High Representative and pursuant to its interpretation hereinunder and by virtue of the said Annex 10, that no liability is capable of being incurred on the part of the Institutions of Bosnia and Herzegovina, and/or any of its subdivisions and/or any other authority in Bosnia and Herzegovina, in respect of any loss or damage allegedly flowing, either directly or indirectly, from such Decision of the High Representative made pursuant to his or her international mandate, or at all.

Article 4: For the avoidance of doubt, it is hereby specifically declared and provided that the provisions of the Order contained herein are, as to each and every one of them, laid down by the High Representative pursuant to his international mandate and are not, therefore, justiciable by the Courts of Bosnia and Herzegovina or its Entities or elsewhere, and no proceedings may be brought in respect of duties in respect thereof before any court whatsoever at any time hereafter".

OHR, *Order on the Implementation of the Decision of the Constitutional Court of Bosnia and Herzegovina in the Appeal of Milorad Bilbija et al, No. AP-953/05,* 23 March 2007.

5.3.2 COURTS BEYOND INTERNATIONALLY ADMINISTERED TERRITORIES

The potential role of courts and other judicial institutions outside the administered territory in enhancing the accountability of ITA missions remains unmapped. The role of local courts outside internationally administered territories has thus far been shaped within the broader context of UN peacekeeping and by the fact that ITA missions are subsidiaries of international organizations.[226] This is not to say that in the state-context states play substantive roles in upholding the accountability amongst each other. Indeed, in principle states are shielded from review by foreign courts based on sovereign immunity; *par in parem non habet imperium*. In addition, as a matter of national rather than international law, in certain jurisdictions the act of state doctrine, posits that "courts of one country cannot sit in judgment on the acts of the

[226] *See* Sections 4.2 and 5.1.3 above.

government of another done within its own territory”[227] demanding that acts of third states should in principle be treated as being valid.[228] It can be argued that these limitations are narrower in nature than the immunity currently protecting ITA missions from appearing before foreign local courts.

> In 2008, the former General Counsel with the Office of the High Representative filed a suit against the OHR and High Representative Miroslav Lajčák for wrongful termination. The suit was filed before the United States District Court For the Northern District of California, California being the plaintiff's place of residence. The defendant sought dismissal for, amongst other things, lack of subject matter jurisdiction by invoking the Foreign Sovereign Immunities Act, 28 U.S.C. 1330. Lack of personal jurisdiction disposed of the case, but the court nevertheless touched upon the defendant's claim to sovereign immunity: “Whether the FSIA applies to an entity such as the OHR, or to the High Representative, presents novel and thorny issues”.
>
> The United States District Court For the Northern District of California, *Sarkis v. Lajcak et al.*, (5:2008cv01911), Order Granting Motion to Dismiss, p. 10, 14 October 2009. At the time of writing, the case was pending appeal before the United States Court of Appeals, Ninth Circuit.

When it comes to international courts, the founding documents of ITA missions do not reserve any role in particular for the ICJ in relation to the international administration of territories.[229] This is in sharp contrast to the Mandate and Trusteeship systems, which consistently incorporated the PCIJ and the ICJ respectively into their framework.[230] By and large, this was possible due to the fact that under these systems, states were administering territories on behalf of the international organizations and could therefore appear before the respective courts. The administration of Danzig shows, however, that even in cases of direct international administration, the ICJ could play a role by issuing advisory

---

[227] The United States Supreme Court, *Underhill v. Hernandez, 168 U.S. 250 (1897)*.

[228] *See also* Perritt (2004), p. 23. In his article on judicial review of decisions by political trustees, Perrit expounds the different obstacles local courts would face if they decided to hear a case involving ITA missions. Perrit mentions the example of a New Jersey company filing a suit against, amongst others, UNMIK and the KTA. On *forum-nonconveniens* grounds, the company dismissed its claim. Perrit, however, discusses possible outcomes in the event the plaintiff had not withdrawn its claim and assesses how various types of immunities (based on the General Convention, the International Organizations Immunities Act of 1945 and the Foreign Sovereign Immunities Act of 1976) would have impacted the proceedings. Finally, Perrit includes the act of state-doctrine in his analysis.

[229] The potential role of the ICJ with respect to review of ITA missions fits into the broader debate on the relationship between the ICJ and the UN Security Council in terms of review. This broader context will not be addressed here. Authors have argued in favour of a more proactive stance by the ICJ in relation to the UN Security Council, *see e.g.* De Wet (2006), p. 65.

[230] *See* Section 3.1.3 above.

opinions, just as the PCIJ did at the time.[231] In practice, the ICJ touched indirectly upon the mandate of UNMIK in *Kosovo*. Despite the fact that the advisory opinion provided some insight into the scope of the UN's mandate, the ICJ's opinion did not contribute to the present ITA accountability debate.[232] Currently, nothing prevents the ICJ from engaging by way of advisory opinion in a more proactive way, while hearing contentious cases involving ITA missions require additional and outside-the-box legal regulation.

Turning to regional courts, the relationship between such courts and territories under international administration is in no way formalized. Courts such as the ECtHR seem *prima facie* suitable for acting as an oversight body with respect to internationally administered territories, not least because of their independence and their proximity to the territories impacted by the exercise of ITA mandates. However, engaging regional courts also poses certain conceptual as well as practical challenges. Primarily, as long as ITA missions are perceived as international organizations, jurisdictional as well as immunity-related issues are bound to occur. Another concern finds its roots in the asymmetric development of regional human rights as treaties and accompanying supervisory mechanisms vary from region to region. Moreover, territories under international administration are not necessarily party to a treaty providing for regional oversight mechanisms, making the level of supervision highly dependent on the territories involved. The relationship between the ECtHR and the OHR and UNMIK – ITA missions within the court's (geographical) reach – is indicative of the described challenges. The relevant landmark decisions of the ECtHR are discussed below in order to illustrate the way in which the ECtHR is currently positioned vis-à-vis situations of territorial administration as well as obstacles preventing the Court from engaging in a more proactive way.

5.3.2.1 The European Court of Human Rights and ITA Missions

Despite the fact that the ECtHR is out of reach for individuals living in internationally administered territories – at least with respect to acts of the international administration – the Court has received several complaints relating to Kosovo and BiH. Different questions shape the space in which the ECtHR was able – or not – to develop as an oversight body with respect to these territories. Is the ECHR applicable in the respective territories? To whom can acts of UNMIK and the OHR be attributed? Are relevant procedural rules flexible enough to accommodate the Court's engagement in this context? On

---

[231] *See* Section 3.2.2 above.

[232] ICJ, *Kosovo*, Advisory Opinion.

several occasions, the Court addressed these issues, two of which are discussed below: attribution and the exhaustion of local remedies-requirement.

Attribution

Most of the uncertainties regarding the relationship between the ECtHR and ITA missions were addressed in the watershed *Behrami* case.[233] Here, the issue of attribution surfaced as a detrimental obstacle in the present context. The facts of the case concern the killing of a child and the wounding of another in 2000 by previously undetonated NATO-dropped cluster-bomb units. Under UN Security Council Resolution 1244 (1999), mine clearing was the responsibility of KFOR and, subsequently, UNMIK. The father of the two children filed a complaint against France as a contributing state alleging breach of Article 2 ECHR.[234] It was first established that mine clearance fell under the authority of UNMIK.[235] The Court went further by stating that both acts of KFOR (in exercising powers delegated under Chapter VII of the UN Charter) and UNMIK (as a subsidiary organ of the UN) are attributable to the UN.[236] Finally, the Court found that the acts of member states carried out on behalf of the UN could not be reviewed.[237] Having arrived at that conclusion, the Court declared the application inadmissible *ratione personae.*

The *Behrami* decision has been criticized on various grounds, one of them being the choice of the Court to approach the case in terms of attribution rather than to focus on the issue of jurisdiction as it did in, for example, *Ilaşcu* and *Loizidou.*[238] According to the Court, although the respondent states exercised the necessary control over Kosovo, the acts were attributable to the UN.[239] Thus, rather than assessing the claim that the applicant was under the required jurisdiction of the respondent state in terms of Article 1 ECHR, the Court focused on whether the complaint was compatible with the ECHR *ratione*

[233] ECtHR, *Behrami. See e.g.* Milanović M. And Papić T. (2009), 'As bad as it gets: the European Court of Human Rights's Behrami and Saramati decision and general international law', 58(2) *International & Comparative Law Quarterly*, pp. 267-296.

[234] Previously, the KFOR claims office had refused Behrami's compensation claim on the grounds that rather than KFOR, UNMIK was responsible for the clearing of mines in Kosovo.

[235] ECtHR, *Behrami*, § 127.

[236] *Id.*, §§ 141 and 143.

[237] *Id.*, § 151.

[238] *See* Section 4.1.1 above.

[239] ECtHR, *Behrami*, §§ 71-72: "71. The Court [considers] that the question raised by the present cases is, less whether the respondent States exercised extra-territorial jurisdiction in Kosovo but far more centrally, whether this Court is competent to examine under the Convention those States' contribution to the civil and security presences which did exercise the relevant control of Kosovo. 72. Accordingly, the first issue to be examined by this Court is the compatibility *ratione personae* of the applicants' complaints with the provisions of the Convention".

personae. Consequently, all remaining questions related to matters such as exhaustion of local remedies, and the further delimitation of extraterritorial applicability of the ECHR remained untouched.

By channeling attribution towards the UN instead of the respondent states, the ECtHR anchored the impossibility of individuals from Kosovo to effectuate their rights in Strasbourg. The trickle-down effect of *Behrami* soon became evident. In *Kusumaj,* Greek KFOR troops occupied a plot of land in 1999 without providing any compensation to the owner. The applicant claimed a continuing violation of Article 1 of Protocol 1 to the ECHR. In *Gajić,* the Court was asked to determine whether Germany was in breach of the same provision, as German KFOR troops had occupied the applicant's apartment. Referring to *Behrami,* the Court in both cases declared the applications inadmissible.[240]

Also with respect to BiH, the ECtHR adopted the *Behrami* approach. In 2004, the OHR removed numerous individuals from public office and barred them from running for election.[241] In *Berić,* the ECtHR was asked to state its position on whether this amounted to a breach of Articles 6, 11 and 13, ECHR and whether BiH could be held responsible. The application differs from the previous cases, as it links the 'host state' to the acts of the international presence rather than one of the contributing states, which in the case of the OHR would have been difficult to determine. The Court concluded that acts of the OHR could not be attributed to BiH, regardless of Bosnia's acceptance of the OHR's civil administration.[242] In the given context, the decision of the Court to declare the application inadmissible was a correct one, taking into account the supra-constitutional position of the OHR vis-à-vis the BiH legal order.[243] However, in adopting the *Behrami* approach, the Court once again effectively upheld the

---

[240] ECtHR, *Kusumaj v. Greece*, No. 6974/05, Decision on Admissibility, 5 July 2007 (*Kusumaj*) and *Gajić v. Germany*, No. 31446/02, Decision on Admissibility, 28 August 2007 (*Gajić*).

[241] *See* Section 5.3.1.2 above.

[242] ECtHR, *Berić et al. v. Bosnia and Herzegovina*, No. 36357/04, 36360/04, 38346/04, 41705/04, 45190/04, 45578/04, 45579/04, 45580/04, 91/05, 97/05, 100/05, 101/05, 1121/05, 1123/05, 1125/05, 1129/05, 1132/05, 1133/05, 1169/05, 1172/05, 1175/05, 1177/05, 1180/05, 1185/05, 20793/05 & 25496/05, Decision on Adbissibility, 16 October 2007 (*Berić*).

[243] In another case, the ECtHR decided that BiH could be held responsible for the contents of the Constitution of Bosnia and Herzegovina, despite the fact that the Constitution is "an annex to the [the Dayton Peace Agreement]. Since it was part of a peace treaty, the Constitution was drafted and adopted without the application of procedures which could have provided democratic legitimacy. It constitutes the unique case of a constitution which was never officially published in the official languages of the country concerned but was agreed and published in a foreign language, English". Though BiH did not enact the Constitution, its Parliamentary Assembly had the power to amend it. Hence, the Court found that BiH was, at the very least, responsible for maintaining the contested constitutional provisions, *see* ECtHR, *Sejdić and Finci v. Bosnia and Herzegovina*, No. 27996/06 & 34836/06, Grand Chamber, 22 December 2009 (*Sejdić and Finci*).

inviolability of decisions taken by an international administrator, *in casu* the OHR.

Exhaustion of Local Remedies

As most attempts to effectuate rights at the international level fail *ratione personae,* other issues relating to enforcement have rarely been addressed by the relevant bodies. Nevertheless, the requirement to exhaust domestic remedies – common to human rights treaties in general – has surfaced as a second obstacle. Taking Kosovo as an example, the question at hand concerns the domestic remedies an inhabitant of Kosovo is expected to exhaust, assuming extraterritorial application was accepted. In other words, does the local-remedies requirement relate to remedies in Kosovo or to the domestic remedies of the respondent state?

The rationale behind the local-remedies requirement, recognized by the ICJ in *Interhandel* as a rule of customary international law, is to give states an opportunity to respond to allegations of wrongdoing within their own legal system.[244] With respect to international organizations, agreement exists that the principle is applicable despite terminological pitfalls; namely, internal remedies available within the legal framework of an organization should be exhausted before a complaint is internationalized.[245]

A strict application of the principle under the given circumstances is problematic from the perspective of the applicant. Namely, the legal system of the respondent state generally coincides with the legal system within which the plaintiff is situated. The wording in *Interhandel* inadvertently reveals this assumption by referring to the *locus* of the violation and the domestic legal system as one:

> Before resort may be had to an international court [...] it has been considered necessary that the State where the violation occurred should have an opportunity to redress it by its own means, within the framework of its own domestic legal system.[246]

However, in the ITA context, strictly speaking the '*locus*' and the 'domestic legal system' are separated. Following the main rationale, the local-remedies rule will refer to remedies available in a sending state rather than mechanisms

[244] ICJ, *Interhandel* (*Switzerland v. Unites States of America*), Judgment, 21 March 1959, p. 27 (*Interhandel*).

[245] *E.g.* ILC, *Sixth report on responsibility of international organizations*, by Special Rapporteur Giorgio Gaja, UN Doc. A/CN.4/597, 1 April 2008, § 16.

[246] ICJ, *Interhandel*, p. 27.

within reach of the applicant, placing a heavy burden on the applicant. In such situations, case-law reflects that applying the domestic remedies-rule is a balancing act between the interests of the applicant and the respondent state.

In *Issa,* the ECtHR had to decide on the admissibility of a claim of six Iraqi women against Turkey concerning Turkey's military activities in northern Iraq. The Court first anchored the rationale that the local-remedies principle, as laid down in Article 35(1) ECHR, refers to remedies as provided for under the jurisdiction of the respondent state. Under the given circumstances, the applicants should have requested the Turkish authorities to initiate an investigation. In particular, complaints mechanisms provided for by the Turkish army in principle qualify as domestic remedies in this particular case. However, the normal effectiveness-threshold applies: the Court held that applying "for an inquiry to the Turkish army authorities in northern Iraq [did not] constitute a remedy the existence of which was sufficiently certain in practice". Turning to the applicants, the Court held that the fact that the applicants were shepherds in northern Iraq lends "credence to the applicants' argument that the judicial mechanism of Turkey, a foreign country, was physically and financially inaccessible to them", thereby concluding that "the applicants were dispensed from trying to institute judicial proceedings in Turkey" and declaring the application admissible.[247] On the merits, the ECtHR found that despite their presence in northern Iraq, the Turkish military forces did not exercise the necessary control in order for the applicants to be considered within the "jurisdiction" of Turkey in terms of Article 1 ECHR.[248]

In *Cyprus v. Turkey,* effective control of Turkey over Northern Cyprus was established.[249] Despite the fact that the case concerned an interstate application, parties invoked the local-remedies principle. The ECtHR concluded that under the given circumstances, courts established as part of the local legal system in the northern part of Cyprus should be regarded as "domestic remedies" of the respondent state.[250] The effectiveness of such remedies, the Court argued, should be determined on a case-by-case basis with respect to each particular allegation.[251] However, no reference is made to remedies within the original territory of the respondent state. Thus, the inference can be drawn that where the

---

[247] ECtHR, *Issa*. In court reasoned in a similar fashion in *Öcalan*, where it ultimately failed to accept the effectiveness of addresing the Mudanya Court of First Instance or a judge belonging to the Ankara National Security Court.
[248] ECtHR, *Issa*, § 82.
[249] ECtHR, *Cyprus v. Turkey*.
[250] *Id.*, § 102: "The Court concludes accordingly that, for the purposes of former Article 26 (current Article 35 para. 1) of the Convention, remedies available in the "TRNC" may be regarded as "domestic remedies" of the respondent State and that the question of their effectiveness is to be considered in the specific circumstances where it arises".
[251] *Id.*, §§ 98-102.

Court finds that jurisdiction of a state has been extended beyond its borders, remedies established under the purview of this extended jurisdiction constitute the domestic remedies of the respondent state.

It must be noted here that the fact that the Court was dealing with a particular state rather than an international territorial administration facilitated the adopted approach. Translated into the context of Kosovo, it is doubtful whether local courts under the PISG or even mechanisms set up by UNMIK could be considered the domestic remedies of any potential respondent state in particular.

In other cases, the issue was brought up by the parties but remained untouched, as the ECtHR reached a decision before addressing the domestic-remedies requirement. In *Banković,* for example, some respondent states claimed that the applicants had failed to exhaust remedies available in the respondent states.[252] In *Behrami,* France argued that local remedies had not been exhausted, but the ECtHR found that it was unnecessary to address the issue, as it had already reached an inadmissibility decision based on other grounds.[253]

The ECtHR seems to do a turnabout in *Gajić.* In that case, the Court accepted the argument made by Germany that the applicant from Kosovo had not exhausted remedies available to him under German law: namely, the applicant had lodged a compensation claim in Germany and could subsequently initiate procedures before German administrative courts. Leaving open the question as to whether the alleged actions "engage the responsibility of the respondent State", the Court concluded that the complaint is "in any event premature and should therefore be declared inadmissible according to Article 35(1) and (4) of the Convention".[254] Thus, in *Gajić* the Court gives precedence to the local-remedies requirement over the approach taken in *Behrami,* where it previously found it unnecessary to discuss Article 35 ECHR.

A small digression in the direction of the ICCPR regime is warranted at this point. A petition was filed with the Human Rights Committee under the first optional protocol of the ICCPR. The plaintiff claimed a violation of Article 2, Paragraph 3(a) of the ICCPR by Spain as a result of alleged misconduct of a Spanish civil police unit of UNMIK.[255] The claimant argued for the extraterritorial application of Spain's obligations under the ICCPR. With respect to the exhaustion of domestic remedies, the claimant argued that neither the UNMIK Police Commissioner nor the Public Prosecutor in the local Peć District Court were willing to accept the complaint. Furthermore, the claimant added,

---

[252] As argued by Hungary, Italy and Poland, *see* ECtHR, *Banković*, § 33.
[253] ECtHR, *Behrami*, §§ 67 and 153.
[254] ECtHR, *Gajić*.
[255] In an e-mail exchange in June 2010, Officers of the Petitions Team of the Office of the High Commissioner for Human Rights in Geneva could not say whether other similar complaints had been filed.

efforts by the OIK to obtain information from UNMIK police were futile. In turn, Spain rejected the notion that obligations under the ICCPR *in casu* had extraterritorial effect. Moreover, Spain pointed out that the claimant should have sought redress by requesting a waiver of immunity and filing for a settlement through the UNMIK claims procedure. Spain also referred to remedies under the Spanish legal order, which argument was accepted. The Human Rights Committee held in *Kurbogaj* that domestic remedies had not been exhausted, and declared the communication inadmissible.[256] Here, unlike the ECtHR's finding in *Issa,* the Human Rights Committee failed to consider the near impossibility of the claimant to address the Spanish authorities from Kosovo, and held that the claimant should have exhausted remedies available to him under Spanish law.

In summary, the requirement to exhaust domestic remedies is interpreted in the light of the circumstances of a particular case. Case law suggests that courts and oversight bodies are sensitive to the specific relationship between individuals falling under the extraterritorial jurisdiction of a state and the local-remedies requirement. While in *Issa* the position of the applicants proved to be decisive, in *Gajić* and *Kurbogaj,* the ECtHR and the Human Rights Committee, respectively considered the respondent state's remedies to be effective and above all readily available. Thus, in cases where ITA-related activities are (*Kurbogaj*) or potentially could be (*Gajić*) linked to a particular state through the extraterritorial effect of treaty-based human rights obligations, the local-remedies requirement remains an obstacle in effectuating such rights.

5.3.3 OTHER INTERNATIONAL AND REGIONAL HUMAN RIGHTS MECHANISMS

Finally, interaction has developed between ITA missions and various international oversight mechanisms developed in the field of human rights law, ranging from treaty-based reporting procedures to non-institutionalized monitoring conducted by NGOs. The interaction is voluntary, and in practice remains limited to oversight processes that can only lead to non-binding observations. Hence, it does not absolve ITA missions from rethinking their approach to accountability; it does not impose a binding legal framework on the exercise of public power; it does not affect the immunity enjoyed by ITA missions and it does not diffuse the concentrated powers vested in the international administrators. It does, however, complement the rudimentary accountability regime by effectuating, to some extent, the patchy legal

256 HRCee, *Kurbogaj and Kurbogaj v. Spain*, Communication No. 1374/2005, Decision on Admissibility, UN Doc. CCPR/C/87/D/1374/2005, 14 July 2006.

framework that has developed over time, and by establishing a certain form of independent review.

Three dimensions of such interaction are discussed below. Firstly, various human rights treaties provide for oversight mechanisms. Through the supervision of 'host-states' such as Indonesia and Serbia, ITA missions are at times indirectly scrutinized by these bodies. While this cannot be considered actual oversight, in practice it has opened the door for a more substantive and immediate interaction between ITA missions and relevant compliance mechanisms. Secondly, ITA missions subject themselves to scrutiny by oversight bodies in a manner similar to the supervision of state-parties. Thirdly, a type of interaction concerns the relationship ITA missions establish with NGOs and international organizations in general.

5.3.3.1 Indirect Scrutiny by International Compliance Mechanisms

Fundamental human rights treaties cited by ITA missions by and large provide for compliance mechanisms ranging from reporting obligations to individual petition rights. For example, Article 40 of the ICCPR regulates the reporting obligation between state parties and the Human Rights Committee while Articles 16 and 17 of the International Covenant on Economic, Social and Cultural Rights (ICESCR) deal with reports submitted to the Committee on Economic, Social and Cultural Rights (CESCR).[257]

From this perspective, the establishment of interaction depends on whether the internationally administered territory is nominally linked to the relevant treaties. If this is the case, supervisory bodies can address the ITA mission indirectly through reports concerning the 'host states' such as Serbia, BiH or Indonesia.

With respect to UNTAET, existing oversight procedures have not been employed. This may be attributed to the situation on the ground, the short period of deployment and the relatively low number of relevant treaties ratified by Indonesia at the time.

---

[257] Art. 9 of the International Convention on the Elimination of All Forms of Racial Discrimination (ICERD) regulates the reporting procedure for the Committee on the Elimination of Racial Discrimination (CERD). Under the Convention on the Elimination of All Forms of Discrimination against Women (CEDAW), reporting to the Committee on the Elimination of Discrimination Against Women (CtEDAW) is regulated by Art. 18. The Convention Against Torture and Other Cruel, Inhuman or Degrading Treatment and Punishment (CAT) regulates reporting to the Committee Against Torture (CtAT) in Art. 19 and the Convention on the Rights of the Child (CRC) does the same in Art. 44 with respect to reports submitted to the Committee on the Rights of the Child (CtRC).

BiH rarely used its reporting obligations to address the powers vested in the OHR; the 2005 initial report submitted by BiH under the ICCPR is an exception.[258] In the context of the right to self-determination, the report emphasizes the manner in which the OHR exercises supreme authority within the legal order of BiH.[259] As well as acknowledging the positive effects of OHR interventions, the report draws attention to certain negative implications of the OHR's persisting supremacy. During the 88th Session of the Human Rights Committee, the representatives of BiH were asked to clarify the sentiment "which seemed to suggest that the presence of the [High Representative] was an obstacle to, rather than a guarantor of, the implementation of human rights in the State party".[260] Subsequent concluding observations as well as follow-up communication by BiH did not provide a meaningful answer to the question.

Conversely, Serbia used its reporting obligations to address the international administration of Kosovo and in effect to trigger the involvement of UNMIK under the available oversight procedures. The initial report submitted by Serbia

---

[258] HRCee, *Consideration of Reports Submitted by States Parties Under Article 40 of the Covenant, Initial report, Bosnia and Herzegovina*, UN Doc. CCPR/C/BIH/1, 24 November 2005.

[259] *Id.*, §§ 15-16, in pertinent part remind the HRCee of the following: "We should point out the fact that after more than nine years after the establishment of the peace in Bosnia and Herzegovina, the Office of the High representative is an institution participating or directly involving in work of the constitutional, legislative, executive and judicial authorities. The practice up to now shows that the High Representative has changed by his decisions the entities' constitutions, made new and changed the existing laws, exerted immediate influence on the judicial and executive authorities through a range of decisions on replacement of certain officials, that is public authority holders, replacement of the entities' presidents, judges and prosecutors, through decisions on establishment of real and territorial jurisdiction of the courts, establishment of the Independent Judicial Commission as a separate body of the Office of the High Representative for Bosnia and Herzegovina and appointment of a number of persons authorized to monitor the court proceedings and similar. Since the establishment of the OHR, four persons have been at the position of the High Representative. This institution, besides constitutional amendments, in 1999, passed 3 laws and seven decisions; in 2000 17 laws and 28 decisions; in 2001 17 decisions, in 2002 24 laws out of total number of 38 passed acts; in 2003 2 laws, 36 decisions, 1 letter on appointment and 1 directive. Grand total makes 58 laws and 92 decisions in the five-year period. Many of the mentioned decisions represent laws in material sense, or else they contain them as attachments. This is the case, for example, with the OHR decision on passing the Law on amendments to the Law on Court of Bosnia and Herzegovina and the Decision passing the Law on Amendments on the Law on Prosecutor's Office of Bosnia and Herzegovina. Only in 2003, 12 such decisions were made. During this period the Parliamentary Assembly of Bosnia and Herzegovina adopted 132 laws. Besides the above mentioned, it should be emphasized that Bosnia and Herzegovina was accepted in the CoE in 2002, that since 1992 (since recognition) it has been the member of UN and that it has its state authorities (institutions) which function in accordance with the Constitution (Annex IV of the General Framework Peace Agreement for Bosnia and Herzegovina)".

[260] HRCee, *Summary Record of the 2402nd meeting*, 88th Session, UN Doc. CCPR/C/SR.2402, 26 October 2006, § 31.

and Montenegro under the ICCPR in 2003 illustrates this approach.[261] Occasionally throughout the report, the Human Rights Committee was reminded that the State Union of Serbia and Montenegro is not in the position to fulfill its obligations under the ICCPR with respect to Kosovo. Moreover, the report included a separate annex devoted to the criminal law system and the human rights situation in Kosovo. In addition to a politically tainted substantive overview of the situation on the ground, issues were addressed such as the influence of UNMIK as the executive on the judiciary, UNMIK's extra-judicial detentions and the immunity of UNMIK. The Human Rights Committee considered these points by asking whether and to what extent UNMIK has an impact on the obligation of Serbia and Montenegro to implement the ICCPR in Kosovo.[262] During the oral consideration of the initial report and the committee's list of issues, delegates from Serbia and Montenegro addressed the question by suggesting that UNMIK should engage in filing reports under the ICCPR.[263] Likewise, UNMIK was discussed indirectly and similar suggestions were made during the consideration of Serbia's reports under the ICESCR, CEDAW, CRC and CAT regime [264]

[261] HRCee, *Consideration of Reports Submitted by States Parties Under Article 40 of the Covenant, Initial report, Serbia and Montenegro*, UN Doc. CCPR/C/SEMO/1, 24 July 2003.
[262] HRCee, *List of Issues to be taken up in connection with the consideration of the initial report of Serbia and Montenegro (CCPR/C/SEMO/2003/1)*, 80th Session, UN Doc. CCPR/C/81/L/SEMO, 7 May 2004, § 4.
[263] HRCee, *Summary Record of the 2207th meeting*, 81st Session, UN Doc. CCPR/C/SR.2207, 27 July 2004, § 27.
[264] CESCR, *Consideration of Reports Submitted by States Parties Under Articles 16 and 17 of the Covenant, Concluding observations of the Committee on Economic, Social and Cultural Rights, Serbia and Montenegro*, 34th Session, UN Doc. E/C.12/1/Add.108, 23 June 2005, § 9 (the CESCR here rejects the suggestions, only to accept UNMIK reports at a later stage, as discussed below); CtEDAW, *Summary record of the 775th meeting*, 38th Session, UN Doc. CEDAW/C/SR.775, 18 July 2007, §§ 11-13; CtRC, *Summary Record of the 1326th meeting*, 48th Session, UN Doc. CRC/C/SR.1325, 18 December 2009, § 8 and CtRC, *Consideration of Reports Submitted by States Parties Under Article 44 of the Convention, Concluding Observations: Republic of Serbia*, 48th Session, UN Doc. CRC/C/SRB/CO/1, 20 June 2008, § 6; CtAT, *Consideration of Reports Submitted by States Parties Under Article 19 of the Convention, Second periodic reports of States parties due in 1999, Serbia*, UN Doc. CAT/C/SRB/2, 8 February 2007; CtAT, *Summary Record (Partial) of the 843rd meeting*, 41st Session, UN Doc. CAT/C/SR.843, 12 November 2008, § 3 and CtAT, *Consideration of Reports Submitted by States Parties Under Article 19 of the Convention, Concluding observations of the Committee against Torture, Serbia,* 41st Session, UN Doc. CAT/C/SRB/CO/1, 21 November 2008, § 22 (in the context of the CAT, it was only noted that Serbia was unable to provide accurate information regarding the situation in Kosovo *i.e.* to fulfill its obligations; no explicit suggestions were made regarding any possible UNMIK reports).

5.3.3.2 Direct Scrutiny by International Compliance Mechanisms

The endorsement of the suggestion by most of the compliance bodies paved the way for the second dimension of interaction – one between UNMIK and the compliance bodies directly. The first UN body to follow Serbia's suggestion was the Human Rights Committee in its concluding observations in 2004, when it "encouraged" UNMIK to engage in the reporting procedure with respect to Kosovo.[265] Not all UN treaty bodies adopted this approach as quickly. In 2005, for example, the CESCR initially rejected the suggestion with respect to the ICESCR, requesting Serbia and Montenegro instead to cooperate with the Secretary-General and UNMIK in order to supplement its own initial report with data pertaining to Kosovo.[266] Later, UNMIK did engage under the ICESCR in the same way as it did under the ICCPR. Up to the moment of writing, February 2011, UNMIK had submitted reports under the ICCPR and the ICESCR regimes.[267] To support the reports, UNMIK filed a core document providing an overview of the overall human rights situation in Kosovo.[268] The inclusion of UNMIK in these regimes triggered the submission of shadow reports by NGOs along with oral discussions, which resulted in concluding observations.[269]

---

[265] HRCee, *Consideration of Reports Submitted by States Parties Under Article 40 of the Covenant, Concluding observations of the Human Rights Committee, Serbia and Montenegro,* 81st Session, UN Doc. CCPR/CO/81/SEMO, 12 August 2004, § 3.

[266] CESCR, *Consideration of Reports Submitted by States Parties Under Articles 16 and 17 of the Covenant, Concluding observations of the Committee on Economic, Social and Cultural Rights, Serbia and Montenegro,* 34th Session, UN Doc. E/C.12/1/Add.108, 23 June 2005, § 9.

[267] HRCee, *Report Submitted by the United Nations Interim Administration Mission in Kosovo to the Human Rights Committee on the Human Rights Situation in Kosovo Since June 1999, Kosovo (Serbia and Montenegro)*, UN Doc. CCPR/C/UNK/1, 13 March 2006 and *Document submitted by the United Nations Interim Administration Mission in Kosovo under articles 16 and 17 of the Covenant, Kosovo (Serbia)*, UN Doc. E/C.12/UNK/1, 15 January 2008.

[268] UN Human Rights Instruments, *Core Document Forming Part of the Reports of States Parties, Kosovo (Serbia)*, UN Doc. HRI/CORE/UNK/2007, 15 January 2008.

[269] For shadow reports, *see e.g.* Internal Displacement Monitoring Centre, *Submission from the Internal Displacement Monitoring Centre (IDMC) to the Human Rights Committee, Issues of concern and recommendations in relation to the report submitted by the United Nations Interim Administration Mission in Kosovo (CCPR/C/UNK/1, 13 March 2006)*, 30 June 2006 and the AI, *Briefing to the Human Rights Committee during the 87th Session in July 2006*, AI Index: Eur 70/007/2006. For concluding observations, *see* HRCee, *Consideration of Reports Submitted by States Parties Under Article 40 of the Covenant, Concluding observation of the HRCee, Kosovo (Serbia)*, 87th Session, UN Doc. CCPR/C/UNK/CO/1, 14 August 2006. Further information was received from UNMIK in 2008, *see* UN Doc. CCPR/C/UNK/CO/1/Add.2. These concluding observations were followed by UNMIK comments, *see* UN Doc. CCPR/C/UNK/CO/1/Add. 1. Under the ICESCR, concluding observations were adopted in 2008, *see* CESCR, *Consideration of Reports Submitted by States Parties Under Articles 16 and 17 of the Covenant, Concluding Observations of the Committee on Economic, Social and Cultural Rights*, UN Doc. E/C.12/UNK/CO/1,

The reports submitted by UNMIK provide an extensive overview of the human rights situation in Kosovo along the lines of the respective legal frameworks. Furthermore, all measures adopted by UNMIK to improve the situation and uphold the rights enshrined by the relevant treaties are presented. However, the reports fail to address the question of whether and to what extent UNMIK might have had a negative impact on human rights protection on the ground. In that sense, the reports contain little or no self-reflection. On a final note, it should be kept in mind that this interaction developed at UNMIK's discretion. Moreover, in a 2010 UN questionnaire, Serbia was asked to give its opinion on whether UNMIK reporting should continue under the ICCPR.[270] This seems to suggest that when it comes to this type of interaction, the UN attaches value to the consent of the nominal 'host state'.

Several of the previously mentioned UN treaty body mechanisms provide for individual complaints to be filed with the respective oversight bodies. For the ICCPR and the CEDAW, this is made possible by optional protocols while under the CAT and CERD regimes, states must submit declarations in order for individual petitions to be considered. Employing these individual complaints mechanisms in order to address ITA missions has not been regulated or agreed upon. The petition that led to the admissibility decision in *Kurbogaj v. Spain* is in this sense exceptional, despite the fact that regulating this option would bring present ITA missions closer to the petition practice as it existed under the Mandate and Trusteeship regimes discussed in Section 3.1.2.[271]

> In the 2008 report under the Universal Periodic Review procedure, Serbia noted that it is unable to provide information about the human rights situation in Kosovo. UNMIK was invited by the government of Serbia to submit relevant information with respect to the situation in Kosovo so that such information could be included in the report. However, UNMIK failed to reply prior to submission of the report.
>
> HRC, Working Group on the Universal Periodic Review, *National report submitted in accordance with paragraph 15 (A) of the annex to Human Rights Council resolution 5/1, Serbia*, 3rd Session, UN Doc. A/HRC/WG.6/3/SRB/1, 23 September 2008, §§ 115-118.

1 December 2008. These concluding observations were preceded by a list of issues and UNMIK replies, *see* UN Doc. E/C.12/UNK/Q/1 and UN Doc. E/C.12/UNK/Q/1/Add.1.

[270] In 2010, the HRCee asked Serbia to indicate whether it still wants the HRCee to invite UNMIK to submit reports under the ICCPR with respect to Serbia's second round of reporting, *see* HRCee, *List of issues to be taken up in connection with the consideration of the second periodic report of Serbia (CCPR/C/SRB/2)*, 98th Session, UN Doc. CCPR/C/SRB/Q/2, 8 April 2010, § 2.

[271] HRCee, *Kurbogaj and Kurbogaj v. Spain*, Communication No. 1374/2005, Decision on Admissibility, UN Doc. CCPR/C/87/D/1374/2005, 14 July 2006.

At the UN level, treaty-based mechanisms are complemented by the network of special procedures as an overarching category of human rights protection mechanisms under the Human Rights Council (and previously the Commission on Human Rights). These special procedures have also proved to be a legal framework within which UNMIK – although not the OHR – has been discussed in terms of achievement as well as accountability. The 'Special Rapporteur of the Commission on Human Rights on the situation of human rights in Bosnia and Herzegovina, the Republic of Croatia, and the Federal Republic of Yugoslavia' discussed the situation in Kosovo in general as well as UNMIK's lack of accountability more in particular.[272] Also, the situation in Kosovo has been addressed and visits to Kosovo have been conducted by Special Rapporteurs with thematic mandates pertaining to, amongst other issues, the freedom of opinion and expression, the elimination of all forms of religious intolerance and human rights defenders.[273]

The potential value of thematic procedures is illustrated in relation to the Roma lead-poisoning situation, which situation was addressed through a joint effort by the Special Rapporteurs on the adverse effects of the illicit movement and dumping of toxic and dangerous products and wastes on the enjoyment of human rights, on adequate housing as a component of the right to an adequate standard of living and on the human rights of internally displaced persons.[274]

---

[272] For assessments on the situation in Kosovo under UNMIK, *see e.g.* CommHR, *Report of Mr. Jiri Dienstbier, Special Rapporteur of the Commission on Human Rights on the situation of human rights in Bosnia and Herzegovina, the Republic of Croatia, and the Federal Republic of Yugoslavia*, 57th Session, UN Doc. E/CN.4/2001/47, 29 January 2001. UNMIK's use of extra-judicial detentions was also criticized in *e.g.* CommHR, *Report of Mr. Jiri Dienstbier, Special Rapporteur of the Commission on Human Rights on the situation of human rights in Bosnia and Herzegovina, the Republic of Croatia, and the Federal Republic of Yugoslavia*, 57th Session, UN Doc. E/CN.4/2001/47/Add.1, 22 March 2001, § 30.

[273] CommHR, *Report submitted by the Special Rapporteur on the promotion and protection of the right to freedom of opinion and expression, Ambeyi Ligabo, Addendum, Mission to the State Union of Serbia and Montenegro,* 61st Session, UN Doc. E/CN.4/2005/64/Add.4, 8 February 2005, §§ 47, 52, 57 and 76 and HRC, *Report of the Special Representative of the Secretary-General on the situation of human rights defenders, Hina Jilani, Addendum, Mission to Serbia, including Kosovo,* 7th Session, UN Doc. A/HRC/7/28/Add.3, 4 March 2008; HRC, *Report of the Special Rapporteur on freedom of religion or belief, Asma Jahangir, Addendum, Mission to the Republic of Serbia, including visit to Kosovo,* 13th Session, UN Doc. A/HRC/13/40/Add.3, 28 December 2009.

[274] UNMIK was contacted regarding the issue in 2005; an appeal was sent to UNMIK in 2006, to which UNMIK responded by letter dated 11 April 2006, informing the Special Rapporteurs on the efforts made to relocate the internally displaced persons. *See e.g.* CommHR, *Report of the Representative of the Secretary-General on the human rights of internally displaced persons, Walkter Kälin, Addendum, Mission to Serbia and Montenegro,* 62nd Session, UN Doc. E/CN.4/2006/71/Add.5, 9 January 2006; CommHR, *Adverse effects of the illicit movement and dumping of toxic and dangerous products and wastes on the enjoyment of human rights, Report of the Special Rapporteur, Okechukwu Ibeanu, Addendum, Summary of communications sent to and replies received from Governments and*

At the regional level as well, UNMIK entered into agreements with the Council of Europe with respect to the 1995 Framework Convention for the Protection of National Minorities (Framework Convention) and the 1987 European Convention for the Prevention of Torture and Inhumane or Degrading Treatment or Punishment (CPT).[275] This was suggested by Council of Europe parliamentarians from Serbia and Montenegro through a motion for recommendation on 29 September 2003.[276] The parliamentarians suggested that UNMIK should enter into agreements with the Council of Europe in order for the Framework Convention and the CPT to be implemented in Kosovo. Moreover, it was suggested that application of the ECHR could be improved if individual petitions from Kosovo were allowed.[277] These steps in effect advocate the applicability of the respective legal frameworks vis-à-vis UNMIK and the subjection of UNMIK to accompanying oversight mechanisms.

Soon thereafter, on 23 August 2004, the SRSG and the Secretary-General of the Council of Europe signed two agreements shaping the relationship between UNMIK and the Council of Europe.[278] Both agreements are similar in content. The preambles refer to, amongst other things, UN Security Council Res. 1244 (1999) and to the Kosovo Constitutional Framework. Moreover, they refer to the fact that Serbia (then Serbia and Montenegro) has ratified the respective treaties, at the same time stating explicitly that the agreements do not make UNMIK a party to the treaties.

Under Article 1 of the Framework Convention Agreement, UNMIK declares – on behalf of the PISG as well – that it will exercise its mandate in compliance with the Framework Convention. A similar provision is lacking in the CPT Agreement due to the different nature of this legal framework, which mainly relates to oversight. The Framework Convention Agreement provides that the

---

other actors during 2005, 62nd Session, UN Doc. E/CN.4/2006/42/Add.1, 27 March 2006, §§ 11-15; HRC, *Report of the Special Rapporteur on the right to adequate housing as a component of the right to an adequate standard of living, Mr. Miloon Kothari, Addendum, Summary of communications sent and replies received from Governments and other actors,* 4th Session, UN Doc. A/HRC/4/18/Add.1, 18 May 2007, §§ 64-66.

275 "Agreement between the United Nations Interim Administration Mission in Kosovo and the Council of Europe on technical arrangements related to the European Convention for the Prevention of Torture and Inhuman or Degrading Treatment or Punishment" (CPT Agreement) and "Agreement between the United Nations Interim Administration Mission in Kosovo (UNMIK) and the Council of Europe on technical arrangements related to the Framework Convention for the Protection of National Minorities" (Framework Convention Agreement), signed in Priština on 23 August 2004.

276 The recommendation called for the CoE Committee of Ministers and UNMIK to agree on a mode of cooperation in the context of the Framework Convention and the CPT.

277 *See* Section 4.1.1 for similar ideas discussed during talks with an official of the Serbian government.

278 CPT Agreement and Framework Convention Agreement, signed in Priština on 23 August 2004.

Committee of Ministers of the Council of Europe shall monitor the implementation of the convention in Kosovo in the same way it does with respect to state parties, by receiving reports from UNMIK, engaging in dialogue and issuing recommendations.[279] In turn, the CPT Agreement regulates the access of the European Committee for the Prevention of Torture and Inhuman or Degrading Treatment of Punishment (CPT Committee) to detention facilities: namely, "to any place in Kosovo where persons are deprived of their liberty by an authority of UNMIK".[280] The modalities of the visits, the grounds on which UNMIK can make representations against CPT Committee visits and the confidential manner in which the findings are communicated are all based on the CPT principles applicable to member states in general.[281]

In practice, the CPT agreement only became operational in June 2006, when a similar agreement was reached between the Council of Europe and NATO with respect to KFOR detention facilities, through an exchange of letters between representatives of both organizations.[282] Pursuant to the CPT Agreement, a visit to Kosovo was conducted in March 2007 which resulted in a report that triggered a response from UNMIK. Both documents were made public at the request of UNMIK.[283] A second visit to Kosovo was conducted in June 2010.[284] Under the Framework Convention Agreement, between 2005 and 2010 UNMIK engaged twice in the reporting system. Each cycle included reports filed by UNMIK,[285] supplementary shadow reports,[286] field visits and

---

279 Framework Convention Agreement, Artt. 2 and 3.

280 CPT Agreement, Art. 1.2.

281 *Id.*, Artt. 3-7.

282 COE, *Council of Europe Anti-Torture Committee gains access to NATO run detention facilities in Kosovo*, Press Release, 19 June 2006, at <http://www.cpt.coe.int/documents/srb/2006-07-19-eng.htm>.

283 CoE, *Report to the United Nations Interim Administration in Kosovo (UNMIK) on the visit to Kosovo carried out by the European Committee for the Prevention of Torture and Inhumane or Degrading Treatment or Punishment (CPT) from 21 to 29 March 2007*, Doc. CPT/Inf(2009)3 and Coe, *Response of the United Nations Interim Administration Mission in Kosovo (UNMIK) to the report of the European Committee for the Prevention of Torture and Inhumane or Degrading Treatment or Punishment (CPT) on the visit to Kosovo from 21 to 29 March 2007*, Doc. CPT/Inf(2009)4, both documents dated 20 January 2009.

284 CoE News Flash, *Council of Europe anti-torture Committee visits Kosovo*, 18 June 2010, at <http://www.cpt.coe.int/documents/srb/2010-06-18-eng.htm>.

285 CoE, *Report Submitted by the United Nations Interim Administration in Kosovo (UNMIK) Pursuant to Article 2.2 of the Agreement Between UNMIK and the Council of Europe Related to the Framework Convention for the Protection of National Minorities*, Doc. ACFC(2005)003, 02 June 2005 and CoE, *Progress Report on the implementation of the Framework Convention for the Protection of National Minorities in Kosovo submitted by the United Nations Interim Administration Mission in Kosovo*, Doc. ACFC(2008)001, 21 July 2008.

286 PRAXIS, *Thematic Shadow Report on the Implementation of the Framework Convention for the Protection of National Minorities in Kosovo*, 24 May 2006 and a shadow report

opinions by the Advisory Committee on the Framework Convention for the Protection of National Minorities and UNMIK observations thereto.[287]

5.3.3.3 Incidental Oversight by International Organizations

A third and final dimension of interaction consists of sporadic reports issued regarding the situation on the ground by various international organizations and NGOs. Various organizations have engaged in such reporting, including Human Rights Watch, the International Committee of the Red Cross and Amnesty International. These organizations have issued reports that, as well as being a substantive assessment of the situation on the ground, directly address the accountability deficit of the respective ITA-engagements.[288]

The Venice Commission reports on BiH and Kosovo, referenced extensively throughout the previous chapters, also illustrate the engagement by the Council of Europe with respect to the accountability situation in the respective territories.[289] Organizations entrusted to carry out parts of the ITA-mandate have

---

submitted in September 2005 as a result of cooperation of various minority working groups coordinated by an OSCE Consultant.

[287] Visits were conducted between 11-15 October 2005 and 27-30 April 2009. The following opinions were rendered: CoE, Advisory Committee on the Framework Convention for the Protection of National Minorities, *Opinion on the Implementation of the Framework Convention for the Protection of National Minorities in Kosovo*, Doc. ACFC/OP/I(2005)004, 25 November 2005 and CoE, Advisory Committee on the Framework Convention for the Protection of National Minorities, *Second Opinion on Kosovo(1)*, Doc. ACFC/OP/II(2009)004, 05 November 2009. UNMIK filed written observations with respect to both opinions: UNMIK, *Observations on the Opinion of the Advisory Committee on the Framework Convention for the Protection of National Minorities (adopted on 25 November 2005)*, submitted on 18 February 2006 and UNMIK, *Comments to the 2nd Opinion on Kosovo (1) of the Advisory Committee on the Framework Convention for the Protection of National Minorities*, 31 May 2010. Ultimately, the first opinion was adopted by the CoE, Committee of Ministers, Resolution ResCMN(2006)9, *On the Implementation of the Framework Convention for the Protection of National Minorities in Kosovo (Republic of Serbia)*, 21 June 2006.

[288] *E.g.* HRW *Kosovo 2007* paper; HRW, *Not on the Agenda. The Continuing Failure to Address Accountability in Kosovo Post-March 2004*, Vol. 18, No. 4(D), May 2006. For AI, *see e.g. Serbia (Kosovo): The challenge to fix a failed UN justice mission*, EUR 70/001/2008, 29 January 2008; *Kosovo (Serbia): The UN in Kosovo – A Legacy of Impunity*, EUR 70/015/2006, November 2006; *Human rights protection in post-status Kosovo/Kosova: Amnesty International's recommendations relating to talks on the final status of Kosovo/Kosova*, EUR 70/008/2006, 24 July 2006; *East Timor: Justice past, present and future*, ASA 57/001/00, July 2001.

[289] *E.g.* Venice Commission Kosovo Report; *Report of the Council of Europe Commissioner for Human Rights' Special Mission to Kosovo(1)*, Doc. CommDH(2009)23, 2 July 2009; Report by Mr. Alvaro Gil-Robles, Commissioner for Human Rights, *Kosovo: The Human Rights Situation and the Fate of Persons Displaced from their Homes*, Doc. CommDH(2002)11, 16 October 2002. With respect to BiH, *see e.g.* Venice Commission OHR Report.

incidentally overstepped their mandate by scrutinizing the activities of their international partners. One such example is the OSCE Mission in Kosovo, tasked to carry out certain parts of the ITA-mandate, which has on occasion issued reports addressing UNMIK policies, especially with respect to criminal justice and human rights protection.[290]

In a context in which other institutionalized oversight mechanisms are lacking, the contribution of these reports to the ITA accountability regime should not be underestimated. The monitoring raises awareness about the situation on the ground, and the reports contain a plethora of information with respect to the overall situation as well as to individual cases of alleged misconduct by the international presence. Moreover, this type of monitoring contributes to the delineation of a legal framework within which ITA missions are expected to operate.

5.4 CONCLUDING REMARKS

Already in 2004, the Venice Commission Kosovo Report considered the establishment of independent review mechanisms for UNMIK and KFOR activities "a matter of urgency".[291] The present chapter addresses the claim that, thus far, the archetypal institutional design of international territorial administrations in general has failed to incorporate meaningful accountability mechanisms. In particular, it has illustrated how the lack of institutionalized public law principles prevents such institutions from being established.

In Section 5.1, it was discussed that upon establishment, ITA missions are embedded in an accountability regime that fails to reach beyond the common peacekeeping accountability benchmarks. The backbone of this *ab initio* applicable accountability regime consists of an internal reporting obligation and internal oversight mechanisms. While the obligation to report is based on a principal-agent relationship between the establishing organization and the particular ITA-mission, the internal oversight procedures are essentially

[290] For example, the OSCE Legal System Monitoring Section of the Human Rights and Rule of Law department criticized various aspects of UNMIK's institutional design. Criticism ranges from the persistent lack of judicial review mechanisms to insufficiencies within UNMIK's criminal justice policy. This was done through reports such as *The Criminal Justice System 1999-2005. Reforms and Residual Concerns*, March 2006 and *Report on the Administrative Justice System in Kosovo*, April 2007; OSCE Mission in Kosovo, Department of Human Rights and Rule of law, *Observations and Recommendations of the OSCE Legal System Monitoring Section: Report No. 6, Extension of Custody Time Limits and the Right of detainees: The Unlawfulness of Regulation 1999/26*, 29 April 2000. *See* also the OSCE Kosovo Remedies Catalogue 1, in which the practice of extrajudicial detentions by SRSG executive decisions is criticized for lacking legal remedies.

[291] Venice Commission Kosovo Report, p. 21.

administrative in nature and could lead to disciplinary action. The founding documents do not prescribe the establishment of additional accountability mechanisms and, moreover, do not impose a coherent and fit-for-purpose legal framework on the ITA missions. The engagement of judicial bodies is not regulated, and any such engagement is framed by stringent immunity provisions and dependent upon the mission-contributing states.

In practice, the reporting obligation remains abstract and remote from the individuals and the local population *in toto* that the missions ultimately aim to protect. Mission-specific internal oversight mechanisms contribute to, amongst other things, the mainstreaming of human rights and the supervising of financial matters, but they have also been subjected to criticism. Human Rights Watch, for example, characterized UNMIK's internal oversight mechanisms as being "either dormant or improperly constituted".[292]

Section 5.2 illustrated a second category of accountability mechanisms. These mechanisms are established based on the acknowledgment that basic peacekeeping-oriented accountability mechanisms do not suffice in the ITA context. This category of mechanisms includes ad hoc established review mechanisms and built-in safeguard procedures that aim to guarantee the adherence to recognized human rights standards. The built-in safeguards are a procedural component of the ITA decision-making process and can only be regarded as a preliminary part of a broader accountability regime. With respect to review procedures, the one feature dominating all discussed mechanisms is the fact that they are not anchored in the founding documents and that, consequently, their establishment and mandate depends on the international administrator's discretion, depriving these institutions of a basic level of independence. The 'Kosovanization' of the OIK and the curbing of the HRAP's mandate through executive interference by the SRSG are clear examples thereof. As the Council of Europe commented on the position of the international administrator vis-à-vis the local judiciary, "[s]uch disregard by the executive for court decisions flouts all accepted principles of the diffusion of powers and the rule of law".[293]

Although a step forward in establishing a comprehensive accountability regime, due to their ad hoc, semi-independent and often weak mandate, these mechanisms overall fail to counterweigh the concentrated authority of the international administrators. Their ability to effectuate change on the ground reaches only as far as the benevolence of the international administration allows. In cases where institutions with the power to review did engage in a proactive

[292] HRW *Kosovo 2007* paper, p. 2

[293] CoE, *Kosovo: The Human Rights Situation and the Fate of Persons Displaced From Their Homes*, Report by Mr. Alvaro Gil-Robles, Commissioner for Human Rights, 16 October 2002, § 81.

way, they have at times met with a less than cooperative attitude on the part of international administration.[294] However, being the only mechanisms mandated to scrutinize the exercise of the ITA mandate, they represent the backbone of the accountability regimes set up over time.[295]

Finally, Section 5.3 entered into uncharted waters, describing the interaction that has developed between ITA missions and preexisting compliance mechanisms and judicial institutions. Courts at times have engaged in what can only be described as judicial activism, by attempting to assume jurisdiction so as to encompass the exercise of public powers by international administrations. In so doing, domestic as well as international courts face various challenges relating to immunity and the supremacy of international institutions vis-à-vis the local judicial system. Moreover, no clearly delineated legal framework is at hand that could be imposed or upheld by these courts, thus resulting in looming legal fragmentation if left unregulated. Other examples of this interaction relate to the atypical cooperation between UNMIK – for various reasons OHR and UNTAET did not engage in such practice – and treaty-based compliance mechanisms. The fact that UNMIK engaged in such cooperation, for example by submitting periodic reports, is praiseworthy. The reports filed by UNMIK, and the opinions rendered by the relevant oversight bodies, provide plenty of information regarding the manner in which the ITA mandate is exercised. The documents touch upon matters such as the Roma IDP camps in the northern part of Kosovo or upon UNMIK's housing policies. In addition, through closer cooperation with the treaty-based bodies, the contours of an applicable legal framework are further shaped. At the same time, practice shows that by engaging in such cooperation, the ITA missions reinforce their state-like appearance: namely, they tend to act like states when it comes to issues such as follow-up or the negotiations concerning access to detention facilities for monitoring purposes.[296] The analyzed interaction displays a reluctance to assume and accept obligations in a consistent way and to establish appropriate accountability mechanisms, thereby further substantiating the call for a mentality shift in this respect.

---

[294] *E.g.* Kosovo Ombudsperson Mr. Marek Nowicki's voiced his concerns during his speech to the CoE Parliamentary Assembly on 25 January 2005. Here, he urged that UNMIK be placed under an obligation to respond timely to the OIK's concerns.

[295] *E.g.* CoE, *Protection of human rights in Kosovo,* Report of the Committee on Legal Affairs and Human Rights, Doc. 10393, 6 January 2005, Section B(ii), § 15.

[296] *E.g.* UNMIK at times has been poor in terms of follow-up, *see* HRCee, *Report of the Special Rapporteur for follow-up on concluding observations*, 95th Session, UN Doc. CCPR/C/95/2/Rev.1, 26 May 2009, p. 18 and HRCee, *Report of the Special Rapporteur for follow-up on concluding observations*, 98th Session, UN Doc. CCPR/C/98/2, 19 April 2010, pp. 6-7.

6 CONCLUDING OBSERVATIONS

> *"The significant problems we face cannot be solved at the same level of thinking with which we created them"*
>
> \- *Albert Einstein*

When international law proves institutionally unequipped to address a recurring legal problem within its own ambit, recourse to other fields of law should be considered. As a case in point, international law is inadequately geared to deal with the persisting accountability deficit of international territorial administrations (ITA missions). Acknowledged time and again by commentators and expert reports, this accountability deficit – which compromises the positive achievements and, ultimately, the legitimacy of ITA missions – served as a point of departure, as this book set out to address the following question: *What is the potential of public law principles in conceptualizing the systemic accountability deficit inherent to missions engaged in international territorial administration?*

More in particular, this book explored two implications of a public law approach to the problem at hand. First, based on the nature of their mandate and on the impact of the exercise thereof, to what extent is it warranted to perceive ITA missions as public entities exercising public power rather than international organizations merely engaged in extensive peacekeeping? Second, if such a paradigm shift is accepted, how does a public law approach influence our understanding of the accountability deficit at hand?

The concluding observations provided in this chapter have the following three objectives. Firstly, premises underlying the public law approach to ITA missions and the manner in which they exercise their mandate are summarized (Section 6.1). Secondly, the main implications of a public law approach are discussed with respect to the ITA accountability deficit (Section 6.2). Finally, in the light of the subject matter of this book and the adopted public law approach, several suggestions are provided for further research (Section 6.3).

6.1 THE LEGITIMACY OF A CALL FOR INCREASED ACCOUNTABILITY OF INTERNATIONAL TERRITORIAL ADMINISTRATIONS

International territorial administration connotes the near-absolute replacement of a state by an international entity (Section 6.1.1). International entities established to that effect are geared with state-like powers. However, the accompanying regime of checks and balances is systemically inadequate, which in turn facilitates the persisting accountability deficit (Section 6.1.2). The fact that international law does not provide a coherent legal framework within which this deficit can be addressed necessitates alternative approaches to how we perceive international territorial administrations and their inherent lack of accountability (Section 6.1.3).

6.1.1 LEGAL INTERACTION OF THE GLOBAL AND THE LOCAL

ITA missions are *sui generis* legal entities, entrusted with an international mandate to administer particular territories through the exercise of state-like public powers. The ramifications of the exercise of this mandate are primarily felt at the national and sub-national level. Compared to other international entities acting at the local level, international administrations operate in a unique environment in which the state as the traditional intermediary between the global and the local has vanished. In other words, in instances of international administration the international legal order has descended to the national level, so to speak, and has substituted the state, thereby bypassing a 'sovereignty context' in which international organizations by and large operate when acting 'on the ground'.

This legal interplay between the global and the local is not wholly unprecedented. Under the Mandate and the Trusteeship systems, the League of Nations and the United Nations respectively assumed the responsibility to administer territories, albeit by appointing states as Mandatories and Trustees. As the Trusteeship system was phased out in the overall context of decolonization and the aims and means of UN peacekeeping efforts steadily expanded, peacekeeping missions increasingly began to include elements of civil administration. It is within this context that international territorial administration resurfaced, culminating in the UN-led administration of East Timor and Kosovo (by UNTAET and UNMIK, respectively) and the administration of BiH by the international community through the establishment of the OHR.[1] This is not to say that the international territorial administration-paradigm is confined to these three missions; indeed, elements of civil administration are scattered amongst various international peace-related efforts. Rather, these particular missions epitomize the variety of legal issues that arise when international entities assume overall responsibility to shape a particular public order at the local level.

6.1.2 THE DIRECT IMPACT OF INTERNATIONALIZED PUBLIC POWERS ON THE INDIVIDUAL

The subjection of territories to international administration is a response to extraordinary circumstances on the ground in which peace is disrupted and public administration has come to a standstill. The necessity of international engagement in such situations was left undisputed in this book. Instead, emphasis was placed on the nature of international engagement and on the impact thereof. The extent of this impact flows from the fact that an ITA mandate facilitates much more than a guarantee for the absence of armed conflict. It empowers international entities with ultimate legislative and executive authority and the responsibility to administer justice. Viewed together, this amounts to a near-complete set of state-like powers.[2] In the words of the *Brahimi* report, ITA missions

> set and enforce the law, establish customs services and regulations, set and collect business and personal taxes, attract foreign investment, adjudicate property disputes and liabilities for war damage, reconstruct and operate all public utilities, create a banking system, run schools and pay teachers and collect the garbage.[3]

Through the exercise of these powers, communities and individuals are impacted in the most direct manner *i.e.* in the way they would otherwise be affected by their state. Consequently, the exercise of an ITA mandate can result in any number of situations in which individuals and other stakeholders might be adversely affected. These situations range from cases of corruption to the individual – criminal – misconduct of office holders. Moreover, these situations include the mandated exercise of public power, which at times might not be in line with certain predominantly human rights-related standards.

---

[1] *See* Section 2.2.2 above.

[2] *See* Section 4.3 above.

[3] *Brahimi* Report, § II.H. The report criticizes the UN's urge to classify ITA as a peace operation and touches upon the question of whether the UN should be engaged in such missions at all.

6.1.3 THE LACK OF A COHERENT LEGAL AND REGULATORY FRAMEWORK

History proves us wrong in assuming that when it comes to the exercise of public power, good intentions lessen the need for checks or balances; at the very least, even "the fullest commitment [to respecting human rights] cannot rule out the possibility of making mistakes".[4] The potentially adverse effects of international territorial administration legitimize a demand for accountability and prompt the question as to how international law, or any other body of law for that matter, regulates the exercise of public powers by ITA missions in relation to this demand for accountability.[5]

This book illustrates that a clear and coherent legal and regulatory framework is lacking within which this demand could be addressed. Sovereignty of the 'host state' is a weak legal framework in this respect, since the scope of ITA-mandates extends to the point where it renders the sovereignty of the 'host state' ineffectual and incapable of imposing any limitations to the manner in which ITA missions operate.[6] A regulatory framework which does apply to the present situation emanates from the UN Charter, which, as a general legal framework, applies to all conduct of UN subsidiaries including UN-led ITA missions. However, no particular provisions in the Charter provide for the substitution of states by international entities.[7] This is in contrast to the legal frameworks which the Covenant of the League of Nations and the UN Charter provided with respect to mandates and trusteeships, respectively. These frameworks regulated the exercise of the particular mandates and trusts, and guaranteed the establishment of certain accountability mechanisms, most notably an extensive individual right to petition.

Several other bodies of law likewise prove to be deficient in terms of addressing the demand for accountability. The applicability of international humanitarian law to international peacekeeping is acknowledged, but it does not go beyond framing the military component of ITA missions. The law of occupation does provide guidelines as to how territories under foreign control should be administered, but it fails to address situations in which control over a territory is lawfully assumed by an international entity. Finally, international human rights law provides a normative framework within which public power

---

[4] Venice Commission Kosovo Report, p. 21.

[5] Here, accountability is defined in general lines as "the extent to which international Organisations, in the fulfillment of their functions as established in their constituent instruments, are and should be subject to, or should exercise, forms of internal and external scrutiny and monitoring, irrespective of potential and subsequent liability and/or responsibility", ILA 2004, p. 5.

[6] *See* Section 2.3.2.2 above.

[7] *See* Sections 2.2 and 2.3 above.

should be exercised and does so increasingly with respect to non-state actors. However, it generally lacks auxiliary mechanisms through which the human rights standards can be upheld in situations where public power is exercised by international organizations.

As a response, a public law-based approach is suggested. The fact that ITA-mandates are exercised by international entities has generally been the point of departure when ITA accountability is addressed, resulting in a legal gridlock and practical impediments in terms of accountability. Rather than focusing on the administering entity, emphasis should be placed on the nature of the powers exercised. The adopted approach draws from the functional parallel between ITA missions and states and posits that since ITA missions and national administrations are similar in terms of the public powers vested in them, their accountability-related concerns will likewise be comparable. Based on this *praesumptio similitudinis,* it is suggested that a public law approach to the exercise of public powers by ITA missions facilitates a better understanding of the related accountability deficit, as public law is the principal 'tool' through which accountability is addressed at the national level. The public law approach also implies a normative claim: if international law was progressive enough to develop to the point where international organizations replace states, the same progressiveness ought to be expected in terms of accepting accompanying responsibilities and oversight mechanisms.

6.2 A Public Law Approach to the Accountability Deficit of International Territorial Administrations

The public law approach builds on the premise that three fundamental public law principles – the rule of law, reviewability and an independent judiciary as a corollary of the diffusion of power – play a paramount role in achieving accountability. Stripped to their core, the three public law principles together convey the following message. Within any particular public order, the exercise of public power should neither be unlimited nor uncontrolled. Sovereign prerogatives should be exercised in accordance with certain procedural and/or substantive norms and regulations, upheld through a coherent regime of checks and balances. A cornerstone of any such regime is a dispersed authority to exercise public power. An independent judicial branch should emanate from this diffusion of power, and be independent in the sense that it can engage in review of the exercise of public power in order to uphold the pre-set limitations, without fearing unreasonable consequences. Finally, the principles require a certain degree of institutionalization in order to serve their accountability-purpose.[8]

From a methodological perspective, focusing on the core values of certain principles instead of on their detailed definitions applicable in national legal systems facilitates the use of such principles on levels and in situations that are considered atypical. In order to facilitate this in the present context, public law principles need to be stripped of technicalities and relieved of their state-connotation. The underlying rationale here is that rather than being linked to states, the principles are linked to the exercise of public power as such. In other words, the public law approach rejects the *faux pas* of applying public law principles in the realm of international law and international organizations, at least to the extent that these organizations in whole or in part substitute a state by exercising public powers. In the words of Sarooshi:

> It is the inextricable link between domestic public law and the activity of governing that mandates in general terms the application of domestic public law principles to those international organizations that exercise conferred powers of government.[9]

The implication of a public law-based approach is twofold. Firstly, by looking at ITA missions through a public law lens, one comes to grips with the nature of the related accountability problems. An assessment of the anatomy of ITA missions from a public law perspective traces the roots of the accountability deficit to a systemic disregard for public law principles (Section 6.2.1). Secondly, the analyses of the established accountability regimes in the ITA-context and the functioning of accountability mechanisms show that there is a link between the ITA accountability deficit and the absence of public law principles in the way ITA missions exercise their public powers (Section 6.2.2).

6.2.1 THE ISSUE: A DISREGARD OF PUBLIC LAW BY INTERNATIONAL TERRITORIAL ADMINISTRATIONS

The ITA accountability deficit emanates from the dichotomy between two distinct mindsets, one of which is centered on states while the other revolves around international organizations. Namely, ITA missions exercise state-like powers and behave like states while at the same time invoking the fact that they are international organizations when they see fit. How this bipolar approach to governing prevents the establishment of a coherent accountability regime is

---

[8] *See* Section 1.4.1 above.

[9] Sarooshi (2005), p. 14, footnote omitted.

understood best through the public law prism. Three main institutional features of ITA missions should be distinguished in this respect: the lack of a clear legal and regulatory framework, near-absolute immunities and an inclusive mandate. This book analyzed the linkages between these three features and the three public law principles, which resulted in three so-called determinants of the accountability-deficit.

The first determinant of the accountability deficit is that the rule of law is difficult to uphold if no consensus exists beforehand on the applicability of a coherent legal framework. Without clear parameters, the scope of the mandate is open for self-interpretation and is confined only by the most basic international legal principles. In particular, no coherent legal framework exists that would act as "a contrivance which not only describes but also confines government".[10] Rather, the mandate of ITA missions is construed as "the floor (but not the ceiling) for everything the mission does".[11]

It was illustrated that the Mandate and Trusteeship systems' legal frameworks provided a more fit-for-purpose set of guidelines and obligations. It is not asserted that these legal frameworks and the overall functioning of the Mandate and Trusteeship systems were immaculate. Rather, what these systems illustrate is the added value of a pre-set legal framework containing obligations that serve as a yardstick for assessing the exercise of the ITA-mandate. Through the available mechanisms, these yardsticks were invoked through the available mechanisms and the substantive standards were upheld.[12] Moreover, the existence and functioning of certain accountability mechanisms was rooted in these pre-set legal frameworks and as a consequence, these mechanisms did not depend on the discretion of the administering power.[13]

Indeed, the internal law of the organization establishes basic substantive guidelines and administrative procedures with respect to the functioning of UN subsidiaries. However, by no means does it regulate the functioning of a de facto state. Certain other legal regimes, international human rights law in particular, nominally provide substantive guidelines. However, the constituent UN Security Council resolutions fail to subject ITA missions explicitly to the international human rights regime and the particular ITA missions in practice have refrained from correcting this omission. Instead, declared adherence to numerous human rights documents remains voluntary, and for the most part cannot be effectuated through related compliance mechanisms. Here, the fact that the administration of

[10] Wormuth F.D. (1949), *The Origins of Modern Constitutionalism*, New York: Harper and Brothers, p. 3.

[11] Jacques Paul Klein, former SRSG for UNTAES and Principal Deputy High Representative with the OHR in BiH, as quoted *in* Chesterman (2003).

[12] *See* Section 3 above.

[13] *See* Section 3.1 above.

a state is in the hands of an international organization makes it difficult to subject ITA missions to a predominantly state-oriented international human rights accountability regime. Phrased more pessimistically, this dichotomy makes it easy for ITA missions to avoid subjection to human rights compliance mechanisms.

The second determinant concerns the review of the exercise of public power by a judicial or quasi-judicial organ, which is made impossible by a near-absolute set of immunities enjoyed by ITA missions. Covering both individuals and the administration *in toto,* the scope of these immunities is determined through an international organizations-mindset. It shields various types of acts and decisions from being subjected to review, even when acts with comparable effect would not enjoy the same privilege in the context of a state. As the Venice Commission observed:

> It is worth underlining at the outset that the main obstacle to setting up a mechanism of review of UNMIK and KFOR is their character as international organisations. [...] Nevertheless, it must be recalled that in Kosovo UNMIK and KFOR carry out tasks which are certainly more similar to those of a State administration than those of an international organisation proper. It is unconceivable and incompatible with the principles of democracy, the rule of law and respect for human rights that they could act as State authorities and be exempted from any independent legal review.[14]

While no archetypal legal system exists with respect to the extent of competences of the judicial branch, the need for a basic degree of judicial and/or constitutional control is generally accepted and is encouraged by the UN through its rule of law-related efforts worldwide. Achieving this basic level of judicial protection in internationally administered territories is made impossible by the immunities at hand; besides hampering the justiciability of various substantive human rights norms, the immunities in and of themselves in some cases result in a violation of the right to an effective remedy and access to justice.[15]

Finally, the all-inclusive ITA mandate attributes all powers to one single institution, which leads to an undesirable concentration of powers. A primary consequence thereof is that no distinction exists between the executive and the judicial branch, so to speak, of the international administration. Rather, the international decision-making structures are concentrated and final, despite the gradual introduction of power-sharing arrangements with the local authorities.

[14] Venice Commission Kosovo Report, pp. 20-21

[15] *See* Section 4.2 above.

Regulations, orders and administrative directions issued by a single person remain the procedural channel through which laws and constitutional amendments are imposed, individual detentions are prolonged and elected office holders are dismissed from office.

Arguments in defence of these ITA features often relate to functional necessity and to the chaos in which ITA missions are required to operate. Indeed, the accumulation of power in one single institution mirrors measures adopted by states in response to an emergency situation on the ground; this is no novelty if one recalls, for example, the appointment of a Roman dictator during the Roman Republic. However, such measures ought to be an extraordinary disruption to an otherwise well-shaped legal system. This is decidedly not the case with ITA missions. The matrix for setting up ITA missions rests on a state-of-emergency mindset. The extraordinary powers attributed to the SRSG's or the OHR are general rather than specific and in continue to apply throughout the duration of the mission, which, in the case of BiH and Kosovo, lasts well beyond the time a state of emergency has ceased to exist. In other words, rule by decree in the ITA-context is not a temporary measure derogating from a mandate which otherwise incorporates checks and balances and facilitates independent review.[16] Rather, the robust nature of the mandate is anchored in the constituent documents, which do not provide opportunities for reconsideration once the emergency situation on the ground has ceased to exist.

In summary, recurring features of ITA missions such as immunity and highly concentrated decision-making procedures, provide the opportunity for public power to be exercised in an outright autocratic manner. While these features might be justified from the perspective of functional necessity, they are troublesome in terms of public law. As the Council of Europe's Commissioner for Human Rights, Thomas Hammarberg, observed:

> [w]hen international organisations exercise executive and legislative control as a surrogate state they must be bound by the same checks and balances as we require from a democratic government.[17]

In the context of this issue, the three determinants together shape a deadlock in which the quest for accountability has found itself. This essentially legal problem is too often addressed by non-legal and contextual arguments. For example, the necessity of an accountability regime is at times downplayed by the benevolence behind the motives of UN administration missions. Likewise,

[16] *See* Sections 4.3 and 4.4 above.

[17] CoE, Commissioner for Human Rights, *International Organisations acting as quasi-governments should be held accountable"*, Viewpoints 2009, at <http://www.coe.int/t/commissioner/Viewpoints/090608_en.asp>.

the need for the ITA missions to be effective is at times misused to counter calls for even the most basic public law guarantees of due process. The predominance of such arguments should be rejected. As Advocate General Maduro stated in his opinion in *Kadi*:

> when the risks to public security are believed to be extraordinarily high, the pressure is particularly strong to take measures that disregard individual rights, especially in respect of individuals who have little or no access to the political process. Therefore, in those instances, the courts should fulfill their duty to uphold the rule of law with increased vigilance.[18]

In other words, arguments aimed at challenging the necessity of judicial review or the viability of legal constraints on ITA missions distract from looking at the accountability deficit as a legal problem and addressing this deficit accordingly *i.e.* by legal means, all to the detriment of accountability. As Morrow and White pointedly stated with respect to the situation in East Timor:

> The interests of the international community and East Timorese alike were best served when the ideals to which the UN is rightly bound and committed were used not dogmatically, but strategically: where the UN, so familiar with the techniques of promoting accountability over sovereignty, acknowledged the existence of the sovereignty-like responsibilities with which it was, itself, now burdened.[19]

6.2.2 THE CONSEQUENCE: IMPROVISED ACCOUNTABILITY

As a consequence of the three determinants, the image on the ground in terms of accountability mechanisms is one of incoherence, improvisation and ad hoc solutions, the success of which depends on benevolence, personal engagement and creativity. The accountability deficit by and large has only been mitigated to the extent allowed for by the international organizations-approach to ITA missions, safe for sporadic outside the box solutions through which accountability was enhanced. The submission of periodic reports by UNMIK under the ICCPR and the ICESCR are examples thereof. Despite the ad hoc nature of these solutions, UNMIK's inclusion into these state-centered compliance mechanisms is remarkable and, on a normative note, commendable.

Upon establishment, ITA missions are geared with a rudimentary set of accountability mechanisms. Reporting obligations that assure accountability to the principal rather than the administered society and internal oversight that

[18] European Court of Justice, *Kadi I*, Opinion of AG Maduro, 16 January 2008, § 35.
[19] Morrow & White (2002), pp. 3-4.

provides for administrative and disciplinary procedures form the backbone of the *ab initio* applicable accountability regime. Engagement of judicial bodies at the local level is conditioned by the waiver of immunity while regional or international judicial bodies are not a component of the accountability regime. These judicial bodies are not awarded a role by the constitutive documents of ITA missions, while various legal obstacles – pertaining, for example, to personal jurisdiction and attribution – in principle prevent judicial bodies such as the ECtHR to engage in the review of acts and omissions of ITA missions *proprio motu*.

Under the Mandate and Trusteeship systems, the PCIJ and the ICJ respectively were assigned a role in dealing with mandates and trusteeship-related issues. As limited as their role may have been, the respective courts did at times pronounce on the way in which particular territories were administered on several occasions.[20] It should be kept in mind that at the time states served as proxies for the international administration of territories and could therefore appear before the judicial bodies instead of the international organizations. Arguably, this would have been different if the international organizations themselves assumed the role of administrator as such direct administration, some suggested at the time, would amount to "paralysis tempered by intrigue".[21] Nevertheless, when the League incidentally did assume the role of direct administrator, the PCIJ proved able to continue to fulfill its supervisory role by rendering advisory opinions with respect to the internationally administrated territories.[22]

In sum, other than the rudimentary accountability regime, no additional mechanisms are envisaged *ab initio* that could adequately address the non-conventional powers vested in by ITA missions.

Measures aimed at addressing the accountability deficit adopted along the way reflect ambivalence rather than commitment on the side of international administrations. Ad hoc established institutions such as Ombudsperson institutions or the Human Rights Advisory Panel in Kosovo illustrate the need for and the potential added value of such institutions. Their fate also illustrates the institutional setting that prevents them from gaining and holding on to momentum. The demise of the Human Rights Advisory Panel is a telling case in point.[23]

---

[20] *See* Sections 3.1.3 and 3.2 above.

[21] Smuts J.C. (1918), *The League of Nations: A Practical Suggestion*, London: Hodder & Stoughton, p. 18. *See also* Van Ginneken (1992), p. 7. For a further analysis of this rejection, *see* Stahn (2008), pp. 76-78.

[22] *See* Section 3.2 above.

[23] *See* Section 5.2.3 above.

Taking all this into account, where does accountability on the part of international territorial administrations stand at this point?

Tapestries of ad hoc established accountability mechanisms are not able to prevent the internationally administered territories from falling into an accountability vacuum. Think back to Agim Behrami or the displaced community in Kosovo suffering from lead contamination. While the harm inflicted upon them is undisputed, the peculiar legal order within which ITA missions operate convoluted their quest for accountability. A variety of legal documents served as a basis for the claims of human rights violations, ranging from provisional local criminal codes to regional and international human rights documents. These documents, however, were either not binding on the international administration or were not enforceable upon it. No pre-set body of norms exists from which clear obligations might have been distilled.

Also in terms of *fora*, the confusion is apparent. From an institutional perspective, the omission to embrace the principle of (judicial) review has led to a mishmash of mechanisms scattered across the local, regional and international legal plains, at times struggling to assume jurisdiction over acts of international administrations. Indeed, the plaintiff's pursuit of accountability in the two respective cases led to a variety of institutions. The path their legal representatives followed in filing submissions on their behalf, however, does not reflect a coherent system of institutions with a clear hierarchy. Rather, the actions taken in search of recourse and redress follow the path of a ball in a pinball machine, its course being decided on the spot and according to no rule in particular: namely, driven by jurisdictional hurdles and immunities.

The lack of a legal framework and institutionalized and independent review mechanisms makes it nearly impossible to uphold the rule of law in terms of the relationship between ITA missions and adversely affected individuals or groups. It results in an "increased risk of litigation in national courts over trustee decisions".[24] In some cases where courts assumed jurisdiction over decisions adopted by the international administrator, it is fair to assume that the courts' 'progressive' attitudes towards the plaintiffs were at times insincere. Consider, for example, the July 2003 *Armando dos Santos* decision of the Dili Court of Appeal, where the court's reasoning was seemingly tainted by political motives.[25] Such instances are certainly not in the interest of justice and can increase fragmentation within an already intricate legal order. The developments before some other courts – for example, the Constitutional Court of BiH – are different and illustrate a real need to compensate for an existing accountability vacuum. However, by and large these attempts eventually failed due to the omnipotence of the international administrators. Attempts by these courts to

[24] *See* Perritt (2004), pp. 14-36.
[25] *See* Section 5.3.1 above.

pierce the ensuing accountability deficit and bypass stringent immunities were quashed by way of executive interference in the realm of the judiciary. While opinions may differ as to the desirability of local courts engaging at all in this type of judicial activism, the course of action taken by the Bosnian Constitutional Court signals, in a *Kadi*-like manner, the need for judicial review and calls for reconsideration of initial choices made with respect to the institutional design of ITA missions.

In response to this situation, a public law approach ought to be adopted, implying a conceptual and terminological 'translation' of ITA missions' features into the 'language' of public law. What does this mean? The necessity for well-coordinated peacekeeping missions is undisputed; in BiH for example, the efforts to restore peace were initially hampered by the uncoordinated number of organizations involved in the endeavour. However, translated in terms of public law, the coordination of peace-related efforts in East Timor, Kosovo or BiH amounted to the exercise of public power by one person, unchecked by an independent judiciary. This protracted supremacy of an international administration, at least in the way they are currently institutionalized, has a detrimental impact on the accountability and ultimately the legitimacy of international administration.[26]

In no way does the call for increased accountability through public law principles diminish the success of ITA missions in bringing about peace, nor does it downplay the difficulties ITA missions face on the ground in doing so; quite to the contrary. The strength of the public law approach lies in its sensitivity to emergency situations on the ground and the ability of public law as such to provide entities that administer territories with the means to address emergency situations as long as required. Furthermore, public law has the potential to 'appease' the two contradicting mindsets which dominate the accountability deficit by focusing on the nature and effect of the exercise of public power by international administrations. All this, through a legal framework that is sensitive to context and, above all, beneficial to the accountability, and ultimately legitimacy, of entities exercising public power.

6.3 FURTHER RESEARCH

The contents of this book as well as developments in practice prompt numerous questions, the answers to which merit further research. Additional inquiry is suggested along the following three themes.

[26] *See e.g.* International Crisis Group, *Bosnia: Europe's Time to Act*, Europe Briefing No. 59, 11 January 2011, where the continuing powers of the OHR are said to have an incapacitating effect on the development of BiH.

The lack of a coherent legal framework surfaced as a recurring obstacle to accountability, prompting various legal problems, including an unclear relationship between individual ITA missions and New York – the UN Department of Peacekeeping Operations in particular – as well as a weak institutional preparedness of the individual ITA missions. Further research is warranted in relation to the formal and material aspects of a potential regulatory framework. The formal aspect relates to the institutional dimension of a possible legal framework. Developments within the UN such as the adoption of the *Brahimi* report and the establishment of the Peacebuilding Commission in 2005 further the structuring of UN peace-related efforts. Whether these developments provide the adequate tools to embed ITA missions in an institutionalized legal framework remains to be seen. Also in terms of judicial institutions, a public law approach could be considered. In a broader context, decisions such as *Kadi I* and *Bosphorus* reflect in a sense a public law approach to the legal issues underlying the respective legal proceedings; regardless of the outcome in these cases, public law-based insights were considered in reshaping existing relationships between legal orders and legal actors. In the context of ITA missions, courts and quasi-judicial bodies at the local level have already attempted to mirror this approach. Existing case-law could be the basis for further research into the potential of a public law approach to the relationship between various judicial bodies and international entities exercising state-like public powers. The material aspect concerns a possible set of substantive obligations which might govern the conduct of ITA missions. The feasibility of including substantive obligations into a legal framework would need to be assessed and an appropriate set of such obligations would need to be determined, keeping in mind the diversity of territories which qualify for international administration. In so doing, the public law approach should not be lost sight of as ITA missions will continue to exercise public powers comparable to those exercised by states.

A second, but related, area of research would explore the nexus between ITA missions and criminal law as a specific component of a possible legal framework. Two dimensions can be distinguished. Upon deployment, ITA missions start reshaping the legal order of the territory they administer. UNMIK's inept determination of Kosovo's applicable law or the unclear status of defamation under the laws applicable in East Timor suggests a lack of preparedness on the part of the respective ITA missions. Criminal law is particularly important in this respect, as a functioning criminal law system is essential for the administered society to move on. The ability to address crimes from the past is furthermore a crucial factor in terms of the ITA-mission's legitimacy. Research is necessary so as to make sure that a pre-set criminal law system strikes the right level of abstraction in order to accommodate the differences on the ground between the various ITA missions. Ideas about a "common United Nations justice package", presented in the *Brahimi* report, should be mentioned in this respect.[27] The second dimension of this area of research involves the ambiguous relationship between international criminal law and the ITA missions themselves. Considering that ITA missions by their very nature operate in post-conflict situations, and keeping in mind the steady proliferation of international criminal tribunals, interaction between these two international legal entities is inevitable. UNMIK's constituent Resolution, for example, demands full cooperation from the international administration with the International Criminal Tribunal for the Former Yugoslavia (ICTY), although it fails to envisage any compliance mechanism in this respect.[28] Practice shows that cooperation comes in many shapes; one can for example think of giving effect to international arrest warrants, providing guarantees for the provisional release of accused persons or the obligation to investigate allegations of serious crimes.[29] In this respect, the ICTY's "concerns regarding the lack of full cooperation provided by [UNMIK]" should not go unmentioned.[30] Hypothetically, elements of ITA missions themselves could also be subjected to investigations of a criminal legal character.[31] Research clarifying the emerging relationship between ITA missions and international criminal law is therefore warranted.

Finally, it is suggested that the implications of the EU's increased engagement in the administration of BiH and Kosovo require assessment. With the establishment of entities such as the EU Special Representative, the International Civilian Office (in Kosovo) and missions like EULEX, entities are created that in terms of authority might prove to be a proverbial wolf in sheep's clothing. On the one hand, EULEX decidedly emphasizes its 'lite' mandate and places emphasis on local ownership. On the other hand, the EU Special Representatives continue to operate under the umbrella of UN mandated Chapter VII peacekeeping efforts. In the case of Kosovo, the supreme authority of the EU Special Representative is furthermore anchored at the local level, for example by Articles 146-147 of Kosovo's Constitution. The legal implications

---

[27] *Brahimi* report, §§ 79-82.
[28] SC Res. 1244 (1999), § 14.
[29] *E.g.* Sense Tribunal, *Eulex issues guarantees for Haradinaj and Brahimaj*, 24 August 2010, at <http://www.sense-agency.com/icty/eulex-issues-guarantees-for-haradinaj-and-brahimaj.29.html?cat_id=1&news_id=11842>; B92, *Albania invites EULEX to investigate*, 22 December 2010, at <http://www.b92.net/eng/news/region-article.php?yyyy=2010&mm=12&dd=22&nav_id=71681>; B92, *Del Ponte: Two options for investigation*, 22 December 2010, at <http://www.b92.net/eng/news/politics-article.php?yyyy=2010&mm=12&dd=22&nav_id=71679>.
[30] ICTY, *Thirteenth Annual Report*, 21 August 2006, § 86.
[31] *E.g.* B92, *Hague Tribunal should investigate UNMIK*, 26 December 2010, at <http://www.b92.net/eng/news/politics-article.php?yyyy=2010&mm=12&dd=26&nav_id=71754>.

of this similarity should be assessed, as problems relating to accountability might prove to be similar to the ones discussed in this book.[32]

6.4 FINAL REMARKS

Imagine an (international) lawyer being asked the following question: Does functional necessity warrant a robust mandate and a thick shield of immunity for international organizations engaged in post-conflict situations? The answer would most probably be affirmative. Now imagine a (constitutional) lawyer being asked a second question: In cases in which excessive use of police force leads to fatalities, or where negligent – one might even argue reckless – acts of public authorities result in the continuing poisoning of a whole community, should recourse and redress be provided to the victims? The answer would probably be affirmative as well.

International territorial administration provides a setting in which the factual backgrounds of these two questions have merged. Consequently, the two affirmative answers collide. The prevalence of the former leads to a systemic accountability deficit. Addressing this accountability concern is crucial in order to increase the level of judicial protection of individuals and communities placed under direct international rule. This is not asking the impossible; while state practice shows that perfection cannot be demanded, it must be pursued. When it comes to accountability of entities exercising public power, deficiencies in the practice of states are not the yardstick and should not prevent us from addressing the systemic problem at hand. An improved accountability record is assumed to have a legitimizing effect on international administrations which due to their nature cannot count on other, more conventional, factors of legitimization. Especially in deeply divided societies, a recurring trait in the ITA-context,

[32] Thus far, the EULEX mission in Kosovo in principle follows the accountability structures as the ones analyzed in Chapter 5. Internal oversight is ensured through internal mechanisms of the EU as well as local units such as the Human Rights and Gender Office, an advisory and policy office mandated to ensure the adherence to human rights standards and gender mainstreaming. For legal proceedings, accountability rests on the local jurisdictions of the participating EU member states and depends on immunity waivers. In terms of reporting, EULEX reports to the EU Council as well as the UN Security Council. Most notably, EULEX established a Human Rights Review Panel (HRRP), similar to the HRAP. The HRRP "is not a judicial or disciplinary body". Rather, the three international panel members decide on individual complaints and decide on whether human rights violations occurred. A first session was held in Priština in May 2010. *See* EULEX Accountability document, at <http://www.eulex-kosovo.eu/en/interactive/accountability.php> and <http://www.hrrp.eu/> and HRRP press release, 6 May 2010.

accountability as a legitimizing factor stands out as demands for accountability transcend the fault lines of ethnic divide.[33]

Turning back to the question pertaining to the potential role of public law principles in conceptualizing the ITA accountability deficit, it can be summarized that direct administration of territories by international organizations is essentially a legal experiment. The same can be argued with respect to the attempts made within international law to address the related accountability deficit. A consideration of the public law dimension of what has been unfolding in East Timor, Kosovo and BiH contributes to a better comprehension of the related accountability concerns. It sharpens our understanding of the obstacles preventing accountability from being achieved – obstacles that, rather than being insurmountable, remain largely man-made legal constructs that can be overcome.

[33] Interviews with members of Kosovo's three major communities were conducted by the author throughout the territory of Kosovo from September to November 2007. All interviewees shared an identical view with respect to UNMIK's lack of accountability. Interviews conducted by HRW corroborate this, *see* HRW *Kosovo 2007* paper, p. 9, n. 6.

NEDERLANDSE SAMENVATTING

Verantwoordingsplicht bij internationaal bestuur van gebieden:

Een publiekrechtelijke invalshoek

Dit boek richt zich op het verantwoordingsdeficit binnen internationaal bestuurde gebieden. Er wordt gesproken van 'internationaal bestuur van gebieden' wanneer internationale entiteiten (bestuursmissies) ten koste van staten het volledige bestuur van een gebied overnemen. In deze situaties worden publieke taken, welke traditioneel aan staten toebehoren, uitgeoefend door bestuursmissies. Het uitgangspunt van dit boek is dat internationaal recht geen adequaat juridisch kader biedt waarbinnen bestuursmissies deze publieke taken uitoefenen. Meer in het bijzonder betekent dit dat binnen het bestaande netwerk van internationaalrechtelijke instellingen en procedures bestuursmissies nauwelijks ter verantwoording kunnen worden geroepen voor de manier waarop zij de toegekende publieke machten uitoefenen.

De mogelijke rol van publiekrechtelijke beginselen bij het conceptualiseren van dit verantwoordingsdeficit staat centraal in dit boek. Daarmee sluit dit onderwerp aan bij het bredere debat over de verantwoordingsplicht – en uiteindelijk de legitimiteit – van internationale organisaties, vooral wanneer deze organisaties publieke taken uitoefenen waardoor (groepen van) individuen direct worden geraakt. Het onderwerp van dit boek wordt behandeld aan de hand van de drie meest representatieve voorbeelden van internationaal bestuur van gebieden: het VN bestuur van Oost-Timor (UNTAET, 1999-2002) en Kosovo (UNMIK, sinds 1999) en het internationale bestuur van Bosnië en Herzegovina (OHR, sinds 1995).

Een publiekrechtelijke invalshoek vormt het uitgangspunt van dit boek aangezien nationale en locale overheden op basis van publiekrechtelijke beginselen en procedures verantwoording afleggen voor de manier waarop zij publieke macht uitoefenen. Het gaat hierbij om drie kernbeginselen: rechtsstatelijkheid (*rule of law*), rechterlijke toetsing (*judicial review*) en een onafhankelijke rechtsmacht (*independent judiciary*). De aanname is dat deze publiekrechtelijke beginselen ook een rol kunnen – en in normatieve zin, dienen – te spelen buiten hun traditionele staatsrechtelijke context *i.e.* in situaties waar de staat effectief vervangen is door een internationale entiteit.

HOOFDSTUK 1 vormt de introductie van het onderwerp waarin een werkbare definitie van het concept van bestuursmissies uiteen wordt gezet aan de hand van twee kenmerken. Ten eerste, het mandaat van bestuursmissies is allesomvattend en behelst wetgevende, uitvoerende en rechtsprekende bevoegdheden. Ten tweede, dit allesomvattende mandaat is ultiem. Daarmee wordt bedoeld dat de uiteindelijke verantwoordelijkheid voor het uitoefenen van dit mandaat bij de internationale entiteit ligt, ook wanneer bepaalde bevoegdheden gedelegeerd worden aan locale instellingen. Het internationale bestuur behoudt namelijk het recht om locaal genomen besluiten te veranderen en/of ongeldig te verklaren. Wanneer voldaan is aan deze twee vereisten ontstaat een unieke rechtsorde. Hierin zijn internationale en locale rechtsregels onlosmakelijk aan elkaar verbonden, genieten besluiten van bestuursmissies hiërarchisch voorrang ten opzichte van de oorspronkelijke locale rechtsorde en werken besluiten van bestuursmissies direct door, waardoor zij alle facetten van de publieke ruimte bepalen en individuen direct (en mogelijk nadelig) beïnvloeden.

Voorts zet het eerste hoofdstuk de methodologie uiteen, welke voortbouwt op principes van rechtsvergelijking. De methodologie is gericht op het toepassen van publiekrechtelijke beginselen buiten hun traditionele staatsrechtelijke context. Hiervoor dienen de beginselen teruggebracht te worden tot hun kern wat het mogelijk maakt om de ratio achter de beginselen te 'transplanteren' naar een internationaalrechtelijke context.

In HOOFDSTUK 2 wordt het internationaal besturen van gebieden als concept nader uitgelicht. Er wordt gekeken naar parallellen met het Mandatenstelsel van de Volkenbond en het Trustschapsstelsel van de VN. In het kader van beide stelsels werden gebieden onder internationaal bestuur geplaatst, met dien verstande dat staten werden aangewezen om onder toeziend oog van de Volkenbond en de VN de mandaatgebieden en de trustgebieden te besturen. Bij het beschouwen van de parallellen wordt ook het *ad hoc* internationale bestuur van Danzig en het Saarland betrokken. In beide gevallen bestuurde de Volkenbond de betreffende gebieden zonder tussenkomst van een staat.

Ook wordt de verhouding tussen bestuursmissies en meer traditionele vredesmissies besproken. De missies in Oost-Timor en Kosovo zijn binnen een brede context van verregaande vredesmissies opgericht. Echter, het juridisch kader dat vredesmissies (van de VN) reguleert is niet toereikend om de unieke, vaak publiekrechtelijke, problemen op te lossen die zich voordoen wanneer internationale missies het complete bestuur van een gebied overnemen.

Het resterende stuk van hoofdstuk 2 voegt hier aan toe dat de juridische basis van bestuursmissies en de soevereiniteit van het 'ontvangende land' ook geen juridisch kader bieden waarbinnen het verantwoordingsdeficit gereguleerd kan worden. Bestuursmissies worden opgericht op basis van Hoofdstuk VII van het VN handvest. In tegenstelling tot het Mandatenstelsel en het Trustschapsstelsel biedt het handvest echter geen specifiek juridisch kader dat verplichtingen van en toezicht op de bestuursmissies reguleert. De bevoegdheden van bestuursmissies zijn bovendien zodanig dat de soevereiniteit van de 'ontvangende staten' niet bepalend is voor de manier waarop de gebieden door de bestuursmissies worden bestuurd; feitelijk is soevereiniteit in situaties van internationaal bestuur opgeschort. De conclusie die in dit hoofdstuk getrokken wordt is dat deze omstandigheden een negatieve invloed hebben op de mate waarin publiekrechtelijke beginselen – in het bijzonder het beginsel van rechtsstatelijkheid – doorgevoerd kunnen worden in de uitoefening van publieke macht door bestuursmissies.

Vervolgens richt het boek zich meer specifiek op het vraagstuk van verantwoording. HOOFDSTUK 3 behandelt de mechanismen waarmee binnen het Mandatenstelsel en het Trustschapsstelsel de verantwoordingsplicht werd gewaarborgd. Drie dimensies van het destijds opgezette verantwoordingsregime worden behandeld. Ten eerste, staten belast met het dagelijkse bestuur van gebieden moesten rapporteren aan de Mandatencommissie en de Trustschapsraad. Ten tweede, een rol was weggelegd voor het Permanente Hof van Internationale Justitie en daarna het Internationale Hof van Justitie. Deze internationale hoven konden zich uitspreken over de overeenkomsten die ten grondslag lagen aan de oprichting van elk mandaat en trustgebied. Deze hoven deden dat ook, zowel via contentieuze zaken als ook door middel van adviezen. Hierdoor kon richting worden gegeven aan de manier waarop gebieden bestuurd werden. De derde, en meest vooruitstrevende, dimensie heeft betrekking op het recht voor individuen om petities in te dienen bij de Volkenbond en de VN. Beide stelsels garandeerden het petitierecht waardoor individuen beklag konden doen over de besturende mogendheid en waardoor een directe juridisch verband werd gelegd tussen individuen en internationaal recht.

Twee algemene kenmerken dienen te worden benadrukt met betrekking tot de behandelde verantwoordingsregimes. Ten eerste, de regimes waren verankerd in de documenten die ten grondslag lagen aan beide stelsels en/of aan de individuele besturen. De meerwaarde hiervan, in termen van recht, is dat de in de regimes opgenomen waarborgen niet door de besturende mogendheid veranderd konden worden. Het bestaan van een dergelijk juridisch kader bracht bovendien met zich mee dat aan het handelen van besturende mogendheden expliciete grenzen werden gesteld. De mogendheden konden aan deze grenzen worden gehouden doormiddel van de rapporten, petities en de procedures voor de internationale hoven. Het tweede kenmerk betreft het feit dat gebieden bestuurd werden door aangewezen staten en niet door de internationale organisaties zelf. Dit was vooral bepalend voor de rol van de internationale hoven, aangezien zich jurisdictie problemen zouden voordoen in het geval van direct bestuur door internationale organisaties. Het hoofdstuk sluit echter af met een beschouwing over de manier waarop de verantwoordingsplicht was geregeld tijdens het internationale bestuur van Danzig en het Saarland. Het hoofdstuk wordt afgesloten met de conclusie dat alle drie de facetten van het verantwoordingsregime, *mutatis mutandis,* ook onder deze omstandigheden bleven functioneren.

In HOOFDSTUK 4 worden drie hoofdeigenschappen van tegenwoordige bestuursmissies 'vertaald' in termen van publiekrecht. Met andere woorden, een verband wordt gelegd tussen institutionele en conceptuele aspecten van bestuursmissies enerzijds en beginselen van publiekrecht anderzijds.

Ten eerste wordt vastgesteld dat het ontbreken van een duidelijk juridisch kader waarbinnen bestuursmissies hun publieke macht uitoefenen tot gevolg heeft dat rechtsstatelijkheid moeilijk kan worden gewaarborgd. Eerder werd vastgesteld dat een eenduidig juridisch kader ontbreekt. Verschillende onderdelen van de internationale rechtsorde blijken niet of maar gedeeltelijk in staat om deze lacune te vullen. Internationaal humanitair recht is weliswaar van toepassing op bestuursmissies, maar reguleert hoofdzakelijk de militaire aspecten van deze missies. Verder wordt in het hoofdstuk de weleens gesuggereerde band tussen bestuursmissies en bezettingsrecht verworpen op grond van conceptuele verschillen. Het internationaal mensenrechten regime werpt zich ten slotte op als een potentieel relevant juridisch kader, vooral met het oog op de aard van het mandaat van bestuursmissies. Hoofdstuk 4 behandelt verschillende manieren waarop gesteld zou kunnen worden dat mensenrechtennormen op bestuursmissies van toepassing zijn, namelijk via het VN handvest, op basis van de gewoonterechtelijke status van bepaalde mensenrechtennormen en via mensenrechtenverdragen. Met betrekking tot deze laatste optie worden de meerwaarde en juridische obstakels ten aanzien van de mogelijke link tussen mensenrechtenverdragen en bestuursmissies verder uitgewerkt. Hieronder vallen opties zoals automatische successie in het geval van verdragen die al eerder geldend recht waren in de bestuurde gebieden en extraterritoriale werking van bepaalde verdragsverplichtingen rustende op staten die deelnemen aan de bestuursmissie, alsook de optie dat bestuursmissies eventueel partij zouden kunnen worden bij mensenrechtenverdragen. Tot slot wordt aandacht besteed aan de rol van nationaal recht als een potentieel juridisch kader voor het handelen van bestuursmissies.

Ten tweede wordt betoogd dat ruime immuniteiten rechterlijke toetsing onmogelijk maken. In het algemeen bestaat er frictie tussen immuniteiten van internationale organisaties en mensenrechten, met name in het licht van het recht op toegang tot de rechter. Om straffeloosheid te voorkomen kunnen internationale organisaties immuniteit opschorten en zijn zij in bepaalde gevallen verplicht om alternatieve procedures ter beschikking te stellen. Ook vanuit de rechtspraak wordt in toenemende mate de immuniteit van internationale organisaties ingeperkt en afgewogen tegen mensenrechtelijke belangen. In het geval van bestuursmissies komt de besproken frictie nog meer tot uiting. Bestuursmissies nemen namelijk publieke taken over en handelen als staten terwijl ze blijven vasthouden aan een immuniteitconcept dat normaliter van toepassing is op internationale organisaties. Het stuk sluit af met een beschouwing over immuniteiten als een van de oorzaken van het verantwoordingsdeficit.

Ten slotte wordt gekeken naar het allesomvattende en geconcentreerde mandaat van bestuursmissies en de daaruit voortvloeiende onmogelijkheid om een onafhankelijke rechtsmacht op te zetten. Hoofdstuk 4 zet de levensloop van bestuursmissie-mandaten uiteen, beginnende bij de attributie van ruime maar onduidelijk begrensde publieke macht, via zelfinterpretatie door de bestuursmissies tot het uiteindelijke delegeren van bepaalde bevoegdheden aan locale overheden door de bestuursmissies met behoud van uiteindelijke verantwoordelijkheid. Het internationale mandaat vertrouwt de bestuursmissie – en het hoofd van de betreffende missie – alle macht toe. Dit betekent dat wetgevende en uitvoerende macht, als ook de verantwoordelijkheid voor de rechtspraak, in de handen ligt van een persoon. Hierdoor kan de uitvoerende macht 'op de stoel van de rechter' zitten en daarmee de onafhankelijkheid van de rechtspraak in het geding brengen.

Deze kenmerken van bestuursmissies worden vaak verdedigd door te wijzen op de uitzonderlijke situatie waarin de bestuurde gebieden zich bevinden. Als gevolg van de 'noodtoestand' zouden de besproken maatregelen en institutionele oplossingen noodzakelijk zijn. Het hoofdstuk sluit af met een beschouwing en uiteindelijke verwerping van dit argument aan de hand van de eisen die worden gesteld door de belangrijkste mensenrechtenverdragen aan het inroepen van de noodtoestand om te kunnen derogeren aan mensenrechtelijke verplichtingen.

In HOOFDSTUK 5 wordt de praktische uitwerking van de kenmerken van bestuursmissies behandeld zoals besproken in hoofdstuk 4. Gekeken wordt naar de bestaande verantwoordingsmechanismen binnen en rondom bestuursmissies.

Ten eerste wordt gekeken naar de mechanismen die *ab initio* worden opgezet en vanaf de oprichting van afzonderlijke bestuursmissies een elementaire verantwoordingsplicht in stand dienen te houden. Dit verantwoordingsregime bestaat uit de plicht om te rapporteren aan de VN Veiligheidsraad en uit interne, in essentie administratiefrechtelijke, procedures. In het geval van VN gestuurde missies zijn deze mechanismen centraal gereguleerd vanuit de VN en zijn ze niet gericht op de bevolking van de bestuurde gebieden als zodanig. Verder steunt de VN op nationale rechtstelsels in gevallen wanneer immuniteit opgeheven wordt en de gang naar de rechter noodzakelijk wordt geacht. Ook worden de bestaande procedures beschouwd die betrekking hebben op privaatrechtelijke schadeclaims die voortvloeien uit schade geleden als gevolg van handelingen van bestuursmissies. In het hoofdstuk wordt geconcludeerd dat dit systeem geen toereikend juridisch kader biedt waarbinnen bestuursmissies ter verantwoording kunnen worden geroepen.

Vervolgens worden *ad hoc* opgerichte mechanismen bestudeerd. Deze instellingen en procedures worden binnen afzonderlijke missies opgericht om gehoor te geven aan de roep voor meer verantwoording. Het gaat hierbij om onderdelen van het besluitvormingsproces die er op moeten toezien dat besluiten van bestuursmissies voeldoen aan bepaalde interne en mensenrechtelijke criteria. Om *ex post* toezicht te bewerkstelligen worden instellingen als de Ombudspersoon en aparte mensenrechten panels opgericht. Deze instellingen hebben een algemene of een specifieke (op een bepaald onderwerp toegespitste) rechtsmacht om besluiten van bestuursmissies te toetsen. In het hoofdstuk wordt geconcludeerd dat deze mechanismen een welkome toevoeging zijn aan het initiële verantwoordingsregime. Deze mechanismen worden echter, in tegenstelling tot het Mandatenstelsel en het Trustschapsstelsel, opgericht door de bestuursmissies zelf. Het hoofdstuk wijst op de nadelige gevolgen hiervan en illustreert hoe deze mechanismen qua bestaan, rechtsmacht en procedure afhankelijk zijn en bepaald worden door de bestuursmissies. Dit verzwakt de onafhankelijkheid van deze quasi-juridische instellingen en leidt in sommige gevallen tot directe inmenging van de bestuursmissie (de wetgevende en de uitvoerende macht) in hun gang van zaken.

Ten slotte wordt de interactie tussen bestuursmissies en bestaande procedures en instellingen geanalyseerd. Hierbij wordt gekeken naar de manier waarop locale overheden en juridische organen reageren op de uitoefening van publieke macht door bestuursmissies. In het hoofdstuk wordt aandacht besteed aan gevallen waarbij locale hoven hebben getracht de macht van bestuursmissies in te perken, alsook aan de manier waarop bestuursmissies daar op hebben gereageerd door zich te beroepen op immuniteiten en door gebruik te maken van hun geconcentreerde mandaat. Ook wordt er gekeken naar de interactie tussen bestuursmissies en internationale en regionale mensenrechtenregimes en bijbehorende juridische instellingen, zoals het Europees Hof voor de Rechten van de Mens en het Mensenrechtencomité van de VN.

HOOFDSTUK 6 biedt, tot slot, enkele samenvattende conclusies en inzichten. De implicaties van een publiekrechtelijke invalshoek worden beschouwd. In het hoofdstuk wordt geconstateerd dat problemen met betrekking tot de verantwoordingsplicht voortvloeien uit het feit dat publiekrechtelijke beginselen onvoldoende in acht worden genomen bij de manier waarop bestuursmissies worden ingericht en bij de besluitvormingsprocessen waarmee bestuursmissies publieke macht uitoefenen. De vaststelling van de juridische contouren van dit verantwoordingsdeficit is gebaat bij een publiekrechtelijke invalshoek. Hierbij spelen publiekrechtelijke beginselen een belangrijke rol aangezien deze beginselen niet het handelen van staten, maar het uitoefenen van publieke macht als zodanig reguleren. Het boek wordt afgesloten met de beschouwing dat juridische obstakels die tot het verantwoordingsdeficit leiden overbrugbaar zijn en dat het betrekken van publiekrechtelijke beginselen bij het zoeken naar een coherente oplossing voor het verantwoordingsdeficit geoorloofd en wenselijk is.

REFERENCES

SELECTED BOOKS AND ARTICLES

Aksu E. (2006), 'International Transitional Administrations: Towards Territorialization of IGOs?', 13(1) *Journal of International and Area Studies*, pp. 37-52.

Allan T. (2001), *Constitutional justice: a Liberal theory of the rule of law*, New York: Oxford University Press.

— (2003), 'Constitutional Dialogue and the Justification of Judicial Review', 23(4) *Oxford Journal of Legal Studies*, pp. 563-584.

— (2004), 'Legislative Supremacy and Legislative Intent: A reply to Professor Craig', 24(4) *Oxford Journal of Legal Studies*, pp. 563-583.

Allott P. (1999), 'The concept of International Law', 10(1) *European Journal of International Law*, pp. 31-50.

Anghie A. (2002), 'Colonialism and the Birth of International Institutions: Sovereignty, Economy, and the Mandate System of the League of Nations', 34 *New York University Journal of International Law and Politics*, pp. 513-634.

Aoi C. *et al.* (eds.)(2007), *Unintended Consequences of Peacekeeping Operations*, New York: United Nations University Press.

Baskin M. (2004), 'Between Exit and Engagement: On the Division of Authority between International and Domestic Institutions in Transitional Administration', 10 *Global Governance*, pp. 119-137.

Battini S. (2005), 'International Organizations and Private Subjects: A Move Toward A Global Administrative Law', 2005/3 *IILJ Working Paper*, pp. 1-30.

Baylis E.A. (2007), 'Parallel Courts in Post-Conflict Kosovo', 32 *Yale Journal of International Law*, pp. 1-59.

Beatty D.M. (2004), *The Ultimate Rule of Law*, New York: Oxford University Press.

Beauvais J.C. (2001), 'Benevolent Despotism, A Critique of U.N. State-Building in East Timor', 33 *New York University Journal of International Law and Politics*, pp. 1101-1178.

Bentwich N. (1929), 'Judicial Interpretation of the Mandate for Palestine', 1 *Zeitschrift für ausländisches öffentliches Recht und Völkerrecht*, pp. 212-222.

Berdal M. & Caplan R. (2004), 'The Politics of International Administration', 10 *Global Governance*, pp. 1-5.

Berman N. (2006), 'Intervention in a "Divided World": Axes of Legitimacy', 17(4) *European Journal of International Law*, pp. 743-769.

Bickel A.M. (1962), *The Least Dangerous Branch: the Supreme Court at the bar of Politics*, Indianapolis: Bobbs–Merrill.

Bisschop W.R. (1924), *The Saar Controversy*, London: Sweet & Maxwell.

Black J. (2007), 'Constructing and contesting legitimacy and accountability in polycentric regulatory regimes', 2007/12 *IILJ Working Paper*, pp. 1-33.

Bodansky D., Brunnee J. & Hey E. (eds.)(2007), *The Oxford Handbook of International Environmental Law*, Oxford: Oxford University Press.

Bogdandy A. (von)(2006), 'Constitutionalism in International Law: Comment on a Proposal from Germany', 47(1) *Harvard International Law Journal*, pp. 223-242.

— (2008), 'General Principles of International Public Authority: Sketching a Research Field', 9(11) *German Law Journal,* pp. 1909-1938.

Bongiorno C. (2002), 'A Culture of Impunity: Applying International Human Rights Law to the United Nations in East Timor', 33 *Columbia Human Rights Law Review*, pp. 623-647.

Bondy W. (1998), *The Separation of Governmental Powers in History, in Theory, and in the Constitutions*, Union: The Lawbook Exchange.

Boon K. (2005), 'Legislative Reform in Post-Conflict Zones: Jus Post Bellum and the Contemporary Occupant's Law-Making Powers', 50 *McGill Law Journal*, pp. 285-326.

Boothby D. (2004), 'The Political Challenges of Administering Eastern Slavonia', 10 *Global Governance*, pp. 37-51.

Borowski M. (2003), 'The Beginnings of Germany's Federal Constitutional Court', 16(2) *Ratio Juris* pp. 155-186.

Bovens M. (2007), 'Analysing and Assessing Accountability: A Conceptual Framework', 13(4) *European Law Journal* pp. 447- 468.

Bowett D.W. (1964), *United Nations Forces; A Legal Study of United Nations Practice*, London: Stevens & Sons Ltd.

Brabandere E. (2009), *Post-conflict Administrations in International Law; International Territorial Administration, Transitional Authority and Foreign Occupation in Theory and Practice*, Leiden: Martinus Nijhoff Publishers.

Bracton H. (1968), *On the Laws and Customs of England, Vol. III*, Cambridge, Massachusetts: Harvard University Press.

Brand M. (2003), *The Development of Kosovo Institutions and the Transition of Authority from UNMIK to Local Self-Government*, Geneva: Centre for Applied Studies in International Negotiations.

Breugel J.W. (1953), 'The Right to Petition an International Authority', 2(4) *International and Comparative Law Quarterly*, pp. 542-563.

Brownlie I. (2008), *Principles of Public International Law*, New York: Oxford University Press.

Butler W.E. (ed.)(1980), *International Law in Comparative Perspective*, Alphen aan den Rijn: Sijthoff & Noordhoff.

ButleRitchie D.T. (2004), 'The confines of modern constitutionalism', 3(1) *Pierce Law Review*, pp. 1-32.

Cannizzaro E. (2005), 'Machiavelli, the UN Security Council and the Rule of Law', *Global Law Working Paper 11/05*, pp. 1-32.

Caplan R. (2002), *A New Trusteeship? The International Administration of War-torn Territories*, Oxford: Oxford University Press.

— (2004)(1), 'International Authority and State Building: The Case of Bosnia and Herzegovina', 10 *Global Governance*, pp. 53-65.

— (2004)(2), 'Partner or Patron? International Civil Administration and Local Capacity-building', 11(2) *International Peacekeeping*, pp. 229-247.

— (2006), *International Governance of War-Torn Territories*, New York: Oxford University Press.

Carey J. (1966), 'The United Nations' Double Standard on Human Rights Complaints', 60(4) *American Journal of International Law*, pp. 792-803.

Cerone J. (2001), 'Minding the Gap: Outlining KFOR Accountability in Post-Conflict Kosovo', 12 *Leiden Journal of International Law,* pp. 469-488.

Charlesworth H. & Wood M. (2001), '"Mainstreaming Gender" in International Peace and Security: The Case of East Timor', 26 *Yale Journal of International Law*, pp. 313-318.

Chesterman S. (2002), *The United Nations as Government: Accountability Mechanisms for Territories Under UN Administration*, Fighting Corruption in Kosovo: Lessons from the Region Conference, Priština, 4-5 March 2002.

— (2003), *You, the People: The United Nations, Transitional Administration, and State-Building,* Final Report, Project on Transitional Administration, International Peace Academy.

— (2005), *You, the People: the United Nations, Transitional Administration and State-Building*, Oxford: Oxford University Press.

— (2008), 'An International Rule of Law?', 56(2) *American Journal of Comparative Law*, pp. 1-39.

Chodosh H.E. (1999), 'Comparing Comparisons: In Search of Methodology', 84 *Iowa Law Review*, pp. 1025-1132.

Chopra J. (2000)(1), 'The UN's Kingdom of East Timor', 42(3) *Survival*, pp. 27-40.

— (2000)(2), 'Introductory Note to UNTAET Regulation 13 (2000)', 39(4) *International Legal Materials*, pp. 936-938.

Chowdhuri R.N. (1955), *International Mandates and Trusteeship Systems: A Comparative Study* (diss. Amsterdam, UvA), The Hague: Martinus Nijhoff.

Cogen M. & Brabandere E. (2007), 'Democratic Governance and Post-conflict Reconstruction', 20 *Leiden Journal of International Law*, pp. 669-693.

Coomans F. & Kamminga M. (2004), *Extraterritorial Application of Human Rights Treaties*, Antwerp: Intersentia.

Corwin E.S. (1928), 'The "Higher Law" Background of American Constitutional Law', 42(2) *Harvard Law Review*, pp. 149-185.

— (1929), 'The "Higher Law" Background of American Constitutional Law', 42(3) *Harvard Law Review*, pp. 365-409.

Craig P. (2004), 'Legislative Intent and Legislative Supremacy: A Reply to Professor Allan', 24(4) *Oxford Journal of Legal Studies*, pp. 585-596.

— (2004), 'The Common Law, Shared Power and Judicial Review', 24(2) *Oxford Journal of Legal Studies*, pp. 237-257.

Crawford J.R. (2006), *The Creation of States in International Law*, Oxford: Oxford University Press.

De Búrca G. & Gerstenberg O. (2006), 'The Denationalization of Constitutional Law', 47(1) *Harvard International Law Journal,* pp. 243-262.

De Búrca G. (2010), 'The European Court of Justice and the International Legal Order after *Kadi*', 51(1) *Harvard International Law Journal,* pp. 1-50.

De Wet E. (2004), 'The Direct Administration of Territories by the United Nations and its Member States in the Post Cold War Era: Legal Bases and Implications for National Law', 8 *Max Planck Yearbook of United Nations Law*, pp. 291-340.

— (2006)(1), 'The International Constitutional Order', 55 *International and Comparative Law Quarterly*, pp. 51-76.

— (2006)(2), 'The Emergence of International and Regional Value Systems as a Manifestation of the Emerging International Constitutional Order', 19 *Leiden Journal of International Law*, pp. 611-632.

— (2008), 'Holding International Institutions Accountable: The Complementary Role of Non-Judicial Oversight Mechanisms and Judicial Review', 9(11) *German Law Journal,* pp. 1987-2011.

Diehl P.F. (2005), *The Politics of Global Governance: International Organizations in an Interdependent World*, Boulder: Lynne Rienner.

Dworkin R. (1978), 'Political Judges and the Rule of Law', 64 *Proceedings of the British Academy*, pp. 1-32.

Dyzenhaus D. (2005), 'The Rule of (Administrative) Law in International Law', 2005/1 *IILJ Working Paper*, pp. 1-43.

Eagleton C. (1928), *The Responsibility of States in International Law*, New York: New York University Press.

Esty D.C. (2006), 'Good Governance at the Supranational Scale: Globalizing Administrative Law', 115 *Yale Law Journal*, pp. 1490-1562.

Evans L.H. (1932), 'The General Principles Governing the Termination of a Mandate', 26(4) *American Journal of International Law*, pp. 735-758.

Everly R. (2007), 'Reviewing Governmental Acts of the United Nations in Kosovo', 8(1) *German Law Journal*, pp. 21-38.

Falk R. & Strauss A. (2000), 'On the Creation of a Global People's Assembly: Legitimacy and the Power of Popular Sovereignty', 36 *Stanford Journal of International Law,* pp. 191-220.

Fassbender B. (1998), 'The United Nations Charter as Constitution of the International Community', 36 *Columbia Journal of Transnational Law,* pp. 529-620.

Fearon J.D. & Laitin D.D. (2004), 'Neotrusteeship and the Problem of Weak States', 28(4) *International Securities*, pp. 5-43.

Feinberg N. (1930), *La Juridiction de la Cour Permanente de Justice Internationale dans le Système des Mandats*, Paris: Rousseau.

Fletcher-Cooke J. (1959), 'Some Reflections on the International Trusteeship System, with Particular Reference to its Impact on the Governments and Peoples of the Trust Territories', 13(3) *International Organization*, pp. 423-430.

Ford C.E. & Oppenheim B.A. (2008), 'Neotrusteeship or Mistrusteeship? The "Authority Creep" Dilemma in United Nations Transitional Administration', 41(1) *Vanderbilt Journal of Transnational Law*, pp. 55-105.

Francesco F. (ed.)(2007), *Access to Justice as a Human Right*, Oxford: Oxford University Press.

Franck T. (1992), 'The Emerging Right to Democratic Governance', 86(1) *American Journal of International Law,* pp. 46-91.

— (1995), *Fairness in International Law and Institutions,* Oxford: Clarendon Press.

Friedrich C.J. (1937), *Constitutional Government and Politics*, New York: Harper and Row.

— (1946), *Constitutional Government and Democracy: theory and practice in Europe and America*, Boston: Ginn and Company.

— (1964), *Transcendent Justice, the religious dimensions of Constitutionalism*, Durham: Duke University Press.

— (1974), *Limited Government: A Comparison*, London: Prentice-Hall; Englewood Cliffs.

Gerber D. (1998), 'System Dynamics: Toward a Language of Comparative Law', 46(4) *American Journal of Comparative Law*, pp. 719-737.

Ginsburg T. (2002), 'Economic Analysis of the Design of Constitutional Courts', 3(1) *Theoretical Inquiries in Law*, pp. 1-38.

Goldstone A. (2004), 'UNTAET with Hindsight: The Peculiarities of Politics in an Incomplete State', 10 *Global Governance*, pp. 83-98.

Goodman R. (2002), 'Human Rights Treaties, Invalid Reservations, and State Consent', 96(1) *American Journal of International Law,* pp. 531-560.

Goodwin M. (2007), 'From Province to Protectorate to State? Speculation on the Impact of Kosovo's Genesis upon the Doctrines of International Law', 8(1) *German Law Journal,* pp. 1-20.

Gorajo P. (2002), 'The Legacy and Lessons of the United Nations Transitional Administration in East Timor', 24 *Contemporary Southeast Asia,* pp. 313-333.

Gordon R. (1997), 'Saving Failed States: Sometimes A Neocolonialist Notion', 12 *American University Journal of International Law & Policy,* pp. 903-974.

— (1999), *Controlling the State – Constitutionalism from Ancient Athens to Today*, Cambridge: Harvard University Press.

Grant R.W. & Keohane R.O. (2004), 'Accountability and Abuses of Power in World Politics', 2004/7 *IILJ Working Paper*, pp. 1-36.

Grant T.D. (1998), 'International Guaranteed Constitutive Order, Cyprus and Bosnia as Predicates for a New Non-traditional Actor in the Society of States', 8 *Journal of Transnational Law and Policy,* pp. 1-55.

Grenfell L. (2006), 'Legal Pluralism and the Rule of Law in Timor Leste', 19 *Leiden Journal of International Law,* pp. 305-337.

Hales J.C. (1937), 'Some Legal Aspects of the Mandate System: Sovereignty: Nationality: Termination and Transfer', 23 *Transactions of the Grotius Society,* pp. 85-126.

Hall D. (1946), 'The British Commonwealth and Trusteeship', 22 *International Affairs*, pp. 199-213.

— (1947), 'The Trusteeship System', 24 *British Yearbook of International Law,* pp. 33-71.

— (1948), *Mandates, Dependencies and Trusteeship*, London: Stevens & Sons Limited.

Harland D. (2004), 'Legitimacy and Effectiveness in International Administration', 10 *Global Governance*, pp. 15-19.

Harlow C. & Rawlings R. (2007), 'Promoting Accountability in Multilevel Governance: A Network Approach', 13(4) *European Law Journal,* pp. 542-562.

Harutyunyan G. & Mavčič A. (1999), *Constitutional Review and its Development in the Modern World: A Comparative Constitutional Analysis*, Ljubljana: Yerevan.

Hayek F. A. (1955), *The Political Ideal of the Rule of Law,* Cairo: National Bank of Egypt Fiftieth Anniversary Commemoration Lectures.

Haynes D.F. (ed.)(2008), *Deconstructing the Reconstruction: Human Rights and Rule of Law in Postwar Bosnia and Herzegovina*, Aldershot: Ashgate.

Helfer L. (2004), 'Constitutional Analogies in the International Legal System', 37 *Loyola Los Angeles Law Review*, pp. 139-238.

Helman G.B. & Ratner S.R. (1993), 'Saving failed states', 89 *Foreign Policy*, pp 3-20.

Herman J. (1994), *Naar de Areopagus: de Volkenbond en het Toezicht op de Volkenrechtelijke Bescherming van Nationale Minderheden in Oost-Europa: Een Interdisciplinaire Benadering* (Towards the Areopagus: the League of Nations and the Supervision of the International Protection of National Minorities in Eastern Europe: An Interdisciplinary Approach) (diss. Utrecht), Utrecht: Universiteit Utrecht, Faculteit Letteren.

Heun W. (2003), 'Supremacy of the Constitution, Separation of Powers, and Judicial Review in Nineteenth-Century German Constitutionalism, 16(2) *Ratio Juris*, pp. 195-205.

Hey E. (1997), 'The World Bank Inspection Panel: Towards the Recognition of a New Legally Relevant Relationship in International Law', 2 *Hofstra Law & Policy Symposium 1997,* p. 61-74.

— (2004), 'International Public Law', 6 *International Law FORUM du Droit International*, pp. 149-162.

Hirsch E.D., Kett J.F. & Trefil J. (2002), *The New Dictionary of Cultural Literacy*, New York: Houghton Mifflin.

Honig F. (1936), 'International Law and the Transfer of Mandated Territories', 18(4) *Journal of Comparative Legislation and International Law*, pp. 204-211.

Hudson M.O. (1921), 'The League of Nations and the Protection of the Inhabitants of Transferred Territories', 96 *Annals of the American Academy of Political and Social Science*, pp. 78-83.

Ignatieff M. (2003), *Empire Lite: Nation Building in Bosnia, Kosovo and Afghanistan,* London: Vintage.

Irmscher T. (2001), 'The Legal Framework for the Activities of the United Nations Interim Administration in Kosovo: The Charter, Human Rights and the Law of Occupation', 44 *German Yearbook of International Law*, pp. 353-395.

Joerges C., Sand I-J. & Teubner G. (eds.)(2004), *Transnational Governance and Constitutionalism,* Oxford: Hart.

Karnavas M. (2003), 'Creating the Legal Framework of the Brčko District of Bosnia and Herzegovina: A Model for the Region and Other Post conflict Countries', 97(1) *American Journal of International Law*, pp. 111-131.

Kelsen H. (1950), *The Law of the United Nations*, London: Stevens & Sons Limited.

Keohane R. & Nye J. (2001), 'Democracy, Accountability, and Global governance', *Harvard University John F. Kennedy School of Government, Politics Research Group Working Papers on International Relations No. 01-4*, 2001.

Keohane R. (2002), 'Commentary on the Democratic Accountability of Non-Governmental Organizations', 3 *Chicago Journal of International Law,* pp. 477-479.

King I. & Mason W. (2006), *Peace at any Price: How the World failed in Kosovo,* New York: Cornell University Press.

Kingsbury B., Krisch N. & Stewart R. (2004), 'The Emergence of Global Administrative Law' 2004/1 *IILJ Working Paper*, pp. 1-48.

Kirgis F.L. (2001), 'Security Council Governance of Post Conflict Societies: A Plea for Good Faith and Informed Decision Making', 95(3) *American Journal of International Law,* pp. 579-582.

Klabbers J. (2004), 'Constitutionalism Lite', 1 *International Organizations Law Review*, pp. 31-58.

Klabbers J., Peters A. & Ulfstein G. (2009), *The Constitutionalization of International Law,* Oxford: Oxford University Press.

Knoll B. (2002), 'UN Imperium: Horizontal and Vertical Transfer of Effective Control and the Concept of Residual Sovereignty in "Internationalized" Territories', 7 *Austrian Review of International and European Law* pp. 3-52.

— (2005), 'From Benchmarking to Final Status? Kosovo and The Problem of an International Administration's Open-Ended Mandate', 16(4) *European Journal of International Law*, pp. 637-660.

— (2006), 'Beyond the *Mission Civilisatrice*: The Properties of a Normative Order within an Internationalized Territory', 19 *Leiden Journal of International Law*, pp. 275-304.

— (2007)(1), 'Legitimacy and UN-Administration of Territory', 8(1) *German Law Journal,* pp. 39-56.

— (2007)(2), 'Bosnia: Reclaiming Local power from International Authority', 3(3) *European Constitutional Law Review*, pp. 357-366.

— (2008), *The Legal Status of Territories Subject to Administration by International Organizations*, New York: Cambridge University Press.

Knoll B. & Uhl R. (2007), 'Too Little, Too Late: The Human Rights Advisory Panel in Kosovo', 5 *European Human Rights Law Review*, pp. 534-549.

Knudsen T. & Laustsen C. (2006), *Kosovo Between War and Peace: Nationalism, Peacebuilding & International Trusteeship,* New York: Routledge.

Kondoch B. (2001), 'The United Nations Administration of East Timor', 6 *Journal of Conflict and Security Law,* pp. 245-265.

Koopmans T. (2003), *Courts and Political Institutions: A Comparative View*, Cambridge: Cambridge University Press.

Korhonen O. (2001), 'International Governance in Post-Conflict Situations', 14 *Leiden Journal of International Law,* pp. 495-529.

Kreijen G. (ed.) (2002), *State, Sovereignty, and International Governance,* Oxford: Oxford University Press.

— (2004), *State Failure, Sovereignty and Effectiveness: Legal Lessons from the Decolonization of Sub-Saharan Africa*, Leiden: Martinus Nijhoff Publishers.

Ku C. & Jacobson H. (eds.) (2003), *Democratic Accountability and the Use of Force in International Law,* Cambridge: Cambridge University Press.

Kumm M. (2004), 'The Legitimacy of International Law: A Constitutionalist Framework of Analysis', 15(5) *European Journal of International Law,* pp. 907-931.

Linton S. (2001), 'Rising From the Ashes: the Creation of a Viable Criminal Justice System in East Timor', 25 *Melbourne University Law Review*, pp. 122-180.

Loughlin M. (2003), *The Idea of Public Law,* New York: Oxford University Press.

Loughlin M. & Walker N. (eds.) (2007), *The Paradox of Constitutionalism*, New York: Oxford University Press.

Macaulay N. (1937), *Mandates: Reasons, Results, Remedies,* London: Methuen & Co.

MacDonald R. & Johnston D.M. (eds.) (2005), *Towards World Constitutionalism: Issues in the Legal Ordering of the World Community*, Leiden: Martinus Nijhoff Publishers.

Marks S. (2003), *The Riddle of All Constitutions; International Law, Democracy, and the Critique of Ideology,* Oxford: Oxford University Press.

Marshall D. & Inglis S. (2003), 'The Disempowerment of Human Rights-based Justice in the United Nations Mission in Kosovo', 16 *Harvard Human Rights Journal*, pp. 95-146.

Martinez M.M. (1996), *National Sovereignty and International Organizations*, The Hague: Kluwer Law International.

Mason J.B. (1946), *The Danzig Dilemma*, California: Stanford University Press.

Matheson M. (2001), 'United Nations Governance of Post Conflict Societies', 95(1) *American Journal of International Law*, pp. 76-85.

McIlwain C.H. (1968), *The Growth of Political Thought in the West: From the Greeks to the End of the Middle Ages*, New York: Cooper Square Publishers.

— (rev.ed. 1947), *Constitutionalism: Ancient and Modern*, Ithaca, New York: Cornell University Press.

McLaughlin R. (2003), 'East Timor, Transitional Administration and the Status of the Territorial Sea', 4 *Melbourne Journal of International Law,* pp. 323-340.

Mégret F. & Hoffmann F. (2003), 'The UN as a Human Rights Violator? Some Reflections on the United Nations Changing Human Rights Responsibilities', 25(2) *Human Rights Quarterly,* pp. 314-342.

— (2005), 'Fostering Human Rights Accountability: An Ombudsman for the United Nations', 11 *Global Governance*, pp. 139-148.

Milano E. (2003), 'Security Council Action in the Balkans: Reviewing the Legality of Kosovo's Territorial Status', 14(5) *European Journal of International Law,* pp. 99-1022.

— (2006), *Unlawful Territorial Situations in International Law: Reconciling Effectiveness, Legality and Legitimacy,* Leiden: Nijhoff.

Milanović M. & Papić T. (2009), 'As Bad as it Gets: The European Court of Human Rights's Behrami and Saramati Decision and General International Law', 58(2) *International & Comparative Law Quarterly*, pp. 267-296.

Momirov A. (2007), 'The Individual Right to Petition in Internationalized Territories: From Progressive Thought to an Abandoned Practice', 9 *Journal of the History of International Law,* pp. 203-232.

Momirov A. & Naudé Fourie A. (2009), 'Vertical Comparative Law Methods: Tools for Conceptualizing the International Rule of Law', 2(3) *Erasmus Law Review,* pp. 291-309.

Morall J. B. (1980), *Political Thought in Medieval Times*, Toronto: University of Toronto Press.

Morrow J. & White R. (2002), 'The United Nations in Transitional East Timor: International Standards and the Reality of Governance', 22 *Australian Yearbook of International Law,* pp. 1-46.

Morrow J. (2005), *History of Western Political Thought: A Thematic Introduction*, New York: Palgrave Macmillan.

Mulgan R. (2000), 'Accountability: An Ever Expanding Concept?', 78 *Public Administration,* pp. 555-573.

Naudé Fourie A. (2009), *The World Bank Inspection Panel and Quasi-Judicial Oversight: In Search of the 'Judicial Spirit' in Public International Law*, Utrecht: Eleven International Publishing.

Nilsson J. (2004), 'UNMIK and the Ombudsperson Institution in Kosovo: Human Rights Protection in a United Nations "Surrogate State"', 22(3) *Netherlands Quarterly of Human Rights*, pp. 389-407.

Pacquée D. & Dewulf S. (2007), 'International Territorial Administrations and the Rule of Law: The Case of Kosovo', 4(1) *Essex Human Rights Review*, pp. 1-14.

Pagani F. (1996), 'L'administration de Mostar par l'Union Européenne', *Annuaire français de Droit International*, pp. 234-254.

Pallis M. (2005), 'The Operation of UNHCR's Accountability Mechanisms' 2005/12 *IILJ Working Paper*, pp. 1-38.

Palmer V.V. (2005), 'From Lerotholi to Lando: Some Examples of Comparative Law Methodology', 53 *American Journal of Comparative Law*, pp. 261-290.

Parker T. (2003), *The Ultimate Intervention: Revitalising the UN Trusteeship Council for the 21st Century*, Paper, Center for European and Asian Studies at Norwegian School of Management, pp. 1-54.

Paulson S.L. (2003), 'Constitutional Review in the United States and Austria: Notes on the Beginnings', 16(2) *Ratio Juris*, pp. 223-239.

Pennock J.R. & Chapman J.W. (eds.)(1979), *Constitutionalism,* New York: New York University Press.

Perritt H.H. (2004), 'Providing Judicial Review for Decisions by Political Trustees', 15(1) *Duke Journal of Comparative and International Law*, pp. 1-74.

Peters A. & Schwenke H. (2000), 'Comparative Law beyond Post-Modernism', 49 *International and Comparative Law Quarterly*, pp. 800-834.

Peters A. (2006), 'Compensatory Constitutionalism: The Function and Potential of Fundamental International Norms and Structures', 19 *Leiden Journal of International Law,* pp. 579-610.

Ramos Romeu F. (2006), 'The Establishment of Constitutional Courts: A Study of 128 Democratic Constitutions', 2(1) *Review of Law and Economics,* pp. 103-135.

Ratner S. (1996), *The New UN peacekeeping: Building peace in lands of conflict after the cold war*, New York: St. Martin's Press.

— (2005), 'Foreign Occupation and International Territorial Administration: The Challenges of Convergence', 16(4) *European Journal of International Law,* pp. 695-719.

Rawski F. (2003), 'To Waive or Not to Waive: Immunity and Accountability in U.N. Peacekeeping Operations', 103 *Connecticut Journal of International Law,* pp. 103-132.

Reif L.C. (2004), *The Ombudsman, Good Governance and the International Human Rights System,* Leiden; Boston: Martinus Nijhoff.

Reimann M. & Zimmerman R. (eds.)(2006), *The Oxford Handbook of Comparative Law*, Oxford: Oxford University Press.

Reinisch A. & Weber U.A. (2004), 'In the Shadow of Waite and Kennedy. The Jurisdictional Immunity of International Organizations, the Individual's Right of access to the Courts and Administrative Tribunals as Alternative Means of Dispute Settlement', 1 *International Organizations Law Review*, pp. 59-110.

— (2001)(1), 'Securing the Accountability of International Organizations', 7 *Global Governance,* pp. 131-149.

— (2001)(2), 'Developing Human Rights and Humanitarian Law Accountability of the Security Council for the Imposition of Economic Sanctions', 95(4) *American Journal of International Law,* pp. 851-872.

Reisman M. (1989), 'Reflections on State Responsibility for Violations of Explicit Protectorate, Mandate, and Trusteeship Obligations', 10(1) *Michigan Journal of International Law,* pp. 231-240.

Rosenblum D. (2007), 'Internalizing Gender: Why International Law Theory Should Adopt Comparative Method', 45 *Columbia Journal of Transnational Law,* pp. 759-828.

Rothert M. (2000), 'UN Intervention in East Timor', 39 *Columbia Journal of Transnational Law,* pp. 257-282.

Ruffert M. (2001), 'The Administration of Kosovo and East Timor by the International Community', 50 *International and Comparative Law Quarterly*, pp. 613-631.

Russel F.M. (1921), 'The Saar Basin Governing Commission', 36(2) *Political Science Quarterly*, pp. 169-183.

— (1966 reprint), *The International Government of the Saar*, New York: University of California publications.

Salamun M. (2005), *Democratic Governance in International Territorial Administration. Institutional Prerequisites for Democratic Governance in the Constitutional Documents of Territories Administered by International Organizations,* Baden-Baden: Nomos.

Sayre F.B. (1919), *Experiments in International Administration*, New York: Harper & Brothers.

Sarooshi D. (2005), *International Organizations and their Exercise of Sovereign Powers,* Oxford: Oxford University Press.

Scheffer D.J. (2003), 'Beyond Occupation Law', 97(4) *American Journal of International Law,* pp. 842-859.

Schermers H.G. & Blokker N.M. (2003), *International Institutional Law*, Boston: Martinus Nijhoff Publishers.

Schilling T. (2005), 'On the Constitutionalization of General International Law', *The Jean Monnet Program Working Paper 06/05*, pp. 1-67.

Schwelb E. (1955), 'The Trieste Settlement and Human Rights', 49(2) *American Journal of International Law,* pp. 240-248.

Scott C. (2000), 'Accountability in the Regulatory State', 27(1) *Journal of Law and Society,* pp. 38-60.

Scott R. & Stephan P. (2006), *The Limits of Leviathan,* New York: Cambridge University Press.

Sealey R. (1982), 'On the Athenian Concept of Law', 77(4) *The Classical Journal,* pp. 289-302.

Shaw M.N. (2008), *International Law,* New York: Cambridge University Press.

Shelton D. (2005), *Remedies in International Human Rights Law,* Oxford: Oxford University Press.

Shraga D. (2000), 'UN Peacekeeping Operations: Applicability of International Humanitarian Law and Responsibility for Operations-related Damage', 94(2) *American Journal of International Law,* pp. 406-412.

Simma B. & Alston P. (1988-89), 'The Sources of Human Rights Law: Custom, Jus Cogens and General Principles', 12 *Australian Yearbook of International Law*, pp. 82-108.

Slaughter A. (2004), 'Sovereignty and Power in a Networked World Order', 40 *Stanford of International Law,* pp. 283-328.

Smuts J.C. (1918), *The League of Nations: A Practical Suggestion*, London: Hodder & Stoughton.

Smyrek D.S. (2006), *Internationally Administered Territories – International Protectorates?: An Analysis of Sovereignty over Internationally Administered Territories with Special Reference to the Legal status of Post-War Kosovo*, Berlin: Duncker & Humblot.

Stahn C. (2001)(1), 'Constitution without a State? Kosovo under the United Nations Constitutional Framework for Self-Government', 14 *Leiden Journal of International Law,* pp. 531-561.

— (2001)(2), 'The United Nations Transitional Administrations in Kosovo and East Timor: A First Analysis', 5 *Max Planck Yearbook of United Nations Law*, pp. 105-183.

— (2001)(3), 'International Territorial Administration in the former Yugoslavia: Origins, Developments and Challenges Ahead', 61 *Zeitschrift für Ausländisches Öffentliches Recht und Völkerrecht,* pp. 107-177.

— (2005)(1), 'The Geometry of Transitional Justice: Choices of Institutional Design', 18 *Leiden Journal of International Law,* pp. 425-466.

— (2005)(2), 'Institutionalizing Brahimi's "Light Footprint". A Comment on the Role and Mandate of the Peacebuilding Commission', 2 *International Organizations Law Review,* pp. 403-415.

— (2005)(3), 'Governance Beyond the State: Issues of Legitimacy in International Territorial Administration', 2(1) *International organizations Law Review,* pp. 9-56.

— (2008), *The Law and Practice of International Territorial Administration*, Cambridge: Cambridge University Press.

Steffek J. (2003), 'The Legitimation of International Governance: A Discourse Approach', 9(2) *European Journal of International Relations*, pp. 249-275.

Stein P. (1999), *Roman Law in European History,* Cambridge: Cambridge University Press.

Steinberg R.H. (2004), 'Who Is Sovereign?', 40 *Stanford Journal of International Law* pp. 329-346.

Steiner Ch. & Ademović N. (eds.) (2010), *Constitution of Bosnia and Herzegovina: Commentary*, Sarajevo: Konrad Adenaur Stiftung e.V.

Stolleis M. (2003), 'Judicial Review, Administrative Review and Constitutional Review in the Weimar Republic', 16(2) *Ratio Juris*, pp. 266-280.

Strohmeyer H. (2001), 'Collapse and Reconstruction of a Judicial System: The United Nations missions in Kosovo and East Timor', 95(1) *American Journal of International Law,* pp. 46-63.

Tamanaha B. Z. (2004), *On the Rule of Law*, Cambridge: Cambridge University Press.

Thallinger G. (2007), 'The UN Peacebuilding Commission and Transitional Justice', 8(7) *German Law Journal,* pp. 681-710.

— (2008), 'The Rule of Exhaustion of Local Remedies in the Context of the Responsibility of International Organisations', 77(4) *Nordic Journal of International Law*, pp. 401-428.

Tomuschat C. (ed.)(2002), *Kosovo and the International Community: A Legal Assessment,* The Hague: Kluwer Law International.

Traub J. (2000), 'Inventing East Timor', 79 *Foreign Affairs,* pp. 74-89.

Tremblay L.B. (2003), 'General Legitimacy of Judicial Review and the Fundamental Basis of Constitutional Law', 23(4) *Oxford Journal of Legal Studies*, pp. 525-562.

Tremper J.M. (2004), 'The Decolonization of Chechnya: Reviving the UN Trusteeship Council', 15(1) *Journal of Public and International Affairs*, pp. 121-141.

Triggs G. (2002), 'Proposed Timor Sea Arrangements between Australia and the East Timor Transitional Administration', 20(1) *Journal of Energy and Natural Resources Law,* pp. 40-49.

Triggs G. & Bialek D. (2002), 'The New Timor Sea Treaty and Interim Arrangements for Joint Development of Petroleum Resources', 3 *Melbourne Journal of International Law,* pp. 322-363.

Turner R.V. (2003), *Magna Carta through the Ages*, Harlow: Pearson Education Limited.

Valcke C. (2004), 'Comparative Law as Comparative Jurisprudence – The Comparability of Legal Systems', 52 *American Journal of Comparative Law,* pp. 713-740.

Van Ginneken A.H.M. (1992), *Volkenbondsvoogdij; Het Toezicht van de Volkenbond op het Bestuur in Mandaatgebieden 1919-1940* (The League of Nations; The Supervision of Mandatory Authority by the League of Nations 1919-1940) (diss. Utrecht), Utrecht: Universiteit Utrecht.

Walker N. (2003), 'Post-National Constitutionalism and the Problem of Translation', 2003/3 *IILJ Working Paper*, pp 1-27.

Waters C. (2007), 'Nationalising Kosovo's Ombudsperson', 12(1) *Journal of Conflict and Security Law,* pp. 139-148.

— (2008), '"Kosovanizing" the Ombudsperson: Implications for Kosovo Peacekeeping', 15(5) *International Peacekeeping*, pp. 648-662.

Wellens K. (2002), *Remedies against International Organizations*, Cambridge: Cambridge University Press.

— (2004), 'Fragmentation of International Law and Establishing an Accountability Regme for International Organizations: The Role of the Judiciary in Closing the Gap', 25 *Michigan Journal of International Law,* pp. 1159-1181.

Werzer J. (2008), 'The UN Human Rights Obligations and Immunity: an Oxymoron Casting a Shadow on the Transitional Administrations in Kosovo and East Timor', 77(1-2) *Nordic Journal of International Law*, pp. 105-140.

White N.D. & Klaasen D. (eds.)(2005), *The UN, Human Rights and Post-Conflict situations*, Manchester: Manchester University Press.

Wiener J.B. (2001), 'Something Borrowed for Something Blue: Legal Transplants and the Evolution of Global Environmental Law', 27 *Ecology Law Quarterly,* pp. 1295-1372.

Williams P.R. & Pecci F.J. (2004), 'Earned Sovereignty: Bridging the Gap Between Sovereignty and Self-Determination', 40 *Stanford Journal of International Law,* pp. 347-386.

Wilde R. (1998), 'Quis Custodiet Ipsos Custodes?: Why and How UNHCR Governance of "Development" Refugee Camps Should be Subject to International Human Rights Law', 1 *Yale Human Rights & Development Law Journal,* pp. 107-128.

— (2001), 'From Danzig to East Timor and Beyond: the Role of International Territorial Administration', 95(3) *American Journal of International Law,* pp. 583-606.

— (2003), 'Taxonomies of International Peacekeeping: An Alternative Narrative', 9 *ILSA Journal of International and Comparative Law,* pp. 391-398.

— (2004), 'Representing International Territorial Administration: A Critique of Some Approaches', 15(1) *European Journal of International Law*, pp. 71-96.

— (2005), 'Legal "Black Hole"? Extraterritorial State Action and International Treaty Law on Civil and Political Rights', 26 *Michigan Journal of International Law,* pp. 739-806.

— (2008), *International Territorial Administration. How Trusteeship and the Civilizing Mission Never Went Away*, Oxford: Oxford University Press.

Williams P.R. & Pecci F.J. (2004), 'Earned Sovereignty: Bridging the Gap Between Sovereignty and Self-Determination', 40 *Stanford Journal of International Law,* pp. 1-40.

Wormuth F.D. (1949), *The Origins of Modern Constitutionalism*, New York: Harper and Brothers.

Wouters J. & Naert F. (2001), 'How Effective is the European Security Architecture? Lessons from Bosnia and Kosovo', 50 *International and Comparative Law Quarterly,* pp. 540-576.

Wouters J., Brems E. & Smis S. (2009), *Accountability of International Organisations for Human Rights Violations,* Antwerp: Intersentia.

Wright Q. (1923), 'Sovereignty of the Mandates', 17(4) *American Journal of International Law* pp. 691-703.

— (1924), 'Status of the Inhabitants of Mandated Territory', 18(2) *American Journal of International Law*, pp. 306-315.

— (1930), *Mandates under the League of Nations*, Chicago: University of Chicago Press (1968 reprint).

Ydit M. (1961), *Internationalised Territories*, Leiden: A.W. Sythoff.

Zakaria F. (2004), *The Future of Freedom*, New York: W.W. Norton and Company Inc.

Zaum D. (2007), *The Sovereignty Paradox. The Norms and Politics of International Statebuilding,* Oxford: Oxford University Press.

Zegveld L. (2000), *Armed Opposition Groups in International Law: The Quest for Accountability*, Cambridge: Cambridge University Press.

Zimmermann A. & Stahn C. (2001), 'Yugoslav Territory, United Nations Trusteeship or Sovereign State? Reflections on the Current and Future Legal Status of Kosovo', 70 *Nordic Journal of International Law,* pp. 423-460.

Zwanenburg M. (2005), *Accountability of peace support operations*, Leiden: Nijhoff.

Zweigert K. & Kötz H. (1998), *An Introduction to Comparative Law*, Oxford: Oxford University Press.

SELECTED REPORTS AND DOCUMENTS

AMNESTY INTERNATIONAL (AI) / http://www.amnesty.org/

East Timor: Building a new country based on human rights, ASA 57/05/00, August 2000.

East Timor: Justice past, present and future, ASA 57/001/00, July 2001.

Iraq: Responsibilities of the occupying powers, MDE 14/089/2003, April 2003.

Kosovo: Protect the right to health and life, News Service No. 189, 13 July 2005.

Human rights protection in post-status Kosovo/Kosova: Amnesty International's recommendations relating to talks on the final status of Kosovo/Kosova, EUR 70/008/2006, July 2006.

Briefing to the Human Rights Committee during the 87th Session, Eur/70/007/2006, July 2006.

Kosovo (Serbia): The UN in Kosovo – A Legacy of Impunity, EUR 70/015/2006, November 2006.

Serbia (Kosovo): The challenge to fix a failed UN justice mission, EUR 70/001/2008, January 2008.

Kosovo: No justice for the February 2007 killings, Public Statement, AI Index: EUR 70/001/2009, 9 February 2009.

COUNCIL OF EUROPE (CoE) / http://www.coe.int/

Opinion on Human Rights in Kosovo: Possible Establishment of Review Mechanisms, European Commission for Democracy through Law, 8-9 October 2004.

Report of the Committee on Legal Affairs and Human Rights, Doc. 10393, 6 January 2005.

Report by the Commissioner for Human Rights Mr. Thomas Hammarberg on his Visit to Bosnia and Herzegovina, 4-11 July 2007, Doc. CommDH(2008)1, 20 February 2008.

Report of the Council of Europe Commissioner for Human Rights' Special Mission to Kosovo(1), Doc. CommDH (2009) 23, 2 July 2009.

Kosovo: Commissioner Hammarberg calls for stop of forced returns and immediate evacuation of Roma from lead-contaminated camps, News Item, 15 February 2010.

EUROPEAN STABILITY INITIATIVE (ESI) / http://www.esiweb.org/

Reshaping International Priorities in Bosnia And Herzegovina – Part I – Bosnian Power Structures, Report, 14 October 1999.

Turning Point: The Brussels PIC Declaration And A State-Building Agenda For Bosnia And Herzegovina, Report, 7 June 2000.

In Search Of Politics: The Evolving International Role in Bosnia And Herzegovina, Report, 1 November 2001.

De-industrialisation and its consequences – A Kosovo story, Report, Lessons Learned and Analysis Unit of the EU Pillar of UNMIK, Priština-Berlin, 1 March 2002.

The Ottoman Dilemma – Power and Property Relations Under the United Nations Mission in Kosovo, Report, Lessons Learned and Analysis Unit of the EU Pillar of UNMIK, Priština-Berlin, 8 August 2002.

Trepča 1965-2000, A report to the European Stability Initiative & the Lessons Learned and Analysis Unit of the EU Pillar of UNMIK in Kosovo by Michael Palairet, 11 June 2003.

On Mount Olympus. How the UN violated human rights in Bosnia and Herzegovina, and why nothing has been done to correct it, Report, 10 February 2007.

Legal Dynamite. How a Bosnian court may bring closer the end of the Bosnian protectorate, Report, 12 March 2007.

The worst in class: How the international protectorate hurts the European future of Bosnia and Herzegovina, Discussion Paper, 8 November 2007.

One year on: the injustice continues, Report, 26 June 2008.

HUMAN RIGHTS WATCH (HRW) / http://hrw.org/

Not on the Agenda. The Continuing Failure to Address Accountability in Kosovo Post-March 2004, Report, Volume 18, No. 4(D), 29 May 2006.

Better Late than Never – Enhancing the Accountability of International Institutions in Kosovo, Report, No. 2, 14 June 2007.

A Human Rights Agenda for a New Kosovo, Report, No. 1, February 2008.

Kosovo: Poisoned by Lead, A Health and Human Rights Crisis in Mitrovica's Roma Camps, Report, 23 June 2009.

INTERNATIONAL CRISIS GROUP (ICG) / http://www.crisisgroup.org/

Finding the Balance: The Scales of Justice in Kosovo, Balkans Report No. 134, 12 September 2002.

Bridging Kosovo's Mitrovica Divide, Europe Report No. 165, 13 September 2005.

Bosnia's Incomplete Transition: Between Dayton and Europe, Europe Report No. 198, 9 March 2009.

ORGANIZATION FOR SECURITY AND CO-OPERATION IN EUROPE (OSCE) / http://www.osce.org

Review 1: The Criminal Justice System in Kosovo (February-July 2000), OSCE Mission in Kosovo, 10 August 2000.

Remedies Catalogue, OSCE Mission in Kosovo, Human Rights and Rule of Law, 2 September 2004.

Report on the Administrative Justice System in Kosovo, OSCE Mission in Kosovo, Department of Human Rights, Decentralization and Communities, Legal System Monitoring Section, 12 April 2007.

Privatization in Kosovo: Judicial Review of Kosovo Trust Agency Matters by the Special Chamber of the Supreme Court of Kosovo, OSCE Mission in Kosovo, Monitoring Department/Rule of Law Division, Legal System Monitoring Section, 21 May 2008.

UNITED NATIONS (UN) / http://www.un.org

COMMISSION ON HUMAN RIGHTS & HUMAN RIGHTS COUNCIL / http://www2.ohchr.org/english/bodies/hrcouncil/

Report of Mr. Jiri Dienstbier, Special Rapporteur of the Commission on Human Rights on the situation of human rights in Bosnia and Herzegovina, the Republic of Croatia, and the Federal Republic of Yugoslavia, Addendum, 57nd Session, UN Doc. E/CN.4/2001/47/Add.1, 22 March 2001.

Adverse effects of the illicit movement and dumping of toxic and dangerous products and wastes on the enjoyment of human rights, Report of the Special Rapporteur, Okechukwu Ibeanu, Addendum, Summary of communications sent to and replies received from Governments and other actors during 2005, 62nd Session, UN Doc. E/CN.4/2006/42/Add.1, 27 March 2006.

Report of the Representative of the Secretary-General on the human rights of internally displaced persons, Walkter Kälin, Addendum, Mission to Serbia and Montenegro, 62nd Session, UN Doc. E/CN.4/2006/71/Add.5, 9 January 2006.

Report of the Special Rapporteur on the right to adequate housing as a component of the right to an adequate standard of living, Mr. Miloon Kothari, Addendum, Summary of communications sent and replies received from Governments and other actors, 4th Session, UN Doc. A/HRC/4/18/Add.1, 18 May 2007.

Special Rapporteur on the promotion and protection of the right to freedom of opinion and expression, Ambeyi Ligabo, Addendum, Mission to the State Union of Serbia and Montenegro, UN Doc. E/CN.4/2005/64/Add.4, 8 February 2005.

Report of the Special Representative of the Secretary-General on the situation of human rights defenders, Hina Jilani, Addendum, Mission to Serbia, including Kosovo, 7th Session, UN Doc. A/HRC/7/28/Add.3, 4 March 2008.

Report of the Special Rapporteur on freedom of religion or belief, Asma Jahangir, Addendum, Mission to the Republic of Serbia, including visit to Kosovo, 13th Session, UN Doc. A/HRC/13/40/Add.3, 28 December 2009.

COMMITTEE ON ECONOMIC, SOCIAL AND CULTURAL RIGHTS / http://www2.ohchr.org/english/bodies/cescr/

Concluding observations of the Committee on Economic, Social and Cultural Rights, Serbia and Montenegro, Consideration of Reports Submitted by States Parties Under Articles 16 and 17 of the Covenant, 34th Session, UN Doc. E/C.12/1/Add.108, 23 June 2005.

Summary Record of the 37th Meeting, 41th Session, UN Doc.E/C.12/2008/SR.37, 20 November 2008.

Document submitted by the United Nations Interim Administration Mission in Kosovo under articles 16 and 17 of the Covenant, Kosovo (Serbia), UN Doc. E/C.12/UNK/1, 15 January 2008.

Concluding Observations of the Committee on Economic, Social and Cultural Rights, Document submitted by the United Nations Interim Administration Mission in Kosovo (UNMIK), Consideration of Reports Submitted by States Parties Under Articles 16 and 17 of the Covenant, 41th Session, UN Doc. E/C.12/UNK/CO/1, 1 December 2008.

HUMAN RIGHTS COMMITTEE / http://www2.ohchr.org/english/bodies/hrc/index.htm

Comments of the Human Rights Committee, United Kingdom of Great Britain and Northern Ireland, Consideration of Reports Submitted by States Parties Under Article 40 of the Covenant, UN Doc. CCPR/C/79/Add.55, 27 July 1995.

General Comment 26, Continuity of Obligations, UN Doc. A/53/40, 12 August 1997.

Concluding observation of the Human Rights Committee, Israel, Consideration of Reports Submitted by States Parties Under Article 40 of the Covenant, 63rd Session, UN Doc. CCPR/C/79/Add.93, 18 August 1998.

General Comment 29, States of Emergency, UN Doc. CCPR/C/21/Rev.1/Add.11, 31 August 2001.

Concluding Observations of the Human Rights Committee, United Kingdom of Great Britain and Northern Ireland and Overseas Territories of the United Kingdom of Great Britain and Northern Ireland, Consideration of Reports Submitted by States Parties Under Article 40 of the Covenant, UN Docs. CCPR/CO/73/UK, CCPR/CO/73/UKOT, 6 December 2001.

Initial report, Serbia and Montenegro, Consideration of Reports Submitted by States Parties Under Article 40 of the Covenant, UN Doc. CCPR/C/SEMO/1, 24 July 2003.

List of Issues to be taken up in connection with the consideration of the initial report of Serbia and Montenegro (CCPR/C/SEMO/2003/1), 80th Session, UN Doc. CCPR/C/81/L/SEMO, 7 May 2004.

General Comment 31 [80], The Nature of the General Legal Obligation Imposed on States Parties to the Covenant, UN Doc. CCPR/C/21/Rev.1/Add.13, 26 May 2004.

Summary Record of the 2207th Meeting, 81th Session, UN Doc. CCPR/C/SR.2207, 27 July 2004.

Concluding observations of the Human Rights Committee, Serbia and Montenegro, Consideration of Reports Submitted by States Parties Under Article 40 of the Covenant, 81th Session, UN Doc. CCPR/CO/81/SEMO, 12 August 2004.

Concluding observation of the Human Rights Committee, Syrian Arab Republic, Consideration of Reports Submitted by States Parties Under Article 40 of the Covenant, 84th Session, UN Doc. CCPR/CO/84/SYR, 9 August 2005.

Report Submitted by the United Nations Interim Administration Mission in Kosovo to the Human Rights Committee on the Human Rights Situation in Kosovo Since June 1999, Kosovo (Serbia and Montenegro), UN Doc. CCPR/C/UNK/1, 13 March 2006.

Concluding observation of the Human Rights Committee, Kosovo (Serbia), Consideration of Reports Submitted by States Parties Under Article 40 of the Covenant, 87th Session, UN Doc. CCPR/C/UNK/CO/1, 14 August 2006.

Summary Record of the 2402nd Meeting, 88th Session, UN Doc. CCPR/C/SR.2402, 26 October 2006.

Document submitted by the United Nations Interim Administration Mission in Kosovo under articles 16 and 17 of the Covenant, Kosovo (Serbia), UN Doc. E/C.12/UNK/1, 15 January 2008.

List of issues to be taken up in connection with the consideration of the second periodic report of Serbia (CCPR/C/SRB/2), 98th Session, UN Doc. CCPR/C/SRB/Q/2, 8 April 2010.

Report of the Special Rapporteur for follow-up on concluding observations, 98th Session, UN Doc. CCPR/C/98/2, 19 April 2010.

Concluding observation of the Human Rights Committee, Israel, Consideration of Reports Submitted by States Parties Under Article 40 of the Covenant, 99th Session, UN Doc. CCPR/C/ISR/CO/3, 29 July 2010.

SECRETARY-GENERAL / http://www.un.org/sg/

'We the Peoples': The Role of the United Nations in the 21st Century, Report, UN Doc. A/54/2000, 27 March 2000.

Administrative and budgetary aspects of the financing of the United Nations peacekeeping operations: financing of the United Nations peacekeeping operations, Report, UN Doc. A/51/903, 21 May 1997.

Financing of the United Nations Transitional Administration in East-Timor, Report, UN Doc. A/55/443, 3 October 2000.

Implementation of the recommendations of the Special Committee on Peacekeeping Operations, 54th Session, Report, UN Doc. A/54/670, 6 January 2000.

The Rule of Law and Transitional Justice in Conflict and Post-conflict Societies, Report, UN. Doc. S/2004/616, 23 August 2004.

OTHER HUMAN RIGHTS BODIES / http://www2.ohchr.org/english/

Committee Against Torture, *Second periodic reports of States parties due in 1999, Serbia*, Consideration of Reports Submitted by States Parties Under Article 19 of the Convention, 41th Session, UN Doc. CAT/C/SRB/2, 8 February 2007.

Committee Against Torture, *Summary Record (Partial) of the 843rd Meeting*, 41th Session, UN Doc. CAT/C/SR.843, 12 November 2008.

Committee Against Torture, *Concluding observations of the Committee against Torture, Serbia*, Consideration of Reports Submitted by States Parties Under Article 19 of the Convention, 41th Session, UN Doc. CAT/C/SRB/CO/1, 21 November 2008.

Committee on the Elimination of Discrimination against Women, *Summary record of the 775th meeting*, 38th Session, UN Doc. CEDAW/C/SR.775, 18 July 2007.

Committee on the Rights of the Child, *Concluding Observations: Republic of Serbia*, Consideration of Reports Submitted by States Parties Under Article 44 of the Convention, 48th Session, UN Doc. CRC/C/SRB/CO/1, 20 June 2008.

Committee on the Rights of the Child, *Summary Record of the 1326th Meeting*, 48th Session, UN Doc. CRC/C/SR.1326, 18 December 2009.

OTHER UN DOCUMENTS

Comprehensive Proposal for the Kosovo Status Settlement, UN Doc. S/2007/168/Add.1, 26 March 2007 (*Ahtisaari Proposal*), at http://www.unosek.org/.

Comprehensive Review of The Situation in Kosovo, UN Doc. S/2005/635, 7 October 2005 (*Eide Report*), at http://www.ico-kos.org/pdf/KaiEidereport.pdf.

Handbook on United Nations Multidimensional Peacekeeping Operations, United Nations, Department of Peacekeeping Operations, Peacekeeping Best Practices Unit, December 2003, at http://www.peacekeepingbestpractices.unlb.org/.

International Criminal Tribunal for the former Yugoslavia, *Thirteenth Annual Report,* 21 August 2006.

International Law Commission, *6th Report on responsibility of international organizations by Special Rapporteur Giorgio Gaja*, UN Doc. A/CN.4/597, 1 April 2008, at http://untreaty.un.org/ilc/guide/9_11.htm.

Report of the Ad Hoc Committee on criminal accountability of United Nations officials and experts on mission, UN Doc. A/63/54, 11 April 2008, at http://www.un.org/law/criminalaccountability/index.html.

Report of the Group of Legal Experts on ensuring the accountability of United Nations staff and experts on mission with respect to criminal acts committed in peacekeeping operations, UN Doc. A/60/980, 16 August 2006, at http://www.un.org/en/ga/sixth/63/CrimAcc.shtml.

Report of the Panel on United Nations Peace Operations, UN Doc. A/55/305-S/2000/809, 21 August 2000 (*Brahimi Report*), at http://www.un.org/peace/reports/peace_operations/.

Report on the Rule of Law at the National and International Levels, UN Doc. A/61/456, 17 November 2006, at http://www.un.org/en/ruleoflaw/index.shtml.

UN Report of the Advisory Committee on Administrative and Budgetary Questions, Financing of the United Nations Transitional Administration in East Timor, UN Doc. A/55/531, 30 October 2000, at http://www.un.org/ga/acabq/index.asp.

Uniting our strengths: Enhancing United Nations support for the rule of law, UN Doc. A/61/636-S/2006/980, 14 December 2006, at http://www.un.org/en/ruleoflaw/index.shtml.

MISCELLANEOUS

The Netherlands' Advisory Council on International Affairs & Advisory Committee on Issues of Public International Law, *Failing States: A Global Responsibility,* No. 35, May 2004, at http://www.aiv-advies.nl/.

Federal Ministry for European and International Affairs of Austria, *The UN Security Council and the Rule of Law. The Role of the Security Council in Strengthening a Rules-based International System*, Final Report and Recommendations from the Austrian Initiative, 2004-2008, at http://www.unrol.org/.

International Center for Transitional Justice, *Property Rights in Kosovo: A Haunting Legacy of a Society in Transition,* Occasional Paper Series, February 2009, at http://www.ictj.org/.

International Commission on Intervention and State Sovereignty (2001), *Report: The Responsibility to Protect,* Ottawa: International Development Research Center, at http://www.iciss.ca/.

International Law Association, *Accountability of International Organisations,* Final Report, Berlin Conference 2004, at http://www.ila-hq.org/.

Society for threatened peoples, *Highest level of lead contamination ever registered in samples of human hair,* Göttingen, December 2005, at http://www.gfbv.de/.

Society for Threatened Peoples, The Kosovo Medical Emergency Group, *Dossier of Evidence Supporting the Call to Take Decisive Action to Implement Immediately an Emergency Evacuation and the Highest Level of Medical Treatment for all Roma, Ashkali and Kosovan-Egyptian Families in the Displaced Persons Camps of North Kosovo,* at http://www.roma-kosovoinfo.com.

United States Institute of Peace, *International Judges and Prosecutors in Kosovo,* Special Report, October 2003, at http://www.usip.org/.

SELECTED DECISIONS, OPINIONS AND RULINGS

INTERNATIONAL

EUROPEAN COURT OF HUMAN RIGHTS (ECTHR) & EUROPEAN COMMISSION ON HUMAN RIGHTS / http://www.echr.coe.int/echr/

ECtHR, *Lawless v. Ireland*, No. 332/57, 1 July 1961 (*Lawless*).

European Commission on Human Rights, *Ilse Hess v. United Kingdom*, No. 6231/73, Decision on Admissibility, 28 May 1975 (*Ilse Hess*).

ECtHR, *Ireland v. the United Kingdom*, No. 5310/71, 18 January 1978 (*Ireland v. the United Kingdom*).

European Commission on Human Rights, *Melchers & Co. v. Federal Republic of Germany*, No. 13258/77, 9 February 1990 (*Melchers*).

ECtHR, *Loizidou v. Turkey* (Preliminary Objections), No. 15318/89, 23 March 1995 (*Loizidou*).

ECtHR, *Aksoy v. Turkey*, No. 21987/93, 18 December 1996 (*Aksoy*).

ECtHR, *Matthews v. United Kingdom*, No. 24833/94, 18 February 1999 (*Matthews*).

ECtHR, *Waite and Kennedy v. Germany*, No. 26083/94, 18 February 1999 (*Waite and Kennedy*).

ECtHR, *Cyprus v. Turkey*, No. 25781/94, 10 May 2001 (*Cyprus v. Turkey*).

ECtHR, *Marshall v. the United Kingdom*, No. 41571/98, Decision on Admissibility, 10 July 2001 (*Marshall*).

ECtHR, *Al-Adsani v. the United Kingdom*, No. 35763/97, 21 November 2001 (*Al-Adsani*).

ECtHR, *Banković et al. v. Belgium and 16 Other Contracting States*, No. 52207/99, Grand Chamber, Decision on Admissibility, 12 December 2001 (*Banković*).

ECtHR, *Ilaşcu et al. v. Moldova and Russia*, No. 48787/99, 8 July 2004 (*Ilaşcu*).

ECtHR, *Issa et al. v. Turkey*, No. 31821/96, 16 November 2004 (*Issa*).

ECtHR, *Öcalan v. Turkey*, No. 46221/99, Grand Chamber, 12 May 2005 (*Öcalan*).

ECtHR, *Bosphorus Hava Yollari Turizm ve Ticaret Anonim Sirketi v. Ireland*, No. 45036/98, 30 June 2005 (*Bosphorus*).

ECtHR, *Jeličić v. Bosnia and Herzegovina, No. 41183/02, Decision on Admissibility,* 15 November 2005 (*Jeličić*).

ECtHR, *Behrami and Behrami v. France, Saramati v. France, Germany and Norway*, No. 71412/01 & 78166/01, Grand Chamber, Decision on Admissibility, 31 May 2007 (*Behrami*)

ECtHR, *Kusumaj v. Greece*, No. 6974/05, Decision on Admissibility, 5 July 2007 (*Kusumaj*).

ECtHR, *Gajić v. Germany*, No. 31446/02, Decision on Admissibility, 28 August 2007 (*Gajić)*.

ECtHR, *Berić et al. v. Bosnia and Herzegovina*, No. 36357/04, 36360/04, 38346/04, 41705/04, 45190/04, 45578/04, 45579/04, 45580/04, 91/05, 97/05, 100/05, 101/05, 1121/05, 1123/05, 1125/05, 1129/05, 1132/05, 1133/05, 1169/05, 1172/05, 1175/05, 1177/05, 1180/05, 1185/05, 20793/05 & 25496/05, Decision on Admissibility, 16 October 2007 (*Berić*).

ECtHR, *Sejdić and Finci v. Bosnia and Herzegovina*, No. 27996/06 & 34836/06, Grand Chamber, 22 December 2009 (*Sejdić and Finci*).

EUROPEAN COURT OF JUSTICE (ECJ) / http://curia.europa.eu/

European Court of Justice, Joined Cases C-402 & 415/05P, *Kadi & Al Barakaat International Found. v. Council of the European Union & Commission of the European Communities*, 3 September 2008 (*Kadi I*).

INTERNATIONAL COURT OF JUSTICE (ICJ) / http://www.icj-cij.org/

International Status of South West Africa, Advisory Opinion, 11 July 1950 (*International Status of South West Africa*).

Voting Procedure on Questions relating to Reports and Petitions concerning the Territory of South West Africa, Advisory Opinion, 7 June 1955 (*Voting Procedure concerning South West Africa*).

Admissibility of Hearings of Petitioners by the Committee on South West Africa, Advisory Opinion, 1 June 1956 (*Admissibility of Hearing of Petitioners*).

Interhandel (*Switzerland v. Unites States of America*), Judgment, 21 March 1959 (*Interhandel*).

South-West Africa (Ethiopia v. South Africa; Liberia v. South Africa), Judgment, 21 December 1962 (*South-West Africa*).

Northern Cameroons (*Cameroon v. United Kingdom*), Judgment, 2 December 1963 (*Northern Cameroons*).

Legal Consequences for States of the Continued Presence of South Africa in Namibia (South West Africa) notwithstanding Security Council Resolution 276 (1970), Advisory Opinion, 21 June 1971 (*Continued Presence of South Africa*).

Applicability of Article VI, Section 22 of the Convention on the Privileges and Immunities of the U.N., Advisory Opinion, 15 December 1989 (*Convention on the Privileges and Immunities of the U.N.*).

Certain Phosphate Lands in Nauru (*Nauru v. Australia*), Judgment, 26 June 1992 (*Certain Phosphate Lands in Nauru*).

Legality of the Threat or Use of Nuclear Weapons, Advisory Opinion, 8 July 1996 (*Nuclear Weapons*)

Difference Relating to Immunity from Legal Process of a Special Rapporteur of the Commission on Human Rights, Advisory Opinion, 29 April 1999 (*Cumaraswamy*).

Legal Consequences of the Construction of a Wall in the Occupied Palestinian Territory, Advisory Opinion, 8 July 2004 (*Palestinian Wall*).

Accordance with International Law of the Unilateral Declaration of Independence in Respect of Kosovo, Advisory Opinion, 22 July 2010 (*Kosovo*).

PERMANENT COURT OF INTERNATIONAL JUSTICE (PCIJ) / http://www.icj-cij.org/

The Mavrommatis Jerusalem Concessions (*Greece v. Great Britain in its capacity as Mandatory for Palestine*), Judgment, Ser. A, No. 5, 26 March 1925 (*Mavrommatis Jerusalem Concessions*).

Polish Postal Service in Danzig, Advisory Opinion, Ser. B, No. 11, 16 May 1925 (*Polish Postal Service*).

Interpretations of article 3, paragraph 2, of the Treaty of Lausanne, Advisory Opinion, Ser. B, No. 12, 21 November 1925 (*Interpretations of Treaty of Lausanne*).

Readaptation of the Mavrommatis Jerusalem Concessions (*Greece v. Great Britain in its capacity as Mandatory for Palestine*), Judgment, Ser. A, No. 11, 10 October 1927 (*Mavrommatis Readaptation*).

Jurisdiction of the Courts of Danzig, Advisory Opinion, Ser. B. No. 15, 3 March 1928 (*Jurisdiction of the Courts of Danzig*).

Free City of Danzig and International Labour Organization, Advisory Opinion, Ser. B, No. 38, 26 August 1930 (*Free City of Danzig and ILO*).

Access to, or Anchorage in, the Port of Danzig, of Polish War Vessels, Advisory Opinion, Ser. A/B, No. 43, 11 December 1931 (*Port of Danzig*).

Treatment of Polish Nationals in the Danzig Territory, Advisory Opinion, Ser. A/B, No. 44, 4 February 1932 (*Treatment of Polish Nationals*).

Legal status of Eastern Greenland, Ser. Judgment, A/B, No. 53, 5 April 1933 (*Legal status of Eastern Greenland*).

Consistency of Certain Danzig Legislative Decrees with the Constitution of the Free City, Advisory Opinion, Ser. A/B, No. 65, 4 December 1935 (*Consistency of Certain Danzig Legislative Decrees*).

Lighthouses in Crete and Samos, Separate Opinion Judge Hudson, Ser. A/B, No. 71, 8 October 1937 (*Lighthouses in Crete and Samos*).

MISCELLANEOUS

Human Rights Committee, *Kurbogaj and Kurbogaj v. Spain,* Communication No. 1374/2005, Decision on Admissibility, UN Doc. CCPR/C/87/D/1374/2005, 14 July 2006.

BOSNIA AND HERZEGOVINA

CONSTITUTIONAL COURT OF BOSNIA AND HERZEGOVINA (CCBH) & THE HUMAN RIGHTS CHAMBER FOR BOSNIA AND HERZEGOVINA & THE HUMAN RIGHTS COMMISSION WITHIN THE CONSTITUTIONAL COURT OF BOSNIA AND HERZEGOVINA / http://www.ccbh.ba/eng/ & http://www.hrc.ba/

Human Rights Chamber for Bosnia and Herzegovina, Case CH/98/1266 (*Dragan Čavić v. Bosnia and* Herzegovina), Decision, 18 December 1998.

Human Rights Chamber for Bosnia and Herzegovina, Case CH/00/4027 and CH/00/4074 (*Municipal council of the municipality South-West Mostar v. The High Representative*), Decision, 9 March 2000.

CCBH, Case U 5/98 (*re the Constitution of the Republika Srpska*), Partial Decisions, 29 January 2000, 18 February 2000, 1 July 2000 and 18 August 2000.

CCBH, Case U 9/00 (*re the Law on State Border Service*), Decision, 3 November 2000.

CCBH, Case U 16/00 (*re Article 8a, paragraph 1 of the Law on the Sale of Apartments with Occupancy Rights*), Decision, 2 February 2001.

CCBH, Case U 25/00 (*re he Decision Amending the Law on Travel Documents of Bosnia and Herzegovina*), Decision, 23 March 2001.

CCBH, Case U 26/01 *(re the Law on the Court of Bosnia and Herzegovina)*, Decision, 28 September 2001.

Human Rights Commission within the Constitutional Court of Bosnia and Herzegovina, Case CH/03/12932 (*Džaferović v. The Federation of Bosnia and Herzegovina*), Decision, 7 May 2004.

CCBH, Case AP 953/05 (*re appeal by Bilbija and Kalinić*), Decision on Admissibility and Merits, 8 July 2006.

MISCELLANEOUS

Sarajevo Municipal Court, Case No. PR-29/03, *Azmir Omerović v. the Ministry of Interior of the Sarajevo Canton*, 6 May 2004.

KOSOVO (UNMIK)

HUMAN RIGHTS ADVISORY PANEL (HRAP) / http://unmikonline.org/human_rights/

Case No. 03/08, *Brahim Sahiti v. UNMIK*, Decision on admissibility, 10 April 2008.

Case No. 04/07, *Balaj et al. v. UNMIK*, Decision on admissibility, 6 June 2008.

Case No. 09/08, *Olga Lajović v. UNMIK*, Decision on admissibility, 16 July 2008.

Case No. 39/08, *Dejan Jovanović v. UNMIK*, Decision on admissibility, 17 October 2008.

Case No. 04/08, *Shaip Canhasi v. UNMIK*, Opinion, 12 November 2008.

Case No. 02/08, *Nexhmedin Spahiu v. UNMIK*, Opinion, 20 March 2009.

Case No. 26/08, *N.M. et al. v. UNMIK*, Decision on admissibility, 5 June 2009.

Case No. 04/07, *Balaj et al. v. UNMIK*, Second Decision on admissibility, 31 March 2010.

Case No. 26/08, *N.M. et al. v. UNMIK*, Second Decision on admissibility, 31 March 2010.

SPECIAL CHAMBER OF THE SUPREME COURT OF KOSOVO ON KOSOVO TRUST AGENCY RELATED MATTERS

Case SCEL 04-001, *Vahdet Kollari et al. v. KTA*, 9 June 2004.

Case SCC 06-0010, *Aleksandar Hadžijević & Vera Frtunić v. KTA and SOE Trepča Hotels*, 20 November 2007.

MISCELLANEOUS

Gnjilane/Gjilan District Court, *Shaban Beqiri and Xhemajl Sejdiu*, 25 July 2000.

Kačanik/Kaçanik Municipal Court, Case No. 2/2001, *Elife Murseli*, 12 March 2001.

Supreme Court of Kosovo, Case No. AC/37/2004, *Bota Sot*, 20 August 2004.

Priština District Court, *Bota Sot*, 16 July 2004 and 14 January 2005.

Priština District Court, Case No. 202/2005, *Florim Ejupi*, 6 June 2008.

EAST TIMOR

Dili District Court, Case No. 01/Pen.Pra/2000/PD.DIL, *Prosecutor v. Victor Alves*, 17 May 2000.

Dili Court of Appeal, Case No. 16/PID.C.G./2001/PD.DIL, *Prosecutor v. Armando dos Santos*, 15 July 2003

Dili District Court, The Special Panels for Serious Crimes, Case No. 18a/2001, *Prosecutor v. Domingos Mendonca*, Decision on the Defence Motion for the Court to order the Public Prosecutor to amend the indictment, 24 July 2003.

Dili District Court, The Special Panels for Serious Crimes, Case No. 1/2002, *The Deputy General Prosecutor for Serious Crimes v. Victor Manuel Alves*, 18 June 2004.

Dili Court of Appeal, Case No. 60/2004 TR, 26 April 2005.

MISCELLANEOUS

Belgium, Brussels Court of Appeal, *Lutchmaya v. Secrétariat général du Groupe des États d'Afrique, des Caraïbes et du Pacifique*, Journal des Tribunaux 2003, 684, ILDC 1363 (BE 2003), 4 March 2003.

British Commonwealth and Empire, Judicial Committee of the Privy Council, *Jerusalem-Jaffa District Governor v. Suleiman Murra*, English Law Reports 1926, Appeals Cases, 3 February 1926.

Denmark, Court of Second Instance for the Eastern Circuit (Østre Landsret), sitting as a court of first instance, Case No U 2000 478 Ø, *Investerings- & Finansieringsselskabet af 11/1 1984 ApS v. UNICEF*, ILDC 64 (DK 1999), 26 August 1999.

France, Court of Cassation, *La Banque Africaine de Développement v. Mr X,* 04-41012, ILDC 778 (FR 2005), 25 January 2005.

Germany, Federal Constitutional Court, *Internationale Handelsgesellschaft mbH v. Einfuhr- und Vorratsstelle für Getreide und Futtermittel,* 37 BVerfGE 271, 29 May 1974 (*Solange I*).

Germany, Federal Constitutional Court, *Wünsche Handelsgesellschaft,* 73 BVerfGE 339, 22 October 1986, (*Solange II*).

Germany, Federal Constitutional Court, *Brunner et al. v. The European Union Treaty*, 89 BVerfGE 155, 12 October 1993 (*Solange III*).

Switzerland, Federal Supreme Court, *Consortium X v. Switzerland,* BGE 130 I 312, ILDC 344 (CH 2004), 2 July 2004.

The Netherlands, The Hague Court of Appeal, Case No. 07-2973*, Mothers of Srebrenica v. The Netherlands and the United Nations,* 30 March 2010.

The United Kingdom, Court of Appeal - Queen's Bench Division, *Bici & Anor v. Ministry of Defence,* [2004] EWHC 786 (QB), 7 April 2004.

The United States, Supreme Court*, Ware v. Hylton,* 3 U.S. (3 Dall.) 190, 7 March 1796.

The United States, Supreme Court*, Marbury v. Madison*, 5 U.S. (1 Cr.) 137, 24 February 1803.

The United States, Supreme Court*, Eakin v. Raub*, 12 S & R Penn. Rep. 330 Pa, 16 April 1825.

The United States, Supreme Court, *Fletcher v. Peck,* 10 U.S. (6 Cr.) 87, 16 March 1810.

The United States, Supreme Court, *Underhill v. Hernandez,* 168 U.S. 250, 29 November 1897.

The United States, Army Court of Criminal Appeal, Crim. App. No. 20000635, *United States v. Ronghi,* 27 May 2003.

The United States, Court of Appeals for the Armed Forces, No. 03-0520, *United States v. Frank J. Ronghi*, 30 June 2004.

The United States, District Court For the Northern District of California, *Sarkis v. Lajcak et al.,* (5:2008cv01911), Order Granting Motion to Dismiss, p. 10, 14 October 2009.

SELECTED ITA-DECISIONS

OFFICE OF THE HIGH REPRESENTATIVE IN BOSNIA AND HERZEGOVINA (OHR) / www.ohr.int

Decision removing Pero Raguz from his position as Mayor of Stolac, 4 March 1998.

Decision removing Drago Tokmakcija from his position as Deputy Mayor of Drvar, 16 April 1998.

Decision on the deadlines for the implementation of the new uniform license plate system, 20 May 1998.

Decision removing Dragan Cavic from his position as a member of the newly elected RS National Assembly, 8 October 1998.

Decision preventing Mijo Tokic from holding any executive position in Canton 10 or any other office, 16 October 1998.

Decision on the interpretation of Article V.5a of Annex 4 of the GFAP in respect of civilian command over armed forces, 19 February 1999.

Brcko Arbitration, Arbitral Tribunal for Dispute over Inter-Entity Boundary in Brcko Area, Final Award, 5 March 1999.

Decision to lift the ban on Dragan Cavic's activities, 30 July 1999.

Decision on the Law on Implementation of the Decisions of the Commission for Real Property Claims of Displaced Persons and Refugees, 27 October 1999.

Decision imposing the Law on State Border Service of Bosnia and Herzegovina, 13 January 2000.

Decision imposing the Law on Judicial and Prosecutorial Service in the Federation, 17 May 2000.

Decision amending the Law on Filling a Vacant Position of a Member of the Presidency of BiH, 7 August 2000.

Decision amending the Federation Law on Pension and Disability Insurance Organisation, providing for financial feasibility and independence, 12 November 2000.

Decision amending the RS Labour Law, reducing compensation payments to employees on 'waiting list', 12 November 2000.

Decision amending the RS Law on Pension and Disability Insurance, providing for financial feasibility and independence, 12 November 2000.

Decision annulling the Amendments on the RS Law on Pension and Disability Insurance from October 2000, 12 November 2000.

Decision establishing the BiH Institute for Accreditation, 12 November 2000.

Decision establishing the BiH Institute for Standards, Metrology and Intellectual Property, 12 November 2000.

Decision establishing the BiH Law on Accreditation, introducing EU Standards, 12 November 2000.

Decision establishing the BiH State Court, 12 November 2000.

Decision imposing the BiH Law on Measuring Units, introducing EU Standards, 12 November 2000.

Decision imposing the BiH Law on Metrology, introducing EU Standards, 12 November 2000.

Decision imposing the BiH Law on Standardisation, introducing EU Standards, 12 November 2000.

Decision imposing the Federation Law on Pension and Disability Insurance Organisation, providing a framework for the merger of the Sarajevo and Mostar Pension Funds, 12 November 2000.

Decision imposing the Law on the State Court of BiH, 12 November 2000.

Decision abolishing the illegal "Municipality of Skelani" and restoring the pre-war boundaries of the Municipality of Srebrenica, 5 December 2000.

Decision removing Edhem Bicakcic from his position as Director of Elektroprivreda for actions during his term as Prime Minister of the Federation of Bosnia and Herzegovina, 23 February 2001.

Decision suspending all judicial and prosecutorial appointments in BiH (except to the BiH and the Entity Const. Courts, the BiH H. Rights Chamber, the BiH Court, and all courts in the Brcko District) pending the restructuring of the judicial system, 4 April 2002.

List of removed and conditionally removed officials by the High Representative, 30 June 2004.

Order on the Implementation of the Decision of the Constitutional Court of Bosnia and Herzegovina in the Appeal of Milorad Bilbija et al, No. AP-953/05, 23 March 2007.

Decision Enacting the Law on Changes and Amendments to the Law on the Council of Ministers in Bosnia and Herzegovina, 19 October 2007.

Drvar Arbitration Award, 16 September 2009.

UNITED NATIONS INTERIM ADMINISTRATION MISSION IN KOSOVO (UNMIK) / http://www.unmikonline.org/

UNMIK Reg. 1999/1, *On the Authority of the Interim Administration in Kosovo*, 25 July 1999.

UNMIK Reg. 1999/24, *On the Law Applicable in Kosovo*, 12 December 1999.

UNMIK Reg. 1999/25, *Amending UNMIK Regulation No. 1999/01, On the Authority of the Interim Administration in Kosovo*, 12 December 1999.

UNMIK Reg. 2000/1, *On the Kosovo Joint Interim Administrative Structure*, 14 January 2000.

UNMIK Reg. 2000/6, *On the Appointment and Removal From Office of International Judges and International Prosecutors*, 15 February 2000.

UNMIK Reg. 2000/38, *On the Establishment of the Ombudsperson Institution in Kosovo*, 30 June 2000.

UNMIK Reg. 2000/47, *On the Status, Privileges and Immunities of KFOR and UNMIK and Their Personnel in Kosovo*, 18 August 2000.

UNMIK Reg. 2000/54, *Amending UNMIK Regulation No. 1999/01 of 25 July 1999, as Amended, On the Authority of the Interim Administration in Kosovo*, 27 September 2000.

UNMIK Reg. 2000/59, *Amending UNMIK Regulation No. 1999/24 of 12 December 1999 On the Applicable Law in Kosovo*, 27 October 2000.

UNMIK Reg. 2001/2, *Amending UNMIK Regulation No. 2000/6, As Amended, On the Appointment and Removal From Office of International Judges and International Prosecutors*, 12 January 2001.

UNMIK Reg. 2001/9, *On a Constitutional Framework for Provisional Self-Government in Kosovo*, 15 May 2001.

UNMIK Reg. 2001/18, *On the Establishment of Detention Review Commission for Extra-Judicial Detention Based on Executive Orders*, 25 August 2001.

UNMIK Reg. 2002/9, *On an Amendment to the Constitutional Framework for Provisional Self-Government*, 3 May 2002.

UNMIK Reg. 2002/13, *On the Establishment of a Special Chamber of the Supreme Court of Kosovo on Kosovo Trust Agency Related Matters*, 13 June 2002.

UNMIK Administrative Direction 2002/18, *Implementing UNMIK Regulation No. 2000/47 on the Status, Privileges and Immunities of KFOR and UNMIK and their Personnel in Kosovo,* 9 September 2002.

UNMIK Executive Decision 2002/10, *Setting Aside of a Decision of the Municipal Assembly of Gjakove/Djakovica of 17 April 2002*, 11 September 2002.

UNMIK Executive Decision 2002/16, *On the Refusal of the Gjakova/Djakovica Municipality to Issue Death Certificates to Ms. Hazbije Geraqina and Mr. Gjergj Hasanaj,* 18 December 2002.

UNMIK Reg. 2003/25, *On the Provisional Criminal Code of Kosovo*, 6 July 2003.

UNMIK Executive Decision 2003/11, *Setting Aside of a Decision of the Municipal Assembly of Fushe Kosove/Kosovo Polje of 25 June 2003*, 27 August 2003.

UNMIK Executive Decision 2004/1, *Setting Aside of a Decision of the Municipal Assembly of Prishtine/Pristina of 30 December 2003*, 18 February 2004.

UNMIK Executive Decision 2004/22, *Setting Aside a Decision of 5 July 2004 of TM Board of Directors*, 7 October 2004.

UNMIK Executive Decision 2004/25, 20 October 2004.

UNMIK Reg. 2005/18, *Amending UNMIK Regulation No. 2002/12 on the Establishment of the Kosovo Trust Agency*, 22 April 2005.

UNMIK Reg. 2006/6, *On the Ombudsperson Institution in Kosovo*, 16 February 2006.

UNMIK Reg. 2006/12, *On the Establishment of the Human Rights Advisory Panel*, 23 March 2006.

UNMIK Administrative Direction 2006/17, *Amending and Replacing UNMIK Administrative Direction 2003/13, Implementing UNMIK Regulation No. 2002/13 on the Establishment of a Special Chamber of the Supreme Court of Kosovo on Kosovo Trust Agency Related Matters,* 6 December 2006.

UNMIK Reg. 2007/29, *On Amendments to the Constitutional Framework for Provisional Self-Government in Kosovo*, 4 October 2007.

UNMIK Reg. 2008/1, *On an Amendment to the Constitutional Framework for Provisional Self-Government in Kosovo*, 8 January 2008.

UNMIK Reg. 2008/4, *Amending UNMIK Regulation No. 2002/13 On the Establishment of a Special Chamber of the Supreme Court of Kosovo on Kosovo Trust Agency Related Matters*, 5 February 2008.

UNMIK Reg. 2008/9, *On an Amendment to the Constitutional Framework for Provisional Self-Government*, 8 February 2008.

UNMIK Reg. 2008/16, *Amending UNMIK Regulation No. 2002/12 on the Establishment of the Kosovo Trust Agency*, 20 March 2008.

UNMIK Reg. 2008/19, *Amending UNMIK Regulation No. 2008/4, amending UNMIK Regulation No. 2002/13 on the Establishment of a Special Chamber of the Supreme Court of Kosovo on Kosovo Trust Agency related Matters*, 31 March 2008.

UNMIK Reg. 2008/27, *Amending UNMIK Regulation No. 2002/12 on the Establishment of the Kosovo Trust Agency*, 27 May 2008.

UNMIK Administrative Direction 2009/1, *Implementing UNMIK Regulation No. 2006/12 on the Establishment of the Human Rights Advisory Panel*, 17 October 2009.

UNITED NATIONS TRANSITIONAL ADMINISTRATION IN EAST TIMOR (UNTAET) / http //www.eastimorlawjournal.org/ & http://www.un.org/en/peacekeeping/missions/past/etimor/UntaetN.htm

UNTAET Reg. 1999/1, *On the Authority of the Transitional Administration*, 27 November 1999.

UNTAET Reg. 1999/2, *On the Establishment of a National Consultative Council*, 2 December 1999.

UNTAET Reg. 1999/3, *On the Establishment of a Transitional Judicial Service Commission*, 3 December 1999.

UNTAET Reg. 2000/10, *On Public Procurement for Civil Administration in East Timor*, 6 March 2000.

UNTAET Reg. 2000/14, *Amending Regulation No. 2000/11*, 10 May 2000.

UNTAET Reg. 2000/17, *On the Prohibition of Logging Operations and Export of Wood from East Timor*, 8 June 2000.

UNTAET Reg. 2000/19, *On Protected Places*, 30 June 2000.

UNTAET Reg. 2000/23, *On the Establishment of the Cabinet of the Transitional Government in East Timor*, 14 July 2000.

UNTAET Reg. 2000/24, *On the Establishment of a National Council*, 14 July 2000.

UNTAET Reg. 2000/33, *Amending Regulations No 2000/24 On the Establishment of a National Council*, 26 October 2000.

UNTAET Reg. 2001/2, *On the Election of a Constituent Assembly to Prepare a Constitution for an Independent and Democratic East Timor*, 16 March 2001.

UNTAET Reg. 2001/15, *On the Establishment of an Authority for the Regulation of Telecommunications in East Timor*, 21 July 2001.

UNTAET Reg. 2001/28, *On the Establishment of the Council of Ministers*, 21 July 2001.

INDEX

G

H

I

J

K

L

M

N

O

P

V

W

ABOUT THE AUTHOR

Aleksandar Momirov was born on 10 August 1980 in Belgrade, Serbia. He studied Dutch law at the Erasmus University Rotterdam (The Netherlands), where he specialized in public international law and obtained his law degree in 2004. He received the Erasmus School of Law's Best Thesis Award 2003/2004 for his LL.M thesis on the topic of accountability of international organizations, which was subsequently published. Between 2002 and 2005, he worked at the International Criminal Tribunal for the Former Yugoslavia where he was involved in several key cases as a member of the respective defense teams. After this period, he remained associated with the Tribunal until 2007 through his incidental engagement in several cases as a legal assistant for the defense. Since 2005, he has been working at the department of Public International Law at the Erasmus School of Law as a PhD-candidate and lecturer (2005-2009) and researcher (2009-2011). As the recipient of the Erasmus 'top-talent' grant in 2007, he spent several months in Priština where he worked with members of the Ombudsperson Institution in Kosovo and carried out research on the topic of international territorial administration. While writing his PhD-thesis at the Erasmus School of Law, he was engaged in teaching, provided guest lectures on the topic of international criminal law at the universities of Ankara and Skopje and published several articles on the topic of international administration of territories.